# 英国文学史及选读

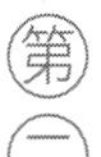

(第二版)

# History and Anthology of English Literature

2ND EDITION

李正栓 吴伟仁 吴晓梅 ◎ 编著

第二册

外语教学与研究出版社
FOREIGN LANGUAGE TEACHING AND RESEARCH PRESS
北京 BEIJING

**图书在版编目（CIP）数据**

英国文学史及选读．第二册 / 李正栓，吴伟仁，吴晓梅编著．-- 2版．-- 北京：外语教学与研究出版社，2021.8（2024.11 重印）
ISBN 978-7-5213-2917-9

Ⅰ．①英… Ⅱ．①李… ②吴… ③吴… Ⅲ．①英语－阅读教学－高等学校－教材②英国文学－文学史－高等学校－教材 Ⅳ．①H319.4：Ⅰ

中国版本图书馆 CIP 数据核字（2021）第 171760 号

出版人　王　芳
项目负责　王　茜
责任编辑　屈海燕
责任校对　王　茜
封面设计　彩奇风
版式设计　锋尚设计
出版发行　外语教学与研究出版社
社　　址　北京市西三环北路 19 号（100089）
网　　址　https://www.fltrp.com
印　　刷　三河市紫恒印装有限公司
开　　本　787×1092　1/16
印　　张　22.5
版　　次　2021 年 10 月第 2 版　2024 年 11 月第 4 次印刷
书　　号　ISBN 978-7-5213-2917-9
定　　价　69.90 元

如有图书采购需求，图书内容或印刷装订等问题，侵权、盗版书籍等线索，请拨打以下电话或关注官方服务号：
客服电话：400 898 7008
官方服务号：微信搜索并关注公众号“外研社官方服务号”
外研社购书网址：https://fltrp.tmall.com

物料号：329170001

# 第二版前言

恩师吴伟仁教授编著的《英国文学史及选读》自1988年出版以来已经长销三十余年。此教材内容选材精当，语言简明流畅，并充分考虑课时等原因而首倡将文学史与文学选读合为一门课程来教授，如今这已成为很多高校英美文学课程较为通行的做法。此外，出版社在教材的编校方面精益求精，也是其畅销和长销的重要原因。

英美文学课程历来是我国英语教学的重要组成部分，因为文学作品呈现了人类最美好的语言，呈现了丰富多彩的世界，呈现了多样的人文素养。经历一段式微历程之后，如今越来越多的专家学者和英语专业教师充分认识到英美文学课程的重要性，呼吁英语类专业建设中传统课程的回归。我们注意到，在新近颁布的《普通高等学校本科外国语言文学类专业教学指南（英语类专业）》中，英国、美国文学史是英语专业方向的必修课程，翻译和商务英语两个新建专业也仍然把英美文学课程列入其中。这说明，无论对哪个专业而言，在提升人文素养、培养合格专业人才方面，文学类课程具有不可估量的价值。

近年来，英美文学教材建设方面成果也很多，分类更为细化，门类更为齐全。除传统的文学导论、文学史教材之外，还出版了多种诗歌、小说、戏剧以及文学理论类教材。此外，还涌现出多个诗歌注释和选读读本、各种戏剧选读读本和小说选读读本。这些教材异彩纷呈，为学生提供了丰富的选择。

遗憾的是，吴伟仁教授的这部教材始终没有大范围修订过。而随着时代变化，我们的人才培养目标有了新的要求，学生的学习需求和课堂环境也发生了变化，新的时代呼唤新的文学史教材。恩师已于2003年仙逝，出版社邀我主持修订工作，我愉快地接受了这个任务，历时数年几易其稿，终于完成了修订任务。

在接受修订任务之初，我与出版社就以下原则达成了一致意见：继承第一版教材特色和整体体例安排，文学史和选读结合，让学生在有限的学时和经济能力可承受的范围内完成英国文学的学习；使用通俗易懂、简明地道的英语来阐述相关内容；更换部分稍显陈旧的选篇，增加现当代作家作品，以期相对完整地呈现英国文学的面貌。

据此，我制订了以下修订方案：

1. 内容的更新与充实。教材在照应篇幅和版面的基础上尽量做到完整和全面，以免造成学生知识上的盲点。对现有部分作家的选篇适当替换和增删之外，重点补充第一版缺失的某些重要作家及其代表作品，尤其是现当代文学的一些内容。适当增加一些文学术语和相关知识，并在此基础上对不同体裁如散文、诗歌、戏剧、小说等稍作讲解，如讲到莎士比亚（William Shakespeare）时介绍一下戏剧方面的相关知识，介绍笛福（Daniel Defoe）时补充一些小说起源发展的相关知识。

2. 结构方面基本遵循第一版“时代背景 + 作家简介 + 作品节选 + 注释”的模式，依据现实课堂教学安排对各章体例适当调整。在生平和作品之外增加简评与鉴赏板块，适当引入文学批评理论术语，对作家整体风格和节选的文学作品作一定的赏析和解读，以引导学生对西方文艺批评理论有一初步的印象，也可以帮助其在今后的学习中更有效地分析作品。在作品选读之后增加思考讨论环节，供学生展开分析讨论，更积极地参与文学作品的赏析与解读过程，从而培养思辨能力并提高文学鉴赏水平；有的思考讨论还涉及与中国文学的比较，使学生在学习外国文学时不忘中国文学，从而深化文明交流互鉴，推动中华文化更好走向世界。

3. 教材形式方面，增加作家图片，使学生对作家作品以及相关历史背景产生更为直观的印象，从而有效地帮助其记忆和理解。改进装帧设计，保留原来的特点又能更美观并且贴近时代和读者。

这次修订历时较长，修订量很大。具体的修订内容包括：

在总体结构方面，教材按照大的历史时期分为几个大部分（Part），各部分底下再按照作家划分若干章节（Chapter）。相比第一版里全书按时间顺序分为若干部分（Part），各部分依次介绍作家的做法，这种划分使其历史线索更加明晰。

在细节安排方面也进行了若干增删调整：

第一版教材把 The Anglo-Saxon Period 和 The Anglo-Norman Period 分成两个部分（Part），第二版则把这两个时期合并为一个部分，但分为两个章节来介绍。这个划分方式更符合历史时期的划分，因为两者同属外族入侵并占领英格兰的时期。

第一版第三部分是 Geoffrey Chaucer，包括乔叟（Geoffrey Chaucer）和各类歌谣。第二版把乔叟单独列为一部分，不仅因为乔叟涵盖歌谣不合适，还因为乔叟和歌谣都值得单独列出。乔叟不仅是英语之父，被人赞誉为英语的北极星，他还是英国文学之父，发明了许多至今仍在使用的格律。他的 *The Canterbury Tales* 在欧洲人文主义尚未进入英国前便开启了英国的人文主义文学与叙事。后世诗人没有不读乔叟的。第二版把歌谣也单独列出。歌谣实际上是英格兰和苏格兰边区反映战争故事和人民生活的歌谣，是一个重要的文学传统，有文化的能听懂看懂，没有文化的也能听懂。歌谣题材也很广泛，有英雄传奇，也有凡人常事，有美丽爱情，也有爱情谋杀，有幽默抒情，也有庄严叙事，值得单独学习。

第一版第四部分是 The Renaissance（文艺复兴），只讲了莎士比亚和培根（Francis Bacon）。第二版将其命名为 The 16th Century: The Age of Drama and Poetry，内容也进行了大幅度调整，新增加七个关键人物。以英国文艺复兴而论，戏剧和诗歌是主体，所以把 16 世纪定性为 The Age of Drama and Poetry。16 世纪不是英国文艺复兴的全部，英国的文艺复兴直到 17 世纪弥尔顿（John Milton）逝世才结束，也是整个欧洲文艺复兴的结束。其实，英国的文艺复兴离不开乔叟、怀亚特（Thomas Wyatt）和霍华德（Henry Howard）这三个人对人文主义思想的解读和译介。乔叟架设了欧洲人文主义文学和思想与英格兰交流的桥梁，准确地说，是乔叟通过译介意大利文学和法国文学从而发展了英国文学，并且以 *The Canterbury Tales* 引发读者对“人”的关注。怀亚特大量地翻译意大利诗歌尤其是彼得拉克

（Francesco Petrarca）的爱情诗，引入了意大利十四行诗，用英语歌颂意大利式的爱情，向世人证明英语原来也这样美丽，击破了一些人认为英语粗糙而对英语进行的恶毒攻击。怀亚特还发明了 abab 的诗节形式，成为英国十四行诗的开端。霍华德继承了怀亚特的遗志，完成了英国十四行诗的格律，创造出 abab cdcd efef gg 这一韵式。有人把这一韵式叫莎士比亚十四行诗，其实这是一种误称，这是霍华德发明的。怀亚特和霍华德还创造了许多后世一直使用的韵式。所以，16 世纪的英国文学不可不讲这两人。至于为什么增加斯宾塞（Edmund Spenser）、罗利（Walter Raleigh）、西德尼（Philip Sidney）、马洛（Christopher Marlowe）和琼生（Ben Jonson），是因为斯宾塞创作了辉煌的、影响后人的 *The Faerie Queene* 等长诗和 89 首十四行诗。罗利不仅是文学家，还是航海家和历史家；他很早就指出海洋的重要性："谁控制了海洋，/ 谁就控制了世界贸易。/ 谁控制了世界贸易，/ 谁就控制了世界的财富，/ 因而就控制了全世界。"西德尼不仅是个著名诗人，他还写过一个非常重要的诗论 *The Defence of Poesy*。马洛在莎士比亚立身之前早已创作几部不朽的戏剧。琼生更是那个时代人人向往的大文豪，是琼生说莎士比亚"不属于一个时代而属于所有世纪"。另外，第二版中这一部分里，莎士比亚名下保留了 *Hamlet*，去掉了 *The Merchant of Venice*，保留了两首十四行诗，替换了一首十四行诗，即用第一首替换了第 106 首，确保学生知道莎士比亚的 154 首十四行诗是如何开始的。其实，第一首到第十七首是很重要的。讲培根时，只保留了"Of Studies"，因为以风格而论，品尝一篇，便知其他。

第一版第五部分是 The 17th Century: The Period of Revolution and Restoration。第二版将其更名为 The 17th Century: Revolution, Restoration and New Poetic Expression，增加了 New Poetic Expression 这个概念。17 世纪是个非凡的时期，有革命也有复辟。社会革命带来经济变化、阶级变化、思想变化、文学变化和其他领域的变化。以文学而论，新格律、新词汇、新意象、新表达层出不穷，以多恩（John Donne）为代表的玄学派诗人使英国文学气象焕然一新，影响后人至深。赫伯特（George Herbert）曾被艾略特（T. S. Eliot）誉为比多恩还高明的玄学派诗人。赫里克（Robert Herrick）及时行乐的主题具有浓厚的人文主义色彩。萨克林（John Suckling）和洛夫莱斯（Richard Lovelace）是保皇派著名诗人。至于马韦尔（Andrew Marvell），虽然很少有人提及他的功劳，但是他保释了弥尔顿，使弥尔顿能完成 *Paradise Lost*、*Paradise Regained*、*Samson Agonistes* 等不朽巨著。在选文方面，多恩的"The Flea"最具玄学派特征，不可不选。

第一版第六部分是 The 18th Century: The Age of Enlightenment in England，第二版将其更名为 The 18th Century: Enlightenment，Neo-classicism and Pre-romanticism，这样更全面，不只是包括启蒙主义文学，还包括新古典主义和前期浪漫主义，从而把 18 世纪出现的主要流派都涵盖了。德莱顿（John Dryden）这样一个大诗人不可不提；要提新古典主义，不能漏掉蒲柏（Alexander Pope），第二版把他们加上了。讲阿迪生（Joseph Addison）时加上了斯蒂尔（Richard Steele），但砍掉一段选文。对笛福和斯威夫特（Jonathan Swift）两位小说家的选段进行了适当删减。讲彭斯（Robert Burns）时，选文部分删掉了"To a Mouse"，增加了"Mary

Morison”和“Scots, Wha Hae”。

第一版第七部分是 The Romantic Period，介绍英国浪漫派诗人。第二版更名为 The First Half of the 19th Century: The Romantic Period，专门讲 19 世纪上半叶，增加了柯尔律治（Samuel Taylor Coleridge）这样一个诗人兼批评家，同时对其他浪漫派作家作品忍痛割爱进行删减。讲华兹华斯（William Wordsworth）时，只保留四首诗；讲拜伦（George Gordon Byron）时，只保留了三首；讲雪莱（Percy Bysshe Shelley）时，只保留了四首；但讲济慈（John Keats）时，增加了一首十四行诗“On the Grasshopper and Cricket”，因为这首诗充分体现济慈是即兴创作的天才。在介绍司各特（Walter Scott）、奥斯丁（Jane Austen）和兰姆（Charles Lamb）时，对选文分别进行删减；由于年代关系，第二版教材把胡德（Thomas Hood）提前到了这一部分，且只保留其“The Song of the Shirt”这首作品。

第一版第八部分是 The Victorian Age，主要介绍英国这一时期的批判现实主义作家作品。第二版将其更名为 The Second Half of the 19th Century: The Victorian Age and Critical Realism，以凸显 19 世纪下半叶的文学特征。对于狄更斯（Charles Dickens）、勃朗特姐妹（Charlotte Brontë and Emily Brontë）、丁尼生（Alfred Tennyson）和勃朗宁夫人（Elizabeth Barrett Browning）等作家的作品或删减或调整。本部分另外增加了三个应当提及的诗人，即阿诺德（Matthew Arnold）、罗塞蒂（Christina Rossetti）和霍普金斯（Gerard Manley Hopkins）。

第一版第九部分是 Twentieth Century Literature，介绍了从 19 世纪到 20 世纪过渡阶段的作家，讲到乔伊斯（James Joyce）为止。第二版将其命名为 The 20th Century Since 1945：Contemporary Literature。增加了叶芝（William Butler Yeats）、艾略特、布鲁克（Rupert Brooke）、格雷夫斯（Robert Graves）、奥登（Wystan Hugh Auden）、托马斯（Dylan Thomas）和贝克特（Samuel Barclay Beckett）等这一时期重要的作家作品。在讲哈代（Thomas Hardy）时，去掉了 *The Son's Veto* 选文，换成一首诗作“The Darkling Thrush”，还原哈代作为诗人的本来面目。

在乔伊斯之后，第二版新增第十部分，介绍 1945 年之后的现当代作家作品，包含了一些必须提及的作家，如莱辛（Doris Lessing）、拉金（Philip Arthur Larkin）、休斯（Ted Hughes）和希尼（Seamus Heaney）。

需要特别说明的是，每一部分命名以时间顺序为主，其次对该期间用文学流派加以说明。作家出现的顺序，则依据其出生年代顺序排列。而关于作家所属的流派不是绝对的，比如把胡德放在第七部分，因为他出生在这个时代，虽然其作品不显示浪漫主义色彩，而更多展示了对社会不公的批评。再如，传统意义上讲批判现实主义以萨克雷（William Makepeace Thackeray）和狄更斯为主，但第二版教材把勃朗特姐妹、丁尼生、勃朗宁夫妇、阿诺德、罗塞蒂和霍普金斯等也放在第八部分了，这是依据他们的出生年代来安排的。诸如此类，不一一列举，大家理解本版教材以时间顺序排列即可。

在本教材编写过程中，我们参考过一些作者的同类书籍以及一些学者的学术观点，并参考了一些专业的文学类网站资料，在此表示诚挚谢意。另外，要感谢外研社各级领导亲自过问并督促本教材的修订工作，特别感谢徐建忠总编辑、常小玲副总编辑和高英分社李会钦社长的关心。感谢吴洋教授对本教材修订工作给予的大力支持。感谢外研社高英分社副社长冯涛和屈海燕、李丹丹两位编辑在本教材编辑过程中所做的大量专业化的细致工作。

由于水平和学识有限，纰漏之处在所难免。敬请指出，以便改正。

李正栓

# 第一版前言

我国高等院校英语专业在高年级课程中，开设有“英美文学史”和“英美文学作品选读”两门课程。讲授“文学史”以伴随“文学作品选读”为宜，否则容易形成脱节现象，或者形成教学中的重复。再者，文学史是根据历史的顺序以系统讲授为主，由于课时的限制，往往重头轻尾，完不成全面教学的任务。“文学作品选读”只能选一部分重要作家和重要作品进行讲授，略古详今。这样，“史”和“选读”分作两门课程讲授，往往不能相辅而行。从时间上说，也有课时不经济的情况。所以，这两门课程最好结合起来：“史”的部分在书中简明扼要地概述，“选读”部分尽可能遴选文学史上的重要作家和重要作品进行讲授。教师根据班级的具体情况，可多选，也可少选，灵活掌握，因材施教。

本套教材编写的体例，除“史”的部分有简明扼要的叙述以外，作家作品部分有：（1）作家生平与创作介绍；（2）作品内容提要（如选文为作品节录时）；（3）选文；（4）注释。在教学中每周以四学时计，共两个学期（有的院校是四个学期），课堂以讲授作品为主，“史”的部分由教师掌握，供学生参考。“史”与“选读”结合，进行教学，可事半功倍，收到良好的教学效果，这是编写《英国文学史及选读》和《美国文学史及选读》的目的。

《英国文学史及选读》分为两册：第一册涵盖盎格鲁–撒克逊时期至 18 世纪英国文学，第二册涵盖浪漫主义时期至 20 世纪英国文学。

本套教材可供高等院校英语专业作为英美文学史和文学作品选读的教学用书或参考书，也可供广大中学英语教师及具有一定程度的英语自学者和英美文学爱好者作为进修读物。

教材定稿前，曾由原国家教委高校外语教材编审委员会召开审稿会。参加审稿会的有主审人张健教授（山东大学）；审稿人孟广龄教授（北京师范大学）、常耀信教授（南开大学）和李乃坤教授（山东大学）。会议期间，审稿人提出了许多有关作家、选文和注释方面的宝贵意见。编者根据这些意见作了必要的修改。在此，对参加审稿的同志表示衷心的感谢。

教材在编写过程中，曾参考了国内外出版的许多文学史和作品选读方面的书籍，注释部分也参照了有关各书的注释，在此不一一列举。由于编者水平有限，书中错误、缺点和考虑不周之处在所难免，恳切希望读者和专家们批评指正。

编　者

# CONTENTS

Part VII

# The First Half of the 19th Century: The Romantic Period

# Introduction

Romanticism is a movement that flourished in literature, philosophy, music and art in Western culture during most of the 19th century, beginning as a revolt against classicism. There have been many varieties of romanticism in many fields and places at different times.

As a literary movement (1798–1832), romanticism came into being in England in the latter half of the 18th century, represented by William Blake and Robert Burns, the spirit of the pre-romanticism.

As is known to all, literature develops with the development of the society and gets strong influences from other social ideologies, especially from politics. Literature reflects or imitates social life, people's mentality and the mental attitudes of a time and a nation. The class struggles and social upheavals also motivate the development of literature. But the most important and decisive factor in the development of literature is economics. These are true of the literature of all countries. The English romanticism is no exception. It was greatly influenced by the Industrial Revolution and the French Revolution.

After the Industrial Revolution that began in the 1760s, Britain became a "workshop of the world" and the English bourgeoisie fattened on world trade, plunder and colonisation. Britain was becoming a powerful country and called itself "an empire where the sun would never set". No country was strong enough to compete with it. The Industrial Revolution pushed the bourgeoisie to the dominant position in the country. It became the ruling class. The aristocratic class retained some prestige and influence in social life and was still prominent in the Parliament and bureaucracy, but had to submit to the rising, powerful bourgeoisie. As the victim of the Enclosure Movement, the peasants became landless and had to find new ways of living. They became hired workers in the countryside and cities. Thus, a new class, proletariat, had sprung into existence. All the working people lived in dreadful poverty. They were mercilessly exploited and in some places sixteen hours' labour would hardly pay for the daily bread. The bourgeoisie got richer and richer while the labourers became poorer and poorer. It was under this unbearable economic condition that the workers' struggle broke out, finding expression in the spontaneous movement of the Luddites, or "frame-breakers" who broke their masters' weaving machines to show their hatred of the capitalists and capitalist exploitation.

The French Revolution that took place on July 14, 1789 was a great event in Europe. The heavily-exploited Parisian people rose and stormed the Bastille, the symbol of feudalism. The Revolution destroyed the feudal economic base, with its influence sweeping all over Europe.

It is almost impossible for those who had no knowledge of the world history of this period to imagine the extraordinary effect of the French Revolution on the life and thought of England in both cultural and political terms.

The French Revolution proclaimed the natural rights of man and the abolition of class distinctions. In Britain the labouring people and the progressive intellectuals hailed the French Revolution and its principle. Clubs and societies such as the London Corresponding Society and other radical organisations multiplied in Britain, all asserting the doctrine of "liberty, equality and fraternity", the watchword of the Revolution. The Revolution had such a strong influence that many writers such as William Blake, Robert Burns, George Gordon Byron, Percy Bysshe Shelley, Charles Lamb and even William Wordsworth and Samuel Taylor Coleridge, to mention a few, got their inspirations from it and wrote beautiful poems or prose. Wordsworth was at first very much excited by the Revolution and had been to France twice. Even after he had lost faith and hope and gained a comfortable income, Wordsworth, when writing about the Revolution, would still say, "Bliss was it in that dawn to be alive, / But to be young was very heaven."

The French Revolution inspired the working (labouring) people and the progressive intellectuals of Britain, but it scared the bourgeoisie, especially its upper stratum, who allowed and had their own revolution but could not bear the idea of another nation having its own revolution. The British government regarded the French Republic as a most dangerous enemy which threatened its very existence with its revolutionary ideas that often spread quickly. Under the banner of patriotism and fighting "Jacobinism", the British government supported and joined the "Holy Alliance" formed in 1815 by the rulers of Russia, Austria and Prussia to suppress the democratic revolutionary movement in Europe. By doing this, the British government turned men's thoughts from their own to their neighbour's affairs and so prevented a threatened revolution at home. The reactionary measures of the British government resulted in the notorious "Peterloo Massacre" in 1819 at St. Peter's Fields, Manchester, when hundreds of workers were killed and wounded by the troops during a mass rally demanding political reform for which the working people had been fighting for many years.

The political writings of the time also reflected the acute struggle. Edmund Burke spoke against the French Revolution and sang elegies for the downfall of the royalty in France. He wrote a pamphlet entitled *Reflections on the Revolution in France* (1790), which soon became an anti-revolutionary manifesto for all reactionaries in Europe. In his picture of the sufferings of French royalty and nobility, as Thomas Paine said, "He pitied the plumage and forgot the dying bird." In answer to this, Thomas Paine, the radical pamphleteer who had always been fighting for freedom, wrote *The Rights of Man*, in which he advocated that politics was the business of the whole mass of common people instead of a governing oligarchy. People would not like a government that failed to secure people "life, liberty and the pursuit of happiness". People had the right to overthrow such a government, if necessary, by revolution. This pamphlet, coming so soon after the destruction of the Bastille, added fuel to the flames kindled in Britain by the French Revolution. *The Rights of Man* was banned and Thomas Paine was found guilty of treason. The government wanted to arrest him. Fortunately, the accused was not taken prisoner. He did not attend the trial for he had been warned by William Blake of the likelihood of immediate arrest and, instead of returning to his lodgings where the police waited with a warrant, had escaped to France.

The English people became more and more dissatisfied with the reality of their country. Fighting for "liberty, equality and fraternity" also became their national spirit and they never stopped demanding reform for many years to come.

Some reforms had been made in England since 1815. The destruction of the African slave trade, the mitigation of horribly unjust laws, which included poor debtors and petty criminals in the same class, the prevention of child labour, the freedom of the press, the extension of manhood suffrage, the abolition of restrictions against Catholics in the Parliament, the establishment of hundreds of popular schools, under the leadership of Andrew Bell and Joseph Lancaster, to mention but a few of the reforms which marked the progress of civilisation in a single half century. The Reform Bill of 1832 shifted the centre of political power to the middle class.

It was amid these social conflicts mentioned above that romanticism arose as a main literary trend, which prevailed in England during the period of 1798–1832, beginning with the publication of Wordsworth's *Lyrical Ballads* (1798), ending with Walter Scott's death (1832).

The age of Wordsworth was decidedly an age of poetry. Its great men of genius were mostly eminent in the poetical field. Distinction was more easily achieved in poetry than in prose. The general taste was decidedly set in the poetic direction. This fact helped to mark it as the second great age in English literary history, for poetry was the highest form of literary expression, and poetry seemed to have been most in harmony with the noblest powers of the English genius, just as the young enthusiasts turned naturally to poetry and singing as happy men in the Elizabethan Age. The glory of the age of Wordsworth was in the poetry of Scott, Wordsworth, Coleridge, Byron, Shelley, Keats, Moore and Southey. Of its prose works, those of Scott alone had attained a very wide reading, though the essays of Charles Lamb and the novels of Jane Austen had also slowly won for their authors a secure place in the history of English literature. Coleridge and Southey (who with Wordsworth formed the trio of so-called Lake Poets) wrote far more prose than poetry; Southey's prose was much better than his verse. There was also a noteworthy development of the novel which was already beginning to establish itself as the favourite literary form of the 19th century. Drama was the only great literary form that was not adequately represented. Many of the great poets, as well as other writers, tried their hands at dramatic work; but there was probably not a single great drama in the stricter sense of the term. The best that we can say is that there was some really noble poetry written in nominally dramatic form. There were many excellent writers, and there was a vast body of excellent works in a wonderful variety of forms.

Chapter 1

# William Wordsworth

## Life and Works

William Wordsworth (1770–1850) was born in a lawyer's family in Cockermouth, Cumberland. He was brought up by relatives who sent him to school at Hawkshead in the beautiful Lake District in Northwestern England, where he spent his happy school days. Out of school hours, he was free and read widely. He also roamed over the mountains. The beauty of nature attracted him so greatly that nature became his best teacher as he said or implied in many of his poems. The flowers, hills, stars, birds and all things of nature were of greater fascination to him. The constant sight of beautiful nature of the Lake District awoke love and reverence in him. Little by little, the glories of nature grew upon him, until his soul seemed flooded with unutterable delight. This profound passion was fostered by his life in these early years, and grew steadily with his youth. This is why he later wrote a lot of nature poems and was called a nature poet.

At seventeen, in 1787, he went to Cambridge. During the four years there, he was influenced by the young republicans there and was politically enthusiastic about and sympathetic with the French Revolution (1789). He visited France twice, the first time in 1790, the second time in 1792. For economic reasons and relationship with his relatives, he had to leave France in 1792. Of course, his poems of this period had a lot of democratic ideas. With the establishment of the Jacobin dictatorship and the rise of Napoleon in France, Wordsworth lost his former political fervour and changed his attitude towards the Revolution.

In 1795 he and his sister Dorothy settled at Racedom in Somersetshire. A bequest of £900 relieved the financial strain which had caused him anxiety, and secured for him and his sister a modest maintenance. He later accepted the office of a distributor of stamps and was made Poet Laureate. He and his sister passed the rest of their lives in the Lake District, except occasional tours. The two places most associated with him are Grasmere, where he wrote the best of his poetry between the years 1798 and 1808, and Rydal Mount, where he lived in his later years.

His sister Dorothy, as an adviser and commentator of William's poems, helped him a lot in his poetic creation. She won him back from his hopelessness over the Revolution and urged upon him the duty of devoting himself to poetry. Their favourite pastime was walking. To remember one walking, Dorothy wrote a very good journal and Wordsworth wrote "I Wandered Lonely as a Cloud", the famous poem in which he said that nature was the cure of loneness and solitude.

It was in 1797 that Wordsworth made friends with Coleridge and a year later they jointly published the *Lyrical Ballads*. The majority of poems in this collection were written by Wordsworth. Many of Wordsworth's poems were devoted to the position of landless and homeless peasants ("Michael", "The Brothers", "The Old Cumberland Beggar" and others). Sincerely sympathising with the poor, he criticised capitalism severely. Coleridge's chief contribution was his masterpiece *The Rime of the Ancient Mariner*.

## Brief Comment

Wordsworth was a spokesman for the common people. He wrote for them and about them, by using their language. He said, "The principle object—was to choose incidents and situations from common life, and to relate or describe them, throughout, as far as was possible in a selection of language really used by men..." To obtain such situations, "Humble and rustic life was generally chosen, because, in that condition, the essential passions of the heart find a better soil in which they can attain their maturity, are less under restraint, and speak a plainer and more emphatic language; because in that condition of life our elementary feelings coexist in a state of greater simplicity, and, consequently, may be more accurately contemplated, and more forcibly communicated; because the manners of rural life germinate from those elementary feelings, and from the necessary character of rural occupations, are more easily comprehended, and are more durable; and, lastly, because in that condition the passions of men are incorporated with the beautiful and permanent forms of nature."

Wordsworth had his own principle of poetry. He declared that "all good poetry is the spontaneous overflow of powerful feeling" and "takes its origin from emotion recollected in tranquility". He appealed directly to individual sensations, i.e. pleasure, excitement and enjoyment as the foundation in the creation and appreciation of poetry. The function of poetry lies in its power to give an unexpected splendour to familiar and commonplace things, to "incidents and situations from common life". All kinds of people, ordinary peasants, children, even outcasts, can enter poetry.

As to language used in poetry, he advocated using the language of the common people. In his poems he aimed at simplicity and purity of the language, fighting against the conventional forms of the 18th-century poetry. A passionate lover of nature, his descriptions of lakes and rivers, of meadows and woods, of skies and clouds are exquisite.

Wordsworth wrote a great many poems, fresh in imagination, simple, plain and vivid in language but profound in meaning. He was especially good at writing about nature, childhood memories and common people. Hence he was called the poet of nature. His later major works, to mention a few here, include "Lines Composed a Few Miles Above Tintern Abbey", "Lucy Poems", "Ode to Duty", *The Excursion* and *The Prelude*. He also wrote a lot of sonnets.

## Selections

### She Dwelt Among the Untrodden Ways

She dwelt among the untrodden ways
  Beside the springs of Dove[1],
A Maid whom there were none to praise
  And very few to love:

A violet by a mossy stone
  Half hidden from the eye!
—Fair as a star, when only one
  Is shining in the sky.

She lived unknown, and few could know
  When Lucy ceased to be;
But she is in her grave, and, oh,
  The difference to me!

## Notes

1. There are several rivers by this name in England, including one in the Lake District.

## For Study and Discussion

1. In this poem, the setting is the untrodden ways. Why did the maid live there? Is it because she loved nature? Was she poor? Was she alone or with her parents? Why did few people praise or love her? The language is simple, but it is hard to understand. Why did the poet write about such a girl?
2. The second stanza is especially touching when the poet compares the girl to a violet. It reminds readers of the image of the lady in Bai Juyi's poem (白居易《琵琶行》) in which there are two lines "千呼万唤始出来，犹抱琵琶半遮面". Compare the above two lines with: "A violet by a mossy stone / Half hidden from the eye!" What feeling can you get when you read them?

3. In the poem, the poet compares Lucy to a violet and a star at the same time. Is she properly compared? Don't you think there is irony here? Why does the poet use the two images to depict Lucy?
4. What is the rhyme scheme of this poem?

## I Wandered Lonely as a Cloud[1]

I wandered lonely as a cloud
That floats on high o'er vales and hills,
When all at once I saw a crowd,
A host, of golden daffodils;
Beside the lake, beneath the trees,
Fluttering and dancing in the breeze.

Continuous as the stars that shine
And twinkle on the milky way,
They stretched in never-ending line
Along the margin of a bay:
Ten thousand saw I at a glance,
Tossing their heads in sprightly dance.

The waves beside them danced; but they
Out-did the sparkling waves in glee:
A poet could not but be gay,
In such a jocund company:
I gazed—and gazed—but little thought
What wealth the show to me had brought:

For oft, when on my couch I lie
In vacant or in pensive mood,
They flash upon that inward eye
Which is the bliss of solitude;
And then my heart with pleasure fills,
And dances with the daffodils.

## Notes

1. According to Dorothy's description in *Grasmere Journals* for April 15, 1802, she and Wordsworth took a walk that day and came across a belt of daffodils. Two years later, Wordsworth recollected that experience in tranquility and wrote down this poem.

## For Study and Discussion

1. This poem best represents the poet's central idea of his creative process—"emotion recollected in tranquility". What do you think of this idea?
2. In this poem, the image of cloud is outstanding and important, so is the image of daffodils. In some sense, they form a contrast: the cloud is lonely and the daffodils are happy. How do they contribute to expressing the mood of the poet?
3. In the third stanza, the poet does not use "I". Instead, he says "A poet could not but be gay". Why does he use "a poet" to stand for "I"? Can you find such phenomena in other poems, either Chinese or foreign?
4. What is the rhyme scheme of this poem? Learn the first stanza by heart.

### Sonnet: Composed upon Westminster Bridge

September 3, 1802[1]

Earth has not anything to show more fair:
Dull would he be of soul who could pass by
A sight so touching in its majesty:
This City now doth, like a garment, wear
The beauty of the morning; silent, bare,
Ships, towers, domes, theaters, and temples lie
Open unto the fields, and to the sky;
All bright and glittering in the smokeless air.
Never did sun more beautifully steep
In his first splendor, valley, rock, or hill;
Ne'er saw I, never felt, a calm so deep!
The river glideth at his own sweet will:
Dear God! the very houses seem asleep;
And all that mighty heart is lying still!

## Notes

1. The date of this experience was not Sept. 3, but July 31, 1802. Its occasion was a trip to France. See Dorothy Wordsworth's *Grasmere Journals* for July, 1802. The conflict of feelings attending Wordsworth's brief return to France, where he had supported the French Revolution, evoked a number of personal and political sonnets.

## For Study and Discussion

1. In the hands of romantic poets, sonnet began to take the task of expressing the poets' feelings about nature and other things rather than merely love. From this sonnet, what can you get about the poet's feeling about London?
2. At what time of the day does the poet write this poem? Find the words that can give you the hint.
3. If you were asked to learn some lines by heart, which lines would you choose? Why?

### The Solitary Reaper[1]

Behold her, single in the field,
Yon solitary Highland Lass!
Reaping and singing by herself;
Stop here, or gently pass!
Alone she cuts and binds the grain,
And sings a melancholy strain;
O listen! for the Vale profound
Is overflowing with the sound.

No Nightingale did ever chaunt
More welcome notes to weary bands
Of travellers in some shady haunt,
Among Arabian sands:
A voice so thrilling ne'er was heard
In spring-time from the Cuckoo-bird,
Breaking the silence of the seas
Among the farthest Hebrides.

Will no one tell me what she sings?[2]
Perhaps the plaintive numbers flow

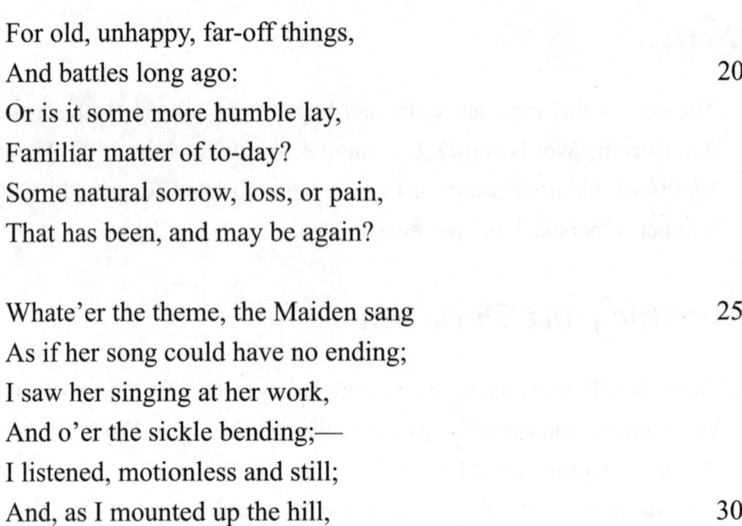

For old, unhappy, far-off things,
And battles long ago:
Or is it some more humble lay,
Familiar matter of to-day?
Some natural sorrow, loss, or pain,
That has been, and may be again?

Whate'er the theme, the Maiden sang
As if her song could have no ending;
I saw her singing at her work,
And o'er the sickle bending;—
I listened, motionless and still;
And, as I mounted up the hill,
The music in my heart I bore,
Long after it was heard no more.

## Notes

1. This is one of the rare poems which were not based on Wordsworth's own experience. Wordsworth said that it was suggested by a passage in Thomas Wilkinson's *Tours to the British Mountains* (1824), which he had seen in manuscript: "Passed by a female who was reaping alone: she sung in Erse (the Gaelic language of Scotland) as she bended over her sickle; the sweetest human voice I ever heard: her strains were tenderly melancholy, and felt delicious, long after they were heard no more."
2. The poet does not understand Erse, the language in which she sings.

## For Study and Discussion

1. Since this poem is not one based on the poet's own experience, why does the poet write this poem? What does he want to express in this poem?
2. What impresses the poet the most?
3. The poet even could not understand what she sings. How can the singing touch him? What view of life does the poem reflect?
4. Learn the last stanza by heart.

Chapter 2

# Walter Scott

## Life and Works

Walter Scott (1771–1832) was born in Edinburgh. He was a weak child, and at three he was taken to Sandyknowe, his grandfather's farm where he heard about the past border wars which he often wrote about later in his poetry. In 1779 he returned to Edinburgh. He attended the high school for a period, and entered university in 1783. He read widely and eagerly, including travels, romances, poetry and old plays, especially fond of ballads. His later poems and novels show that he was susceptible to the beauty of nature that he saw when he was young. In 1786 he entered his father's law office. Six years later, in 1792, he was called to the Scottish bar. Also in 1792 he began to study German. In 1796 he published his translation of Burger's *Lenore and Wild Huntsman*. In 1802 his *Minstrelsy of the Scottish Border* was published. *The Lay of the Last Minstrel* was published in 1805, and it appealed to the public. So he gave up his profession and devoted himself to writing. In 1808 *Marmion* was published; and in 1810, his long poem *Lady of the Lake* brought him unexpected fame. In June, 1814 *Waverley* came out and it revolutionised the English novel. Moreover, besides raising the novel to a higher level, Scott put into it a new element by telling pleasant stories about people in history, thus creating the historical novel. In some sense, he is father of the historical novel. He introduced into his novels historical characters, who then became minor characters. Between 1814 and 1819 he wrote the "Waverly" novels centring on the history of Scotland. *Guy Mannering*, *The Black Dwarf*, *Old Mortality*, *Rob Roy* and *Ivanhoe* followed in succession. In 1820 he was conferred upon the rank of baronet. But in January, 1826, the publishing house of the Ballantynes (of which he was a partner) went bankrupt and he fell heavily into debts. So he worked very hard to pay the debts and make a living. He wrote novels, tales, histories in rapid succession. Because of overwork, symptoms of paralysis appeared. He went to Italy, October 1831, and returned to Abbostsford in 1832. He died there on September 21, 1832. His death marked the end of the English romanticism.

His historical novels cover a period, ranging from the Middle Ages to the 18th century. *Waverley*, *Guy Mannering*, *The Antiquary*, *The Black Dwarf*, *Old Mortality*, *Rob Roy*, and *The Heart of Midlothian* describe Scotland in the 18th century. *The Bride of Lammermoor* and *A Legend of Montrose* describe things of the 17th century. *Ivanhoe* deals with English history of the 12th century. *The Monastery*, *The Abbot* and *Kenilworth* describe the things of the 16th century. *The Pirate*, *The Fortunes of Nigel*, and *Peveril of the Peak* tell stories of Scotland and England in the 17th century. *Quentin Durward* describes things in France during the reign of Louis XI, the 15th century. *St. Ronan's Well* is the only contemporary novel among the works of Scott. It is a satire on the idle aristocratic society of his time.

## Brief Comment

Walter Scott was the creator and a great master of the historical novel. His novels give a panorama of the feudal society from its early stages to its downfall. He describes the different phases of this epoch: the Crusades, the rise of absolute monarchy, the bourgeois revolution in England and the attempts to restore feudalism in the 18th century.

Scott was greatly interested in writing about the fate of the people, especially of the peasants. His historical approach to life was a result of the great changes brought about by the Industrial Revolution in England and the Revolution in France.

The main heroes of his novels are young men of bravery and valour. They are usually of noble birth. However, they appear as common men, poor, persecuted and faced with innumerable hardships. They are thrown into a close friendship with ordinary people. But in the end the heroes acquire their titles and return to the prosperous life of the ruling class.

The great realists of the 19th century made use of, and developed, the method of a realistic presentation of the past in their description and treatment of contemporary life. Thus we may say that Walter Scott's historical novels paved the path for the development of the realistic novel of the 19th century.

## Selections

### **Rob Roy**

### The Story

The scene of the novel is England and Scotland in the first quarter of the 18th century.

A young man, Francis Osbaldistone, the only son and heir of the head of a well-known London firm named Osbaldistone and Tresham, returns home from France, where he received his education. With a strong urge and love for poetry, he refuses to enter into his father's business, which upset and angered his father Mr. Osbaldistone so he sends Francis to his brother

Sir Hildebrand, living in Scotland, with the intention of taking one of his sons to fill up the lucrative situation in the counting house which was made vacant by Francis' obstinacy.

Sir Hildebrand and his sons lead the typical life of feudal lords, and drinking bouts and hunting exhaust all their interests. The only exception is the younger son, Rashleigh, who is to go to London to take Francis' place in Osbaldistone and Tresham. He is well-educated, clever, but malicious and cruel. A quarrel over a trifle which breaks out between him and Francis passes into an irreconcilable enmity.

Of all the household Francis confides in Diana Vernon, a young relative of Sir Hildebrand's wife. The young people fall in love, and Diana proves her devotion by helping Francis out of various risky situations into which he gets involved due to his inexperience.

Soon Rashleigh leaves for London to assume his duties in the firm. One day, he takes the opportunity of Mr. Osbaldistone's absence and absconds with a large sum of money and securities.

At the news that this embezzlement threatens to undermine the firm's credit, Francis sets off in search of Rashleigh who is known to be somewhere in Scotland. Before his departure Diana Vernon gives him a letter which he is to open only in case of an emergency. Simultaneously, the chief clerk of Osbaldistone and Tresham, Owen, is dispatched from London in pursuit of Rashleigh.

Francis arrives in the commercial centre of Scotland—Glasgow. Attending a mass at the cathedral, he meets a mysterious stranger who makes an appointment with him for 12 o'clock midnight on the bridge.

The meeting between them takes place at the appointed time (see selection) and the stranger conducts the astonished Francis to a prison. There Francis finds the loyal clerk Owen. The latter is imprisoned by Scotch merchants connecting with Osbaldistone and Tresham, who learn of the insolvency of the firm. Told by the clerk that his father's business is on the verge of bankruptcy, Francis in despair tears open Diana's letter. The addressee turns out to be his mysterious guide whom he identifies as his casual fellow-traveller on the way from London to his uncle's castle.

The stranger is none other than MacGregor (Rob Roy), the leader of a company of free highlanders, who terrorise all the land-owners in the country. Enlisting his support with the help of Diana's letter, Francis sets forth into the interior of the mountainous country. There he finds out that Rashleigh committed the crime in order to use the money for the uprising.

Diana Vernon and her father, Sir Frederick, one of the initiators and leaders of the conspiracy, induce Rashleigh to refund the money and the securities to Francis.

Travelling in the mountains, Francis and his companions, one of them being the Bailie, are taken prisoners by a detachment of English soldiers who suspect them of participation in the brewing insurrection.

In the ensuing skirmish (see selection) the detachment is annihilated and the prisoners are set free. After numerous adventures in the highlands, Francis returns home safe and sound to restore honour and fortune to his father.

Rashleigh, in the time, betrays the cause and perishes from Rob Roy's vengeful hand.

The story ends in the depiction of the consequences of the ill-fated rebellion on the characters of the book. The uprising is suppressed, Sir Frederick dies, and Francis marries Diana.

## Chapter XXI

Evening had now closed, and the growing darkness gave to the broad, still, and deep expanse of the brimful river, first a hue sombre and uniform—then a dismal and turbid appearance, partially lighted by a waning and pallid moon. The massive and ancient bridge which stretches across the Clyde was now but dimly visible, and resembled that which Mirza, in his unequalled vision[1], has described as traversing the valley of Bagdad. The low-browed arches, seen as imperfectly as the dusky current which they bestrode, seemed rather caverns which swallowed up the gloomy waters of the river, than apertures contrived for their passage. With the advancing night, the stillness of the scene increased. There was yet a twinkling light occasionally seen to glide along by the stream, which conducted home one or two of the small parties, who, after the abstinence and religious duties of the day, had partaken of a social supper,—the only meal at which the rigid Presbyterians[2] made some advance to sociality on the Sabbath. Occasionally, also, the hoofs of a horse were heard, whose rider, after spending the Sunday in Glasgow, was directing his steps towards his residence in the country. These sounds and sights became gradually of more rare occurrence; at length they altogether ceased, and I was left to enjoy my solitary walk on the shores of the Clyde in solemn silence, broken only by the tolling of the successive hours from the steeples of the churches. But as the night advanced, my impatience at the uncertainty of the situation in which I was placed increased every moment, and became nearly ungovernable. I began to question whether I had been imposed upon by the thick of a fool, the raving of a madman, or the studied machination of a villain, and paced the little quay or pier adjoining the entrance to the bridge in a state of incredible anxiety and vexation. At length the hour of twelve o'clock swung its summons over the city from the belfry of the metropolitan church of St Mungo, and was answered and vouched by all the others like dutiful diocesans. The echoes had scarcely ceased to repeat the last sound, when a human form—the first I had seen for two hours—appeared passing along the bridge from the southern shore of the river. I advanced to meet him, with a feeling as if my fate depended on the result of the interview, so much had my anxiety been wound up by protracted expectation. All that I could remark of the passenger, as we advanced towards each other, was, that his frame was rather beneath than above the middle size, but apparently strong, thickset, and muscular; his dress, a horseman's wrapping coat. I slackened my pace, and almost paused as I advanced, in expectation that he would address me. But to my inexpressible disappointment he passed without speaking, and I had no pretence for being the first to address one who, notwithstanding his appearance at the very hour of appointment, might nevertheless be an absolute stranger. I stopped when he had passed me, and looked after him, uncertain whether I ought not to follow him. The stranger walked on till near the northern end of the bridge, then paused, looked back, and, turning round, again advanced towards me. I resolved that this time he should not have the apology for silence proper to apparitions, who, it is vulgarly supposed, cannot speak until they are spoken to. "You walk late, sir," said I, as we met a second time.

"I bide tryste"[3] was the reply; "and so I think do you, Mr. Osbaldistone."

"You are then the person who requested to meet me here at this unusual hour?"

"I am," he replied. "Follow me, and you shall know my reasons."

"Before following you, I must know your name and purpose," I answered.

"I am a man," was the reply; "and my purpose is friendly to you."

"A man!" I repeated. "That is a very brief description."

"It will serve for one who has no other to give," said the stranger. "He that is without name, without friends, without coin, without country, is still at least a man; and he that has all these is no more."

"Yet this is still too general an account of yourself, to say the least of it, to establish your credit with a stranger."

"It is all I mean to give, howsoe'er; you may choose to follow me, or to remain without the information I desire to afford you."

"Can you not give me that information here?" I demanded.

"You must receive it from your eyes, not from my tongue;—you must follow me, or remain in ignorance of the information which I have to give you."

There was something short, determined, and even stern, in the man's manner, not certainly well calculated to conciliate undoubting confidence.

"What is it you fear?" he said, impatiently. "To whom, think ye, is your life of such consequence, that they should seek to bereave ye of it?"

"I fear nothing," I replied firmly, though somewhat hastily. "Walk on—I attend you."

We proceeded, contrary to my expectation to reenter the town, and glided like mute spectres, side by side, up its empty and silent streets. The high and gloomy stone fronts, with the variegated ornaments and pediments of the windows, looked yet taller and more sable by the imperfect moonshine. Our walk was for some minutes in perfect silence. At length my conductor spoke. "Are you afraid?"

"I retort your own words," I replied; "wherefore should I fear?"

"Because you are with a stranger—perhaps an enemy, in a place where you have no friends and many enemies."

"I neither fear you nor them; I am young, active, and armed."

"I am not armed," replied my conductor; "but no matter, a willing hand never lacked weapon. You say you fear nothing; but if you knew who was by your side, perhaps you might underlie a tremor[4]."

"And why should I?" replied I. "I again repeat, I fear nought that you can do."

"Nought that I can do?—Be it so. But do you not fear the consequences of being found with one whose very name whispered in this lonely street would make the stones themselves rise up to apprehend him—on whose head half the men in Glasgow would build their fortune as on a found treasure, had they the luck to grip him by the collar—the sound of whose apprehension were as welcome at the Cross of Edinburgh as ever the news of a field stricken and won in Flanders[5]?"

"And who then are you, whose name should create so deep a feeling of terror?" I replied.

"No enemy of yours, since I am conveying you to a place, where, were I myself recognised and identified, iron to the heels, and hemp to the crag, would be my brief dooming[6]."

I paused and stood still on the pavement, drawing back so as to have the most perfect view of my companion which the light afforded, and which was sufficient to guard me against any sudden motion of assault.

"You have said," I answered, "either too much or too little—too much to induce me to confide in you as a mere stranger, since you avow yourself a person amenable to the laws of the country in which we are—and too little, unless you could show that you are unjustly subjected to their rigour."

As I ceased to speak, he made a step towards me. I drew back instinctively, and laid my hand on the hilt of my sword.

"What," said he, "on an unarmed man, and your friend?"

"I am yet ignorant if you are either the one or the other," I replied; "and, to say the truth, your language and manner might well entitle me to doubt both."

"It is manfully spoken," replied my conductor; "and I respect him whose hand can keep[7] his head.—I will be frank and free with you—I am conveying you to prison."

"To prison!" I exclaimed; "by what warrant, or for what offence?—You shall have my life sooner than my liberty—I defy you, and I will not follow you a step farther."

"I do not," he said, "carry you there as a prisoner; I am," he added, drawing himself haughtily up, "neither a messenger nor sheriff's officer. I carry you to see a prisoner from whose lips you will learn the risk in which you presently stand. Your liberty is little risked by the visit; mine is in some peril; but that I readily encounter on your account, for I care not for risk, and I love a free young blood, that kens[8] no protector but the cross o' the sword."

While he spoke thus, we had reached the principal street, and were pausing before a large building of hewn stone, garnished, as I thought I could perceive, with gratings of iron before the windows.

"Muckle[9]," said the stranger, whose language became more broadly national as he assumed a tone of colloquial freedom—"Muckle wad[10] the provost and bailies o' Glasgow gie[11] to hae[12] him sitting with iron garters to his hose within their tolbooth[13], that now stands wi' his legs as free as the red deer's on the outside on' t[14]. And little wad it avail them; for an if they had me there wi' a stane's[15] weight o' iron at every ankle, I would show them a toom[16] room and a lost lodger before tomorrow. But come on, what stint ye for[17]?"

## Chapter XXX

We approached within about twenty yards of the spot where the advanced guard had seen some appearance of an enemy. It was one of those promontories which run into the lake, and round the base of which the road had hitherto winded in the manner I have described. In the present case, however, the path, instead of keeping the water's edge, scaled the promontory by one or two rapid zigzags, carried in a broken track along the precipitous face of a slaty gray rock, which would otherwise have been absolutely inaccessible. On the top of this rock, only to be approached by a road so broken, so narrow, and so precarious, the corporal declared he had seen the bonnets and long-barrelled guns of several mountaineers, apparently touched among the long heath and brush-wood which crested the eminence. Captain Thornton ordered him to move forward with three files, to dislodge the supposed ambuscade, while at a more slow but steady pace, he advanced to his support with the rest of his party.

The attack which he meditated was prevented by the unexpected apparition of a female upon the summit of the rock. "Stand!" she said, with a commanding tone, "and tell me what ye seek in MacGregor's country?"

I have seldom seen a finer or more commanding form than this woman. She might be between the term of forty and fifty years, and had a countenance which must once have been of a masculine cast of beauty; though now, imprinted with deep lines by exposure to rough weather, and perhaps by the wasting influence of grief and passion, its features were only strong, harsh, and expressive. She wore her plaid, not drawn around her head and shoulders, as is the fashion of the women in Scotland, but disposed around her body as the Highland soldiers wear theirs. She had a man's bonnet, with a feather in it, and unsheathed sword in her hand, and a pair of pistols at her girdle.

"It's Helen Campbell, Rob's wife," said the Bailie, in a whisper of considerable alarm; "and where will be broken heads among us or it's lang[18]."

"What seek ye here?" she asked again of Captain Thornton, who had himself advanced to reconnoitre.

"We seek the outlaw, Rob Roy MacGregor Campbell," answered the officer, "and make no war on women; therefore offer no vain opposition to the king's troops, and assure yourself of civil treatment."

"Ay," retorted the Amazon[19], "I am no stranger to your tender mercies.

Ye have left me neither name nor fame—my mother's bones will shrink aside in their grave when mine are laid beside them.—Ye have left me and mine neither house nor hold[20], blanket nor bedding, cattle to feed us, or flocks to clothe us—Ye have taken from us all—all!—The very name of our ancestors have ye taken away, and now ye come for our lives."

"I seek no man's life," replied the Captain; "I only execute my orders. If you are alone, good woman, you have nought to fear—if there are any with you so rash as to offer useless resistance, their own blood be on their own heads. Move forword, sergeant."

"Forward—march!" said the non-commissioned officer.—"Huzza, my boys, for Rob Roy's head and a purse of gold!"

He quickened his pace into a run, followed by the six soldiers;—but as they attained the first traverse[21] of the ascent, the flash of a dozen of firelocks from various parts of the pass parted in quick succession and deliberate aim.

The sergeant, shot through the body, still struggled to gain the ascent, raised himself by his hands to clamber up the face of the rock, but relaxed his grasp, after a desperate effort, and falling, rolled from the face of the cliff into the deep lake, where he perished. Of the soldiers three fell, slain or disabled; the others retreated on their main body, all more or less wounded.

## Notes

1. Mirza, in his unequalled vision: It refers to Joseph Addison's story "The Vision of Mirza", which contains an allegoric description of a bridge of human life spanning the ocean of eternity.
2. Presbyterians: followers of Protestant doctrine which originated in Great Britain in the 17th century. Presbyterianism rejected the authority of the bishops and invested presbyters (elders) with all power.
3. I bide tryste: I have an appointment.
4. underlie a tremor: be seized with tremor
5. the news of a field stricken and won in Flanders: the news of a victory in Flanders
6. iron to the heels, and hemp to the crag, would be my brief dooming: I would be immediately put in irons and hanged.
   hemp: rope
   crag: (Scotch) neck
7. keep: defend
8. kens: (Scotch) knows, understands
9. muckle: (Scotch) much, a large amount
10. wad: (Scotch) would
11. gie: (Scotch) give
12. hae: (Scotch) have
13. tolbooth: (Scotch) jail
14. on' t: of it
15. stane: (Scotch) stone
16. toom: (Scotch) empty
17. what stint ye for: why did you stop
18. or it's lang: before long
19. Amazon: a fabulous race of female warriors in Greek mythology. Here it refers to Helen, Rob's wife.
20. hold: land

21. traverse: bend

## For Study and Discussion

1. In Chapter XXI, one can see a mysterious "meeting at night" which is never romantic as that of Robert Browning. What is the thought of the speaker "I"? What is he afraid of?
2. What is your opinion of the stranger in Chapter XXI? What can you learn about him from his words? What kind of person is the stranger? Why does he suddenly speak in Scottish dialect in the last paragraph of the selection?
3. What caused the suspense in Chapter XXI?
4. What image of the woman in Chapter XXX can you form? Does your image of her remind you of some woman guerrilla in Chinese literature, for example, "the elderly woman with double pistols"?
5. Why are Helen and her fellows against the king's troops?
6. What is the result of the charge at Helen and her fellows? Learn the last paragraph of this selection by heart.

### *Ivanhoe*

## The Story

Night was drawing near when Prior Aymer of Jorvaux and the haughty Templar, Brian de Bois-Guilbert, overtook a swineherd and a fool by the roadside and asked directions to Rotherwood, the dwelling of Cedric the Saxon. The answers of these serfs so confused the Templar and the Prior that they would have gone far afield had it not been for a pilgrim from the Holy Land whom they encountered shortly afterward. The pilgrim was also travelling to Rotherwood, and he brought them safely to Cedric's ball, where they claimed lodging for the night. The custom of those rude days afforded hospitality to all benighted travellers, and so Cedric gave a grudging welcome to the Norman lords.

There was a feast at Rotherwood that night. On the dais beside Cedric the Saxon sat his ward, the lovely Lady Rowena, descendant of the ancient Saxon princes. It was the old man's ambition to wed her to Athelestane of Coningsburgh of the line of King Alfred. Because his son, Wilfred of Ivanhoe, had fallen in love with Rowena, Cedric had banished him, and the young knight had gone with King Richard to Palestine. None in the banquet hall that night suspected that the pilgrim was Ivanhoe himself.

Another traveller who had claimed shelter at Rotherwood that night was an aged Jew, Isaac of York. Hearing some orders the Templar muttered to his servants as the feast ended, Ivanhoe warned the old Jew that Bois-Guilbert had designs on his moneybag or his person.

Without taking leave of their host the next morning, the disguised pilgrim and Isaac of York left Rotherwood and continued on their way to the nearby town of Ashby de la Zouche.

Many other travellers were also on their way to the town, for a great tournament was to be held there. Prince John, Regent of England in King Richard's absence, would preside. The winner of the tournament would be allowed to name the Queen of Love and Beauty and receive the prize of the passage of arms from her hands.

Ivanhoe attended the tournament with the word Disinherited written upon his shield. Entering the lists, he struck the shield of Bois-Guilbert with the point of his lance and challenged that knight to a mortal combat. In the first passage both knights splintered their lances but neither was unhorsed. At the second passage Ivanhoe's lance struck Bois-Guilbert's helmet and upset him. Then one by one Ivanhoe vanquished five knights who had agreed to take on all comers. When the heralds declared the Disinherited Knight victor of the tourney, Ivanhoe named Rowena the Queen of Love and Beauty.

In the tournament on the following day Ivanhoe was pressed hard by three antagonists, but he received unexpected help from a knight in black, whom the spectators had called the Black Sluggard because of his previous inactivity. Ivanhoe, because of his earlier triumphs during the day, was named champion of the tournament once more. In order to receive the gift from Lady Rowena, Ivanhoe had to remove his helmet. When he did so, he was recognised. He received the chaplet, his prize, kissed the hand of Lady Rowena, and then fainted from loss of blood. Isaac of York and his daughter, Rebecca, were sitting nearby, and Rebecca suggested to her father that they nurse Ivanhoe until he was well. Isaac and his daughter started for their home with the wounded knight carried in a horse litter. On the way they joined the train of Cedric the Saxon, who was still ignorant of the Disinherited Knight's identity.

Before the travellers had gone far, however, they were set upon and captured by a party led by three Norman knights, Bois-Guilbert, Maurice de Bracy, and Reginald Front de Boeuf. They were imprisoned in Front de Boeuf's castle of Torquilstone. De Bracy had designs upon Lady Rowena because she was an heiress of royal lineage. The Templar desired to possess Rebecca. Front de Boeuf hoped to extort a large sum of money from the aged Jew. Cedric was held for ransom. The wounded knight was put into the charge of an ancient hag named Ulrica.

Isaac and his daughter were placed in separate rooms. Bois-Guilbert went to Rebecca in her tower prison and asked her to adopt Christianity so that they might be married. But the plot of the Norman nobles with regard to their prisoners was thwarted by an assault on the castle by Richard the Lion-Hearted, the Black Sluggard of the tournament at Ashby, in company with Robin Hood and his outlaws. Ulrica aided the besiegers by starting a fire within the castle walls. Robin Hood and his men took the prisoners to the forest along with the Norman nobles. In the confusion, however, Bois-Guilbert escaped with Rebecca, and Isaac made preparation to ransom her from the Templar. De Bracy was set free and he hurried to inform Prince John that he had seen and talked with Richard. John plotted to make Richard his prisoner.

Isaac went to the establishment of the Knights Templar and begged to see Bois-Guilbert. Lucas de Beaumanoir, the grand master of the Templars, ordered Isaac admitted to his presence. Isaac was frightened when the grand master asked him his business with the Templar. When he told his story, the grand master learned of Bois-Guilbert's seizure of Rebecca. It was suggested that Bois-Guilbert was under a spell cast by Rebecca. Condemned as a witch, she was sentenced to be burned at the stake. In desperation she demanded, as was her right, a champion to defend her against the charge. Lucas de Beaumanoir agreed and named Bois-Guilbert champion of the Temple.

The day arrived for Rebecca's execution. A pile of wood had been laid around the stake. Rebecca, seated in a black chair, awaited the arrival of her defender. Three times the heralds called upon her champion to appear. At the third call a strange knight rode into the lists and announced himself as Rebecca's champion. When Bois-Guilbert realised that the stranger was Ivanhoe, he at first refused combat because Ivanhoe's wounds were not completely healed. But the grand master gave orders for the contest to begin. As everyone expected, the tired horse of Ivanhoe and its exhausted rider went down at the first blow, so that Ivanhoe's lance merely touched the shield of the Templar. Then to the astonishment of all, Bois-Guilbert reeled in his saddle and fell to the ground. Ivanhoe arose from where he had fallen and drew his sword. Placing his foot on the breast of the fallen knight, he called upon Bois-Guilbert to yield himself or die on the spot. There was no answer from Bois-Guilbert, for he was dead, a victim of the violence of his own passions. The grand master declared that Rebecca was acquitted of the charge against her.

At that moment the Black Knight appeared followed by a band of knights and men-at-arms. It was King Richard, who had come to arrest Rebecca's accusers on a charge of treason. The grand master saw the flag of the Temple hauled down and the royal standard raised in its place.

King Richard had returned in secret to reclaim his throne. Robin Hood became his true follower. Athelestane relinquished his claims to Lady Rowena's hand so that she and Ivanhoe could be married. Cedric the Saxon, reconciled at last with his son, gave his consent, and Richard himself graced their wedding.

Isaac and Rebecca left England for Granada, hoping to find in that foreign land greater happiness than could ever be theirs in England.

## Chapter XIII

The name of Ivanhoe was no sooner pronounced than it flew from mouth to mouth with all the celerity with which eagerness could convey and curiosity receive it. It was not long ere it reached the circle of the Prince, whose brow darkened as he heard the news. Looking around him, however, with an air of scorn, "My lords," said he, "and especially you, Sir Prior, what think ye of the doctrine the learned tell us concerning innate attractions and antipathies? Methinks that I felt the presence of my brother's minion, even when I least guessed whom yonder suit of armour inclosed."

"Front-de-Boeuf must prepare to restore his fief of Ivanhoe," said De Bracy, who, having discharged his part honourably in the tournament, had laid his shield and helmet aside, and again mingled with the Prince's retinue.

"Ay," answered Waldemar Fitzurse, "this gallant is likely to reclaim the castle and manor which Richard assigned to him, and which your Highness's generosity has since given to Front-de-Boeuf."

"Front-de-Boeuf," replied John, "is a man more willing to swallow three manors such as Ivanhoe than to disgorge one of them. For the rest, sirs, I hope none here will deny my right to confer the fiefs of the crown upon the faithful followers who are around me, and ready to perform the usual military service, in the room of those who have wandered to foreign countries, and can neither render homage nor service when called upon."

The audience were too much interested in the question not to pronounce the prince's assumed right altogether indubitable. "A generous prince, a most noble lord, who thus takes upon himself the task of rewarding his faithful followers!"

Such were the words which burst from the train, —expectants, all of them, of similar grants at the expense of King Richard's followers and favourites, if indeed they had not as yet received such.

Waldemar, whose curiosity had led him towards the place where Ivanhoe had fallen to the ground, now returned. "The gallant," said he, "is likely to give your Highness little disturbance, and to leave Front-de-Boeuf in the quiet possession of his gains. He is severely wounded."

"Whatever becomes of him," said Prince John, "he is victor of the day; and were he tenfold our enemy, or the devoted friend of our brother, which is perhaps the same, his wounds must be looked to. Our own physician shall attend him."

A stern smile curled the prince's lip as he spoke. Waldemar Fitzurse hastened to reply that Ivanhoe was already removed from the lists, and in the custody of his friends.

"I was somewhat afflicted," he said, "to see the grief of the Queen of Love and Beauty, whose sovereignty of a day this event has changed into mourning. I am not a man to be moved by a woman's lament for her lover; but this same Lady Rowena suppressed her sorrow with such dignity of manner that it could only be discovered by her folded hands and her tearless eye, which trembled as it remained fixed on the lifeless form before her."

"Who is this Lady Rowena," said Prince John, "of whom we have heard so much?"

"A Saxon heiress of large possessions," replied the Prior Aymer, "a rose of loveliness and a jewel of wealth, the fairest among a thousand, a bundle of myrrh and a cluster of camphire."

"We shall cheer her sorrows," said Prince John, "and wed her to a Norman. She seems a minor, and must therefore be at our royal disposal in marriage. —How sayst thou, De Bracy? What thinkst thou of gaining fair lands and livings by wedding a Saxon, after the fashion of the followers of the Conqueror?"

"If the lands are to my liking, my lord," answered De Bracy, "it will be hard to displease me with a bride; and deeply will I hold myself bound to your Highness for a good deed, which will fulfil all promises made in favour of your servant and vassal."

"We will not forget it," said Prince John; "and that we may instantly go to work, command our seneschal presently to order the attendance of Lady Rowena and her company; that is, the rude churl her guardian, and the Saxon ox whom the Black Knight struck down in the tournament, upon this evening's banquet. —De Bigot," he added to his seneschal, "thou wilt word this our second summons so courteously as to gratify the pride of these Saxons, and make it impossible for them again to refuse; although, by the bones of Becket, courtesy to them is casting pearls before swine."

Prince John had proceeded thus far, and was about to give the signal for retiring from the lists, when a small billet was put into his hand.

"From whence?" said Prince John, looking at the person by whom it was delivered.

"From foreign parts, my lord, but from whence I know not," replied his attendant. "A Frenchman brought it hither, who said he had ridden night and day to put it into the hands of your Highness."

The prince looked narrowly at the superscription, and then at the seal, placed so as to secure the flex-silk with which the billet was surrounded, and which bore the impression of three fleurs-de-lis. John then opened the billet with apparent agitation, which visibly and greatly increased when he had perused the contents, which were expressed in these words: —

"Take heed to yourself for the devil is unchained!"

The prince turned as pale as death, looked first on the earth and then to heaven, like a man who has received news that sentence of execution has been passed upon him. Recovering from the first effects of his surprise, he took Waldemar Fitzurse and De Bracy aside, and put the billet into their hands successively. "It means," he added in a faltering voice, "that my brother Richard has obtained his freedom."

"This may be a false alarm or a forged letter," said De Bracy.

"It is France's own hand and seal," replied Prince John.

"It is time, then," said Fitzurse, "to draw our party to a head, either at York or some other centrical place. A few days later, and it will be indeed too late, Your Highness must break short this present mummery."

"The yeomen and commons," said De Bracy, "must not be dismissed discontented for lack of their share in the sports."

"The day," said Waldemar, "is not yet very far spent. Let the archers shoot a few rounds at the target and the prize be adjudged. This will be an abundant fulfilment of the prince's promises, so far as this herd of Saxon serfs is concerned."

"I thank thee, Waldemar," said the prince; "thou remindest me, too, that I have a debt to pay to that insolent peasant who yesterday insulted our person. Our banquet also shall go forward tonight as we proposed. Were this my last hour of power, it should be an hour sacred to revenge and to pleasure. Let new cares come with tomorrow's new day."

The sound of the trumpets soon recalled those spectators who had already begun to leave the field; and proclamation was made that Prince John, suddenly called by high and peremptory public duties, held himself obliged to discontinue the entertainments of tomorrow's festival; nevertheless, that, unwilling so many good yeomen should depart without a trial of skill, he was pleased to appoint them, before leaving the ground, presently to execute the competition of archery intended for the morrow. To the best archer a prize was to be awarded, being a bugle-horn mounted with silver, and a silken baldric richly ornamented with a medallion of St Hubert, the patron of silvan sport.

More than thirty yeomen at first presented themselves as competitors, several of whom were rangers and underkeepers in the royal forests of Needwood and Charnwood. When, however, the archers understood with whom they were to be matched, upwards of twenty, withdrew themselves from the contest, unwilling to encounter the dishonour of almost certain defeat; for in those days the skill of each celebrated marksman was as well known for many miles round him as the qualities of a horse trained at Newmarket are familiar to those who frequent that well-known meeting.

The diminished list of competitors for silvan fame still amounted to eight. Prince John stepped from his royal seat to view more nearly the persons of these chosen yeomen, several of whom wore the royal livery. Having satisfied his curiosity by this investigation, he looked for the object of his resentment, whom he observed standing on the same spot, and with the same composed countenance which he had exhibited upon the preceding day.

"Fellow," said Prince John, "I guessed by thy insolent babble thou wert no true lover of the longbow, and I see thou darest not adventure thy skill among such merry men as stand yonder."

"Under favour, sir," replied the yeoman, "I have another reason for refraining to shoot besides the fearing discomfiture and disgrace."

"And what is thy other reason?" said Prince John, who, for some cause which perhaps he could not himself have explained, felt a painful curiosity respecting this individual.

"Because," replied the woodsman, "I know not if these yeomen and I are used to shoot at the same marks; and because, moreover, I know not how your Grace might relish the winning of a third prize by one who has unwittingly fallen under your displeasure."

Prince John coloured as he put the question, "What is thy name, yeoman?"

"Locksley," answered the yeoman.

"Then, Locksley," said Prince John, "thou shalt shoot in thy turn, when these yeomen have displayed their skill. If thou carriest the prize, I will add to it twenty nobles; but if thou losest it, thou shalt be stripped of thy Lincoln green, and scourged out of the lists with bowstrings, for a wordy and insolent braggart."

"And how if I refuse to shoot on such a wager?" said the yeoman. "Your Grace's power, supported as it is by so many men-at-arms, may indeed easily strip and scourge me, but cannot compel me to bend or to draw my bow."

"If thou refusest my fair proffer," said the prince, "the provost of the lists shall cut thy bowstring, break thy bow and arrows, and expel thee from the presence as a faint-hearted craven."

"This is no fair chance you put on me, proud prince," said the yeoman, "to compel me to peril myself against the best archers of Leicester and Staffordshire, under the penalty of infamy if they should overshoot me. Nevertheless, I will obey your pleasure."

"Look to him close, men-at-arms," said Prince John. "His heart is sinking. I am jealous lest he attempt to escape the trial. —And do you, good fellows, shoot boldly round. A buck and a butt of wine are ready for your refreshment in yonder tent when the prize is won."

A target was placed at the upper end of the southern avenue which led to the lists. The contending archers took their station in turn at the bottom of the southern access, the distance between that station and the mark allowing full distance for what was called a "shot at rovers". The archers, having previously determined by lot their order of precedence, were to shoot each three shafts in succession. The sports were regulated by an officer of inferior rank, termed the "provost of the games"; for the high rank of the marshals of the lists would have been held degraded had they condescended to superintend the sports of the yeomanry.

One by one the archers, stepping forward, delivered their shafts yeomanlike and bravely. Of the twenty-four arrows, shot in succession, ten were fixed in the target, and the others ranged so near it, that, considering the distance of the mark, it was accounted good archery. Of the ten shafts which hit the target, two within the inner ring were shot by Hubert, a forester in the service of Malvoisin, who was accordingly pronounced victorious.

"Now, Locksley," said Prince John to the bold yeoman with a bitter smile, "wilt thou try conclusions with Hubert, or wilt thou yield up bow, baldric, and quiver to the provost of sports?"

"Sith it be no better," said Locksley, "I am content to try my fortune, on condition that, when I have shot two shafts at yonder mark of Hubert's, he shall be bound to shoot one at that which I shall propose."

"That is but fair," answered Prince John, "and it shall not be refused thee. —If thou dost beat this braggart, Hubert, I will fill the bugle with silver pennies for thee."

"A man can do but his best," answered Hubert, "but my grandsire drew a good longbow at Hastings, and I trust not to dishonour his memory."

The former target was now removed, and a fresh one of the same size placed in its room. Hubert, who, as victor in the first trial of skill, had the right to shoot first, took his aim with great deliberation, long measuring the distance with his eye, while he held in his hand his bended bow, with the arrow placed on the string. At length he made a step forward, and raising the bow at the full stretch of his left arm, till the centre or grasping-place was nigh level with his face, he drew his bowstring to his ear. The arrow whistled through the air, and lighted within the inner ring of the target, but not exactly in the centre.

"You have not allowed for the wind, Hubert," said his antagonist, bending his bow, "or that had been a better shot."

So saying, and without showing the least anxiety to pause upon his aim, Locksley stepped to the appointed station, and shot his arrow as carelessly in appearance as if he had not even looked at the mark. He was speaking almost at the instant that the shaft left the bowstring, yet it alighted in the target two inches nearer to the white spot which marked the centre than that of Hubert.

"By the light of Heaven!" said Prince John to Hubert, "and thou suffer that runagate knave to overcome thee, thou art worthy of the gallows!"

Hubert had but one set speech for all occasions. "And your Highness were to hang me," he said, "a man can but do his best. Nevertheless, my grandsire drew a good bow—"

"The foul fiend on thy grandsire and all his generation!" interrupted John. "Shoot, knave, and shoot thy best, or it shall be the worse for thee!"

Thus exhorted, Hubert resumed his place, and, not neglecting the caution which he had received from his adversary, he made the necessary allowance for a very light air of wind which had just arisen, and shot so successfully that his arrow alighted in the very centre of the target.

"A Hubert, a Hubert!" shouted the populace, more interested in a known person than in a stranger. "In the clout, in the clout! A Hubert forever!"

"Thou canst not mend that shot, Locksley," said the prince with an insulting smile.

"I will notch his shaft for him, however," replied Locksley.

And letting fly his arrow with a little more precaution than before, it lighted right upon that of his competitor, which it split to shivers. The people who stood around were so astonished at his wonderful dexterity that they could not even give vent to their surprise in their usual clamour. "This must be the Devil, and no man of flesh and blood," whispered the yeomen to each other. "Such archery was never seen since a bow was first bent in Britain."

"And now," said Locksley, "I will crave your Grace's permission to plant such a mark as is used in the North Country, and welcome every brave yeoman who shall try a shot at it to win a smile from the bonny lass he loves best."

He then turned to leave the lists. "Let your guards attend me," he said, "if you please—I go but to cut a rod from the next willow-bush."

Prince John made a signal that some attendants should follow him in case of his escape; but the cry of "Shame! Shame!" which burst from the multitude, induced him to alter his ungenerous purpose.

Locksley returned almost instantly with a willow wand about six feet in length, perfectly straight, and rather thicker than a man's thumb. He began to peel this with great composure, observing, at the same time, that to ask a good woodsman to shoot at a target so broad as had hitherto been used was to put shame upon his skill. "For his own part," he said, "and in the land where he was bred, men would as soon take for their mark King Arthur's Round Table, which held sixty knights around it." "A child of seven years old," he said, "might hit yonder target with a headless shaft; but," added he, walking deliberately to the other end of the lists, and sticking the willow wand upright in the ground, "he that hits that rod at five-score yards, I call him an archer fit to bear both bow and quiver before a king, and it were the stout King Richard himself."

"My grandsire," said Hubert, "drew a good bow at the battle of Hastings, and never shot at such a mark in his life; and neither will I. If this yeoman can cleave that rod, I give him the bucklers; or, rather, I yield to the devil that is in his jerkin, and not to any human skill. A man can but do his best, and I will not shoot where I am sure to miss. I might as well shoot at the edge of our parson's whittle, or at a wheat straw, or at a sunbeam, as at a twinkling white streak which I can hardly see."

"Cowardly dog!" said Prince John. "Sirrah Locksley, do thou shoot; but, if thou hittest such a mark, I will say thou art the first man ever did so. Howe'er it be, thou shalt not crow over us with a mere show of superior skill."

"I will do my best, as Hubert says," answered Locksley; "no man can do more."

So saying, he again bent his bow, but on the present occasion looked with attention to his weapon, and changed the string, which he thought was no longer truely round, having been a little frayed by the two former shots. He then took his aim with some deliberation, and the multitude awaited the event in breathless silence. The archer vindicated their opinion of his skill: his arrow split the willow rod against which it was aimed. A jubilee of acclamations followed; and even Prince John, in admiration of Locksley's skill, lost for an instant his dislike to his person. "These twenty nobles," he said, "which, with the bugle, thou hast fairly won, are thine own. We will make them fifty, if thou wilt take livery and service with us as a yeoman of our body guard, and be near to our person. For never did so strong a hand bend a bow, or so true an eye direct a shaft."

"Pardon me, noble Prince," said Locksley, "but I have vowed, that if ever I take service, it should be with your royal brother King Richard. These twenty nobles I leave to Hubert, who has this day drawn as brave a bow as his grandsire did at Hastings. Had his modesty not refused the trial, he would have hit the wand as well as I."

Hubert shook his head as he received with reluctance the bounty of the stranger, and Locksley, anxious to escape further observation, mixed with the crowd, and was seen no more.

The victorious archer would not perhaps have escaped John's attention so easily, had not that prince had other subjects of anxious and more important meditation pressing upon his mind at that instant. He called upon his chamberlain as he gave the signal for retiring from the lists, and commanded him instantly to gallop to Ashby, and seek out Isaac the Jew. "Tell the dog," he said, "to send me, before sundown, two thousand crowns. He knows the security, but thou mayest show him this ring for a token. The rest of the money must be paid at York within six days. If he neglects, I will have the unbelieving villain's head. Look that thou pass him not on the way, for the circumcised slave was displaying his stolen finery amongst us."

So saying, the prince resumed his horse, and returned to Ashby, the whole crowd breaking up and dispersing upon his retreat.

## For Study and Discussion

1. From this selection, what can you know about Prince John? Who is he?
2. How is Lady Rowena described?
3. Why does the prince feel uneasy when reads the billet? What does it mean?
4. When all agreed that the contest should continue, the prince said to Waldemar, "Were this my last hour of power, it should be an hour sacred to revenge and to pleasure. Let new cares come with tomorrow's new day." What can you perceive about the prince?
5. Who is Locksley? How does Prince John trigger him to shoot? Why does Locksley refuse to shoot?
6. Who is King Richard? Try to find some historical facts about him.
7. What is a historical novel? Some people say the historical novels of Walter Scott bear interesting similarities to those of Louis Cha (金庸). Do you agree with it? Why or why not?

# Chapter 3

# Samuel Taylor Coleridge

## Life and Works

Samuel Taylor Coleridge (1772–1834) is mainly remembered for his masterpiece *The Rime of the Ancient Mariner*. But today he is also recognised as one of the important critics who even influenced later literary criticism.

He was born in Devonshire. When he was only ten years old, his father died. He was sent to study in London where he was enthusiastic and brilliant. In 1791, he went to Cambridge University where he, to people's dismay, neglected his study and fell into idleness, carelessness and debt. In 1793 he left Cambridge and joined the army in which he had a miserable life. His brothers sent him back to Cambridge. But he left it again in 1794.

In 1797 he met William Wordsworth and began the happiest period of his life. He and Wordsworth published *Lyrical Ballads* in collaboration in 1798. *The Rime of the Ancient Mariner* is the first and only poem of Coleridge in this collection. This alone won him the honour of a great poet. According to their plan, Coleridge's task was to write about supernatural things or people.

In 1798 he went to Germany with Wordsworth and Dorothy. At the University of Gottingen, he began his lifelong study of Kant and other German philosophers.

Coleridge was a great poet. Though a romantic poet, he is, in some sense, a medievalist, fond of the unusual and supernatural things. As a romantic poet, his imaginative power is intense and his language melodious. His fancy cannot be matched. His early poetry shows the influence of Gray and Blake, especially of the latter. But in his later poems his imagination is bridled by thought and study.

He was also an influential critic, the first critic of the romantic school, highly praised even today. An eloquent speaker of the romantic age, he was good at giving lectures. Between 1808 and 1815 he delivered a series of lectures on Shakespeare, which were later collected in his *Lectures and Notes on Shakespeare and Other English Poets*. His most important work of criticism written in prose is *Biographia Literaria*, which gave the romantic poetry a new principle of criticism: the task of a critic being not to judge but to appreciate and interpret. This is still important today because he rightly pointed out the way from a poetry reader, to an appreciator, interpreter and critic. He also explained the function and nature of a poet and a critic. According to Coleridge, the poet was a creator and the critic was an assistant in the work of creation. The poet, as a man endowed with imaginative genius and fine perception, must be allowed to present the truth in his own without regard to rules or models. And the critic must enter into the poet's purpose and art, and interpret ideas and beauty for the benefit of the reader. This principle of criticism is useful even today.

His ideas on poetry writing, together with the ideas of Keats, influenced the aesthetic theory of T. S. Eliot though Eliot was generally against Wordsworth's idea that all good poetry is a spontaneous overflow of powerful feeling recollected in tranquility. In this respect, Eliot was not unreasonable in that Wordsworth was different from Coleridge and Keats in terms of poetic theory though they were all romantic poets.

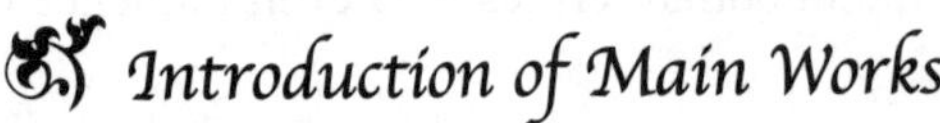

## Introduction of Main Works

### *The Rime of the Ancient Mariner*

*The Rime of the Ancient Mariner* is his masterpiece. It tells a strange story in the form of ballad. Three guests are going to a wedding party, but one of them is detained by an ancient mariner who insists on telling him of his adventures on the sea. As the mariner says, when his ship sails towards the South Pole, an albatross comes through the snow-fog and perches on the rigging. The mariner kills it. Then misfortune falls on the ship. The whole crew, with the exception of the mariner, dies of thirst as a punishment for the act of inhospitality. The spell breaks only when the mariner repents his cruelty.

*The Rime of the Ancient Mariner* is a story of sin and redemption. This is also a story asking us to respect the ecological balance between man and nature. The tale's mysteriousness is perplexing to many readers. Some readers track the appearance of the sun and the moon as symbols of evil and good. Different readers may find different explanations. But the greatest appeal is to the imagination.

### *Kubla Khan*

*Kubla Khan* or *A Vision in a Dream* is said to have been composed in the summer of 1797. According to the poet, this fragment of the poem was inspired by fancy. The poet fell asleep after taking "two grains of opium" as medicine which was prescribed to him for his health. He fell asleep while he was reading about Kubla Khan from an old book of travels entitled *Purchas his Pilgrimage*: "In Xamdu did Kubla Khan build a stately palace, encompassing sixteen miles of plain ground with a wall, wherein are fertile meadows, pleasant springs, delightful streams, and all sorts of beasts of chase and game, and in the midst thereof a sumptuous house of pleasure." He continued for about three hours in profound sleep and formed several hundred lines, between two hundred and three hundred lines in his mind. When he awoke he immediately began to write them down. But he had written fifty lines when he was interrupted by a person on business from Porlock and detained by him more than an hour. On his return to his room, he found, to his great surprise, that…with the exception of eight or ten scattered lines and images, all the rest had passed away like the images on the surface of a stream into which a stone had been cast. So the poem was left a fragment.

About the place of Xamdu, it is uncertain. Some people say it referred to Shangdu in present Inner Mongolia. Some people think it referred to Dadu, the present Beijing, capital of the Yuan Dynasty. The poem described this place as one where the Mongol ruler Kubla Khan, grandson of Genghis Khan, built a pleasure dome on the river Alph. This "sacred river" arises from a violent waterfall in a deep chasm in the side of a hill. After descending from its tumultuous beginning the river winds for about five miles through wood and dale and alongside the palace of Kubla Khan. Then it disappeared into underground caverns.

*Kubla Khan* is more suggestive than coherent. It is so suggestive that no one can unravel its mystery. The names of places, for example, Xamdu, Abyssinia, Mount Abora, are associated with different places in the ancient world. The lush description contains great emotion, as if some violent and fearful events were to happen. The mystery of this poem is always the source of pleasure to readers and critics.

## Selections

### *The Rime of the Ancient Mariner*[1]

Part I

It is an ancient Mariner,
And he stoppeth one of three.
"By thy long grey beard and glittering eye,
Now wherefore stopp'st thou me?

The Bridegroom's doors are opened wide,
And I am next of kin;
The guests are met, the feast is set:
May'st[2] hear the merry din."

He holds him with his skinny hand,
"There was a ship," quoth he.
"Hold off! unhand me, grey-beard loon!"
Eftsoons[3] his hand dropt he.

He holds him with his glittering eye—
The wedding-guest stood still,
And listens like a three years' child:
The Mariner hath his will.

The wedding-guest sat on a stone:
He cannot choose but hear;
And thus spake on that ancient man,
The bright-eyed Mariner.

"The ship was cheered, the harbour cleared,
Merrily did we drop
Below the kirk[4], below the hill,
Below the light house top.

The sun came up upon the left,
Out of the sea came he!
And he shone bright, and on the right
Went down into the sea.

Higher and higher every day,
Till over the mast at noon[5]—"
The wedding-guest here beat his breast,
For he heard the loud bassoon.

The bride hath paced into the hall,
Red as a rose is she;
Nodding their heads before her goes
The merry minstrelsy.

The wedding-guest he beat his breast,
Yet he cannot choose but hear;
And thus spake on that ancient man,
The bright-eyed Mariner.

"And now the storm-blast came, and he
Was tyrannous and strong:
He struck with his o'ertaking wings,
And chased us south along.

With sloping masts and dipping prow,
As who pursued with yell and blow
Still treads the shadow of his foe,
And forward bends his head,
The ship drove fast, loud roared the blast,
And southward aye we fled.

And now there came both mist and snow,
And it grew wondrous cold:
And ice, mast-high, came floating by,
As green as emerald.

And through the drifts[6] the snowy clifts[7]
Did send a dismal sheen:
Nor shapes of men nor beasts we ken—
The ice was all between.

The ice was here, the ice was there,
The ice was all around:
It cracked and growled, and roared and howled,
Like noises in a swound[8]!

At length did cross an Albatross,
Thorough[9] the fog it came;
As if it had been a Christian soul,
We hailed it in God's name.

It ate the food it ne'er had eat[10],
And round and round it flew.
The ice did split with a thunder-fit;
The helmsman steered us through!

And a good south wind sprung up behind;
The Albatross did follow,
And every day, for food or play,
Came to the mariner's hollo!

In mist or cloud, on mast or shroud[11],
It perched for vespers[12] nine;

Whiles all the night, through fog-smoke white,
Glimmered the white moon-shine."

"God save thee, ancient Mariner!
From the fiends, that plague thee thus!—
Why look'st thou so?"—With my cross-bow
I shot the Albatross.

## Notes

1. The selection is Part I of the long poem. It begins with one of wedding guests trying in vain to get away and join the wedding party. The mariner insists on telling the guest his story. He was a seaman, on a ship driven by storms to the Antarctic and blocked in ice. At this time the ship was visited by an albatross, a great sea bird. They were glad to see it and hailed it "in God's name". Then their luck improved: the ice broke up and a breeze from the south pushed them north through the fog. But suddenly, in an act of perverse cruelty, the mariner shot the benevolent bird. Misfortunes were to happen.
2. May'st: you may
3. Eftsoons: at once
4. kirk: church
5. over…noon: The ship reaches the equator.
6. drifts: mists
7. clifts: icebergs
8. swound: swoon
9. Thorough: through
10. eat: old form of "eaten"
11. shroud: rope of the rigging
12. vespers: evenings

## For Study and Discussion

1. Why does the ancient mariner insist on telling his story?
2. How would the wedding guest feel when he was forced to listen to the story of the mariner?
3. The language of this poem is not difficult to understand. But the atmosphere of the poem is mysterious and terrifying. Cite words, phrases and vivid images that contribute to the creation of the atmosphere.

Chapter 4

# Jane Austen

## Life and Works

Jane Austen (1775–1817) was born in Hampshire, England. She was educated at home, and spent her life quietly and cheerfully while doing small domestic duties. She began to write at an early age, very often on a little table in the family sitting-room.

In 1801, the family moved to Bath, a resort city. In 1806, her father died. The family moved first to Southampton and then back to Hampshire. Austen remained single all her life. She spent her life making visits to the homes of relatives and writing novels.

But publishing the novels was difficult. Her *Pride and Prejudice* waited 16 years to be published. *Northanger Abbey* was sold for a small sum of money to a publisher who laid it aside and forgot it. Only *Sense and Sensibility* brought her success, which helped her other novels to be published. When *Emma* was published in 1815, somebody wrote and published a favourable review anonymously in the *Quarterly Review*, which brought fame to Jane Austen. Later people came to know that it was written by Walter Scott.

Austen died at Winchester in 1817, quietly, known by few as few knew how she lived. Today few people do not know her.

Chronologically, Austen as a novelist belonged to the romantic period. Her life was ordinary and uneventful, but she could show the beauty and charm of commonplace things. She completed six novels, *Northanger Abbey*, *Persuasion*, *Sense and Sensibility*, *Pride and Prejudice*, *Mansfield Park* and *Emma*. Each is perfect, and there is no choosing between them for one who enjoys her quiet irony and her simple delicate analysis of character. There are no heroic passions nor astounding adventures. *Northanger Abbey* is a gentle satire on the mysterious tale of haunted castles. In all her novels the courtship of young people, though serious and sympathetic, is subduced by humour to the ordinary plane of emotion. She is the founder of the novel which deals with unimportant middle-class people and of which there are many fine examples in later English fiction. Her style is easy and effortless, a perfect example of what De Quincey meant when he said that one should havc to turn to the prose of the cultivated gentlewoman for English uncorrupted by the slang and cant of the world.

## Brief Comment

Jane Austen did not write about great events. She was not even influenced by the French Revolution. Her novels are calm pictures of social life, untouched by the ugliness of the outside world. She understood the importance of family in human affairs, and brought the novel of family life to its highest point of perfection. She kept the action to scenes familiar to her. Her knowledge was limited, but deep and true. She managed her characters with a master's touch. Elizabeth Bennet in *Pride and Prejudice* is as delightful as Austen called her. Mr. Bennet is nearly as delightful, and most of other leading characters in the novel are first-class literary creations. The famous opening sentence can never be forgotten by readers.

About the scope of her novels, it is commonly agreed that Austen deliberately restricted the scope to the realms of her rather limited experience. She dealt with the social relationships among families of the small-town gentry, whose lives were taken up with visiting, walking in the countryside, and attending parties and picnics.

The action of each novel involves a problem of courtship. The heroine must avoid suitors and, without violating the restraints of modesty, attract the right marriage partner. The tone of each novel is ironic. Austen satirised the pride, snobbishness and foolish sentimentality of her characters. But Austen did not deal with questions of social justice or political inequality. In this respect, she belonged to the classical age that had just ended.

In her novels, the plots are simple and grow naturally out of the characters and their ordinary relations, but incidents as well as characters are handled with perfect sureness of touch and with the perfect mastery of assured knowledge. One of the fine points of her art shown in her novels is her skill in the treatment of conversation. The characters are made to reveal themselves through their own words, and Austen seemed always able to find the precise expression that accurately fits the character and the occasion. In possession of neat humour and a satirical touch, her style is an almost perfect instrument for her purpose—simple, clear, quiet, precise, keen, suggestive and mildly ironical.

## Selections

### ***Pride and Prejudice***

### The Story

*Pride and Prejudice,* finished in 1797, has been regarded as Jane Austen's masterpiece. With a carefully constructed plot, it is written in an elegant style. The first sentence of the novel sets the tone of it. The theme of marriage centres on the conflict between the "prejudice" of

Elizabeth and the "pride" of Mr. Darcy. Her other novels are of essentially the same type. The story goes as follows.

The chief business of Mrs. Bennet's life was to find suitable husbands for her five daughters. Consequently she heard with elation that Netherfield Park, one of the great houses in the neighbourhood, had been let to a London gentleman named Mr. Bingley. Gossip such as Mrs. Bennet loved reported him a rich and altogether eligible young bachelor. Mr. Bennet heard the news with his usual dry calmness, suggesting in his mild way that perhaps Bingley was not moving into the county for the single purpose of marrying one of the Bennet daughters.

Mr. Bingley's first public appearance in the neighbourhood was at a ball. With him were his two sisters, the husband of the older, and Mr. Darcy, Bingley's friend. Bingley was an immediate success in local society, and he and Jane, the oldest Bennet daughter, a pretty girl of sweet and gentle disposition, were attracted to each other at once. His friend, Darcy, however, created a bad impression, seeming cold and extremely proud. In particular, he insulted Elizabeth Bennet, a girl of spirit and intelligence and her father's favourite. He refused to dance with her when she was sitting down for lack of a partner, and he said in her hearing that he was in no mood to prefer young ladies slighted by other men. On future occasions, however, he began to admire Elizabeth in spite of himself. At a later ball she had the satisfaction of refusing him a dance.

Jane's romance with Bingley flourished quietly, aided by family calls, dinners and balls. His sisters pretended great fondness for Jane, who believed them completely sincere. The more critical and discerning Elizabeth suspected them of hypocrisy, and quite rightly, for they made great fun of Jane's relations, especially her vulgar, garrulous mother and her two ill-bred officer-mad younger sisters. Miss Caroline Bingley, who was eager to marry Darcy and shrewdly aware of his growing admiration for Elizabeth, was especially loud in her ridicule of the Bennet family. Elizabeth herself became Caroline's particular target when she walked three muddy miles to visit Jane, who was sick with a cold at Netherfield Park after a ride through the rain to accept an invitation from the Bingley sisters. Until Jane was able to be moved home, Elizabeth stayed to nurse her. During her visit Elizabeth received enough attention from Darcy to make Caroline Bingley long sincerely for Jane's recovery. Nor were her fears ill-founded. Darcy admitted to himself that he would be in some danger from the charm of Elizabeth, if it were not for her interior family connections.

Elizabeth now acquired a new admirer in the person of Mr. Collins, a ridiculously pompous clergyman and a distant cousin of the Bennets, who would some day inherit Mr. Bennet's property. Mr. Collins' patroness, Lady Catherine de Bourgh, had urged him to marry, and he, always obsequiously obedient to her wishes, hastened to comply. The entail gave him Mr. Bennet's property, which caused a lot of hardship for the Bennet sisters. Thinking to alleviate it, Mr. Collins first proposed to Elizabeth. Much to her mother's displeasure and her father's joy she firmly and promptly rejected him. He almost immediately transferred his affections to Elizabeth's best friend, Charlotte Lucas, who, twenty-seven and somewhat homely, accepted at once his offer of marriage.

During Mr. Collins' visit, the younger Bennet sisters, Kitty and Lydia, on one of their many walks to Meryton, met a fascinating new officer, Mr. Wickham, stationed with the regiment there. Outwardly charming, he became a favourite among the ladies, even with Elizabeth. She was willing to believe the story that he had been cheated out of an inheritance left him by his godfather, Darcy's father. Her suspicions of Darcy's arrogant and grasping nature deepened when Wickham did not come to a ball given by the Bingleys, a dance at which Darcy was present.

Soon after the ball, the entire Bingley party suddenly left Netherfield Park. They departed with no intention of returning, as Caroline wrote Jane in a short farewell note which hinted that Bingley might soon become engaged to Darcy's sister. Jane accepted this news at face value and believed that her friend Caroline was telling her gently that her brother loved elsewhere, and that she must cease to hope. Elizabeth, however, was sure of a plot by Darcy and Bingley's sisters to separate him from Jane. She persuaded Jane that Bingley did love her and that he would return to Hertfordshire before that winter was over. Jane almost believed her until she received a letter from Caroline assuring her that they were all settled in London for the winter. Even after Jane told her this news, Elizabeth remained convinced of Bingley's affection for her sister, and deplored the lack of resolution which made him putty in the hands of his designing friend.

About that time Mrs. Bennet's sister, Mrs. Gardiner, an amiable and intelligent woman with a great deal of affection for her two oldest nieces, arrived for a Christmas visit. She suggested to the Bennets that Jane return to London with her for a rest and change of scene and—so it was understood between Mrs. Gardiner and Elizabeth—to renew her acquaintance with Bingley. Elizabeth, not too hopeful for the success of the plan, pointed out that proud Darcy would never let his friend call on Jane in the unfashionable London street on which the Gardiners lived. Jane accepted the invitation, however, and she and Mrs. Gardiner set out for London.

The time drew near for the wedding of Elizabeth's friend, Charlotte Lucas, to the obnoxious Mr. Collins. Charlotte asked Elizabeth to visit her in Kent. In spite of her feeling that there could be little pleasure in such a visit, Elizabeth promised to do so. She felt that in taking such a husband Charlotte was marrying simply for the sake of an establishment, as was indeed the case. Since she herself could not sympathise with her friend's action, Elizabeth thought their days of real intimacy were over. As March approached, however, she found herself eager to see her friend, and she set out with pleasure on the journey with Charlotte's father and sister. On their way, the party stopped in London to see the Gardiners and Jane. Elizabeth found her sister well and outwardly happy, though she had not seen Bingley and his sisters had paid only one call. Elizabeth was sure Bingley had not been told of Jane's presence in London and blamed Darcy for keeping it from him.

Soon after arriving at the Collins' home, the whole party was honoured, as Mr. Collins repeatedly assured them, by a dinner invitation from Lady Catherine de Bourgh, Darcy's aunt and Mr. Collins' patroness. Elizabeth found Lady Catherine a haughty, ill-mannered woman and her daughter thin, sickly, and shy. Lady Catherine was extremely fond of inquiring into the affairs of others and giving them unasked advice. Elizabeth turned off the meddling old woman's questions with cool indirectness, and saw from the effect that she was probably the first who had dared to do so.

Soon after Elizabeth's arrival, Darcy came to visit his aunt and cousin. He called frequently the parsonage, and he and Elizabeth resumed their conversational fencing matches. His rather stilted attentions were suddenly climaxed by a proposal of marriage, but one couched in such proud and condescending terms that Elizabeth indignantly refused him. When he requested her reason for such an emphatic rejection, she mentioned his part in separating Bingley and Jane, and also his mistreatment of Wickham. Angry, he left abruptly, but the next day brought a letter answering her charges. He did not deny his part in separating Jane and Bingley, but he gave as his reasons the improprieties of Mrs. Bennet and her younger daughters, and also his sincere belief that Jane did not love Bingley. As for his alleged mistreatment of Wickham, he proved that he had in reality acted most generously toward the unprincipled Wickham, who had repaid his kindness by attempting to elope with Darcy's young sister. Elizabeth, at first incensed at the proud tones in which he wrote, was at length forced to acknowledge the justice of all he said, and her prejudice against him began to weaken. Without seeing him again, she returned home.

She found her younger sisters clamouring to go to Brighton, where the regiment formerly stationed at Meryton had been ordered. When an invitation came to Lydia from a young officer's wife, Lydia was allowed to accept it over Elizabeth's protests. Elizabeth herself was asked by the Gardiners to go with them on a tour which would take them into Derbyshire, Darcy's home county. She accepted, reasoning that she was not very likely to meet Darcy merely by going into the same county with him. While they were there, however, Mrs. Gardiner decided they should visit Pemberly, Darcy's home. Elizabeth made several excuses, but her aunt was insistent. Then, learning that the Darcy family was not at home, Elizabeth consented to go.

At Pemberly, an unexpected and most embarrassing meeting took place between Elizabeth and Darcy. He was more polite than Elizabeth had ever known him to be, and asked permission for his sister to call upon her. The call was duly paid and returned, but the pleasant intercourse between the Darcy's and Elizabeth's party was suddenly cut short when a letter came from Jane telling Elizabeth that Lydia had run away with Wickham. Elizabeth told Darcy what had happened, and she and the Gardiners left for home at once. After several days the runaway couple was located and a marriage arranged between them. When Lydia came home as heedless as ever, she told Elizabeth that Darcy had attended her wedding. Elizabeth, suspecting the truth, learnt from Mrs. Gardiner that it was indeed Darcy who brought about the marriage by giving Wickham money.

Soon after Lydia and Wickham left, Bingley came back to Netherfield Park, and with him came Darcy. Elizabeth, now more favourably inclined to him than ever before, hoped his coming meant that he still loved her, but he gave no sign. Bingley and Jane, on the other hand, were still obviously in love with each other, and became engaged, to the great satisfaction of Mrs. Bennet. Soon afterwards Lady Catherine paid the Bennets an unexpected call. She had heard it rumoured that Darcy was engaged to Elizabeth. Hoping to marry her own daughter to Darcy, she had charged down with characteristic bad manners to order Elizabeth not to accept his proposal. The spirited girl was not to be intimidated by the bullying Lady Catherine and coolly refused to promise not to marry Darcy. She was far from sure whether she would have another chance, but she had not long to wonder. Lady Catherine, unluckily for her own purpose, repeated to Darcy the substance of her conversation with Elizabeth, and he knew Elizabeth well enough to surmise that her feelings towards him had greatly changed. He returned to Netherfield Park, and he and Elizabeth became engaged. Pride had been humbled and prejudice dissolved.

## Chapter I

It is a truth universally acknowledged that a single man in possession of a good fortune must be in want of a wife.

However little known the feelings or views of such a man may be on his first entering a neighbourhood, this truth is so well fixed in the minds of the surrounding families, that he is considered as the rightful property of some one or other of their daughters.

"My dear Mr. Bennet," said his lady to him one day, "have you heard that Netherfield Park[1] is let at last?"

Mr. Bennet replied that he had not.

"But it is," returned she; "for Mrs. Long[2] has just been here, and she told me all about it."

Mr. Bennet made no answer.

"Do you not want to know who has taken it?" cried his wife impatiently.

"*You* want to tell me, and I have no objection to hearing it."

This was invitation enough.

"Why, my dear, you must know, Mrs. Long says that Netherfield is taken by a young man of large fortune from the north of England; that he came down on Monday in a chaise and four[3] to see the place, and was so much delighted with it that he agreed with Mr. Morris[4] immediately; that he is to take possession before Michaelmas, and some of his servants are to be in the house by the end of next week."

"What is his name?"

"Bingley."

"Is he married or single?"

"Oh! Single, my dear, to be sure! A single man of large fortunes; four or five thousand a year. What a fine thing for our girls!"

"How so? How can it affect them?"

"My dear Mr. Bennet," replied his wife, "how can you be so tiresome! You must know that I am thinking of his marrying one of them."

"Is that his design in settling here?"

"Design! Nonsense, how can you talk so! But it is very likely that he *may* fall in love with one of them, and therefore you must visit him as soon as he comes."

"I see no occasion for that. You and the girls may go, or you may send them by themselves, which perhaps will be still better, for as you are as handsome as any of them, Mr. Bingley might like you the best of the party."

"My dear, you flatter me. I certainly *have* had my share of beauty, but I do not pretend to be anything extraordinary now. When a woman has five grown-up daughters, she ought to give over thinking of her own beauty."

"In such cases a woman has not often much beauty to think of."

"But, my dear, you must indeed go and see Mr. Bingley when he comes into the neighbourhood."

"It is more than I engage for, I assure you."

"But consider your daughters. Only think what an establishment it would be for one of them. Sir William and Lady Lucas[5] are determined to go, merely on that account, for in general, you know, they visit no newcomers. Indeed you must go, for it will be impossible for *us* to visit him if you do not."

"You are over-scrupulous, surely. I daresay Mr. Bingley will be very glad to see you; and I will send a few lines[6] by you to assure him of my hearty consent to his marrying whichever he chooses of the girls; though I must throw in a good word for my little Lizzy[7].

"I desire you will do no such thing. Lizzy is not a bit better than the others; and I am sure she is not half so handsome as Jane[8], nor half so good-humoured as Lydia[9]. But you are always giving *her* the preference."

"They have none of them much to recommend them," replied he; "they are all silly and ignorant like other girls; but Lizzy has something more of quickness than her sisters."

"Mr. Bennet, how *can* you abuse your own children in such a way? You take delight in vexing me. You have no compassion on my poor nerves."

"You mistake me, my dear. I have a high respect for your nerves. They are my old friends. I have heard you mention them with consideration these twenty years at least."

"Ah, you do not know what I suffer."

"But I hope you will get over it, and live to see many young men of four thousand a year come into the neighbourhood."

"It will be no use to us, if twenty such should come, since you will not visit them."

"Depend upon it, my dear, that when there are twenty, I will visit them all."

Mr. Bennet was so odd a mixture of quick parts[10], sarcastic humour, reserve, and caprice, that the experience of three-and-twenty years had been insufficient to make his wife understand his character. Her mind was less difficult to develop. She was a woman of mean understanding, little information, and uncertain temper. When she was discontented, she fancied herself nervous. The business of her life was to get her daughters married; its solace was visiting and news.

## Notes

1. Netherfield Park: the name of an estate in the neighbourhood where the Bennets lived
2. Mrs. Long: a neighbour of the Bennets
3. a chaise and four: a lightweight carriage drawn by four horses
4. Mr. Morris: the cheery and sprightly owner of Netherfield park
5. Sir William and Lady Lucas: Sir William Lucas and his wife, neighbours of the Bennets
6. a few lines: short note, a short letter
7. Lizzy: Mr. Bennet's second daughter
8. Jane: Mr. Bennet's eldest daughter
9. Lydia: Mr. Bennet's youngest daughter
10. quick parts: wits

## For Study and Discussion

1. What do you think of the first paragraph in this selection? Do you think it is a truth? Learn the first paragraph of the novel by heart.
2. Can you say something about the humour of Mr. Bennet? Can you tell how he teases his wife? What is your impression of Mrs. Bennet?
3. Through the dialogue in this opening chapter, what can you perceive about the relationship in the neighbourhood?

## Chapter 5

# Charles Lamb

### Life and Works

Charles Lamb (1775–1834) was born in London. His father was a clerk and confidential attendant of Samuel Salt, a lawyer, whose house in Crown Office Row was Lamb's birthplace and his home during his youth. His grandmother, Mrs. Field, was a housekeeper at Blakesware (near Ware), the "Blakesmoor" described in *Essays of Elia* and in *Mrs. Leicester's School*. Lamb was educated at Christ's Hospital, a charity school, where he met Samuel Taylor Coleridge and formed an enduring friendship with him.

Charles Lamb also became a clerk. After a few months' employment at the Sea House, he obtained, at 17, an appointment in the East India House, a huge trading enterprise, where he remained from 1792 to 1825. In 1796 his mother was killed by his sister Mary who was in a fit of insanity. Lamb sympathised with his sister's condition. When Mary was released from a hospital for the insane, Lamb made a home with her and began to take care of her, who remained subject to periodic seizures, and repaid him with her sympathy and affection. Neither of them got married. When she suffered recurrent attacks, he took her back to the hospital. He himself was for a short time mentally deranged, and the curse of madness acted as a shadow on his life. But most of their life was spent as compatible companions.

Lamb was of the first generation of romantics. He was about the same age as Wordsworth and Coleridge. But Lamb was city-born and city-bred and had no desire to live in the beautiful countryside. Lamb indeed enjoyed the city sights and social life of the city. Lamb liked to drink and play jokes. He enjoyed theaters and tried to revive interest in plays of the Renaissance and Restoration periods. He and his sister Mary worked on Shakespeare's plays and wrote *Tales from Shakespeare*, a retelling for children of the stories from Shakespeare's plays. Lamb adapted the tragedies; his sister Mary adapted the comedies. This was his first successful literary adventure. This work still has a large readership even today. While presenting the charm of their own language, they kept the beauty of Shakespeare's language. The works of Lamb divide themselves naturally into three periods.

First, there are his early literary efforts, including the poems signed "C. L." in Coleridge's

*Poems on Various Subjects* (1796); his romance *A Tale of Rosamund Gray and Old Blind Margaret* (1798); his poetical drama *John Woodvil* (1802); and various other immature works in prose and poetry.

The second period was given largely to literary criticism; and the *Tales from Shakespeare* (1807) was regarded as his first successful literary venture. The book was written primarily for children. But so thoroughly had the brother and sister steeped themselves in the literature of the Elizabethan period that young and old alike were delighted with this new version of Shakespeare's stories, and the *Tales* is still regarded as the best of their kind in English literature. In 1808 appeared his *Specimens of English Dramatic Poets Who Lived about the Time of Shakespeare*. A selection of scenes from Elizabethan dramas, it had a considerable influence on the style of 19th-century English verse.

The third period includes Lamb's criticism of life, which are gathered together in his *Essays of Elia* (1823), and his *Last Essays of Elia*, which was published ten years later. These famous essays began in 1820 with the appearance of the new *London Magazine*, and were continued for many years, such subjects as the "A Dissertation upon Roast Pig", "Old China", "The Praise of Chimney Sweepers", "Imperfect Sympathies", "A Chapter on Ears", "Mrs. Battle's Opinions on Whist", "Mackery End", "Grace Before Meat", "Dream Children" and many others being chosen apparently at random, but all leading to a delightful interpretation of the life in London. In the first and last essays, "A Dissertation upon Roast Pig" and "Dream Children", contain the extremes of Lamb's humour and pathos.

## Brief Comment

Charles Lamb is a great master of familiar essays which are different from those of Francis Bacon. Essays flourished partly because there was a new market for them and people began to understand essays as a form of literature. In the first place Joseph Addison and Richard Steele socialised the essay, and brought it into everyday life and made it familiar and delightful to the multitude. In the hands of imitators like Henry Fielding, Samuel Johnson, Oliver Goldsmith and others, the essay remained popular, though less distinguished, throughout the century of its rebirth. Early in the 19th century it became more definitely a means of intimate self-expression in the hands of Charles Lamb, William Hazlitt, Thomas De Quincey and Leigh Hunt. Of these four men, Lamb remains the most beloved, and, not only among his contemporaries, but in all English prose literature. One of the reasons that essays came to be popular with the readers is that in the early decades of the 19th century there appeared several new reviews and magazines which most of the middle-class readers could enjoy. The periodicals contained literary as well as political writings and provided the readers with the essays of many writers who developed the essay form in their ways.

The style of all his essays is gentle, old-fashioned, irresistibly attractive. Though these essays are all criticism or appreciation of the life of his age, they are all intensely personal. In other words, they are an excellent picture of Lamb and of humanity. Without a trace of vanity or self-assertion, Lamb began with himself, with some purely personal mood or experience, and from this he led the reader to see life and literature as he saw it. It is this wonderful combination of personal and universal interests together with Lamb's rare old-style and quaint humour that makes the essays remarkable. They continue the best tradition upheld by Addison and Steele, the first great essayists; but their sympathies are broader and deeper, and their humour more delicious, than any which preceded them.

## Selections

### Dream Children: A Reverie

Children love to listen to stories about their elders, when *they* were children; to stretch their imagination to the conception of a traditionary great-uncle or grandame, whom they never saw. It was in this spirit that my little ones crept about me the other evening to hear about their great-grand-mother Field[1], who lived in a great house in Norfolk[2] (a hundred times bigger than that in which they and papa lived) which had been the scene—so at least it was generally believed in that part of the country—of the tragic incidents which they had lately become familiar with from the ballad "Children in the Wood"[3]. Certain it is that the whole story of the children and their cruel uncle was to be seen fairly carved out in wood upon the chimney-piece of the great hall, the whole story down to the Robin Redbreasts[4], till a foolish rich person pulled it down to set up a marble one of modern invention in its stead, with no story upon it. Here Alice put out one of her dear mother's looks, too tender to be called upbraiding. Then I went on to say, how religious and how good their great-grandmother Field was, how beloved and respected by everybody, though she was not indeed the mistress of this great house, but had only the charge of it (and yet in some respects she might be said to be the mistress of it too) committed to her by the owner, who preferred living in a newer and more fashionable mansion which he had purchased somewhere in the adjoining country; but still she lived in it in a manner as if it had been her own, and kept up the dignity of the great house in a sort while she lived, which afterwards came to decay[5], and was nearly pulled down, and all its old ornaments stripped and carried away to the owner's other house, where they were set up, and looked as awkward as if someone were to carry away the old tombs they had seen lately at the Abbey[6], and stick them up in Lady C.'s tawdry gilt drawing-room. Here John smiled, as much as to say, "that would be foolish indeed". And then I told how, when she came to die, her funeral was attended by a concourse of all the poor, and some of the gentry too, of the neighbourhood for many miles round, to show their respect for her memory, because she had been such a good and religious woman; so good indeed that she knew all the Psaltery[7] by heart, ay, and a great part of the Testament[8] besides. Here little Alice spread her hands. Then I told what a tall, upright, graceful person their great-grandmother Field once was; and how in her youth she was esteemed the best dancer—here Alice's little right foot played an involuntary movement, till upon my looking grave, it desisted—the best dancer, I was saying, in the county, till a cruel disease, called a cancer, came, and bowed her down with pain; but it could never bend her good spirits, or make them stoop, but they were still upright, because she was so good and religious. Then I told how she was used to sleep by herself in a lone chamber of the great lone house; and how she believed that an apparition of two infants[9] was to be seen at midnight gliding up and down the great staircase near where she slept, but she said "those innocents would do her no harm"; and how frightened I used to be, though in those days I had my maid to sleep with me, because I was never half so good or religious as she and yet I never saw the infants. Here John expanded all his eyebrows and tried to look courageous. Then I told how good she was to all her grand-children, having us to the great house in the holidays, where I in particular used to spend many hours by myself, in gazing upon the old busts of the Twelve Caesars[10], that had been Emperors of Rome, till the old marble heads would seem to live again, or I to be turned into marble with them; how I never could be tired with roaming about that huge mansion, with its vast empty rooms, with their worn-out hangings, fluttering tapestry, and carved oaken panels, with the gilding almost rubbed out—sometimes in the spacious old-fashioned gardens, which I had almost to myself, unless when now and then a solitary gardening man would cross me—and how the nectarines and peaches hung upon the walls, without my ever offering to pluck them, because they were forbidden fruit, unless now and then, —and because I had more pleasure in strolling about among the old melancholy looking yew trees, or the firs, and picking up the red berries, and the fir apples, which were good for nothing but to look at—or in lying about upon the fresh grass, with all the fine garden smells around me—or basking in the orangery, till I could almost fancy myself ripening too along with the oranges and the limes in that grateful warmth—or in watching the dace that darted to and fro in the fishpond, at the bottom of the garden, with here and there a great sulky pike hanging midway down the water in silence, as if it mocked at their impertinent friskings, —I had more pleasure in these busy-idle diversions than in all the sweet flavours of peaches, nectarines, oranges, and such like common baits of children. Here John slyly deposited back upon the plate a bunch of grapes, which, not unobserved by Alice, he had meditated dividing with her, and both seemed willing to relinquish them for the present as irrelevant. Then in somewhat a more heightened tone, I told how, though their great-grandmother Field loved all her grand-children, yet in an especial manner she might be said to love their uncle John L.[11], because he was so handsome and spirited a youth, and a king to the rest or us; and, instead of moping about in solitary corners, like some of us, he would mount the most mettlesome horse he could get, when but an imp no bigger than themselves, and make it carry him half over the county in a morning, and join the hunters when there were any out—and yet he loved the old great house and gardens too, but had too much spirit to be always pent up within their boundaries—and how their uncle grew up to man's estate as brave as he was handsome, to the admiration of everybody, but of their great-grandmother Field most especially; and how he used to carry me upon his back when I was a lame-footed boy[12]—for he was a good bit older than me—many a mile when I could not walk for pain;—and how in after life he became lame-footed too, and I did not always (I fear) make allowances enough for him when he was impatient, and in pain, nor remember sufficiently how considerate he had been to me when I was lame-footed; and how when he died, though he had not been dead an hour, it seemed as if he had died a great while ago, such a distance there is betwixt life and death; and how I bore his death as I thought pretty well at first, but afterwards it haunted and haunted me; and though I did not cry or take it to heart as some do, and as I think he would have done if I had died; yet I missed him all day long, and knew not till then how much I had loved him. I missed his kindness, and I missed his crossness, and wished him to be alive again, to be quarrelling with him (for we quarrelled sometimes), rather than not have him again, and was as uneasy without him, as he, their poor uncle, must have been when the doctor took off his limb[13]. Here the children fell a crying, and asked if their little mourning which they had on was not for uncle John, and they looked up, and prayed me not to go on about their uncle, but to tell them some stories about their pretty dead mother. Then I told how for seven long years, in hope sometimes, sometimes in despair, yet persisting ever, I courted the fair Alice W—n[14]; and, as much as children could understand, I explained to them what coyness, and difficulty, and denial meant in maidens—when suddenly, turning to Alice, the soul of the first Alice looked out at her eyes with such a reality of representment, that I became in doubt which of them stood there before me, or whose that bright hair was; and while I stood gazing, both the children gradually grew fainter to my view, receding, and still receding till nothing at last but two mournful features were seen in the uttermost distance, which, without speech, strangely impressed upon me the effects of speech; "We are not of Alice, nor of thee, nor are we children at all. The children of Alice call Bartrum father. We are nothing; less than nothing; and dreams. We are only what might have been, and must wait upon the tedious shores of Lethe[15] millions of ages before we have existence, and a name"—and immediately awaking, I found myself quietly seated in my bachelor armchair, where I had fallen asleep, with the faithful Bridget unchanged by my side—but John L. (or James Elia)[16] was gone for ever.

## Notes

1. Field: Mary Field, Lamb's grandmother, was a housekeeper for more than fifty years at the Blakesware in Hertfordshire, the seat of the Plumers. William Plumer, who lived in another family seat (also in Hertfordshire) and dismantled Blakesware, was still living when "Dream Children" was published, and this may have been the reason why Lamb altered the name of the county to Norfolk, the scene of the legend of "Children in the Wood".
2. Norfolk: a county in England
3. "Children in the Wood": This is a popular ballad collected in Thomas Percy's *Reliques of Ancient English Poetry*. It is the story of the little son and daughter of a Norfolk gentleman,

who were left with a considerable fortune in the care of an uncle. He, in order to secure the property, hired two ruffians to murder the children. But one of them relented and killed his companion. The little ones were, however, left in the Wayland Wood, where they perished at night of cold and terror.

4. Robin Redbreasts: the robins which at the end of the ballad covered the bodies of the children with leaves
5. which afterwards came to decay: John E. Cussans says in his *A History of Hertfordshire* that the Blakesware house was pulled down in 1822. The "other house" was Gilston, the principal seat of the Plumers, some miles distant.
6. the Abbey: the Westminster Abbey
7. Psaltery: the Book of Psalms. "Psalter" is the more usual and correct form.
8. the Testament: the New Testament
9. an apparition of two infants: There was a legend in the Plumer family about the mysterious disappearance of two children in the 17th century.
10. the old busts of the Twelve Caesars: These were among the things removed by Mr. Plumer from Blakesware.
11. John L.: John Lamb, elder brother of Charles, who died in October, 1821
12. a lame-footed boy: It is not known whether Lamb was ever temporarily lame in his boyhood. John Lamb's lameness was caused by the fall of a stone in 1796, just before the tragedy (Mary Lamb killed her mother in a fit of insanity) which made such a difference in Charles Lamb's life.
13. took off his limb: a detail supplied by Lamb's imagination
14. Alice W—n: Lamb explained that Alice W—n stood for Alice Winterton, the name of a village girl, but the name was feigned. The girl "with the bright yellow Hertfordshire hair, and eyes of watchet hue" was probably Ann Simmons. She was the sweetheart of Lamb in his boyhood and lived in one of the cottages near Blakesware. She seemed to have married Mr. Bartram, or Bartrum, a London pawnbroker, and thus "the children of Alice call Bartrum father".
15. Lethe: the river of Hades, which made those who drank the water in it completely forget their past life
16. Bridget and James Elia are the names which Lamb gives to his sister and brother in "My Relations".

## For Study and Discussion

1. Why do children love to listen to stories about their elders?
2. What is the tone of this speaker? Is this story-telling like free chatting or a monologue?
3. Describe the image of the great grandmother Field in your own words. It seems that the great grandmother is the central figure in this story. Why does Lamb talk so fondly of her?

4. What is the speaker's feeling towards John Lamb? What is John Lamb like according to the speaker?
5. The ending of the essay leaves the reader in great sympathy for the speaker. Why do the children call Bartrum father? Why does Lamb speak of his bygone times in the form of dreams?

# Chapter 6

# George Gordon Byron

## Life and Works

George Gordon Byron (1788–1824) was born into an aristocratic but impoverished family. His father died when he was only three years old. He was brought up by his mother. When he inherited the title Lord Byron, he also inherited some wealth from one of his uncles. He studied in Harrow School and Cambridge University.

Byron was extremely handsome and attractive, but he was born lame with a clubfoot, which often caused him unhappiness.

At nineteen, he published a volume of poems entitled *Hours of Idleness*, but was ridiculed by a critic in the *Edinburgh Review*. He took his revenge by publishing *English Bards and Scotch Reviewers*. In this poem he attacked not only his enemies, the critics, but also nearly all literary celebrities of his day.

In 1809 he went to travel in Europe and Asia Minor, visiting Malta, Greece and the Near East. He wrote the first two cantos of *Childe Harold's Pilgrimage*. On his tour he did many things, some good and kind, some romantic and lovely.

He also wrote lurid verse-romances, namely, *The Giaour*, *The Corsair*, *Lara* and others. These Oriental tales were crude and melodramatic, but they appealed to the popular taste. *Childe Harold's Pilgrimage* made Byron famous and popular. He made several speeches in the House of Lords supporting the oppressed workers. His condemnation on the unjust society and his sympathy for the oppressed people was easily seen in his poems such as "An Ode to the Framers of the Frame Bill" and "Song for the Luddites".

Byron created a type of hero called Byronic hero. A Byronic hero is a handsome young man who maintains an attitude of pride and cynicism. The Byronic hero conceals his inner misery behind a careless facade. Many of Byron's readers equated Byron with the characters he created. He married Annabella Milbanke in 1815. The marriage proved to be a failure, for they often quarrelled bitterly over many things and they divorced in 1816. Byron found himself surrounded by scandals and repelled by the society. He left England on April 25, 1816, and would never see England again.

He spent the rest of his years in Switzerland and Italy. To this period belong his most important works, the later cantos of *Childe Harold's Pilgrimage*, the dramatic works such as *Manfred* and *Cain*, and his satiric masterpiece, *Don Juan*. In 1824 he went to Greece as a leader of the revolutionary forces against the tyranny of the Sultan. He died from a fever.

## Brief Comment

Byron is one of the most excellent representatives of the English romanticism. As one of the most influential poets of his time, his literary career was closely linked with the struggle and progressive movements of his age. He opposed oppression and slavery, and had an ardent love for liberty. He praised the people's revolutionary struggles. His poems are favourites of the British workers and the labouring people of other countries. His influence has shown itself in the works of the chartist poets in England and the progressive poets in many other countries.

His poems show energy and vigour, romantic daring and powerful passion. Though he was a romantic, he had stronger ties to the 18th-century writers than any of his contemporaries. He admired Dryden and Pope, but he was lacking in Pope's care for artistic finish.

Byron's influence was felt not only in his own time, but also in later times. Byron's rejection by the English high society made him all the more alluring to liberal thinkers among the artistic and intellectual community of Europe. Thus Byron's influence derived from his poetry and from his personality as well. Those freedom-loving people took him as a role model. His "The Isles of Greece" was translated into Chinese by Ma Junwu, Su Manshu, Hu Shi and others. The translation of this poem deeply influenced the Chinese youths in the beginning of the 20th century.

## Introduction of Some Main Works

***Childe Harold's Pilgrimage***

*Childe Harold's Pilgrimage*, in the form of the Spenserian stanza, is a travelogue narrated by an eloquent tourist. The name of the hero in the poem stresses his ancient and noble origin. (Childe is an archaic appellation used in its time to designate a young knight.)

*Childe Harold's Pilgrimage* consists of four cantos written in various periods of Byron's life. He wrote most of the first two cantos on the tour through Spain, Portugal, Albania and Greece. He published them in 1812 and they made him the best known English poet at one stroke. He took up *Childe Harold's Pilgrimage* again in 1816, during the European tour after his divorce. Canto III, published in 1816, moved through Belgium, up the Rhine, then to Switzerland and the Alps. Canto IV, published in 1818, described the great cities and monuments of Italy.

The first canto is devoted to Portugal and Spain. Byron regarded these countries with wonder and Portugal in particular as "the delicious land", yet he was not blind to the poverty of the people. He depicted the fight of the Spanish people against foreign invasion which he witnessed during his stay in that country between 1809 and 1810.

The second canto deals with Albania and Greece. Byron told of the picturesque "dark blue sea", moonlit nights and places famous in ancient history. He hailed the past great Albanian warriors and champions of liberty. The vivid episode of the Albanians helping Childe Harold in his distress reflects Byron's own adventure in Albania where he experienced the generosity and hospitality of its people. Byron described the "Fair Greece" with pathos. He lamented her fallen state and spoke of her former glory and power, her brave men and heroic deeds. "The Isles of Greece" is the best example of this.

The third canto begins and ends with the touching address of the poet to his daughter, Ada. From personal sorrows Byron passed to the sufferings of the oppressed people. In describing Waterloo he raised his voice against the restored forces of reaction in Europe after Napoleon was defeated. The canto is mostly devoted to describing Switzerland with philosophical reflections and vivid portraitures. Byron had an exquisite portrayal of the great French writers and philosophers such as Rousseau and Voltaire who prepared the way for the French Revolution. He glorified the Revolution and grieved at the failure of its ideals.

The fourth canto sings of the beauty of Italy. Byron described her nature, her art and literature. He paid tribute to the Italian people who had given the world such men as Petrarch, Dante, Boccaccio, Tasso and Galileo. He addressed Italy of his own time, holding that her former greatness was a pledge of her future glory. He exposed the contemporary reactionaries, particularly the Holy Alliance, and expressed his belief in the ultimate victory of the people in their struggle for liberty.

***Don Juan***

*Don Juan*, Byron's greatest work, in ottava rima, an eight-line iambic pentameter stanza with the rhyme scheme abab abcc, was written in the prime of his creative power, in the years 1818–1823.

*Don Juan* is a long satiric epic, in which Byron made the hero see a lot of the world, comment on, criticise and satirise the world.

*Don Juan* is a loose narrative held together only by the hero Don Juan and the narrator and poet Byron himself. Byron himself said that he had no plot as he wrote, and he continued to add episodes as long as he lived, completing 16 cantos before he died.

The action of the poem took place in the latter quarter of the 18th century, but Byron added sentiments, ideas and events of his own time into the narrative, thus creating a broad picture of European life.

Byron realised the fact that the life of an individual was revealed in its relations with social, political and historical surroundings. Therefore the adventures of Don Juan in all the leading countries of Europe were described against varied social background, and the hero was made to participate in different historical events.

The poem opens with scenes from the hero's childhood which passes in an aristocratic

Spanish family. Juan falls in love with Donna Julia, the beautiful wife of the old and respectable Don Alfonso. But the love affair is soon discovered, after which Julia is cloistered and Juan's mother sends her son abroad "to mend his former morals".

The ship is caught in a storm and sinks several days after its departure. Juan escapes in a boat, and swims to the shore of an island, where lives a famous smuggler and pirate named Lambro. Juan is found very weak and taken care of by Haidee, the only daughter of Lambro. The young people fall in love. But the happy life is broken by Lambro's sudden return. The lovers are separated. Juan is sold to Turkey and Haidee dies in sorrow.

Juan is bought in the slave market of the Turkish capital by the order of the Sultana who has taken a fancy to him. Delivered to the harem in the guise of a woman, Juan lives through many vicissitudes and adventures. At last he makes his escape and gets to the Russian camp near Ismail, a Turkish fortress sieged by Souvorov's armies.

When Ismail is taken, Juan is dispatched to St. Petersburg with the news of the victory and is well received by Empress Catherine. Then he leaves Russia with a secret mission from Catherine, travels through Europe, and finally lands in England.

The end of the poem is planned to take Juan on the tour in Europe, make him participate in the French Revolution and die fighting against the old regime.

In *Don Juan*, Byron found a form suited to his taste and ability. He allowed himself as narrator the freedom to comment ironically on the action and characters, to digress into personal allusion, and to instruct the reader how to read and judge the poem. With a seemingly endless supply of incidents and comments, Byron might have gone on and on forever, but the poem was cut short by his heroic death.

## Selections

### When We Two Parted

When we two parted
In silence and tears,
Half broken-hearted
To sever for years,
Pale grew thy cheek and cold,
Colder thy kiss;
Truly that hour foretold
Sorrow to this.

The dew of the morning
Sunk chill on my brow—
It felt like the warning

Of what I feel now.
Thy vows are all broken,
And light is thy fame;
I hear thy name spoken,
And share in its shame.

They name thee before me,
A knell to mine ear;
A shudder comes o'er me—
Why wert thou so dear?
They know not I knew thee,
Who knew thee too well—
Long, long shall I rue thee,
Too deeply to tell.

In secret we met—
In silence I grieve,
That thy heart could forget,
Thy spirit deceive.
If I should meet thee
After long years,
How should I greet thee?—
With silence and tears.

## For Study and Discussion

1. What kind of person is the mock listener (the woman in the poem)? Choose some of the lines that support your opinion of the listener.
2. What is the feeling of the poet (or the speaker)?
3. Learn the stanza you like best by heart.

### She Walks in Beauty[1]

1

She walks in beauty, like the night
    Of cloudless climes and starry skies;
And all that's best of dark and bright
    Meet in her aspect and her eyes:

Thus mellow'd to that tender light
  Which heaven to gaudy day denies.

2

One shade the more, one ray the less,
  Had half impair'd the nameless grace
Which waves in every raven tress,
  Or softly lightens o'er her face;
Where thoughts serenely sweet express
  How pure, how dear their dwelling place.

3

And on that cheek, and o'er that brow,
  So soft, so calm, yet eloquent,
The smiles that win, the tints that glow,
  But tell of days in goodness spent,
A mind at peace with all below,
  A heart whose love is innocent!

## Notes

1. One of the lyrics in *Hebrew Melodies* (1815), written to be set to adaptations of traditional Jewish tunes by the young musician Isaac Nathan. Byron wrote the lines the morning after he had met his beautiful young cousin, Mrs. Robert John Wilmot, who wore a black mourning gown brightened with spangles.

## For Study and Discussion

1. Some people say that this poem is reminiscent of the Renaissance love lyric in which the lady's physical beauty is seen as an indication of her inner beauty and purity of soul. Do you agree with this? Give your reason.
2. What does the poet compare the lady's beauty to? How does her appearance express her thoughts and past experience?
3. How do you understand the line "One shade the more, one ray the less"?
4. Choose some lines that you like best and paraphrase them in your own words.

## The Isles of Greece

from Canto II of *Don Juan*

1

The isles of Greece, the isles of Greece!
  Where burning[1] Sappho[2] loved and sung.
Where grew the arts of war and peace,
  Where Delos[3] rose, and Phoebus[4] sprung!
Eternal summer gilds them yet,
But all, except their sun, is set.

2

The Scian and the Teian[5] muse,
  The hero's harp, the lover's lute,[6]
Have found the fame your shores refuse:
  Their place of birth alone is mute
To sounds which echo further west
Than your sires' "Islands of the Blest"[7].

3

The mountains look on Marathon[8]—
  And Marathon looks on the sea;
And musing there an hour alone,
  I dream'd that Greece might still be free;
For standing on the Persians' grave,
I could not deem myself a slave.

4

A king[9] sate on the rocky brow
  Which looks o'er sea-born Salamis[10];
And ships, by thousands, lay below,
  And men in nations; —all were his!
He counted them at break of day—
And when the sun set where were they?

5

And where are they? and where art thou,
  My country? On thy voiceless shore
The heroic lay is tuneless now—

The heroic bosom beats no more!
And must thy lyre, so long divine,
Degenerate into hands like mine?

6

'Tis something, in the dearth of fame,
Though link'd among a fetter'd race,
To feel at least a patriot's shame,
Even as I sing, suffuse my face;
For what is left the poet here?
For Greeks a blush—for Greece a tear.

7

Must we but weep o'er days more blest?
Must we but blush? —Our fathers bled.
Earth! render back from out thy breast
A remnant of our Spartan dead!
Of the three hundred grant but three,
To make a new Thermopylae[11]!

8

What, silent still? and silent all?
Ah! no; —the voices of the dead
Sound like a distant torrent's fall,
And answer, "Let one living head,
But one arise, —we come, we come!"
'Tis but the living who are dumb.

9

In vain—in vain: strike other chords;
Fill high the cup with Samian wine[12]!
Leave battles to the Turkish hordes,
And shed the blood of Scio's vine!
Hark! rising to the ignoble call—
How answers each bold Bacchanal[13]!

10

You have the Pyrrhic[14] dance as yet;
Where is the Pyrrhic phalanx gone?

Of two such lessons, why forget
The nobler and the manlier one?
You have the letters Cadmus[15] gave—
Think ye he meant them for a slave?

11

Fill high the bowl with Samian wine!
We will not think of themes like these!
It made Anacreon's song divine:
He served—but served Polycrates—
A tyrant; but our masters then
Were still, at least, our countrymen.

12

The tyrant of the Chersonese[16]
Was freedom's best and bravest friend;
That tyrant was Miltiades!
Oh! that the present hour would lend
Another despot of the kind!
Such chains as his were sure to bind.

13

Fill high the bowl with Samian wine!
On Suli's[17] rock, and Parga's[18] shore,
Exists the remnant of a line
Such as the Doric[19] mothers bore;
And there, perhaps, some seed is sown,
The Heracleidan[20] blood might own.

14

Trust not for freedom to the Franks[21]—
They have a king who buys and sells;
In native swords, and native ranks,
The only hope of courage dwells;
But Turkish force, and Latin fraud,
Would break your shield, however broad.

15

Fill high the bowl with Samian wine!

Our virgins dance beneath the shade—
I see their glorious black eyes shine;
But gazing on each glowing maid,
My own the burning tear-drop laves,
To think such breasts must suckle slaves.

16

Place me on Sunium's [22] marbled steep,
Where nothing, save the waves and I,
May hear our mutual murmurs sweep;
There, swan-like[23], let me sing and die:
A land of slaves shall ne'er be mine—
Dash down yon cup of Samian wine!

## Notes

1. burning: passionate, ardent
2. Sappho: Greek poetess (about 600 BC), who was renowned for her love lyrics
3. Delos: a small island in the Aegean Sea, the birthplace of Apollo according to the Greek mythology
4. Phoebus: epithet of Apollo, the Greek sun god and god of music and poetry
5. The Scian and the Teian: pertaining to Scio and Teos. Scio, a small Greek island, was supposed to be the birthplace of Homer, and Teos, one of the ancient Ionian cities on the coast of Asia Minor, the birthplace of Anacreon, a famous lyric poet.
6. the hero's harp, the lover's lute: alluding to Homer, who in his epics recounted the brave deeds of heroes, and Anacreon, who in his lyrics sang praises of love and wine.
7. "Islands of the Blest": Elysium, the place where the blessed were supposed to reside after death, which Homer placed in the Western Ocean.
8. Marathon: a plain in Greece, where the Persian invaders were completely annihilated by the Greeks in 490 BC
9. A king: referring to Xerxes, king of Persia, who invaded Greece by sea and land in 480 BC
10. Salamis: a Greek island in the Gulf of Aegina. In the Battle of Salamis (480 BC) the Greeks, by outmaneuvering the Persian fleet which numbered 2000 vessels as against 380 Greek ships, succeeded in completely destroying it.
11. Thermopylae: a narrow mountain pass in Greece, where three hundred valiant Spartans fought against the whole army of the Persian invaders
12. Samian wine: famous wine produced on the Isle of Samos, one of the principal islands of the Aegean Sea
13. Bacchanal: worshipper or Bacchus, the god of wine; a drunkard or reveller

14. Pyrrhic: referring to Pyrrhus, king of Epirus, who was the greatest warrior of his time. The Pyrrhic dance (a mimic war-dance) and the Pyrrhic phalanx (a body of heavy-armed infantry firmed in close ranks) were attributed to him.
15. Cadmus: the legendary founder of Thebes, who is said to have introduced into Greece from Phoenicia the alphabet
16. The tyrant of the Chersonese: Miltiades (around 500 BC), once tyrant of the Chersonese Peninsula, later became a general and statesman of Athens. He was an ardent patriot and contributed much to the victory of the Battle of Marathon.
17. Suli: a mountain district in Albania, the home of a militant people, who were among the first to take up arms against the Turks
18. Parga: a seaport on the Ionian Sea
19. Doric: pertaining to the Dorians, a division of the Greek race who settled in Greece in the 12th century BC. The Spartans, renowned for their valour and heroism, were the chief representatives of the Dorians.
20. Heracleidan: referring to Hercules, one of the most celebrated heroes in Greek mythology. The Spartans claimed to be his descendants.
21. the Franks: here meaning the Western Europeans in general
22. Sunium: a promontory near Athens, on which was situated the temple of Poseidon
23. swan-like: from the ancient belief that the swan sings beautifully just before its death

## For Study and Discussion

1. In this song poem, the poet talks about the past glory of ancient Greece. What is the purpose of the poet?
2. What contrast of thought and behaviour between the ancient Greeks and the Greeks of Byron's time does the poet provide the readers with?
3. Lu Xun (鲁迅) talked about the relationship between Byron and Greece in this way: "裴伦平时，又至有情愫于希腊，思想所趣，如磁指南。特希腊时自由悉丧，入突厥版图，受其羁縻，不敢抗拒。诗人惋惜悲愤，往往见于篇章，怀前古之光荣，哀后人之零落，或与斥责，或加激励，思使之攘突厥而复兴，更睹往日耀灿庄严之希腊……" Can you justify Lu Xun's comment with what you can find in this poem?
4. Find some translations of this poem and make your comment on the Chinese versions.
5. Choose the stanza you like best and learn it by heart.

# Chapter 7

# Percy Bysshe Shelley

## Life and Works

Percy Bysshe Shelley (1792–1822) was born into an aristocratic family. He was sent to Eton, a famous private school, where his sensitive nature was thrown into a fever of rebellion. He was called "Mad Shelley" by his schoolmates, and he remained "mad" to the end of his life. It was at Eton that Shelley first became determined to fight against injustice and oppression. In 1810 he went to Oxford University. At Oxford, he published a pamphlet, in which he thought that God's being could not be provable. For this he was expelled after only six months at Oxford.

Shelley then went to London, where he fell in love and eloped with the 16-year-old Harriet Westbrook who Shelley thought was being oppressed by her father. Both families were unhappy about the marriage. So Shelley and Harriet had to live on their own with little money. They went to Ireland for a time to work for Catholic emancipation and improved living conditions for the poor.

Returning to London, Shelley joined the circle of the radical social and revolutionary philosopher and novelist William Godwin. This led him to write *Queen Mab*, a poem attacking dogmatic religion, government, industrial tyranny and war. In 1814 Shelley fell in love with Mary, the brilliant daughter of Godwin and Mary Wollstonecraft. Committed to the idea that human relationships should not be restricted by law or social convention, Shelley went to live with Mary and her stepsister, Claire Clairmont, daughter of Godwin's second wife, in France for a time. The mad Shelley even wrote to invite Harriet Westbrook to live with them in France, totally ignorant of Harriet's feelings.

He was happiest living abroad. He spent the summer of 1816 on the shores of Lake Geneva, in Switzerland, where he was visited by and became friends with Byron.

But when he returned with Mary to England, he found himself branded a social outcast. And a crisis arose later that year when his wife Harriet drowned herself in a fit of despair. He was drowned in criticism and enmity and felt himself an alien in his own country. In 1818, soon after he and Mary were married, they left England for Italy, where Shelley would live for the rest of his life.

His four years in Italy, from 1818 until his death in 1822, were a time of poor health, of financial difficulty, of restless moving about from place to place, and of further personal tragedy. In 1818 and 1819 two of his children by Mary, Clara and William, died, from which his wife suffered a lot. Yet Shelley was able to produce an astonishing amount and range of magnificent poetry. In 1818 he began the philosophical drama that many readers consider his masterpiece, *Prometheus Unbound.* In 1819 he completed *Prometheus Unbound* and the same year he finished *The Cenci*, a drama intended for the stage, and written in much more simple and everyday language than his other works.

From 1818 to 1822, Shelley wrote a great deal of short lyrics, political and personal, on love and nature. Among his lyrics, the greatest political lyric is "Song to the Men of England" and the two best-known lyrics on nature are "Ode to the West Wind" and "To a Sky-Lark". His love lyrics include mainly "Love's Philosophy", "I Fear Thy Kisses, Gentle Maiden", "One Word Is Too Often Profaned" and "When the Lamp Is Shattered". In his love lyrics, he regards love as the noblest thing in the universe, as the thing of extreme purity and as a feeling of devotion and worship. He believes that the noblest love in the human world may lead mankind to a state of harmony, happiness, peace and perfection. He advocates that love should be elevated high above the vulgar, practical attitude towards it.

In 1820 he produced a satire entitled *The Masque of Anarchy* and a philosophical nature-fable entitled *The Sensitive Plant*. In 1821 he published *Adonais*, a great elegy on the death of John Keats. Considering its poetic quality, the nobility of sentiment, its genuine personal grief, the interest of its subject, and the poetic friendship which it values, there is no elegy better written than this.

In 1822 he completed *Hellas*, a lyrical drama about the Greek war of liberation against the Turks. At his death he was at work on *The Triumph of Life*. In addition to these major works, Shelley wrote in each of these years many of the intense, beautifully crafted shorter lyrics for which he is so well known.

In 1822, Shelley was drowned off Leghorn, in a violent storm. Shelley's ashes were buried in the Protestant cemetery at Rome, near the grave of Keats.

## Brief Comment

Shelley is a contradictory and challenging figure. His writing is at once the most passionate and intense of all the romantic poets, and yet the most intellectual, the fullest of philosophical speculation and technical experiment.

Shelley's short poems on nature and love form an important part of his literary output. To him nature exists as an unseen life of the universe and his love of nature is almost boundless. Shelley's love is not limited to mankind, but extended to every living creature. Flowers, trees, seas, mountains and clouds are not only personified but also inspired or spiritualised. Shelley holds passionate communion with the universe. He becomes one with the lark, with the cloud, and with the west wind. This passionate love of nature is but an expression of the poet's eager aspiration for something free from the sordid reality.

Intellectually, he was an immensely learned and well-read man capable of more refined and original philosophical thinking than any other English romantic poets, including Coleridge. And as a poet, as Wordsworth said, "Shelley is one of the best artists of us all: I mean in workmanship of style."

In *The Condition of the Working Class in England* Engels wrote: "Shelley, the genius, the prophet, Shelley, and Byron, with his glowing sensuality and his bitter satire upon our existing society, find most of their readers in the proletariat."

## Introduction of Some Main Works

### *Queen Mab*

*Queen Mab* is Shelley's first long poem of importance. It expresses almost all his major political ideas. It is written in the form of a fairy tale dream. The fairy Queen Mab carries off in her celestial chariot a beautiful and pure maiden called Ianthe, and shows her the past, present and future of mankind. Through the mouth of the fairy queen the poet attacks the tyranny of gold, militarism and religious superstition. The poem has nine cantos. The first two cantos deal with a vision of the woeful past, the last two with an ideal view of the happy future: the fairy queen comforts Ianthe by a glimpse of the happy future when science and love will make a paradise of earth, while the five middle cantos are devoted to a fierce attack on the social evils of the day. Among them, in the third canto the idle life of the exploiting class is exposed; in the fourth canto the ruling class is attacked and criticised. Shelley points out that plunderous war is used as a weapon by the oppressors to attain their selfish ends, and state apparatus is used as a tool in suppressing the people; in the fifth canto the miserable life of the poor people and their hatred for tyranny are described.

### *Prometheus Unbound*

*Prometheus Unbound*, a lyrical drama, is Shelley's masterpiece. The story is taken from Greek mythology. According to the Greek myth, Prometheus stole fire from heaven and taught men how to use it. For this he was punished by Zeus, the supreme god, who chained him to a rock on Mt. Caucasus, where during the daytime a vulture fed on his liver, which was restored each succeeding night.

The theme of this poetical drama is borrowed from the Greek tragedian Aeschylus' play *Prometheus Bound*. But the two plays are quite different in ending. Aeschylus made Prometheus finally reconcile with Zeus. This ending could not be accepted by Shelley. In order to express his faith in the ultimate victory of the people, Shelley made Prometheus the representative of mankind, who has four noble qualities: man's shaping intellect, his heroic endurance, his defiance against tyranny and his love for mankind. Though chained to the rock, he has "great allies" in the world. Mother Earth supports him by giving him strength to endure all sufferings and sending the spirits of heroes and martyrs to cheer him. Lovely shapes of Faith and Hope hover around him. His bride Asia waits for him in the distance. With a firm confidence in the final triumph of his just cause, Prometheus is perfectly calm in his sufferings. He knows that the reign of Zeus is but a passing period in the life of the universe, so he refuses to yield. Finally Zeus is overthrown by Demogorgon, the symbol of change and revolution, and driven into the eternal abyss. Prometheus is set free by Hercules, the most valiant hero in Greek mythology. As Prometheus throws off his fetters, the whole world joins in a chorus to celebrate his liberation. Prometheus' triumph symbolises the victory of mankind over tyranny and oppression.

***The Masque of Anarchy***

*The Masque of Anarchy* is one of Shelley's political lyrics. It deals with the infamous Peterloo Massacre which happened in 1819. In that event hundreds of jobless workers were killed or wounded. Shelley used this poem to reveal the essential nature of the so-called "free competition" under capitalism. In the poem, kings, priests, bankers and lawyers all crowd to welcome Anarchy as their "Law and God". So "Anarchy" in this poem means the tyranny of a handful of oppressors and exploiters over the masses. The first part of the poem describes the contemporary rules of England. In the second part the poet sings of the men of England, their strength and future victory, and calls upon them to rise against the oppressors and blood-suckers.

## Selections

### A Song: "Men of England"[1]

Men of England, wherefore plough
For the lords who lay ye low?
Wherefore weave with toil and care
The rich robes your tyrants wear?

Wherefore feed and clothe and save
From the cradle to the grave
Those ungrateful drones who would
Drain your sweat—nay, drink your blood?

Wherefore, Bees of England, forge

Many a weapon, chain, and scourge,
That these stingless drones may spoil
The forced produce of your toil?

Have ye leisure, comfort, calm,
Shelter, food, love's gentle balm?
Or what is it ye buy so dear
With your pain and with your fear?

The seed ye sow, another reaps;
The wealth ye find, another keeps;
The robes ye weave, another wears;
The arms ye forge, another bears.

Sow seed—but let no tyrant reap;
Find wealth—let no impostor heap;
Weave robes—let not the idle wear;
Forge arms—in your defence to bear.

Shrink to your cellars, holes, and cells—
In halls ye deck another dwells.
Why shake the chains ye wrought? Ye see
The steel ye tempered glance on ye.

With plough and spade and hoe and loom
Trace your grave and build your tomb
And weave your winding-sheet—till fair
England be your Sepulchre.

## Notes

1. This poem was written at a time of turbulent unrest, expressing Shelley's hope for a proletarian revolution. Originally planned as one of a series for working men, it had become, as the poet wished, a hymn of the British labor movement.

   This song contains eight quatrains, with each line containing four accented syllables. The rhyme scheme for each stanza is uniformly aabb.

## For Study and Discussion

1. Discuss the rhetorical devices used in the poem. What are their functions?
2. What is the theme of the poem?
3. In your eyes, which stanza is most exciting? Why?

### Ode to the West Wind[1]

1

O wild West Wind, thou breath of Autumn's being,
Thou, from whose unseen presence the leaves dead
Are driven, like ghosts from an enchanter fleeing,

Yellow, and black, and pale, and hectic[2] red,
Pestilence-stricken multitudes: O Thou,
Who chariotest to their dark wintry bed

The winged seeds, where they lie cold and low,
Each like a corpse within its grave, until
Thine azure sister of the Spring[3] shall blow

Her clarion[4] o'er the dreaming earth, and fill
(Driving sweet buds like flocks to feed in air)
With living hues and odours plain and hill:

Wild Spirit, which art moving everywhere;
Destroyer and Preserver; hear, O hear!

2

Thou on whose stream, 'mid the steep sky's commotion,
Loose clouds like Earth's decaying leaves are shed,
Shook from the tangled boughs of Heaven and Ocean[5],

Angels of rain and lightning: there are spread
On the blue surface of thine aery surge,
Like the bright hair uplifted from the head

Of some fierce Maenad[6], even from the dim verge

Of the horizon to the zenith's height,
The locks of the approaching storm. Thou Dirge

Of the dying year, to which this closing night
Will be the dome of a vast sepulchre,
Vaulted with all thy congregated might

Of vapours[7], from whose solid atmosphere
Black rain and fire and hail will burst: O hear!

3

Thou who didst waken from his summer dreams
The blue Mediterranean, where he lay,
Lulled by the coil of his crystalline streams[8],

Beside a pumice isle in Baiae's bay[9],
And saw in sleep old palaces and towers
Quivering within the wave's intenser day,[10]

All overgrown with azure moss and flowers
So sweet, the sense faints picturing them! Thou
For whose path the Atlantic's level powers

Cleave themselves into chasms, while far below
The sea-blooms and the oozy woods which wear
The sapless foliage of the ocean, know

Thy voice, and suddenly grow grey with fear,
And tremble and despoil themselves:[11] O hear!

4

If I were a dead leaf thou mightest bear;
If I were a swift cloud to fly with thee;
A wave to pant beneath thy power, and share

The impulse of thy strength, only less free
Than thou, O Uncontrollable! If even
I were as in my boyhood, and could be

The comrade of thy wandering over Heaven,
As then, when to outstrip thy skiey speed
Scarce seemed a vision; I would ne'er have striven

As thus with thee in prayer in my sore need.
Oh! lift me as a wave, a leaf, a cloud!
I fall upon the thorns of life! I bleed!

A heavy weight of hours has chained and bowed
One too like thee: tameless, and swift, and proud.

5

Make me thy lyre[12], even as the forest is:
What if my leaves are falling like its own!
The tumult of thy mighty harmonies

Will take from both a deep, autumnal tone,
Sweet though in sadness. Be thou, Spirit fierce,
My spirit! Be thou me, impetuous one!

Drive my dead thoughts over the universe
Like withered leaves to quicken a new birth!
And, by the incantation of this verse,

Scatter, as from an unextinguished hearth
Ashes and sparks, my words among mankind!
Be through my lips to unawakened Earth

The trumpet of a prophecy![13] O Wind,
If Winter comes, can Spring be far behind?

## Notes

1. "This poem was conceived and chiefly written in a wood that skirts the Arno, near Florence, and on a day when that tempestuous wind, whose temperature is at once mild and animating, was collecting the vapors which pour down the autumnal rains" (Shelley's note). As in other major romantic poems—for example, the opening of Wordsworth's "The Prelude", Coleridge's "Dejection: An Ode", and the conclusion to Shelley's *Adonais*—the rising wind, linked with the cycle of the seasons, is presented as the outer correspondent to an inner change from apathy to

spiritual vitality, and from imaginative sterility to a burst of creative power which is parallelled to the inspiration of the Biblical prophets. In Hebrew, Latin, Greek and many other languages, the words for wind, breath, soul and inspiration are all identical or related. Thus Shelley's west wind is a "spirit", the "breath of Autumn's being", which destroys in the autumn in order to revive in the spring. Around this central image the poem weaves various cycles of death and regeneration—vegetational, human and divine.

The ode is a lyric poem of some length, dealing with a lofty theme in a dignified manner and originally intended to be sung. The stanza used in this ode was developed by Shelley from the interlaced three-line units of the Italian *terza rima*: aba, bcb, cdc, etc. Shelley's stanza consists of a set of four such tercets, closed by a couplet rhyming with the middle line of the preceding tercet: aba, bcb, cdc, ded, ee.

2. hectic: the kind of fever which occurs in tuberculosis
3. Thine azure sister of the Spring: the west wind that will blow in the spring
4. clarion: a high, shrill trumpet
5. the tangled boughs of Heaven and Ocean: the fragmentary clouds ("leaves") are torn by the wind from the larger and higher clouds ("boughs"), which are formed by a union of air with vapour drawn up by the sun from the ocean. "Angels" (Line 18) suggests the old sense of messengers, harbingers.
6. Maenad: a female votary who danced frenziedly in the worship of Dionysus (Bacchus), the Greek god of wine and vegetation. As vegetation god, he was fabled to die in the fall and to be resurrected in the spring.
7. vapours: clouds
8. crystalline streams: the currents that flow in the Mediterranean Sea, sometimes with a visible difference in colour
9. pumice: a porous volcanic stone. "Baiae's bay", west of Naples, was the locale of imposing villas erected by Roman emperors.
10. Shelley once observed that, when reflected in water, colours are "more vivid yet blended with more harmony".
11. "The vegetation at the bottom of the sea sympathises with that of the land in the change of seasons" (Shelley's note).
12. lyre: the Eolian lyre, which responds to the wind with alternating musical chords
13. trumpet of a prophecy: a reference to the "clarion" of Line 10

## For Study and Discussion

1. In the first stanza, the poet calls the wind both "destroyer" and "preserver". What does he mean by this?
2. In the second stanza, the images of the sky are developed. In what way are the clouds presented? What are the clouds compared to?

3. In the third stanza, the images of the ocean and water plants are presented. How do they respond to the power of the wind? What does this mean?
4. In the fourth stanza, the poet supposes that if he were a leaf, a cloud, or ocean wave he would be moved by the power of the west wind. Why does he recall himself as a boy? Why does he say: "I fall upon the thorns of life! I bleed."?
5. In the last stanza, the metaphor of wind as power and inspiration is shifted to the Eolian lyre or wind harp. The poet asks to be made an instrument on which the wind can play "mighty harmonies". The poet wants the windlike power to scatter and spread his ideas across the earth. Can we say that by singing praise of the west wind the poet wants to eulogise himself and his revolutionary ideas?
6. The last couplet contains the famous philosophical sentence "O Wind, / If Winter comes, can Spring be far behind?". Comment on it.

## To a Sky-Lark[1]

Hail to thee, blithe Spirit!
  Bird thou never wert—
That from Heaven, or near it,
  Pourest thy full heart
In profuse strains of unpremeditated art.

Higher still and higher
  From the earth thou springest
Like a cloud of fire;
  The blue deep thou wingest,
And singing still dost soar, and soaring ever singest.

In the golden lightning
  Of the sunken Sun—
O'er which clouds are brightning,
  Thou dost float and run;
Like an unbodied joy whose race is just begun.

The pale purple even
  Melts around thy flight,
Like a star of Heaven
  In the broad day-light
Thou art unseen,—but yet I hear thy shrill delight.

Keen as are the arrows
  Of that silver sphere[2],
Whose intense lamp narrows
  In the white dawn clear
Until we hardly see—we feel that it is there.

All the earth and air
  With thy voice is loud,
As when Night is bare
  From one lonely cloud
The moon rains out her beams—and Heaven is overflowed.

What thou art we know not;
  What is most like thee?
From rainbow clouds there flow not
  Drops so bright to see
As from thy presence showers a rain of melody.

Like a Poet hidden
  In the light of thought,
Singing hymns unbidden,
  Till the world is wrought
To sympathy with hopes and fears it heeded not:

Like a high-born maiden
  In a palace-tower,
Soothing her love-laden
  Soul in secret hour,
With music sweet as love—which overflows her bower:

Like a glow-worm golden
  In a dell of dew,
Scattering unbeholden
  Its aerial hue
Among the flowers and grass which screen it from the view:

Like a rose embowered
  In its own green leaves

By warm winds deflowered—
   Till the scent it gives
Makes faint with too much sweet heavy-wingèd thieves[3]:

Sound of vernal showers
   On the twinkling grass,
Rain-awakened flowers,
   All that ever was
Joyous, and clear and fresh, thy music doth surpass.

Teach us, Sprite[4] or Bird,
   What sweet thoughts are thine;
I have never heard
   Praise of love or wine
That panted forth a flood of rapture so divine:

Chorus Hymeneal[5]
   Or triumphal chaunt
Matched with thine would be all
   But an empty vaunt,
A thing wherein we feel there is some hidden want.

What objects are the fountains
   Of thy happy strain?
What fields or waves or mountains?
   What shapes of sky or plain?
What love of thine own kind? what ignorance of pain?

With thy clear keen joyance
   Languor cannot be—
Shadow of annoyance
   Never came near thee;
Thou lovest—but ne'er knew love's sad satiety.

Waking or asleep,
   Thou of death must deem
Things more true and deep
   Than we mortals dream,
Or how could thy notes flow in such a crystal stream?

We look before and after,
And pine for what is not—
Our sincerest laughter
With some pain is fraught—
Our sweetest songs are those that tell of saddest thought.

Yes if we could scorn
Hate and pride and fear;
If we were things born
Not to shed a tear,
I know not how thy joy we ever should come near.

Better than all measures
Of delightful sound—
Better than all treasures
That in books are found—
Thy skill to poet were, thou Scornet of the ground!

Teach me half the gladness
That thy brain must know,
Such harmonious madness
From my lips would flow
The world should listen then—as I am listening now.

## Notes

1. The European skylark is a small bird that sings only in flight, usually when it is too high to be visible. The bird, freed from the bonds of earth and soaring beyond the reach of all the physical senses except hearing, is made the emblem of a nonmaterial spirit of pure joy, beyond the possibility of empirical knowledge. (see Lines 15, 31)
2. silver sphere: the morning star
3. sweet heavy-winged thieves: the "warm winds" (Line 53)
4. Sprite: spirit
5. Hymeneal: marital (from Hymen, Greek god of marriage)

## For Study and Discussion

1. In the first four stanzas, the poet describes the bird as flying off to the setting sun. Even though he can no longer see the bird, he still hears its song. What kind of feeling does the poet express

by saying "an unbodied joy"?

2. In the poem, the poet creates a series of analogies. To what does the poet successively compare the bird?
3. Does the poet want to describe the bird's joy to contrast with miserable human conditions? Why?
4. Line 90 says "Our sweetest songs are those that tell of saddest thought". What difference is there between the sky-lark's song and the song of the poet? Why in the final stanza does the poet ask the sky-lark to "Teach me half the gladness / That thy brain must know"?
5. Learn the first and the last stanza of the poem by heart.

## A Song[1]

A widow bird[2] sat mourning[3] for her love
  Upon a wintry bough[4];
The frozen wind[5] crept on above
  The freezing stream[6] below[7].

There was no leaf upon the forest bare[8],
  No flower upon her ground,[9]
And little motion in the air
  Except the mill-wheel's sound.

## Notes

1. This is a short poem written in two quatrains rhyming abab, cdcd.
2. A widow bird: a female bird without companion
3. mourning: grieving
4. wintry bough: bough in the winter. A wintry bough usually has no leaves. Here both a bird without companion and a bough without leaves show a woeful state.
5. frozen wind: here the poet uses the wind that was frozen to show the cold weather
6. freezing stream: stream becoming frozen
7. below: in contrast to "above" in the third line. The images above and below are all of coldness.
8. the forest bare: the bare forest
9. No flower upon her ground: There is no flower in the forest.

## *For Study and Discussion*

1. How does the setting help express the meaning of the poem?
2. Compare this poem with the famous Chinese poem "Autumn" by Ma Zhiyuan (马致远《天净沙 • 秋思》). What are the similarities between the two poems?
3. Learn this poem by heart, and appreciate the contrast in the last stanza.

# Chapter 8

# John Keats

## Life and Works

John Keats (1795–1821) died when he was only twenty-six. The brevity and intensity of Keats' career as a poet are unmatched in English history. It is a wonder. He achieved so much at such a young age that readers would always speculate about his potential had he lived to reach his artistic maturity.

Keats came from very humble origins. His father was a livery-stable keeper and died from a fall from a horse when Keats was eight. His mother remarried soon but died of tuberculosis six years later when he was fourteen. So when Keats was only fourteen he became the head of the four Keats children. The Keats children were left some money from their grandfather but the trustee of the estate, Richard Abbey, withheld from them the full extent of their inheritance so that they were often short of money.

Keats had been fortunate enough as a boy to attend an excellent private school near London, run by John Clarke, whose son Charles Cowden Clarke became his teacher and mentor who introduced him to poetry, music and the theatre. But soon after his mother died, his guardian removed him from school and as a practical plan for Keats' future, made him an apprentice to a surgeon and apothecary. In 1815 Keats continued his study of medicine more formally at Guy's Hospital in London. He passed his medical examinations and qualified himself the next year to practise as an apothecary, but it was at this time that he decided, much to his guardian's displeasure, to devote his life to poetry.

Keats became a close friend of Leigh Hunt, a well-known literary critic, essayist, poet, political radical, and editor of *The Examiner*, who encouraged him to be a serious writer. Hunt introduced Keats to a literary circle, including Hazlitt, Lamb and Shelley, where his talents found encouragement. Hunt and the circle provided Keats with a friendly and encouraging audience.

In 1817 Keats published a little volume of verse entitled *Poems*, most of it crude and immature enough, but containing the magnificent sonnet "On First Looking into Chapman's Homer" which revealed one source of his inspiration.

From the beginning of his literary career, his imagination had turned to the ancient Greek world. In 1818, he published *Endymion*, a long mythological poem whose beginning line is "A thing of beauty is a joy forever", a sentence bearing Keats' concept of beauty and attitude towards life. Endymion is the Latmian shepherd loved by the moon-goddess. For this poem he was severely attacked by the reviewers, and at least some of their criticisms were justified. Though there are many beautiful ideas and lines in this long poem, yet as a whole *Endymion* is chaotic, and is overfilled with ornament. Keats himself knew this clearly, as was indicated both by his letters and by the proudly humble preface in which he described the poem as a "feverish attempt rather than a deed accomplished", and hoped that "while it is dwindling I may be plotting and fitting myself for verses fit to live".

The year 1818 was difficult for Keats. Apart from the unfriendly and even negative reviews of *Endymion*, some other problems began to weigh heavily on him. As the oldest of four children, Keats felt a special responsibility and closeness to his two brothers and his sister. When his brother George, who had immigrated to America, ran into financial difficulties, Keats worked hard to earn money to help him. His younger brother Tom contracted tuberculosis, and Keats cared for him constantly, running the risk of contracting the disease himself. In the autumn of 1818, Keats fell desperately in love with Fanny Brawne, a pretty, lively and lovely girl to whom he soon became engaged. However, he was too poor both in health and finance to get married. But Keats wrote a lot of poems related to her, to complaint or to praise, some so beautiful, some so woeful that some critics said that Keats could never have written so touching love poems had he not fallen in love with Brawne. To some extent, it was she who gave Keats much inspiration for his love poetry. The year came to a dismal end with Tom's death in December.

In 1820, he published another volume of poetry, entitled *Lamia, Isabella, The Eve of St. Agnes, and Other Poems*. Besides the pieces named, it contained the great odes, "Ode on Melancholy", "Ode on a Grecian Urn", "Ode to Psyche", "Ode to a Nightingale" and the heroic fragment, *Hyperion*. During two years he deepened and strengthened his gift. He turned from Spenser to the great masculine poets of the 17th century, Shakespeare, Webster, Milton and Dryden, in whom he found the iron which he lacked in his earlier intellect, and learned the lessons of artistic calmness and severity, without sacrifice of the mellow sweetness native to him. He added strength to charm.

But Keats' career was to be cut tragically short just as he was beginning to realise his full potential. Before the 1820 volume was published, the first clear signs of the tuberculosis he had always feared became apparent in February 1820. Facts proved that Keats was attacked by tuberculosis, the disease his mother and younger brother Tom got. In September of 1820 he sailed for Italy under the care of his faithful friend, Joseph Severn. Early in the spring of 1821, on February 23, he died in Rome, and was buried in the Protestant cemetery. On his tomb are carved, according to his own request, the words: "Here lics one whose name was writ in water."

## Brief Comment

Keats learned the art of poetry mainly from the poets of the English Renaissance, such as Spenser, Shakespeare and Milton. The artistic aim in his poetry was always to create a beautiful world of imagination as opposed to the sordid reality. He sought to express beauty in all his poems. His leading principle was: "Beauty is truth, truth beauty." He expressed the delight which came not only through the eye and the ear but also through the senses of touch, taste and smell. His poetry is distinguished by sensuousness and the perfection of form. So Keats has often been regarded as a sensuous poet, whose ability to appeal to the senses through language is matchless.

Keats' letters to his brothers and friends are of great value, and they are important sources of his literary principles. His ideas such as the negative capability and the objective existence of the poet (i.e. a poet has no identity) influenced later literary critics and became the base of some of the theories. In some of his letters, he frequently talked about imagination, beauty, truth and poetry. In his eyes, poets give something to mankind which philosophers cannot give, because to confine oneself to what the logical understanding could prove is to ignore other means of access to truth, especially the imagination. To poets, imagination, or intuitive apprehension, is the necessary means of perceiving beauty. To find something beautiful means to find something true. To discern and to reveal the beauty of a phenomenon, or some aspect of human experience, does not mean merely to represent it in a manner which might strike contemporary taste as pretty in colour, sound, or form; it means to disclose its inward nature and purpose in the light of eternal values. Thus beauty, being that quality of an object which is discerned when its essential nature is seen, is a mode of truth. The immortality of great works of art rests upon that fact: they survive not because they happen to please the generations in which they are produced, but because the interpretation which they give of their subjects proves permanently true.

## Introduction of Some Main Works

Among Keats' longer poems, the more important ones are *Lamia*, *The Eve of St. Agnes* and *Isabella*. All these poems deal with the theme of love and the cost of true love in the society of tyranny and oppression.

***The Eve of St. Agnes***

*The Eve of St. Agnes*, with a medieval background, tells a story which is similar to Shakespeare's *Romeo and Juliet*. Keats realised his ambition to write a romance. Keats made use of the legend of Saint Agnes, the patron of virgins. On January 20, the Saint Agnes' Eve, a young girl was supposed to perform certain rites before going to bed in order to have a dream of her future husband. The scene is set in an old castle where people are having a party. Madeline the heroine takes no notice of those young men who want to dance with her. She only thinks of how to have the dream of meeting her future husband. Meanwhile, Porphyro approaches the castle. He plans to sneak in and finds Madeline. Entering a remote part of the castle, he meets his only friend Angela there. He asks about Madeline. She tells him of Madeline's plan to pray to St. Agnes for a vision. He determines to enact the vision Madeline expects. Angela has to help him carry out this plan. She leads him to Madeline's bedchamber. Porphyro hides in the closet. Madeline enters her room and begins to pray. Then she undresses and goes to bed. Porphyro begins to prepare for dream image. Madeline is lost in her dream. When she opens her eyes she sees him in the room. He "melted" into her dream. Outside the castle, a cold windstorm has arisen. He urges her to escape with him from the hostile castle. She agrees and they two leave for a new life.

The poem works through a series of contrasts in imagery: light and dark, warm and cold, noise and silence, young beauty and aged deformity, to present contrast between hate and love, dream and reality, passion and death.

***Isabella***

The story in *Isabella* is taken from *Decameron* by Giovanni Boccaccio, a great Italian writer in the period of Renaissance. Isabella loves Lorenzo, a young man of a lower social rank than that of Isabella's family. In order to separate Isabella from Lorenzo, Isabella's brothers murder Lorenzo. Isabella loves Lorenzo so much that she digs up his head from under the earth and buries it in a flowerpot, but her cruel brothers discover this and take the pot away. Isabella dies of a broken heart. Through the descriptions of the devoted lovers fighting for the realisation of their love against their enemies and oppressors, Keats showed his great sympathy for unfortunate lovers and his deep hatred of the brutal oppressors.

## Selections

### On First Looking into Chapman's Homer[1]

Much have I travell'd in the realms of gold,
   And many goodly states and kingdoms seen;
   Round many western islands have I been
Which bards in fealty to Apollo hold.
Oft of one wide expanse had I been told
   That deep-brow'd Homer ruled as his demesne[2];
   Yet did I never breathe its pure serene[3]
Till I heard Chapman speak out loud and bold:
Then felt I like some watcher of the skies
   When a new planet swims into his ken;

Or like stout Cortez when with eagle eyes
He star'd at the Pacific[4]—and all his men
Look'd at each other with a wild surmise—
Silent, upon a peak in Darien.

## Notes

1. Keats' former schoolteacher, Charles Cowden Clarke, introduced him to the robust translation of Homer by the Elizabethan poet George Chapman. They read through the night, and Keats walked home at dawn. This sonnet, his first great poem, reached Clarke by the ten o'clock mail that same morning.
2. demesne: realm, feudal possession
3. pure serene: clear expanse of air
4. It was Balboa, not Cortez, who caught his first sight of the Pacific from the heights of Darien, Panama.

## For Study and Discussion

1. What is the rhyme scheme of this sonnet?
2. What metaphors does the poet use in the first eight lines? To what does the poet compare his reading of great poets?
3. To what does Keats compare his delight in finding and reading Homer?
4. Which metaphor impresses you the most? Why?
5. Learn the whole sonnet by heart.

### On the Grasshopper and Cricket[1]

The poetry of earth is never dead:
When all the birds are faint with the hot sun,
And hide in cooling trees, a voice will run
From hedge to hedge about the new-mown mead;
That is the Grasshopper's—he takes the lead
In summer luxury—he has never done
With his delights; for when tired out with fun
He rests at ease beneath some pleasant weed.
The poetry of earth is ceasing never:
On a lone winter evening, when the frost
Has wrought a silence, from the stove there shrills

The Cricket's song, in warmth increasing ever,
  And seems to one in drowsiness half lost,
  The Grasshopper's among some grassy hills.

## Notes

1. Keats had a friend called Leigh Hunt, a poet, critic and editor. Leigh Hunt often invited his friends and poets to his home and wrote poems for fun and competition. One evening, when they were talking, they suddenly touched upon the topic of grasshopper, comparing it to a merry cricket by a stove. Hunt suggested that they write on this topic. He and Keats began to write. Amy Lowell, an imagist poet and critic as well as translator, praised it as fresh and enjoyable in many ways. She said, "The opening is an excellent picture, vivid and suggestive; one can see it, feel it, and smell it."

## For Study and Discussion

1. What tone can you perceive from this poem? Why does the poet say that the poetry of earth is never dead?
2. What is the theme of this sonnet? How are the first eight lines and the last six lines related?
3. In what ways are the Grasshopper and the Cricket similar? In what way is it important to the development of the theme of this sonnet?
4. Learn the whole sonnet by heart.

### Ode to a Nightingale[1]

1

My heart aches, and a drowsy numbness pains
    My sense, as though of hemlock[2] I had drunk,
Or emptied some dull opiate to the drains
    One minute past, and Lethe-wards[3] had sunk:
'Tis not through envy of thy happy lot,
    But being too happy in thine happiness,—
        That thou, light-winged Dryad of the trees,
            In some melodious plot
    Of beechen green, and shadows numberless,
        Singest of summer in full-throated ease.

2

O, for a draught of vintage! that hath been
    Cool'd a long age in the deep-delved earth,
Tasting of Flora[4] and the country green,
    Dance, and Provencal song[5], and sunburnt mirth!
O for a beaker full of the warm South,
    Full of the true, the blushful Hippocrene[6],
        With beaded bubbles winking at the brim,
            And purple-stained mouth;
    That I might drink, and leave the world unseen,
        And with thee fade away into the forest dim:

3

Fade far away, dissolve, and quite forget
    What thou among the leaves hast never known,
The weariness, the fever, and the fret
    Here, where men sit and hear each other groan;
Where palsy shakes a few, sad last gray hairs,
    Where youth grows pale, and spectre-thin, and dies;[7]
        Where but to think is to be full of sorrow
            And leaden-eyed despairs,
    Where Beauty cannot keep her lustrous eyes,
        Or new Love pine at them beyond to-morrow.

4

Away! away! for I will fly to thee,
    Not charioted by Bacchus and his pards,
But on the viewless wings of Poesy[8],
    Though the dull brain perplexes and retards:
Already with thee! tender is the night,
    And haply, the Queen-Moon is on her throne,
        Cluster'd around by all her starry Fays[9];
            But here there is no light,
    Save what from heaven is with the breezes blown
        Through verdurous glooms and winding mossy ways[10].

5

I cannot see what flowers are at my feet,
    Nor what soft incense hangs upon the boughs,

But, in embalmed[11] darkness, guess each sweet
    Wherewith the seasonable month endows
The grass, the thicket, and the fruit-tree wild;
    White hawthorn, and the pastoral eglantine[12];
        Fast fading violets cover'd up in leaves;
            And mid-May's eldest child,
    The coming musk-rose, full of dewy wine,
        The murmurous haunt of flies on summer eves.

6

Darkling[13] I listen; and, for many a time
    I have been half in love with easeful Death,
Call'd him soft names in many a mused rhyme[14],
    To take into the air my quiet breath;
Now more than ever seems it rich to die,
    To cease upon the midnight with no pain,
        While thou art pouring forth thy soul abroad
            In such an ecstasy!
    Still wouldst thou sing, and I have ears in vain—
        To thy high requiem become a sod.

7

Thou wast not born for death, immortal Bird!
    No hungry generations tread thee down;
The voice I hear this passing night was heard
    In ancient days by emperor and clown:
Perhaps the self-same song that found a path
    Through the sad heart of Ruth[15], when, sick for home,
        She stood in tears amid the alien corn;
            The same that oft-times hath
    Charm'd magic casements, opening on the foam
        Of perilous seas, in faery lands forlorn[16].

8

Forlorn! the very word is like a bell
    To toll me back from thee to my sole self!
Adieu! the fancy[17] cannot cheat so well
    As she is fam'd to do, deceiving elf.
Adieu! adieu! thy plaintive anthem[18] fades

Past the near meadow, over the still stream,
Up the hill-side; and now 'tis buried deep
In the next valley-glades:
Was it a vision, or a waking dream?
Fled is that music:—Do I wake or sleep?

## Notes

1. Charles Brown, with whom Keats was then living in Hampstead, wrote: "In the spring of 1819 a nightingale had built her nest near my house. Keats felt a tranquil and continual joy in her song; and one morning he took his chair from the breakfast table to the grass plot under a plum tree, where he sat for two or three hours. When he came into the house, I perceived he had some scraps of paper in his hand, and these he was quietly thrusting behind the books. On inquiry, I found those scraps, four or five in number, contained his poetic feeling on the song of our nightingale."
2. hemlock: a poisonous herb, not the North American evergreen tree
3. Lethe-wards: towards Lethe, the river in Hades whose water causes forgetfulness
4. Flora: Roman goddess of flowers, or the flowers themselves
5. Provencal song: Provence, a part of south-east France, famous during the Middle Ages for chivalry and poetry. Provencal, native or inhabitant of Provence.
6. Hippocrene: (=the horse-fountain) This is the fountain of the Muses, on Mount Helicon. This spring ran with wine instead of water.
7. Where youth grows pale, and spectre-thin, and dies: Keats' brother, Tom, wasted by tuberculosis, had died the previous winter.
8. on the viewless wings of Poesy: not by getting drunk on wine, but on the invisible wings of the poetic fancy
9. starry Fays: fairies
10. verdurous glooms and winding mossy ways: green-foliaged
11. embalmed: perfumed
12. eglantine: sweetbrier, or honeysuckle
13. Darkling: in the darkness
14. mused rhyme: in carefully-pondered, thought-out poems
15. Ruth: According to the biblical Book of Ruth, she was the ancestress of King David. After the death of her husband, she left her own people with her mother-in-law. She had picked up the grain in the fields of Baoz of Bethlehem and then became the wife of Baoz. She is celebrated for her devotion to her mother-in-law, Maomi. The next line "She stood in tears amid the alien corn" is the fancy of Keats.
16. forlorn: lonely, miserable
17. fancy: "the viewless wings of Poesy" (Line 33)

18. anthem: the song or hymn

## For Study and Discussion

1. In the first stanza, the poet talks about his feeling when he hears the bird singing. What is his feeling? Why does the "full-throated ease" have such an effect?
2. In the second stanza, the poet calls for a drink. Why does the poet do so?
3. The third stanza tells us that he wants to flee from the society. What is the reality that the poet wants to escape from? What makes the poet so sick of the society?
4. In the fourth stanza, the poet rejects wine and prefers to travel through imagination. Why does he rely on imagination?
5. The fifth stanza describes the image of darkness. Why does the poet put himself in darkness?
6. The sixth stanza discusses the poet's wish for death. Why does he have such a wish?
7. Why does the poet return to the idea of life in the seventh stanza?
8. Why does the poet ask "Was it a vision, or a waking dream?"?
9. Learn the first stanza by heart.

### Ode on a Grecian Urn[1]

1

Thou still unravish'd bride of quietness,
　Thou foster-child of silence and slow time,
Sylvan[2] historian, who canst thus express
　A flowery tale more sweetly than our rhyme:
What leaf-fring'd legend haunts about thy shape
　Of deities or mortals, or of both,
　　In Tempe or the dales of Arcady[3]?
　What men or gods are these? What maidens loth?
What mad pursuit? What struggle to escape?
　　What pipes and timbrels? What wild ecstasy?

2

Heard melodies are sweet, but those unheard
　Are sweeter; therefore, ye soft pipes, play on;
Not to the sensual ear[4], but, more endear'd,
　Pipe to the spirit ditties of no tone:
Fair youth, beneath the trees, thou canst not leave

Thy song, nor ever can those trees be bare;
Bold lover, never, never canst thou kiss,
Though winning near the goal—yet, do not grieve;
She cannot fade, though thou hast not thy bliss,
For ever wilt thou love, and she be fair!

3

Ah, happy, happy boughs! that cannot shed
Your leaves, nor ever bid the spring adieu;
And, happy melodist, unwearied,
For ever piping songs for ever new;
More happy love! more happy, happy love!
For ever warm and still to be enjoy'd,
For ever panting, and for ever young:
All breathing human passion far above,
That leaves a heart high-sorrowful and cloy'd,
A burning forehead, and a parching tongue.

4

Who are these coming to the sacrifice?
To what green altar, O mysterious priest,
Lead'st thou that heifer lowing at the skies,
And all her silken flanks with garlands drest?
What little town by river or sea shore,
Or mountain-built with peaceful citadel,
Is emptied of this folk, this pious morn?
And, little town, thy streets for evermore
Will silent be; and not a soul to tell
Why thou art desolate, can e'er return.

5

O Attic[5] shape! Fair attitude! with brede
Of marble men and maidens overwrought[6],
With forest branches and the trodden weed;
Thou, silent form, dost tease us out of thought
As doth eternity: Cold Pastoral!
When old age shall this generation waste,
Thou shalt remain, in midst of other woe
Than ours, a friend to man, to whom thou say'st,

"Beauty is truth, truth beauty,"[7]—that is all
Ye know on earth, and all ye need to know.

## Notes

1. This urn, with its sculptured reliefs of Dionysian ecstasies, panting young lovers in flight and pursuit, a pastoral piper under spring foliage, and the quiet celebration of communal pieties, resembles parts of various vases, sculptures and paintings; but it existed in all its particulars only in Keats' imagination. In the urn—which captures moments of intense experience in attitudes of grace and freezes them into marble immobility—Keats found the perfect correlative for his persistent concern with the longing for permanence in a world of changes. The interpretation of the details with which Keats develops this concept, however, is hotly disputed, all the way from the opening phrase—is "still"an adverb ("as yet") or an adjective "motionless"? —to the two concluding lines, an ending which has already accumulated much critical discussion. But these disputes testify to the enigmatic richness of meaning in the five short stanzas, and show that the ode has become a central point of reference in the criticism of the English lyric.
2. sylvan: rustic, representing a woodland scene
3. Tempe or the dales of Arcady: Tempe is a beautiful valley in Greece, which has come to represent supreme rural beauty. The dales of Arcady are the valleys of Arcadia, a state in ancient Greece often used as a symbol of the pastoral ideal.
4. the sensual ear: the ear of sense (as opposed to that of the "spirit" or imagination)
5. Attic: Attica was the region of Greece in which Athens was located.
6. overwrought: ornamented all over with an interwoven pattern ("brede")
7. "Beauty is truth, truth beauty": The quotation marks around this phrase are found in the volume of poems Keats published in 1820; but there are no quotation marks in the version printed in *Annals of the Fine Arts*, that same year, or in the four transcripts of the poem made by Keats' friends. This discrepancy has encouraged the diversity of critical interpretations of the last two lines. Leading critics disagree whether the whole of these lines is said by the urn, or "Beauty is truth, truth beauty" by the urn and the rest by Keats or else by an invented lyric speaker; whether the "ye" in the last line is addressed to the lyric speaker, to the readers, to the urn, or to the figures on the urn; whether, "all ye know" is that beauty is truth, or this plus the statement in Lines 46–48; and whether "beauty is truth" is a universal and profound metaphysical proposition, or an over-statement uttered in the course of a dramatic dialogue, or simply nonsense.

## For Study and Discussion

1. What are the two qualities of the urn according to the poet?
2. The scene described in the first stanza is one of carnival. Can you tell about the happy scene?
3. The poet seems to believe that the unfulfilled kiss is better than the reality and the maiden. The

moment of pursuit is recorded in the work of art. What role does art play in this case?

4. The third stanza presents a scene of pure joy. Which word is repeated six times? Why is it repeated? How is the happiness contrasted with the panting and passions of human beings?
5. What scene is presented in the fourth stanza? What are people doing? What is the poet's imagination?
6. Comment on the line "Beauty is truth, truth beauty". Do you think this is ambiguous? State your reasons.
7. Learn the second stanza by heart.

## To Autumn[1]

1

Season of mists and mellow fruitfulness,
   Close bosom-friend of the maturing sun;
Conspiring with him how to load and bless
   With fruit the vines that round the thatch-eves run;
To bend with apples the moss'd cottage-trees,
   And fill all fruit with ripeness to the core;
      To swell the gourd, and plump the hazel shells
   With a sweet kernel; to set budding more,
And still more, later flowers for the bees,
Until they think warm days will never cease,
      For summer has o'er-brimm'd their clammy cells.

2

Who hath not seen thee oft amid thy store?
   Sometimes whoever seeks abroad may find
Thee sitting careless on a granary floor,
   Thy hair soft-lifted by the winnowing[2] wind;
Or on a half-reap'd furrow sound asleep,
   Drows'd with the fume of poppies, while thy hook[3]
      Spares the next swath and all its twined flowers:
And sometimes like a gleaner thou dost keep
   Steady thy laden head across a brook;
   Or by a cyder-press, with patient look,
      Thou watchest the last oozings hours by hours.

3

Where are the songs of spring? Ay, where are they?
　Think not of them, thou hast thy music too,—
While barred clouds bloom the soft-dying day,
　And touch the stubble-plains with rosy hue;
Then in a wailful choir the small gnats mourn
　Among the river sallows[4], brone aloft
　　Or sinking as the light wind lives or dies;
And full-grown lambs loud bleat from hilly bourn[5];
　Hedge-crickets sing; and now with treble soft
　The red-breast whistles from a garden-croft;
　　And gathering swallows twitter in the skies.

## Notes

1. Two days after this serene and gracious ode was composed, Keats wrote on September 22, 1819 to John Hamilton Reynolds: "I never liked stubble fields so much as now—Aye, better than the chilly green of the spring. Somehow a stubble plain looks warm—in the same way that some pictures look warm—this struck me so much in my Sunday's walk that I composed upon it."
2. winnowing: To "winnow" is to fan the chaff from the grain.
3. hook: scythe
4. sallows: willows
5. bourn: region

## For Study and Discussion

1. Some critics describe the three stanzas in this way. The first stanza talks about the autumn tints (秋色); the second people in autumn (秋人); the third sound in autumn (秋声). Although the title of this poem does not name it "ode", this is a perfect ode, a tribute to the autumn, a feeling of fullness, completion and calm pleasure. Can you find some Chinese poems on autumn? Compare them and find what different moods they convey.
2. Find the images presented in the first stanza. In what ways do they contribute to show the maturity and harvest of autumn?
3. How is autumn presented in the image of a female?
4. Why does the third stanza begin with a question asking where the songs of spring are?
5. Learn the first stanza by heart.

## Bright Star[1]

Bright star! would I were stedfast as thou art—
  Not in lone splendour hung aloft the night,
And watching, with eternal lids apart,
  Like nature's patient, sleepless eremite[2],
The moving waters at their priestlike task
  Of pure ablution[3] round earth's human shores,
Or gazing on the new soft-fallen mask
  Of snow upon the mountains and the moors;
No—yet still stedfast, still unchangeable,
  Pillow'd upon my fair love's ripening breast,
To feel for ever its soft swell and fall,
  Awake for ever in a sweet unrest,
Still, still to hear her tender-taken breath,
And so live ever—or else swoon to death.[4]

## Notes

1. While on a tour of the lake country in 1818, Keats had said that the austere scenes "refine one's sensual vision into a sort of north star which can never cease to be open lidded and steadfast over the wonders of the great Power". This is what he told his brother Tom in his letter in June 1818. This thought developed into this sonnet. Keats drafted this poem in 1819 and then copied it into his volume of Shakespeare's poems, while on the way to Italy in September, 1820. So it was often misunderstood as his last poem.
2. eremite: hermit, religious solitary
3. ablution: washing, as part of a religious rite
4. And so live ever—or else swoon to death: In the earlier version: "Half passionless, and so swoon on to death."

## For Study and Discussion

1. What is the image presented in the first eight lines? What meaning does the poet want to convey by this image?
2. How does the poet express his wishes for love in the last six lines?
3. What is the theme of this sonnet?
4. Learn the sonnet by heart.

# Chapter 9

# Thomas Hood

## Life and Works

Thomas Hood (1799–1845) was born into a book-seller's family in London. Hood left his private school at 14 and was admitted into the counting house of a friend of his family. This uncongenial profession affected his health. Later he began to study engraving. The labour of engraving was no better for his health than the counting house had been, and Hood was sent to his father's relations at Dundee, Scotland. He stayed in the house of his maternal aunt, Jean Keay, for some months and then, after a falling out with her he moved on to the boarding house of one of her aunt's friends, Mrs. Butterworth, where he lived for the rest of his time in Scotland. It was also during his time here that Hood began to seriously write poetry and had his first published work.

His work as an engraver and his study of drawing were good to his illustrating his comic writings. In 1821, John Scott, the editor of *The London Magazine*, was killed in a duel, and the periodical passed into the hands of some friends of Hood, who proposed to make him sub-editor. So at the age of twenty-two he started working as a magazine editor, and edited various periodicals, namely, *The London Magazine*, *The Gem*, *The Comic Annual*, *The New Monthly Magazine*, and finally *Hood's Magazine*.

Not all Hood's poems were popular with readers, but some poems were so popular that they were introduced to readers of other countries and translated into German immediately after they were published because of his minute descriptions of the miserable life of the English people.

His famous works include "Miss Killmansegg and Her Precious Leg", a satirical poem holding up to ridicule the worship of gold by the bourgeoisie, "The Song of the Shirt", one of the best poems on the hard life of the labourers under capitalism, and "The Bridge of Sighs", a poem on the miserable fate of the poor women.

## Brief Comment

Most of Hood's works were humorous poems, containing topical comments on contemporary events and manners. They had lost their appeal later, but a few of his serious poems retained a permanent place in English literature. In these works Hood expressed his protest against the social injustice. As a petty bourgeois humanist he went no further than to lament over the fate of the oppressed and express his sympathy for their sufferings.

Hood wrote humorously on many contemporary issues. One of the most important issues in his time was grave robbing and selling of corpses to anatomists. On this serious and perhaps cruel issue, he wrote humorously: "Don't go to weep upon my grave, / And think that there I be. / They haven't left an atom there / Of my anatomie." Hood's most widely-known work during his lifetime was "The Song of the Shirt", which was a lament for a poor London seamstress who had been compelled to sell shirts she had made in order to feed her malnourished and ailing child. This poem appeared in one of the very first editions of *Punch* in 1843 and quickly became a public sensation, being turned into a popular song and inspiring social activists in defense of the countless labouring women who lived in abject poverty despite their constant industriousness.

## Selections

### The Song of the Shirt

With fingers weary and worn,
    With eyelids heavy and red,
A woman sat, in unwomanly rags,
    Plying her needle and thread—
Stitch! stitch! stitch!
    In poverty, hunger, and dirt,
And still with a voice of dolorous pitch
    She sang the "Song of the Shirt!"

"Work! work! work!
    While the cock is crowing aloof!
And work—work—work—
    Till the stars shine through the roof!
It's O! to be a slave
    Along with the barbarous Turk,
Where woman has never a soul to save,
    If this is Christian work!

"Work—work—work—!
    Till the brain begins to swim!
Work—work—work—
    Till the eyes are heavy and dim!
Seam, and gusset, and band,
    Band, and gusset, and seam,—
Till over the buttons I fall asleep,
    And sew them on in a dream!

"O! men with sisters dear!
    O! men with mothers and wives!
It is not linen you're wearing out,
    But human creatures' lives!
Stitch—stitch—stitch—
    In poverty, hunger, and dirt,—
Sewing at once with a double thread,
    A shroud as well as a shirt!

"But why do I talk of Death—
    That phantom of grisly bone?
I hardly fear its terrible shape,
    It seems so like my own—
It seems so like my own,
    Because of the fasts I keep;
O God! that bread should be so dear,
    And flesh and blood so cheap!

"Work—work—work—!
    My labour never flags;
And what are its wages? A bed of straw,
    A crust of bread—and rags,
That shatter'd roof—and this naked floor—
    A table—a broken chair—
And a wall so blank, my shadow I thank,
    For sometimes falling there!

"Work—work—work—!
    From weary chime to chime,
Work—work—work

As prisoners work for crime!
Band, and gusset, and seam,
Seam, and gusset, and band,
Till the heart is sick and the brain benumb'd,
As well as the weary hand.

"Work—work—work—!
In the dull December light,
And work—work—work
When the weather is warm and bright!
While underneath the eaves
The brooding swallows cling,
As if to show me their sunny backs
And twit me with the Spring.

"O! but to breathe the breath
Of the cowslip and primrose sweet—
With the sky above my head,
And the grass beneath my feet!
For only one short hour
To feel as I used to feel,
Before I knew the woes of want,
And the walk that costs a meal!

"O! but for one short hour—
A respite however brief!
No blessed leisure for Love or Hope,
But only time for Grief!
A little weeping would ease my heart;
But in their briny bed
My tears must stop, for every drop
Hinders needle and thread!

"Seam, and gusset, and band,
Band, and gusset, and seam,
Work—work—work
Like the Engine that works by Steam!
A mere machine of iron and wood
That toils for Mammon's[1] sake—

Without a brain to ponder and craze,
    Or a heart to feel and break!"

With fingers weary and worn,
    With eyelids heavy and red,
A woman sat in unwomanly rags,
    Plying her needle and thread—
Stitch! stitch! stitch!
    In poverty, hunger, and dirt,
And still with a voice of dolorous pitch,
Would that its tone could reach the rich!
    She sang this "Song of the Shirt!"

## Notes

1. Mammon: the devil of covetousness, riches

## For Study and Discussion

1. What is the tone of the poet when he describes the woman in the first stanza?
2. How do you understand the images of the cock and the stars? Why does the poet mention "Turk" and "Christian"?
3. How is the woman described in the third stanza?
4. Why does the poet say that the woman is sewing "a shroud as well as a shirt"?
5. Which word is repeated again and again? What effect does the repetition have?

# Part VIII

# The Second Half of the 19th Century: The Victorian Age and Critical Realism

# Introduction

## History of the Period

The Victorian period refers to the years between Queen Victoria's accession in 1837 and her death in 1901.

Among many social and political forces of this age, four things stood out clearly. First, the long struggle of the Anglo-Saxons for personal liberty was settled, and democracy became the established order. The king and the nobles were stripped of power and became figureheads of the past civilisation. The last trace of personal government and of the divine right of rulers disappeared. The House of Commons became the ruling power in England and a series of new reform bills extended the suffrage, until the English people chose for themselves the men who would represent them. Second, the age of democracy brought the age of popular education, of religious tolerance, of growing brotherhood, and of profound social unrest. The slaves had been freed in 1833, but in the middle of the century England awoke to find that slaves were not necessarily the black people, but the multitudes of victims of a more terrible industrial and social slavery. To free these slaves also, the unwilling victims of unnatural competitive methods, had been the growing purpose of the Victorian Age. Third, the age of democracy and education brought about the age of relative peace. England began to think less of the pomp and false glitter of fighting, and more of its moral evils. The nation realised that it was the common people who bore the burden, the sorrow and the poverty of war, while the privileged classes reaped most of the financial and political rewards. Moreover, with the growth of trade and of friendly foreign relations, it became evident that the social equality for which England was fighting for at home belonged to the whole mankind. Brotherhood was universal, not insular. Justice was never settled by fighting. War was horror and barbarism. Fourth, the Victorian Age was especially remarkable for its rapid progress in all arts, sciences and mechanical inventions. A glance at any record of the industrial achievements and inventions of the 19th century will show how vast they were.

Chartism is a key term to understand the English history of this period.

During the years after 1832, the major contradiction on the political stage became more definitely that between labour and capital. The years between 1832 and the early 1850s saw an important series of events known as the Chartist Movement. Chartism arose out of the increasing strength and a greater confidence of the working class as well as their increasing miseries in life. Chartism was, as Lenin said, "the first broad, really mass, politically formed, proletarian revolutionary movement." The Chartist Movement sprang from "the social degradation produced by the unregulated growth of industry and by the subordination of human to commercial interests". According to the new Poor Law of 1834, the system of workhouses was applied to the whole country to make provisions for the poor. The Corn Laws made bread too expensive for the poor, and then intensified exploitation of men, women and even children in that the working people had to work long hours at low wages. All these led to the demand of the workers for social justice and a better life. In 1836 the London Workingmen's Association determined to embark upon a campaign of political rights and drew up a "Charter" (the People's Charter 1837) which embodied and enlarged upon the demands in the petitions of 1819. Of the six "points" in the chartists' program, four, namely, manhood suffrage, the removal of property qualifications for membership in the House of Commons, the payment of members and the secret ballot, had long since become part of English law, while the two others—annual Parliaments and equal electoral districts—remained to this day unrealised. The basic purpose of the chartists was the redress of social grievances which could, they held, be accomplished only when workingmen had representation in the Parliament. There were two conflicting elements in chartism—the men who relied upon moral suasion and those who advocated the use of threats and force. For want of possessing votes with which pressure could be brought upon their governors, and also for want of wise leadership, a unified purpose and funds, the movement ended in failure. During the "Hungry Forties" it hung over England like a threatening cloud, while in the minds of the ruling classes two fears were ever present—terror of pestilence and terror of a rising of the "mob". The revival of chartism in 1846–1848, when a "monster petition" of nearly two million signatures was presented to the Parliament, was the last flicker of what had once threatened to become a conflagration.

All the important events of the Chartist Movement, especially the class contradictions underlying these events, found their expression in the novels of the critical realists like Dickens (*Hard Times*), Charlotte Brontë (*Shirley*) and Mrs. Gaskell (*Mary Barton*, *North and South*) etc. Though it failed, chartism signified the first great political movement of the proletariat in English history.

## Literary Current

The critical realism of the 19th century flourished in the 1840s and in the beginning of 1850s. The realists first and foremost set themselves the task of criticising capitalist society from a democratic viewpoint and delineated the crying contradictions of bourgeois reality. Karl Marx gave the following characterisation of the works of critical realists:

"The present brilliant school of novelists in England, whose graphic and eloquent descriptions have revealed more political and social truths to the world than have all the politicians, publicists, and moralists added together, has pictured all sections of the middle class, beginning with the 'respectable' rentier and owner of government stocks, who looks down on all kinds of 'business' as being vulgar, and finishing with the small shopkeeper and lawyer's clerk. How have they been described by Dickens, Thackeray, Charlotte Brontë and Mrs. Gaskell? As full of self-conceit, prudishness, petty tyranny and ignorance. And the civilised world confirmed their verdict in a damning epigram which it has pinned on that class, that it was servile to its social superiors and despotic to its social inferiors."

The greatest English realist of the time was Charles Dickens. With a striking force and truthfulness, he created pictures of bourgeois civilisation, describing the misery and sufferings of common people.

Another critical realist, William Makepeace Thackeray, was a no less severe exposer of contemporary society. Thackeray's novels mainly contain a satirical portrayal of the upper stratum of society.

Further adherents to the method of critical realism were Charlotte Brontë and Elizabeth Gaskell. In her novel *Mary Barton*, Gaskell described the inhuman conditions of life of English workers and the birth of Chartist Movement as the inevitable result of the monstrous exploitation.

The greatness of the English realists lies not only in their satirical portrayal of bourgeoisie and the exposure of the greed and hypocrisy of the ruling classes, but also in their profound humanism reflected in their sympathy for the labouring people. These writers created positive characters who were quite alien to the vices of the rich and who were chiefly common people.

In the best works of the realist writers, the world of greed and cruelty is contrasted to a world where the unwritten laws of humanism rule in defiance of all the sorrows and inflictions that befall the heroes. This juxtaposition determines the character and function of humour and satire in the realistic novel of the 19th century. Humourous scenes may attend the actions of the positive characters, but this humour is tinged with lyricism and serves to stress the human qualities, the sincerity and kindness of such characters. At the same time, bitter satire and even grotesque are used to expose and criticise the seamy side of reality.

In the fifties and sixties the realistic novel entered a stage of decline. During this period of political reaction, the crisis of realism found its reflection in the works of George Eliot, Anthony Trollope (1815–1882) and others. George Eliot described the life of the labouring people and criticised the privileged classes, however, expository tendencies were much weaker in her works. She raised the problem of class contradictions more seldom and less forcibly. The significance of Eliot's works lies in the portrayal of the pettiness and stagnancy of English provincial life.

The critical realists of the 19th century did not and, due to their world outlook, could not find a way to eradicate social evils.

They did not rise to the realisation of the necessity of changing the contemporary social system radically. They strived for no more than improving it by means of reforms, which brought them to a futile attempt of reconciling the antagonistic class forces—the bourgeoisie and proletariat.

The English working class, however, created a literature of its own which can be, in full justice, called the chartist literature, for it developed among the participants of the Chartist Movement before and after the revolutionary events of 1848. The chartist writers introduced a new theme into English literature—the struggle of the proletariat for its rights.

The second half of the 19th century in England produced a number of outstanding poets such as Alfred Tennyson, Robert Browning, Algernon Charles Swinburne (1837–1909). The greatest of them was Robert Browning. Adhering in his best works to the ideas of humanism, Browning created a gallery of inspired painters, musicians and scientists. Many of his poems were devoted to the glorification of Italy, of its people, nature and art. In his masterpiece *An Italian in England* Browning portrayed an Italian revolutionary fighting for the freedom of the country.

# Chapter 10

# Elizabeth Barrett Browning

## Life and Works

Elizabeth Barrett Browning (1806–1861) was born at Coxhoe Hall, Durham, England. She was the first born of the twelve children. She was educated at home and began to read Shakespeare, Milton, ancient Greek poets and Hebrew literature when she was in her teens. She loved riding, but a fall from a horse injured her backbone when she was 15, which paralysed her for 24 years until the love from Robert Browning made her stand up again.

In 1826, she published a collection of poems anonymously. Her poems attracted Robert Browning who was six years her junior. They fell in love and wrote letters (574 letters in all) to each other. But their love was opposed by her father, Edward Barrett Moulton Barrett, so they had to elope to Florence in Italy in August 1846. Their married life was happy, and she recovered from the backbone injury. In 1849 they gave birth to a boy whom they named Robert Wideman Browning. She died on June 29, 1861, happily and calmly in the arms of her loving husband who thought she just fell into a sleep.

Her most perfect work is the *Sonnets from the Portuguese* (1850), which contains the record of courtship and marriage. Her other works include *The Seraphim* (1838), *Poems* (1844), which show in many places the defects of unreality and of overwrought emotion natural to work produced in the loneliness of a sick-chamber. The best known of her early poems are perhaps "Lady Geraldine's Courtship", where she worked under the influence of Tennyson's idylls, and "The Cry of the Children", where she voiced the humanitarian protest against the practice of employing child labour in mines and factories.

She was deeply interested in the struggle of Italy to shake off her bondage to Austria, as was shown by her *Casa Guidi Windows*, published in 1851. In 1857 appeared her most ambitious work, *Aurora Leigh*, a kind of versified novel of modern English life, with a social reformer and humanitarian, of aristocratic lineage, for the hero, and a young poetess, in large part a reflection of Mrs. Browning's own personality, for the heroine. *Aurora Leigh* showed the influence of a great novel-writing age, when the novel was becoming more and more imbued with social purpose. It attempts unsuccessfully to perform in verse the social function which Charles Dickens, George Eliot and others, strove to perform in prose.

## Brief Comment

Mrs. Browning's technique is uncertain, and she never freed herself from her characteristic faults of vagueness and unrestraint. But her sympathy with noble causes, the elevation and ardour of her moods of personal emotion, and the distinction of her utterance at its best, tempt readers to overlook her technical limitations. She shared her husband's strenuousness and optimism, but she spoke always from the feminine vantage-ground. Her characteristic note is that of intimate, personal feeling; even *Casa Guidi Windows* has been aptly called "a woman's love making with a nation".

During the years of her marriage to Robert Browning, her literary reputation far surpassed that of her poet-husband; when visitors came to their home in Florence, she was invariably the greater attraction. She had a wide following among cultured readers in England and in the United States. She was called Sappho of England and was the idol of Emily Dickinson. A framed portrait of Barrett Browning hung in the bedroom of Emily Dickinson, whose life had been transfigured by the poetry of "that Foreign Lady".

## Selections

### *Sonnets from the Portuguese*

21

Say over again, and yet once over again,
That thou dost love me. Though the word repeated
Should seem "a cuckoo song", as thou dost treat it,
Remember, never to the hill or plain,
Valley and wood, without her cuckoo strain
Comes the fresh Spring in all her green completed.
Belovèd, I, amid the darkness greeted
By a doubtful spirit voice, in that doubt's pain
Cry, "Speak once more—thou lovest!" Who can fear
Too many stars, though each in heaven shall roll,
Too many flowers, though each shall crown the year?
Say thou dost love me, love me, love me—toll
The silver iterance!—only minding, Dear,
To love me also in silence with thy soul.

## For Study and Discussion

1. Why does the speaker compare the repetition of his words of love to "a cuckoo song"? She calls for his love as the darkness of the night calls for dawn. Which lines support this idea?
2. What is the function of the images of stars and flowers?
3. What is equally important besides speaking out his love repeatedly?

22

When our two souls stand up erect and strong,
Face to face, silent, drawing nigh and nigher.
Until the lengthening wings break into fire
At either curvèd point—what bitter wrong
Can the earth do to us, that we should not long
Be here contented? Think. In mounting higher,
The angels would press on us and aspire
To drop some golden orb of perfect song
Into our deep, dear silence. Let us stay
Rather on earth, Belovèd,—where the unfit
Contrarious moods of men recoil away
And isolate pure spirits, and permit
A place to stand and love in for a day,
With darkness and the death-hour rounding it.

## For Study and Discussion

1. What is the idea expressed in the first six lines?
2. Where would the speaker choose to stay in comparison with the angels? What place is the earth like as described in the last five lines?
3. To the speaker and her love, what can conquer the unfit earth?

32

The first time that the sun rose on thine oath
To love me, I looked forward to the moon
To slacken all those bonds which seemed too soon
And quickly tied to make a lasting troth.
Quick-loving hearts, I thought, may quickly loathe;
And, looking on myself, I seemed not one
For such man's love!—more like an out-of-tune
Worn viol, a good singer would be wroth

To spoil his song with, and which, snatched in haste,
Is laid down at the first ill-sounding note.
I did not wrong myself so, but I placed
A wrong on *thee*. For perfect strains may float
'Neath master-hands, from instruments defaced—
And great souls, at one stroke, may do and dote.

## For Study and Discussion

1. Why does the speaker use the images of the sun and the moon? What is her attitude to quick-loving hearts?
2. What is the image of music used here for in Lines 7–10?

43

How do I love thee? Let me count the ways.
I love thee to the depth and breadth and height
My soul can reach, when feeling out of sight
For the ends of Being and ideal Grace.
I love thee to the level of everyday's
Most quiet need, by sun and candlelight.
I love thee freely, as men strive for Right;
I love thee purely, as they turn from Praise.
I love thee with the passion put to use
In my old griefs, and with my childhood's faith.
I love thee with a love I seemed to lose
With my lost saints—I love thee with the breath,
Smiles, tears, of all my life!—and, if God choose,
I shall but love thee better after death.

## For Study and Discussion

1. In what ways does the speaker love her husband?
2. What would she still do after her death?
3. In China there is "A Pledge" in the *Yuefu Poetry*（《乐府诗・上邪》, "上邪，我欲与君相知，长命无绝衰……"）. Compare this sonnet with "A Pledge" and give your comments.

Chapter 11

# Alfred Tennyson

## Life and Works

Alfred Tennyson (1809–1892) was born at Somersby Rectory, Lincolnshire. His father was a vicar of the Church of England, holding several livings by gift from landed proprietors. So Tennyson was from birth in close connection with the main conservative interests of England. In 1830, when he was still an undergraduate at Cambridge, he published his first volume of poems. Two years later he published a second volume, showing a control of both medieval and classical stories in such poems as "The Lady of Shalott" and "The Lotos-Eaters" and in certain others such as "The Palace of Art", giving indication of his ambition to be not a singer merely, but also a teacher. In "The Miller's Daughter" and "The May Queen", he began his long series of idylls of English life, short narratives richly pictured and melodiously tuned, with which he was destined to win the public all the more easily perhaps because of their touches of sentimentality and unreality.

In 1836 Tennyson went to live near London, where he came into contact with Carlyle, and was stirred by his spirit of social protest. He also found in the latter's spiritual view of the universe a support for his religious faith, which was to be sorely tried by doubt. For ten years he published nothing but brooded and worked away in his London lodgings until, in 1842, he came forth with two volumes which took the critics and the world by storm. In these two volumes the range and variety of work was remarkable. Almost every province of poetry was touched upon, from the lyric simplicity of "Break, Break, Break" to the largely moulded epic narrative "Morte d'Arthur". In one of these poems, "Locksley Hall", he uttered the protest which young men like himself, of good though not noble birth, were feeling in the presence of class distinctions which subordinated love to rank, and of an industrial civilisation which made gold the supreme test of success.

Five years later, in 1847, his long poem *The Princess* came out. It was Tennyson's contribution to the question, then beginning to be widely discussed, of the higher education of women. The subtitle is *A Medley*, and no description could be more just.

In 1850 he published *In Memoriam*, which was written in memory of Arthur Hallam, a beloved friend and college-mate of Tennyson's, who had died in 1833. The poem is often considered Tennyson's greatest poetic achievement. It is a stunning and profoundly moving long poem consisting of a prologue, 131 cantos/stanzas, and an epilogue. However, there is no single unified theme in this elegy. Grief, loss and renewal of faith, survival and other themes compete with one another.

## Brief Comment

In 1850 Tennyson became the poet-laureate. A government pension enabled him to marry and to settle in the Isle of Wight. From this time until his death in 1892, he stood as the spokesman of his people in times of national sorrow or rejoicing. In such poems as "The Charge of the Light Brigade", "The Revenge" and "Ode on the Death of the Duke of Wellington", he ministered to national pride, stoked the fires of imperialism, and brought poetry nearer to the national life than it had been since Shakespeare. In the *Idylls of the King* he painted the character of the first English national hero, King Arthur, and gave a new meaning to the legends which had grown up in the Middle Ages about the knights of the Round Table. In no way did he illustrate more conspicuously his tendency to forsake pure romance for romantic treatment of present realities. In these poems, which are full of suggestions of modern moral and social problems, King Arthur's attempt to bring civilisation to his realm through the devotion of his knights failed because of sins which Tennyson felt to be the peculiar danger of his own age.

Tennyson's later works consisted largely of the series of dramas, for the most part based on English history, *Queen Mary*, *Harold* and *Becket*. He was not highly successful in mastering the dramatic form, but his example recalled the former greatness and dignity of the drama and gave an early sign of its recovery. In a number of poems he recalled his old manner—in the classic beauty of "Demeter and Persephone" and "The Death of Oenone"; in the allegory of noble striving towards the light in "Merlin and the Gleam". "Crossing the Bar" may be taken as his farewell word spoken with solemn gladness as he put off into the mysterious sea of death.

Tennyson's use of dramatic dialogue is worth noticing. He and Browning brought this form to an independent type, though it was already used by Renaissance poets such as John Donne and others.

## Selections

### Break, Break, Break

Break, break, break,
  On thy cold gray stones, O Sea!
And I would[1] that my tongue could utter

The thoughts that arise in me.

O, well for the fisherman's boy,
That he shouts with his sister at play!
O, well for the sailor lad,
That he sings in his boat on the bay!

And the stately ships go on
To their haven under the hill;
But O for the touch of a vanished hand[2],
And the sound of a voice that is still[3]!

Break, break, break,
At the foot of thy crags, O Sea!
But the tender grace of a day that is dead
Will never come back to me.

## Notes

1. I would: I wish
2. a vanished hand: the hand of the poet's dead friend Arthur Hallam
3. a voice that is still: the voice of Arthur Hallam

## For Study and Discussion

1. Why does the speaker tell the sea to break on the cold gray stones? Why does he stress that the stones are cold and gray? What impression does the first line leave on you?
2. What scene does the second stanza create? Why does the speaker wish to be the fisherman's boy or the sailor lad?
3. What is the difference between a ship and a still voice?
4. What is the tone of this poem?
5. Learn the first two stanzas by heart.

### The Eagle[1]

He clasps the crag with crooked hands;
Close to the sun in lonely lands,
Ringe'd with the azure world, he stands.

The wrinkled sea beneath him crawls;
He watches from his mountain walls,
And like a thunderbolt he falls.

## Notes

1. This poem was written in 1851 in memory of Arthur Hallam, Tennyson's friend who had been engaged to his sister but died in 1833.

## For Study and Discussion

1. What is the rhyme scheme of this short poem? In the first line, alliteration is used. How does it contribute to the sound effect of this poem?
2. What does "lonely lands" refer to? Is he lonely in life? What is the significance of the words "close to the sun"?
3. How do you understand the image of the "wrinkled sea"? What is the significance of the sea crawling beneath him?
4. The eagle falls like a thunderbolt, presenting the sudden death of the poet's friend. One can sense that the poet compared his friend to the eagle. What is your understanding of this image?

### Crossing the Bar[1]

Sunset and evening star,
   And one clear call for me!
And may there be no moaning of the bar,[2]
   When I put out to sea,

But such a tide as moving seems asleep,
   Too full for sound and foam,
When that which drew from out the boundless deep
   Turns again home.

Twilight and evening bell,
   And after that the dark!
And may there be no sadness of farewell,
   When I embark;

For though from out our bourne[3] of Time and Place
The flood may bear me far,
I hope to see my Pilot face to face
When I have crossed the bar.

## Notes

1. Although not the last poem written by Tennyson, "Crossing the Bar" appears, at his request, as the final poem in all collections of his work.
2. And may there be no moaning of the bar: Mournful sound of the ocean beating on a sand bar at the mouth of a harbour
3. bourne: boundary

## For Study and Discussion

1. What are the images of the sunset and evening star symbolic of? Why does the speaker feel they are calling for him?
2. The image of home seems to be crucial in the second stanza. Please talk about the significance of it. To the speaker, where is home?
3. What does the speaker mean by talking of embarking?
4. The word "bar" is a central one in this poem. "Crossing the bar" is certainly symbolic of something. Of what? Who will be the speaker's pilot?
5. Learn the first and the third stanzas by heart.

# Chapter 12

# William Makepeace Thackeray

## Life and Works

William Makepeace Thackeray (1811–1863), the only child of an Englishman in the Indian Civil Service, was born in Calcutta in 1811. In 1817, after his father's death, he was sent to England to a succession of preparatory schools which he hated, and then to a public school at the Charterhouse, where he was made even more miserable by bullying and flogging. After six years he left to enter the Trinity College, Cambridge, in 1829, where he remained for a little more than a year. He enjoyed the University more than the Charterhouse, but in both places his achievements were social rather than academic. At Cambridge he wrote for *The Snob*, an undergraduate journal to which he contributed a burlesque of Alfred Tennyson's prize poem, "Timbuctoo". He formed lasting friendships with Tennyson, Edward FitzGerald (translator of *Rubaiyat of Omar Khayyam*), and William Brookfield. There he debated at the Union, spent a great deal of money, and left without a degree.

Having a comfortable income from his father's estate, he could afford to take an active part in the society he always enjoyed so much, and to travel. The year he left Cambridge he spent some months in pleasant dilettantism at Weimar, where he was introduced to Goethe. On his return to London he began to study for the bar, but the law was distasteful to him, and he abandoned it after a year's desultory work. He lost a considerable sum of money in 1833 by buying and editing a short-lived paper, *The National Standard*. Extravagance and unwise investments dissipated the rest of his inheritance, and by 1834 he was compelled to earn his living. He always had a flair for drawings, so he decided to study painting in Paris, but was no more successful than his other ventures, although he did become a competent cartoonist and later illustrated several of his own works. When *The Pickwick Papers* were appearing in 1836 he applied unsuccessfully to Dickens for employment in illustrating them.

On the strength of eight guineas a week which he was earning as Paris correspondent for *The Constitutional*, a radical newspaper of which his stepfather was the director, Thackeray married an Irish girl, Isabella Shawe, in August 1836. Three daughters were born to them, of whom two survived; the eldest, Anne, later Lady Ritchie, became a novelist and essayist.

After the birth of her third child, Mrs. Thackeray's mind became progressively deranged until in 1842 she had to be confined; she survived her husband more than thirty years without recovering her sanity. In the wreck of his marriage Thackeray was left to supervise the rearing of his daughters. While his wife lived he was not free to remarry, of course, and the rest of his domestic life was frequently sad and lonely.

*The Constitutional* failed some months after Thackeray's marriage, and he turned to hack work for several journals, including *The Times*. To the new *Fraser's Magazine* he contributed his first important success, *The Yellowplush Correspondence*, fictional memoirs of a pushing and self-important footman, of which the theme was one he later used frequently: the ridiculousness of pretension. Reviews, sketches and novels followed in *Fraser's*, notably: *Catherine*, written to satirise such "Newgate Calendar" novels of crime similar to *Oliver Twist* and Harrison Ainsworth's *Jack Sheppard*; *The Great Hoggarty Diamond*, a story of corruption and speculation in business; and *Barry Lyndon*, the supposed autobiography of an 18th-century Irish adventurer, which covered his career from rascally youth to death in prison. To the newly founded magazine *Punch* Thackeray began contributing in 1842. There he published *The Snob Papers*, later collected as *The Book of Snobs*, which made his reputation as a social satirist.

When he was working on *The Snob Papers*, he was engaged on a long novel, which turned out to be his masterpiece, *Vanity Fair*. Its setting was England during and after the Napoleonic Wars, but its panoramic view of folly and vanity was universal. Rebecca Sharp, the unscrupulous governess whose adventures dominate the book, is generally recognised as one of the most vividly drawn characters in English novels. Hard on the heels of *Vanity Fair* came the publication in numbers of *Pendennis*, the history of an amiable and extravagant young man whose early career was a clear parallel to Thackeray's own.

Thackeray was always gregarious, and he loved the easy life of the upper class, with whom he was friendly but who were frequently the butts for his satire. His wife's incurable illness made him still more dependent upon his friends' hospitality. For several years after her breakdown he found comfort in the home of one of his closest Cambridge friends, William Brookfield. Gradually he fell deeply but innocently in love with Mrs. Brookfield. In the autumn of 1851 Mr. Brookfield wisely insisted that his wife see less of his friend. The loss of a companionship on which he had depended heavily was to him one of the most severe emotional blows of life.

In an effort to forget the hurt and to make his daughters financially secure he began lecturing, although suffered much embarrassment in speaking in public; his six lectures on the English humourists of the 18th century were so well received that he decided to repeat them in America. Before sailing he published *The History of Henry Esmond*, a historical novel for which his studies of the humourists had provided the background. It was set in the period of history he loved best, the reign of Queen Anne, but the love story of Esmond and Lady Castlewood was in part a reflection of his own feeling for Mrs. Brookfield. Perhaps because it was the only one of his novels not published serially, it had a finish and structural organisation greater than any of his other works. Unlike Dickens, he enjoyed his American visit in the winter of 1852–1853, quite aside from the 2500 pounds which he took back to England with him.

His delightful fairy tale, *The Rose and the Ring*, was published in 1855 at the same time when *The Newcomes* was appearing in numbers. The central character of *The Newcomes* was another view of Thackeray himself as a young man of good instincts which were thwarted by his own shortcomings.

The last of his great novels, *The Virginians*, continued the fortunes of the Esmond family in the persons of the American twin grandsons of Henry Esmond, in a setting divided between the fast and fashionable society of England and America of the Revolution.

By this time his popularity rivalled that of Dickens, with whom he was friendly if not intimate; their only quarrel was healed just before Thackeray's death. The sentimentality which he shared with Dickens over scenes of suffering, and the occasionally maudlin quality of his "good" women were tempered in his work with a satirical, sometimes cynical, view of society which perhaps has more appeal today than in his own time. Thackeray had considerable skill in parody, of which his best example was the burlesque of his contemporary writers in the series of *Mr. Punch's Prize Novelists*, republished as *Novels by Eminent Hands* (1856). He never thought of himself as a poet, but some of his light verse, such as "The Ballad of Bouillabaisse", was among the best of its kind.

A huge salary tempted him into becoming the first editor of *The Cornhill Magazine* in 1860, a task he performed adequately, although he was not well fitted for the position. His editorial standards of taste were those of his age; he once rejected a poem by Mrs. Browning because it contained "an account of unlawful passion felt by a man for a woman". His own reputation (and the prices paid by *Cornhill*) helped him get such contributors as Matthew Arnold, Tennyson, Trollope, John Ruskin—and his own daughter Anne. To the magazine he contributed his last three novels: *Lovel the Widower*, a short fictionalised version of an earlier unsuccessful two-act play; *The Adventures of Philip*, the last in the series of young heroes molded in the image of Thackeray's early life; and the unfinished *Denis Duval*, a historical romance in which he returned to his beloved 18th century. He also wrote for *Cornhill* the finest work of his late years, the amusing series of gossipy, familiar editorial essays, *The Roundabout Paper*; like most of his finest works they were mellowly reminiscent and autobiographical.

The ill health from which he had suffered for more than ten years ended in his sudden death at Kensington, London, in December, 1863.

# Selections

### *Vanity Fair*

## The Story

*Vanity Fair* is Thackeray's masterpiece, taking the title from the fair in Bunyan's *The Pilgrim's Progress,* where all sorts of cheats are displayed for sale. The novel presents a panorama of the society of the English upper-middle class in the 19th century. What is more important, none of his other novels can rival it in width of social life, and in depth of social criticism.

The subtitle of the novel—*A Novel Without a Hero*—points to the author's intention to portray not individuals singly but the whole of the notorious "Vanity Fair", the English bourgeois and aristocratic society.

With biting irony Thackeray exposed the vices of this society: hypocrisy, money-worship, and moral degradation. This accounts for the fact that the novel has very few positive characters.

The scene of the story is England in the first half of the 19th century. The book opens with the departure of two young girls from the Academy for Young Ladies on Chiswick Mall, situated in a London suburb, where they have studied for six years. One of them is Amelia Sedley, the daughter of a wealthy London merchant. The other is Rebecca Sharp, an orphan, who is obliged to become governess in the family of a certain baronet, Sir Pitt Crawley. Rebecca Sharp, shrewd and unscrupulous, sophisticated beyond her years, is determined to worm her way into high society at all costs. But she fails in her first attempt to inveigle into matrimony Amelia's rich brother Joseph Sedley.

Coming to Queen's Crawley, Sir Pitt's country seat, Rebecca Sharp finds herself in an atmosphere of avarice, hypocrisy and immorality. She does her best to gain the confidence of her employers and makes herself agreeable. She soon gains the favour of Sir Pitt Crawley, who is captivated by her charms to such a degree that after the death of his wife he proposes to her. But Rebecca has to forfeit this dazzling chance, having rushed into precipitate marriage only two days before with Sir Pitt's younger son Rawdon Crawley.

Amelia Sedley is about to be married to young lieutenant George Osborne, a light-minded man-about-town, pampered by an untroubled and well-to-do life. The two families have long been on friendly terms, Mr. Sedley having launched Osborne in business. Meanwhile, Amelia's father unexpectedly goes bankrupt and leaves his daughter penniless. Old Osborne turns his back on his former friend and benefactor and orders his son to break with Amelia. George Osborne has an intimate friend Captain Dobbin who is secretly and hopelessly in love with Amelia. Wishing to see Amelia happy, the Captain arranges the match between her and George and, as a result, the infuriated old Osborne disowns his son. George goes off to war with Napoleon and is killed in the Battle of Waterloo. In this part of the novel the author draws vivid pictures of various representatives of English society who followed the English army to the continent. The description of the Battle of Waterloo is brief but intense and vigorous.

Widowed Amelia gives birth to a son and entirely devotes herself to his upbringing.

In the meantime, Rebecca, after a number of adventures, insinuates herself into the graces of "good society" and enters into a liaison with Lord Steyne, a cynical old reprobate and rake. The illicit lovers are discovered by Rebecca's husband. As a consequence, Rawdon Crawley breaks with his wife. Being in the rank of a colonel, he obtains an appointment as governor to one of the British colonies and leaves England for good. Shortly after his arrival there he contracts fever and dies.

After many vicissitudes and wanderings, Rebecca attains respectability and a position of comparative ease. On meeting her former friend Amelia, who still reverently holds dear the memory of her dead husband, Rebecca discloses an old secret, bringing to light a proof of George's unfaithfulness to his marriage vows. Amelia's idol shattered, she decides to reward Dobbin's many-year fidelity by consenting to marry him.

## Brief Comment on the Novel

Thackeray drew a broad panorama of social life in his novel, criticising money-worship, cruelty and unscrupulousness ruthlessly. As the subtitle of the novel suggests, the story is neither with a plot nor a hero. Its whole action revolves two women, Amelia Sedley and Rebecca Sharp.

The central figure, Rebecca Sharp, is a perfect embodiment of the spirit of Vanity Fair as her only aspiration in life is to gain wealth and position by any means: through lies, mean actions and unscrupulous speculating with every sacred ideal. Drawing the striking character of Rebecca Sharp, Thackeray did not, however, regard her as an exception. Everyone wishes to gain something in the Vanity Fair and acts almost in the same manner as her. The character of Rebecca Sharp is drawn with admirable skill. She is full-blooded and many-sided, an unprincipled adventurer, a gifted woman with a keen sense of humour and deep understanding of people. Cringing to the rich and titled snobs, clever Rebecca at the same time perceives how shallow, vain and worthless they are.

Amelia and Dobbin may be considered as the positive characters of the novel. Amelia is gentle and virtuous, but too simple-hearted and naive to oppose the plots of the selfish and calculating personages that surround her. The author's portrayal of Amelia is tinged with subtle irony. She is duped at every turn, and only Dobbin, the one character worthy of the author's positive estimate, is faithful to her.

The inferences drawn by the author at the end of the novel are not consoling. Evil rules the world, and though it should be opposed to a reasonable extent, it is on the whole remediless. In the course of the narrative Thackeray often digressed from the plot to express his own attitude towards the events and characters described.

In *Vanity Fair* Thackeray made use of the device to blend his own remarks with the narration of the story and those of the characters. Besides, Thackeray distinguished himself to be a master of pure and simple style. His style is characterised by its ease, refinement and an exquisite naturalness, with which he was able to express his thoughts, emotions and movement of consciousness perfectly.

## Chapter XXXVI
## How to Live Well on Nothing a Year

I suppose there is no man in this Vanity Fair of ours so little observant as not to think sometimes about the worldly affairs of his acquaintances, or so extremely charitable as not to wonder how his neighbour Jones, or his neighbour Smith, can make both ends meet at the end of the year. With the utmost regard for the family, for instance (for I dine with them twice or thrice in a season), I cannot but own that the appearance of the Jenkinses in the Park, in the large barouche[1] with the grenadier-footmen, will surprise and mystify me to my dying day: for though I know the equipage is only jobbed, and all the Jenkins people are on board wages, yet those three men and the carriage must represent an expense of six hundred a year at the very least—and then there are the splendid dinners, the two boys at Eton[2], the prize governess and masters for the girls, the trip abroad, or to Eastbourne or Worthing[3], in the autumn, the annual ball with a supper from Gunter's (who, by the way, supplies most of the *first-rate* dinners which J. gives, as I know very well, having been invited to one of them to fill a vacant place, when I saw at once that these repasts are very superior to the *common* run of entertainments for which the *humbler* sort of J.'s acquaintances get cards)—who, I say, with the most good-natured feelings in the world, can help wondering how the Jenkinses make out matters? What *is* Jenkins? We all know—Commissioner of the Tape and Sealing Wax Office, with £1200 a year for a salary. Had his wife a private fortune? Pooh!—Miss Flint—one of eleven children of a small squire in Buckinghamshire. All she ever gets from her family is a turkey at Christmas, in exchange for which she has to board two or three of her sisters in the off season; and lodge and feed her brothers when they come to town. How does Jenkins balance his income? I say, as every friend of his must say. How is it that he has not been outlawed long since; and that he ever came back (as he did to the surprise of everybody) last year from Boulogne[4]?

"I," is here introduced to personify the world in general—the Mrs. Grundy of each respected reader's private circle—every one of whom can point to some families of his acquaintance who live nobody knows how. Many a glass of wine have we all of us drunk, I have very little doubt, hob-and-nobbing with the hospitable giver, and wondering how the deuce he paid for it.

Some three or four years after his stay in Paris, when Rawdon Crawley and his wife[5] were established in a very small comfortable house in Curzon Street, May Fair[6], there was scarcely one of the numerous friends whom they entertained at dinner that did not ask the above question regarding them. The novelist, it has been said before, knows everything, and as I am in a situation to be able to tell the public how Crawley and his wife lived without any income, may I entreat the public newspapers which are in the habit of extracting portions of the various periodical works now published, *not* to reprint the following exact narrative and calculations—of which I ought, as the discoverer (and at some expense, too), to have the benefit? My son, I would say, were I blessed with a child—you may by deep inquiry and constant intercourse with him, learn how a man lives comfortably on nothing a year. But it is best not to be intimate with gentlemen of this profession, and to take the calculations at second-hand, as you do logarithms, for to work them yourself, depend upon it, will cost you something considerable.

On nothing per annum[7] then, and during a course of some two or three years, of which we can afford to give but a very brief history, Crawley and his wife lived very happily and comfortably at Paris. It was in this period that he quitted the Guards, and sold out of the army.[8] When we find him again, his mustachios and the title of Colonel on his card are the only relics of his military profession.

It has been mentioned that Rebecca, soon after her arrival in Paris, took a very smart and leading position in the society of that capital, and was welcomed at some of the most distinguished houses of the restored French nobility. The English men of fashion in Paris courted her, too, to the disgust of the ladies their wives, who could not bear the parvenue[9]. For some months the salons of the Faubourg St. Germain[10], in which her place was secured, and the splendours of the new Court, where she was received with much distinction, delighted, and perhaps a little intoxicated Mrs. Crawley, who may have been disposed during this period of elation to slight the people—honest young military men mostly—who formed her husband's chief society.

But the Colonel yawned sadly among the duchesses and great ladies of the Court. The old women who played *écarté*[11] made such a noise about a five-franc piece, that it was not worth Colonel Crawley's while to sit down at a card-table. The wit of their conversation he could not appreciate, being ignorant of their language. And what good could his wife get, he urged, by making curtsies every night to a whole circle of Princesses? He left Rebecca presently to frequent these parties alone, resuming his own simple pursuits and amusements amongst the amiable friends of his own choice.

The truth is, when we say of a gentleman that he lives elegantly on nothing a year, we use the word "nothing" to signify something unknown; meaning, simply, that we don't know how the gentleman in question defrays the expenses of his establishment. Now, our friend the Colonel had a great aptitude for all games of chance: and exercising himself, as he continually did, with the cards, the dice-box, or the cue, it is natural to suppose that he attained a much greater skill in the use of these articles than men can possess who only occasionally handle them. To use a cue at billiards well is like using a pencil, or a German flute, or a small-sword—you cannot master any one of these implements at first, and it is only by repeated study and perseverance, joined to a natural taste, that a man can excel in the handling of either. Now Crawley, from being only a brilliant amateur, had grown to be a consummate master of billiards. Like a great general, his genius used to rise with the danger, and when the luck had been unfavourable to him for a whole game, and the bets were consequently against him, he would, with consummate skill and boldness, make some prodigious hits which would restore the battle, and come in a victor at the end, to the astonishment of everybody—of everybody, that is, who was a stranger to his play. Those who were accustomed to see it were cautious how they staked their money against a man of such sudden resources, and brilliant and overpowering skill.

At games of cards he was equally skilful; for though he would constantly lose money at the commencement of an evening, playing so carelessly and making such blunders, that new-comers were often inclined to think meanly of his talent; yet, when roused to action, and awakened to caution by repeated small losses, it was remarked that Crawley's play became quite different, and that he was pretty sure of beating his enemy thoroughly before the night was over. Indeed, very few men could say that they ever had the better of him.

His successes were so repeated that no wonder the envious and the vanquished spoke sometimes with bitterness regarding them. And as the French say of the Duke of Wellington[12], who never suffered a defeat, that only an astonishing series of lucky accidents enabled him to be an invariable winner; yet even they allow that he cheated at Waterloo[13], and was enabled to win the last great trick: so it was hinted at headquarters in England, that some foul play must have taken place in order to account for the continuous successes of Colonel Crawley.

Though Frascati's and the Salon[14] were open at that time in Paris, the mania for play was so widely spread, that the public gambling-rooms did not suffice for the general ardour, and gambling went on in private houses as much as if there had been no public means for gratifying the passion. At Crawley's charming little *réunions*[15] of an evening this fatal amusement commonly was practised—much to good-natured little Mrs. Crawley's annoyance. She spoke about her husband's passion for dice with the deepest grief; she bewailed it to everybody who came to her house. She besought the young fellows never, never to touch a box; and when young Green of the Rifles, lost a very considerable sum of money, Rebecca passed a whole night in tears, as the servant told the unfortunate young gentleman, and actually went on her knees to her husband to beseech him to remit the debt, and burn the acknowledgment. How could he? He had lost just as much himself to Blackstone of the Hussars, and Count Punter of the Hanoverian Cavalry. Green might have any decent time; but pay?—of course he must pay; to talk of burning IOU's was child's play.

Other officers, chiefly young—for the young fellows gathered round Mrs. Crawley—came from her parties with long faces, having dropped more or less money at her fatal card-tables. Her house began to have an unfortunate reputation. The old hands warned the less experienced of their danger. Colonel O'Dowd, of the—the regiment, one of those occupying in Paris, warned Lieutenant Spooney of that corps. A loud and violent fracas[16] took place between the infantry-colonel and his lady, who were dining at the Café de Paris, and Colonel and Mrs. Crawley, who were also taking their meal there. The ladies engaged on both sides. Mrs. O'Dowd snapped her fingers in Mrs. Crawley's face, and called her husband "no better than a blackleg".

Colonel Crawley challenged Colonel O'Dowd, C.B. The Commander-in-Chief hearing of the dispute sent for Colonel Crawley, who was getting ready the same pistols "which he shot Captain Marker", and had such a conversation with him that no duel took place. If Rebecca had not gone on her knees to General Tufto, Crawley would have been sent back to England; and he did not play, except with civilians, for some weeks after.

But, in spite of Rawdon's undoubted skill and constant successes, it became evident to Rebecca, considering these things, that their position was but a precarious one, and that, even although they paid scarcely anybody, their little capital would end one day by dwindling into zero. "Gambling," she would say, "dear, is good to help your income, but not as an income itself. Some day people may be tired of play, and then where are we?" Rawdon acquiesced in the justice of her opinion; and in truth he had remarked that after a few nights of his little suppers, etc., gentlemen *were* tired of play with him, and, in spite of Rebecca's charms, did not present themselves very eagerly.

Easy and pleasant as their life at Paris was, it was after all only an idle dalliance and amiable trifling; and Rebecca saw that she must push Rawdon's fortune in their own country. She must get him a place or appointment at home or in the colonies; and she determined to make a move upon England as soon as the way could be cleared for her. As a first step she had made Crawley sell out of the Guards, and go on half-pay. His function as aide-de-camp[17] to General Tufto had ceased previously. Rebecca laughed in all companies at that officer, at his toupee (which he mounted on coming to Paris), at his waistband, at his false teeth, as his pretensions to be a lady-killer above all, and his absurd vanity in fancying every woman whom he came near was in love with him. It was to Mrs. Brent, the beetle-browed wife of Mr. Commissary Brent, to whom the General transferred his attentions now—his bouquets, his dinners at the restaurateurs', his opera-boxes, and his knick-knacks. Poor Mrs. Tufto was no more happy than before, and had still to pass long evenings alone with her daughters, knowing that her General was gone off scented and curled to stand behind Mrs. Brent's chair at the play. Becky had a dozen admirers in his place, to be sure; and could cut her rival to pieces with her wit. But, as we have said, she was growing tired of this idle social life: opera-boxes and restaurateur-dinners palled upon her; nose-gays could not be laid by as a provision for future years; and she could not live upon knick-knacks, laced handkerchiefs and kid gloves. She felt the frivolity of pleasure, and longed for more substantial benefits.

At this juncture news arrived which was spread among the many creditors of the Colonel at Paris, and which caused them great satisfaction. Miss Crawley, the rich aunt from whom he expected his immense inheritance, was dying; the Colonel must haste to her bedside. Mrs. Crawley and her child would remain behind until he came to reclaim them. He departed for Calais[18], and having reached that place in safety, it might have been supposed that he went to Dover[19]; but instead he took the diligence to Dunkirk, and thence travelled to Brussels, for which place he had a former predilection. The fact is, he owed more money at London than at Paris; and he preferred the quiet little Belgian city to either of the more noisy capitals.

Her aunt was dead. Mrs. Crawley ordered the most intense mourning for herself and little Rawdon. The Colonel was busy arranging the affairs of the inheritance. They could take the premier[20] now, instead of the little entresol[21] of the hotel which they occupied. Mrs. Crawley and the landlord had a consultation about the new hangings, an amicable wrangle about the carpets, and a final adjustment of everything except the bill. She went off in one of his carriages; her French *bonne* with her; the child by her side; the admirable landlord and landlady smiling farewell to her from the gate. General Tufto was furious when he heard she was gone, and Mrs. Brent furious with him for being furious; Lieutenant Spooney was cut to the heart; and the landlord got ready his best apartments previous to the return of the fascinating little woman and her husband. He serréd[22] the trunks which she left in his charge with the greatest care. They had been especially recommended to him by Madame Crawley. They were not, however, found to be particularly valuable when opened some time after.

But before she went to join her husband in the Belgic capital, Mrs. Crawley made an expedition into England, leaving behind her her little son upon the Continent, under the care of her French maid.

The parting between Rebecca and the little Rawdon did not cause either party much pain. She had not, to say truth, seen much of the young gentleman since his birth.

After the amiable fashion of French mothers, she had placed him out at nurse in a village in the neighbourhood of Paris, where little Rawdon passed the first months of his life, not unhappily, with a numerous family of foster-brothers in wooden shoes. His father would ride over many a time to see him here, and the elder Rawdon's paternal head glowed to see him rosy and dirty, shouting lustily, and happy in the making of mud-pies under the superintendence of the gardener's wife, his nurse.

Rebecca did not care much to go and see the son and heir. Once he spoiled a new dove-coloured pelisse of hers. He preferred his nurse's caresses to his mamma's, and when finally he quitted that jolly nurse and almost parent, he cried loudly for hours. He was only consoled by his mother's promise that he should return to his nurse the next day; indeed the nurse herself, who probably would have been pained at the parting too, was told that the child would immediately be restored to her, and for some time awaited quite anxiously his return.

In fact, our friends may be said to have been among the first of that brood of hardy English adventurers who have subsequently invaded the Continent, and swindled in all the capitals of Europe. The respect, in those happy days of 1817–1818, was very great, for the wealth and honour of Britons. They had not then learned, as I am told, to haggle for bargains with the pertinacity which now distinguishes them. The great cities of Europe had not been as yet open to the enterprise of our rascals. And whereas there is now hardly a town of France or Italy in which you shall not see some noble countryman of our own, with that happy swagger and insolence of demeanour which we carry everywhere, swindling inn-landlords, passing fictitious cheques upon credulous bankers, robbing coachmakers of their carriages, goldsmiths of their trinkets, easy travellers of their money at cards, —even public libraries of their books: —

thirty years ago you needed but to be a Milor Anglais[23], travelling in a private carriage, and credit was at your hand wherever you chose to seek it, and gentlemen, instead of cheating, were cheated. It was not for some weeks after Crawleys' departure that the landlord of the hotel which they occupied during their residence at Paris, found out the losses which he had sustained; not until Madame Marabou, the milliner, made repeated visits, with her little bill for articles supplied to Madame Crawley; not until Monsieur Didelot from the Boule d'Or in the Palais Royal had asked half-a-dozen times whether cette charmante Miladi[24], who had bought watches and bracelets of him, was de retour[25]. It is a fact that even the poor gardener's wife, who had nursed Madame's child, was never paid after the first six months for that supply of the milk of human kindness with which she had furnished the lusty and healthy little Rawdon. No, not even the nurse was paid—the Crawleys were in too great a hurry to remember their trifling debt to her. As for the landlord of the hotel, his curses against the English nation were violent for the rest of his natural life. He asked all travellers whether they knew a certain Colonel Lor Crawley—avec sa femme—une petite dame, très spirituelle[26]. "*Ah, Monsieur*!" he would add—"*ils m'ont affreusement volé.*"[27] It was melancholy to hear his accents as he spoke of that catastrophe.

Rebecca's object in her journey to London was to effect a kind of compromise with her husband's numerous creditors, and by offering them a dividend of nine pence or a shilling in the pound, to secure a return for him into his own country. It does not become us to trace the steps which she took in the conduct of this most difficult negotiation; but, having shown them to their satisfaction, that the sum which she was empowered to offer was all her husband's available capital, and having convinced them that Colonel Crawley would prefer a perpetual retirement on the Continent to a residence in this country with his debts unsettled; having proved to them that there was no possibility of money accruing to him from other quarters, and no earthly chance of their getting a larger dividend than that which she was empowered to offer, she brought the Colonel's creditors unanimously to accept her proposals, and purchased with fifteen hundred pounds of ready money, more than ten times that amount of debts.

Mrs. Crawley employed no lawyer in the transaction. The matter was so simple, to have or to leave, as she justly observed, that she made the lawyers of the creditors themselves do the business. And Mr. Lewis representing Mr. Davids, of Red Lion Square, and Mr. Moss acting for Mr. Manasseh of Cursitor Street (chief creditors of the Colonel's), complimented his lady upon the brilliant way in which she did business, and declared that there was no professional man who could beat her.

Rebecca received their congratulations with perfect modesty; ordered a bottle of sherry and a bread cake to the little dingy lodgings where she dwelt, while conducting the business, to treat the enemy's lawyers: shook hands with them at parting, in excellent good humour, and returned straightway to the Continent, to rejoin her husband and son, and acquaint the former with the glad news of his entire liberation. As for the latter, he had been considerably neglected during his mother's absence by Mademoiselle Geneviève, her French maid; for that young woman, contracting an attachment for a soldier in the garrison of Calais, forgot her charge in the society of this *militaire*[28], and little Rawdon very narrowly escaped drowning on Calais sands at this period, where the absent Geneviève had left and lost him.

After a stay at Brussels, where they lived in good fashion with carriages and horses, and giving pretty little dinners at their hotel, the Colonel and his lady again quitted that city, from which slander pursued them as it did from Paris, and where it is said they left a vast amount of debt behind them. Indeed, this is the way in which gentlemen who live upon nothing a year, make ends meet.

From Brussels, Colonel and Mrs. Crawley came to London; and it is at their house in Curzon Street, May Fair, that they really showed the skill which must be possessed by those who would live on the resources above named.

## Notes

1. barouche: carriage
2. Eton: college preparatory to Oxford for the sons of the aristocracy
3. Eastbourne and Worthing are both health resorts on the south coast of England.
4. Boulogne: the French port and health resort
5. Rawdon Crawley and his wife: "His wife" refers to Rebecca Sharp, who is a governess in the house of her relatives, the rich Crawleys. They get married secretly and on the discovery of this are thrown out of the house. During the war with Napoleon, Rawdon serves in the army.
6. Curzon Street, May Fair: It was located in the aristocratic part of London.
7. per annum: (Latin) per year
8. To become an officer one had to buy a commission; when retiring, the officer sold out his commission.
9. parvenue: (French) an upstart
10. Faubourg St. Germain: aristocratic quarter of Paris
11. *écarté*: a French card game
12. the Duke of Wellington: the English military leader, who defeated Napoleon at the Battle of Waterloo in 1815
13. Waterloo: a village in Belgium, near which the forces of Britain and Prussia won a decisive battle against Napoleon in 1815
14. Frascati's and the Salon: gambling houses in Paris
15. *réunions*: (French) gatherings
16. fracas: (French) noisy quarrel
17. aide-de-camp: (French) adjutant
18. Calais: the French port, from which ships cross the Channel for Britain
19. Dover: the English port on the Channel serving the routes to the Continent
20. premier: (French) the first floor in a house

21. entresol: (French) the low storey between the first and ground floor. It was a sign of prosperity and wealth to occupy the first floor.
22. serréd: (French) packed
23. Milor Anglais: (French) English lord
24. cette charmante Miladi: (French) this charming Lady
25. de retour: (French) to return
26. avec sa…très spirituelle: (French) with his wife, a little lady with high spirit
27. The whole sentence in French means that "Ah, Sir, they have robbed me terribly."
28. *militaire*: (French) military man

## For Study and Discussion

1. The opening paragraph of this chapter serves the title very well. What's the main point of this paragraph? Is it true or reasonable? What is the author's attitude towards this point?
2. "The novelist, it has been said before, knows everything, and as I am in a situation to be able to tell the public how Crawley and his wife lived without any income, may I entreat the public newspapers which are in the habit of extracting portions of the various periodical works now published…" This is apparently the words of the author who often makes comments on what he has been writing about while narrating the story. What is the advantage of using this technique rather than the purely third personal point of view?
3. Tell how Rebecca became popular with the people. What proves that she is sophisticated? What is her attitude towards her husband? How does she treat her son?
4. What do you think of Rawdon Crawley?
5. The author uses a lot of French words when he describes the landlord of the hotel. What does this mean? Why does the landlord of the hotel curse the English nation? Why does the author allow this to happen?

## Chapter 13

# Charles Dickens

### Life and Works

Charles Dickens (1812–1870) was born at Landport of Portsmouth, Hampshire, where his father was a Navy pay office clerk who had a lovable, improvident nature. Charles had no regular education, but he supplemented it with constant reading, particularly of the 18th-century novels in his father's small library. When Charles was still a child, his father was transferred to London, where the expenses of a large family so overtaxed the resources of Mr. Dickens that he was at last committed to the Marshalsea, a debtors' prison. Charles, then twelve, had to look after himself. With the help of a relative, he found a job pasting labels on bottles in a blacking warehouse. He was poorly clothed, ill-fed, forced to live in the cheapest place, and to associate with the roughest kind of companions. This experience was so bitter and galling to the sensitive boy that he was much impressed. Years later, when he was a successful, happy man, he could not look back upon it without tears in his eyes. His father's imprisonment and his own child labour gave him both a driving ambition to rise out of poverty and a sympathetic understanding of the poor people. So it is no wonder that he later became a great portrayer of child life and suffering children. Owing to a rupture between his employer and the elder Mr. Dickens, Charles was removed from this place and sent to school. But his schooling was cut short when he was fifteen. This time he got a job as a lawyer's office boy, studying shorthand and reading at the British Museum in his spare time. His skill at shorthand got him employment reporting debates in the House of Commons for the daily newspapers. And he became a writer of light sketches of contemporary life for magazines.

His first published sketch appeared in the *Monthly Magazine* in 1833, when he was twenty-one, and a series of his stories and sketches followed in that magazine and in the *Evening Chronicle*. They were collected in 1836 as *Sketches by Boz*, for which he took his pseudonym from a family nickname. In this year he married Catherine Hogarth, daughter of the owner of the *Evening Chronicle*.

At the time of his marriage he was writing a series of humourous stories to accompany illustrations of Cockney sporting life by a well-known artist. The artist's death after the appearance of the first number left Dickens a freer hand to develop the richly comic adventures of the Pickwick Club in the English countryside. The sales of the *Pickwick Papers* were slow at first, but they jumped with the introduction into the story of the engaging Cockney servant, Sam Weller, and by 1837, when its publication in numbers was completed, Dickens had risen in a year from obscurity to a position of popularity unequalled in England before or since. This year he was twenty-five years old. His success with the comic *Pickwick Papers* established Dickens as a popular humourist.

Dickens was extremely industrious. Before *Pickwick* was finished, he began to publish *Oliver Twist* in a monthly magazine. This is his first true novel and has a carefully worked-out plot, in contrast to the picaresque series of incidents in *Pickwick Papers*. It is also the most autobiographical of his novels. Its picture of the workhouses created under the New Poor Law and the description of the criminal slums of London in which young Oliver lived brought Dickens a new class of serious reader interested in social reform.

While *Oliver Twist* was still being published in series Dickens started to publish *Nicholas Nickleby*. *Nicholas Nickleby* begins as an exposure of the cruelty and neglect of boarding schools in Yorkshire, but it owes its vitality to the high spirits in which Dickens created such comic characters as the provincial theatrical troupe of Mr. Crummles and Mrs. Nickleby, for whom Dickens' mother in her less agreeable moments furnished the model. All Dickens' major novels were published either in numbers, like *Nicholas Nickleby*, or in installments in magazines, which frequently accounted for the episodic quality of his work.

In 1840 Dickens began a weekly paper, *Master Humphrey's Clock*, patterned on the *Spectator* and *Tatler*. The reader's interests were less in the familiar essays than in the stories which Dickens was providing. Gradually the paper became only the framework for the publication of two novels, *The Old Curiosity Shop* and *Barnaby Rudge*. In the former, the interest in which the present readers find is the humourous characters, but what Dickens' contemporaries loved were the pathos of the sufferings and death of Little Nell, who was created in the image of Dickens' sister-in-law, who had died in 1837, and to whom he was devoted. *Barnaby Rudge*, his first historical novel, was set in the period of the Gordon antipoverty riots of 1780. These two novels are stories of great humour that feature the neglected or orphaned children.

His first trip to America in 1842 began with an enthusiastic and uncritical reception which slowly soured as Dickens began to speak out against slavery and the American publishers' piracy of English books. He, in turn, was disgusted by the crudeness of life and manners in America, and in particular by his own lack of privacy there. His *American Notes*, published on his return to England, provoked great resentment in the United States. In his next novel, *Martin Chuzzlewit*, he once more used his observations on the trip to draw the ludicrous characters of the American episodes of the book, and again it aroused protest from America. The novel was concerned with the evils of the love of money, but Dickens embroidered the tale with the humour of some of his most comic characters, such as the old nurse Sara Gamp and the hypocritical Pecksniff.

His first and best classic Christmas book, *A Christmas Carol* failed to sell as well as he expected. But it was the first of an annual series of Christmas books.

Both his family (he had five children by this time) and his expenses were increasing, so he spent the years 1844 and 1845 in Italy to economise and to rest. He had always had a great love for the stage, and on his return to England he began to act in private theatricals, an activity which took a lot of his time and energy. He went to the Continent for several months in 1846, and in Switzerland he began to write *Dombey and Son*, which was a great financial success. Most critics, however, agreed that this study of middle-class pride and the decline of the merchant house of Dombey was hardly one of his best works.

*David Copperfield*, however, pleased everyone. Many of the events of its hero's childhood and his romance with Dora were clearly reminiscences of Dickens' youth. The mellow vein of memory provided a range of characterisation he never surpassed, and such characters as the marvelous Micawber and the cringing Uriah Heep made this novel the most popular of all his works.

In March, 1850, Dickens began a weekly family magazine, *Household Words*, from which he excluded politics and anything which would shock his readers. The magazine sold well, and in it he printed many of his own works and works of other writers.

*Bleak House* is a satire on the abuses of the Court of Chancery. It shows Dickens at his best in handling complex narrative and interlocking plots, but the prevailing mood of somberness was new to his readers. *Hard Times* is an earnest attack on the vulgarity and materialism of the rising middle-class industrialists. In *Little Dorrit*, the most vivid scenes are those in the debtors' prison, remembered from his father's stay in the Marshalsea. The satire on bureaucracy, the scenes on the Continent and the contrived mystery woven into the plot show Dickens at his gloomiest and in his least successful vein.

Because his publishers, who controlled both magazines, refused to let him republish his defense of position in separating his wife, Dickens left them to start a new and similar magazine, *All the Year Round*. Its first number in 1859 contained the beginning of his historical novel of the French Revolution, *A Tale of Two Cities*. The story of redemption through devotion shows his ability at handling pure narrative, and it has always been one of his most popular novels, although it lacks his characteristic humour.

By this time his reputation was great. His concern for the oppressed poor, his sentiment (which sometimes slipped into sentimentality), his flair for narrative, often melodramatic, and, above all, his invention of comic characters, combined to make him more popular than any other English novelist. His royalties were large, but the expenses of a big family, the upkeep of a country house, and his private philanthropy kept him pressed for money. After the separation from his wife, he began to give public readings from his works to increase his income. He had a natural talent for acting, and his reading tours were enormously successful, but the addition of this work and burden to his already heavy load of writing harmed his health.

*Great Expectations* is told in the first person by Pip, a young man who learns through adversity to discard his own superficial snobbishness. Because of the unity of interest, the centering on the chief character, and the credible quality of its romantic story, many critics considered it the best of his novels. *Our Mutual Friend*, the immediate successor of *Great Expectations*, was set in the early 1860s, one of the few times when Dickens used a contemporary setting. The characterisation was as carefully developed as any Dickens created, but the plot, centred on a young man who watched the effect of his supposed death upon society, was so loosely constructed that the book was hardly one of his major successes.

In spite of repeated warnings about his health, he continued his public readings. Late in 1867 he sailed for America, where he stayed four months. He had his hosts let bygones pass, he complimented the Americans on their progress, and they turned out in such numbers to hear his readings that he made nearly £20,000 on his tour. With his health dangerously harmed by his American trip he continued the high pressure of his readings on his return to England, until he was forced by his physician to stop. In the autumn of 1869 he began his last book, *The Mystery of Edwin Drood*, of which the first number appeared in April, 1870. While working on the still unfinished story at his country house, Gade Hill Place, on June 8, 1870, he suffered a stroke of apoplexy and died a day later. After a funeral service which was as simple as possible to conform to his own wishes, England entombed her favourite novelist in Westminster Abbey.

## Brief Comment

Of Dickens' fictional art, the most distinguished feature is his successful characterisation. With his well-worked-out plots, Dickens displayed great skills in the handling of the broad and intricate construction, in giving his characters exactly the actions and words that fit them in their positions in life and in their given environment, and in his successful use of irony or obvious exaggeration to achieve the penetrating effect of satire. It is all proper to say that Charles Dickens is a great master in the development of English literature.

Dickens liked to use sudden discovery technique in his novels. With this sudden discovery, he usually ended his novels with relative happy scenes. He always tried to soften the problems and wished for reforms rather than revolution.

*Oliver Twist* is a good example to express Dickens' wish for a better society. He used this novel to publicise the kind and the beautiful nature of mankind. He also believed in benevolence. The benevolent people always hoped to create a harmonious life by helping the miserable and the pitiable. He seemed to criticise the thieves and robbers on the surface, but he was actually criticising the environment that made them. One can also find that Dickens advocated that both the kind and the evil get their due fate. Also, he preferred comic ending to tragic ending. In the story of Harry Maylie and Rose Maylie, Dickens told the readers that love could turn a wastrel son or a prodigal not only to a good man but also a divine minister. In this novel, one can also learn something about the heritage system, which might also foster evil ideas and behaviour in the case of Monks. He gave a sympathetic description of even a street girl named Nancy, which presented Dickens' humanistic viewpoint.

*Oliver Twist* is a novel worth reading many times if one wants to know the conditions of life in the then England, Dickens' humanitarian thought and his viewpoint on virtue.

## Selections

### *Oliver Twist*

## The Story

Oliver Twist was born in the lying-in room of a parochial workhouse about seventy-five miles north of London. His mother's name was not known. She had been found unconscious by the roadside, exhausted by a long journey on foot, and she died leaving as the only tokens of her child's identity a locket and a ring. These were stolen by old Sally, a pauper present at her death.

Oliver owned his name to Bumble, the parish beadle and a bullying official of the workhouse, who always named his unknown waifs in the order of an alphabetical system he had devised. Twist was the name between Swubble and Unwin on Bumble's list. Oliver Twist was thus named.

An offered reward of ten pounds would be provided to discover his parentage. But this failed. So he was sent to a nearby poor farm, where he passed his early childhood in neglect and near starvation. At the age of nine he was moved back to the workhouse. Always hungry, he asked for a second serving of porridge one day. The scandalised authorities put him in solitary confinement and posted a bill offering five pounds to any master who would take him off the parish.

Oliver was apprenticed to a man named Sowerberry, a casket maker, to learn a trade. Sowerberry employed little Oliver, dressed in miniature mourning clothing, at attendant at children's funerals. Another employee of Sowerberry, Noah Claypole, teased Oliver about his parentage. Oliver, goaded beyond endurance, fiercely attacked Claypole and was subsequently locked in the cellar by Mrs. Sowerberry. Sowerberry released Oliver, who, that night, bundled up his meager belongings and started out for London.

In a London suburb, Oliver, worn out from walking and weak from hunger, met Jack Dawkins, sharp-witted slum gamin. Dawkins, known as the Artful Dodger, offered Oliver lodgings in the city, and Oliver soon found himself in the midst of a gang of young thieves, led by a miserly old Jew, Fagin. Oliver was trained as a pickpocket. On his first mission he was caught and taken to the police station. There he was rescued by kindly Mr. Brownlow, the man whose pocket Oliver was accused of having picked. Mr. Brownlow, his gruff friend Grimwig and the old housekeeper Mrs. Bedwin cared for the sickly Oliver. They marveled at the boy's resemblance to a portrait of a young lady in Mr. Brownlow's possession. Oliver's health recovered. One day, he was given some books and money to take to a bookseller. Grimwig wagered that Oliver would not return. Meanwhile Fagin and his gang had been on constant lookout for the boy's appearance, and he was intercepted by Nancy, a young street girl associated with the gang.

Bumble, on parochial business in London, saw Mr. Brownlow's advertisement for word leading to Oliver's recovery. Hoping to profit, he hastened to Mr. Brownlow and reported that Oliver was incorrigible. After receiving this information, Mr. Brownlow refused to have Oliver's name mentioned in his presence.

Once more Oliver was in the hands of Fagin. During his absence the gang had been studying a house in Chertsey, west of London, preparatory to breaking into it at night. The time came for the adventure, and Oliver, much to his horror, was chosen to participate. He and Bill Sikes, brutal young co-leader of the gang, met Toby Crackit, another housebreaker. The trio, in the dark of early morning, pried open a small window of the house. Oliver entered, determined to warn the occupants. The robbers were discovered and the trio fled. Oliver was wounded by gunshot.

In fleeing, Sikes threw the wounded Oliver into a ditch and covered him with a cape. Toby Crackit, the other housebreaker, returned and reported to Fagin. The old thief-trainer was more than ever interested in Oliver after an important conversation with one named Monks. This discussion, overheard by Nancy, concerned Oliver's parentage and Monks' wish to have the boy made a youthful felon.

Oliver crawled feebly to the house into which he had gone the night before. He was taken in by the owner Mrs. Maylie and Rose, her adopted daughter. Oliver's story aroused their sympathy and he was saved from police investigation by Dr. Losberne, friend of the Maylies. Upon his recovery the boy went with the doctor to seek out Mr. Brownlow, but it was learned that the old gentleman, his friend Grimwig, and Mrs. Bedwin had gone to the West Indies.

Meanwhile Bumble courted the widow Corney. During one of their conversations, Mrs. Corney was called out to attend the death of old Sally, who had stood by at the death of Oliver's mother. After old Sally died, Mrs. Corney removed a pawn ticket from her hand. In Mrs. Corney's absence, Bumble appraised her property to his satisfaction. He proposed marriage.

The Maylies moved to the country, where Oliver studied gardening, read, and took long walks. During this holiday Rose Maylie fell sick and nearly died. After her recovery, Harry Maylie the wastrel son of Mrs. Maylie joined the group. Harry, in love with Rose, asked for her hand in marriage. Rose refused on two grounds; she could not marry him before she discovered who she was, and she could not marry him unless he mended his ways. One night, Oliver was frightened when he saw Fagin and Monks peering through the study window.

Bumble had discovered that married life with the former Mrs. Corney was not all happy, for she dominated him completely. When Monks went to the workhouse seeking information about Oliver, he met with Mr. and Mrs. Bumble and learned that Mrs. Bumble had redeemed a locket and a wedding ring with the pawn ticket she had recovered from Sally. Monks bought the trinkets from Mrs. Bumble and threw them in the river.

Monks told Fagin that he had disposed of the tokens of Oliver's parentage. Again Nancy overheard the two villains. After drugging Bill Sikes, whom she had been nursing to recovery from gunshot wounds received in the ill-fated venture at Chertsey, she went to see Rose Maylie whose name and address she had overheard in the conversation between Fagin and Monks. Nancy told Rose everything she had heard concerning Oliver. Rose was unable to understand fully the various connections of the plot nor could she see Monks' connection with Oliver. She offered the miserable girl the protection of her own home, but Nancy refused, knowing that she could never leave Bill Sikes. The two young women agreed on a time and place for later meetings. Rose and Oliver went to call on Mr. Brownlow, whom Oliver had glimpsed in the street. The reunion of the boy, Mr. Brownlow, and Mrs. Bedwin was a joyous one. Even old Grimwig gruffly expressed his pleasure at seeing Oliver again. Rose told Mr. Brownlow Nancy's story.

In the meantime, Noah Claypole and Charlotte, maid-servant of the Sowerberrys, had run away from the casket maker and arrived in London, where they went to the public house which was the haunt of Fagin and his gang. Fagin flattered Noah into his employ, Noah's job being to steal small coins from children on household errands.

At the time agreed upon for her appointment with Rose Maylie, Nancy was unable to leave the demanding Bill Sikes. Noticing Nancy's impatience, Fagin decided that she had tired of Sikes and that she had another lover. Fagin hated Sikes because of the younger man's power over the gang, and he saw this situation as an opportunity to rid himself of Sikes. Fagin set Noah on Nancy's trail.

The following week Nancy got free with the aid of Fagin. She went to Rose and Mr. Brownlow and revealed to them the haunts of all the gang except Sikes. Noah, having overheard all this, secretly told Fagin, who in turn told Sikes. In his rage Sikes brutally murdered Nancy, never knowing that the girl had been faithful to him. He fled, pursued by the vision of murdered Nancy's staring eyes. Frantic from fear, he attempted to kill his dog, whose presence might betray him. The dog ran away.

Monks was arrested and he confessed to Mr. Brownlow the plot against Oliver. Oliver's father, Edward Leeford, had married a woman older than himself. Their son, Edward Leeford, was the man now known as Monks. After several years of unhappiness, the couple separated. Monks and his mother stayed on the continent and Mr. Leeford returned to England. Later Leeford met a retired naval officer and fell in love with his seventeen-year-old daughter who had a younger sister aged three. Leeford contracted to marry the girl, but before the marriage could be performed he was called to Rome where an old friend had died. On the way to Rome he stopped at the house of Mr. Brownlow, his best friend, and left a portrait of his betrothed. He himself fell sick in Rome and died. His former wife seized his papers.

When Leeford's young wife-to-be, who was pregnant, heard of Leeford's death, she ran away to hide her condition. Her father died soon afterward and the younger sister was eventually adopted by Mrs. Maylie. She was Rose Maylie, Oliver's aunt. Monks lived a prodigal life. When his mother died, he went to the West Indies, where Mr. Brownlow had gone in search of him. But Monks had already returned to track down Oliver, whose part of his father's settlement he wished to keep from his young half-brother. It was Monks who had offered the reward at the workhouse for information about Oliver's parentage, and it was Monks who had paid Fagin to see that the boy remained with the gang as a common thief.

After Fagin and the Artful Dodger had been seized, Bill Sikes and the remainder of the gang met on Jacob's Island in the Thames River. They intended to stay there in a deserted house until the hunt had died down. But Sikes' dog led their pursuers to the hideout. Bill Sikes hanged himself accidentally with the rope he was using as a means of escape. The other robbers were captured. Fagin was hanged publicly at Newgate after he had revealed to Oliver the location of papers concerning the boy's heritage. Monks had entrusted these papers to the Jew for safekeeping.

Harry Maylie, who had become a minister, married Rose Maylie. Mr. Brownlow adopted Oliver and took up residence near the church of the Reverend Harry Maylie. Mr. and Mrs. Bumble lost their parochial positions and soon became inmates of the workhouse which once had been their domain. Monks, allowed to retain his share of his father's property, went to America and eventually died in prison. Oliver's years of hardship and unhappiness were at an end.

## Chapter II

Oliver had not been within the walls of the workhouse[1] a quarter of an hour, and had scarcely completed the demolition of a second slice of bread, when Mr. Bumble[2], who had handed him over to the care of an old woman, returned; and, telling him it was a board night, informed him that the board had said he was to appear before it forthwith.

Not having a very clearly defined notion of what a live board was, Oliver was rather astounded by this intelligence, and was not quite certain whether he ought to laugh or cry. He had no time to think about the matter, however; for Mr. Bumble gave him a tap on the head, with his cane, to wake him up, and another on the back to make him lively, and bidding him follow, conducted him into a large whitewashed room where eight or ten fat gentlemen were sitting round a table, at the top of which, seated in an arm-chair rather higher than the rest, was a particularly fat gentleman with a very round, red face.

"Bow to the board," said Bumble. Oliver brushed away two or three tears that were lingering in his eyes, and seeing no board[3] but the table, fortunately bowed to that.

"What's your name, boy?" said the gentleman in the high chair.

Oliver was frightened at the sight of so many gentlemen, which made him tremble; and the beadle gave him another tap behind, which made him cry; and these two causes made him answer in a very low and hesitating voice; whereupon a gentleman in a white waistcoat said he was a fool, which was a capital way of raising his spirits, and putting him quite at his ease.

"Boy," said the gentleman in the high chair, "listen to me. You know you're an orphan, I suppose?"

"What's that, Sir?" inquired poor Oliver.

"The boy *is* a fool—I thought he was," said the gentleman in the white waistcoat, in a very decided tone. If one member of a class be blessed with an intuitive perception of others of the same race, the gentleman in the white waistcoat was unquestionably well qualified to pronounce an opinion on the matter.

"Hush!" said the gentleman who had spoken first. "You know you've got no father or mother, and that you are brought up by the parish, don't you?"

"Yes, Sir," replied Oliver, weeping bitterly.

"What are you crying for?" inquired the gentleman in the white waistcoat. And to be sure it was very extraordinary. What *could* the boy be crying for?

"I hope you say your prayers every night," said another gentleman in a gruff voice, "and pray for the people who feed you, and take care of you, like a Christian."

"Yes, Sir," stammered the boy. The gentleman who spoke last was unconsciously right. It would have been *very* like a Christian, and a marvellously good Christian, too, if Oliver had prayed for the people who fed and took care of *him*. But he hadn't, because nobody had taught him.

"Well, you have come here to be educated, and taught a useful trade," said the red-faced gentleman in the high chair.

"So you'll begin to pick oakum tomorrow morning at six o'clock," added the surly one in the white waistcoat.

For the combination of both these blessings in the one simple process of picking oakum, Oliver bowed low by the direction of the beadle, and was then hurried away to a large ward, where, on a rough hard bed, he sobbed himself to sleep. What a noble illustration of the tender laws[4] of this favoured country!—they let the paupers go to sleep!

Poor Oliver! He little thought, as he lay sleeping in happy unconsciousness of all around him, that the board had that very day arrived at a decision which would exercise the most material influence over all his future fortunes. But they had. And this was it:—

The members of this board were very sage, deep, philosophical men; and when they came to turn their attention to the workhouse, they found out at once, what ordinary folks would never have discovered—the poor people like it! It was a regular place of public entertainment for the poorer classes—a tavern where there was nothing to pay—a public breakfast, dinner, tea, and supper all the year round—a brick and mortar elysium, where it was all play and no work. "Oho!" said the board, looking very knowing; "we are the fellows to set this to rights; we'll stop it all in no time." So, they established the rule, that all poor people should have the alternative (for they would compel nobody, not they) of being starved by a gradual process in the house, or by a quick one out of it. With this view, they contracted with the water-works to lay on an unlimited supply of water, and with a corn-factor to supply periodically small quantities of oatmeal; and issued three meals of thin gruel a day, with an onion twice a week, and half a roll on Sundays. They made a great many other wise and humane regulations having reference to the ladies, which it is not necessary to repeat; kindly undertook to divorce poor married people, in consequence of the great expense of a suit in Doctors' Commons[5]; and, instead of compelling a man to support his family as they had theretofore done, took his family away from him, and made him a bachelor! There is no telling how many applicants for relief under these last two heads would not have started up in all classes of society, if it had not been coupled with the workhouse. But they were long-headed men, and they had provided for this difficulty. The relief was inseparable from the workhouse and the gruel, and that frightened the people.

For the first six months after Oliver Twist was removed, the system was in full operation. It was rather expensive at first, in consequence of the increase of the undertaker's bill, and the necessity of taking in the clothes of all the paupers, which fluttered loosely on their wasted, shrunken forms, after a week or two's gruel. But the number of workhouse inmates got thin as well as the paupers, and the board were in ecstasies.

The room in which the boys were fed was a large stone hall, with a copper at one end, out of which the master, dressed in an apron for the purpose, and assisted by one or two women, ladled the gruel at mealtimes; of which composition each boy had one porringer, and no more—except on festive occasions, and then he had two ounces and a quarter of bread besides. The bowls never wanted washing—the boys polished them with their spoons till they shone again; and when they had performed this operation, (which never took very long, the spoons being nearly as large as the bowls) they would sit staring at the copper with such eager eyes as if they could devour the very bricks of which it was composed; employing themselves meanwhile in sucking their fingers most assiduously, with the view of catching up any stray splashes of gruel that might have been cast thereon. Boys have generally excellent appetites. Oliver Twist and his companions suffered the tortures of slow starvation for three months; at last they got so voracious and wild with hunger, that one boy, who was tall for his age, and hadn't been used to that sort of thing, (for his father had kept a small cook's shop) hinted darkly to his companions, that unless he had another basin of gruel per diem[6], he was afraid he should some night eat the boy who slept next him, who happened to be a weakly youth of tender age. He had a wild, hungry eye, and they implicitly believed him. A council was held; lots were cast who should walk up to the master after supper that evening, and ask for more; and it fell to Oliver Twist.

The evening arrived; the boys took their places; the master in his cook's uniform stationed himself at the copper; his pauper assistants ranged themselves behind him; the gruel was served out, and a long grace was said over the short commons[7]. The gruel disappeared, and the boys whispered to each other and winked at Oliver, while his next neighbours nudged him. Child as he was, he was desperate with hunger and reckless with misery. He rose from the table, and advancing, basin and spoon in hand, to the master, said, somewhat alarmed at his own temerity—

"Please, Sir, I want some more."

The master was a fat, healthy man, but he turned very pale. He gazed in stupefied astonishment on the small rebel for some seconds, and then clung for support to the copper. The assistants were paralysed with wonder, and the boys with fear.

"What!" said the master at length, in a faint voice.

"Please, Sir," replied Oliver, "I want some more."

The master aimed a blow at Oliver's head with the ladle, pinioned him in his arms, and shrieked aloud for the beadle.

The board were sitting in solemn conclave when Mr. Bumble rushed into the room in great excitement, and addressing the gentleman in the high chair, said—

"Mr. Limbkins, I beg your pardon, Sir;—Oliver Twist has asked for more." There was a general start. Horror was depicted on every countenance.

"For *more*!" said Mr. Limbkins. "Compose yourself, Bumble, and answer me distinctly. Do I understand that he asked for more, after he had eaten the supper allotted by the dietary?"

"He did, Sir," replied Bumble.

"That boy will be hung," said the gentleman in the white waistcoat; "I know that boy will be hung."

Nobody controverted the prophetic gentleman's opinion. An animated discussion took place. Oliver was ordered into instant confinement; and a bill was next morning pasted on the outside of the gate, offering a reward of five pounds to anybody who would take Oliver Twist off the hands of the parish. In other words, five pounds and Oliver Twist were offered to any man or woman who wanted an apprentice to any trade, business, or calling.

"I never was more convinced of anything in my life," said the gentleman in the white waistcoat, as he knocked at the gate and read the bill next morning—"I never was more convinced of anything in my life, than I am that that boy will come to be hung."

As I purpose to show in the sequel whether the white waist-coated gentleman was right or not, I should perhaps mar the interest of this narrative (supposing it to possess any at all) if I ventured to hint just yet, whether the life of Oliver Twist had this violent termination or no.

## Chapter III

For a week after the commission of the impious and profane offence of asking for more, Oliver remained a close prisoner in the dark and solitary room to which he had been consigned by the wisdom and mercy of the board. It appears, at first sight, not unreasonable to suppose, that, if he had entertained a becoming feeling of respect for the prediction of the gentleman in the white waistcoat, he would have established that sage individual's prophetic character, once and for ever, by tying one end of his pocket-handkerchief to a hook in the wall, and attaching himself to the other. To the performance of this feat, however, there was one obstacle, namely, that pocket-handkerchiefs being decided articles of luxury, had been, for all future times and ages, removed from the noses of paupers by the express order of the board in council assembled, solemnly given and pronounced under their hands and seals. There was a still greater obstacle in Oliver's youth and childishness. He only cried bitterly all day; and when the long, dismal night came on, he spread his little hands before his eyes to shut out the darkness, and crouching in the corner, tried to sleep: ever and anon waking with a start and tremble, and drawing himself closer and closer to the wall, as if to feel even its cold hard surface were a protection in the gloom and loneliness which surrounded him.

Let it not be supposed by the enemies of "the system", that, during the period of his solitary incarceration, Oliver was denied the benefit of exercise, the pleasure of society, or the advantages of religious consolation. As for exercise, it was nice cold weather, and he was allowed to perform his ablutions every morning under the pump, in a stone yard, in the presence of Mr. Bumble, who prevented his catching cold, and caused a tingling sensation to pervade his frame, by repeated applications of the cane; as for society, he was carried every other day into the hall where the boys dined, and there sociably flogged as a public warning and example; and so far from being denied the advantages of religious consolation, he was kicked into the same apartment every evening at prayer time, and there permitted to listen to, and console his mind with, a general supplication of the boys, containing a special clause therein inserted by authority of the board, in which they entreated to be made good, virtuous, contented, and obedient, and to be guarded from the sins and vices of Oliver Twist, whom the supplication distinctly set forth to be under the exclusive patronage and protection of the powers of wickedness, and an article direct from the manufactory of the devil himself.

## Notes

1. workhouse: a public institution for reception of paupers in a parish or group of parishes. The inhabitants of workhouses were subjected to most brutal exploitation. In the novel Dickens gave a realistic picture of the horrible existence in workhouses.
2. Mr. Bumble: a tyrannical parish beadle who put Oliver into the workhouse
3. Note the pun on the word "board".
4. the tender laws: It alludes to the Poor Laws passed by the Parliament in 1834, which cut down relief received by the paupers and established workhouses into which the needy people were driven and where they were terribly exploited.
5. Doctors' Commons: a court of Civil Law in London, dealing with suits concerning wills, marriages, licenses and divorce proceedings
6. per diem: (Latin) per day
7. short commons: scanty daily food

## For Study and Discussion

1. Where is the humour when Oliver is asked to bow to the board?
2. What is the capital way of raising Oliver's spirits?
3. What is a Christian like according to the board members? Why does Dickens say "It would have been very like a Christian, and a marvelously good Christian, too, if Oliver had prayed for the people who fed and took care of him. But he hadn't, because nobody had taught him."?
4. What is the living condition of the workhouse?
5. When Dickens describes how the children in the workhouse are fed, he says, "The bowls never wanted washing." What does this mean?
6. What makes Oliver ask for some more food? What is the result? What is the board members' response? What decision is made about Oliver?

# Chapter 14

# Robert Browning

## Life and Works

Robert Browning (1812–1889) was born in London. Mingled with the English and Scottish blood in his veins was a more distant strain of German and Creole, a fact of value in considering the cosmopolitan range of his imagination. He passed his boyhood and youth in the suburb of Camberwell, near enough to London to make the great smoky city on the horizon a constant reminder of the complex human life he was to interpret as subtly and deeply as any poet had done since the Elizabethan age. His first stimulus to poetic creation was given by a volume of Shelley which he picked up by chance on a London book-stall in his fourteenth year. His first long poem, *Pauline*, published in 1833, was a half-dramatic study of the type of spiritual life which Shelley's career embodied; and Shelley's influence was clearly traceable both in its thought and in its style. After a trip to Russia and Italy, Browning published *Paracelsus* in 1835. This, like *Pauline*, was the "history of a soul". In it Browning's wonderful endowments are already suggested: his knowledge of the causes of spiritual growth and decay, his subtle analysis of motive and countermotive, his eloquence in pleading a cause, the enkindled power and beauty of his language when blown upon by noble passion. The hindrances from which he suffered are also only too clear, especially his tendency to lose himself in tangled thought and to grow harsh and obscure in pursuing the secondary suggestions of his theme. In *Sordello* these faults smothered down the clear fire of poetry into a torpid smoke. In *Pippa Passes*, however, he shook himself free from these faults of manner, and produced a dramatic poem of sustained beauty, as clear as sunlight, a work of simple, melodious, impassioned art. Between 1840 and 1845 Browning was chiefly occupied with attempts to write actable plays; of these the most interesting were perhaps *Colombe*'s *Birthday*, *A Blot in the 'Scutcheon* and *The Return of the Druses*. He had also begun those short poems dealing with special moments in the lives of various men and women, historical or imaginary, which constituted the most important division of his works. These were included in such collections as *Dramatic Lyrics*, *Dramatic Romances* and *Men and Women*.

In 1846 Browning eloped with Elizabeth Barrett, whose poetic reputation was then far greater than his, and went to live in Italy. The pair settled in Florence, in the house called "Casa Guidi", from which was taken the title of Mrs. Browning's long poem on the Italian Liberation, *Casa Guidi Windows* (1851). Here Browning continued his great series of dramatic monologues. After Mrs. Browning's death in 1861, he began *The Ring and the Book*. This is the crowning effort of his genius for the vastness of its scope and its grasp of human nature, though it lacks the spontaneous grace and charm which the best of his shorter pieces share with *Pippa Passes*, that perfect fruit of his youthful imagination. After the death of his wife, Browning spent most of his time in England. He wrote much, with a steady gain in intellectual subtlety, but with a corresponding loss of poetic beauty. He made a more and more deliberate sacrifice of form to matter, wrenching and straining the verse-fabric in order to pack into it all the secondary meanings of the theme. To the last, however, his genius continued to throw out bursts and jets of exquisite music, colour and feeling. Such, for instance, are the little pieces called "Wanting is—What?" and "Never the Time and the Place", written at the age of 71; and such is "Summum Bonum", written just before the pen dropped from his hand in 1889. He had to wait long for recognition, but during the latter years of his life his fame overshadowed even that of Tennyson, and his works were studied and made a cult of, with an enthusiasm seldom accorded to a living poet.

## Brief Comment

Robert Browning, who disputed with Tennyson the first place among Victorian poets, was Tennyson's opposite in almost every respect but fame and length of years. His genius was preeminently dramatic; his interest lay, not in universal law, but in individual passion. And his style, instead of being eclectic and carefully elaborated, was highly individual, and often more intent on meaning than on form. Browning was strong where Tennyson was weak, weak where Tennyson was strong. Both shared almost equally in the Victorian tendency towards reflection, and towards a didactic aim; but their reflection was exercised upon very different phenomena, and their teaching was widely opposed.

The greatest contribution of Browning to English poetry is his skillful and unmatched use of dramatic monologue. A dramatic monologue is a poem in which a speaker, clearly separate from the poet, speaks to a mock listener, or an implied audience who does not speak but seems to be clearly present in the scene so that he or she triggers the speaker to talk. The purpose of the monologue (or the soliloquy) is not so much to make a statement about its declared subject matter, but to develop the character of the speaker. Each character in the poem exposes his or her innermost thoughts and emotions through monologues one by one.

Dramatic monologue was already much used by poets in the 16th and 17th century. John Donne and other poets are some of the best examples. So it is not proper to say that Browning or Tennyson invented the dramatic monologue. But we can say that Browning and Tennyson made it better known.

By using this technique, Browning created different types of character and displayed the psychology of all sorts of people. The dramatic monologue used by Alfred Tennyson and others tends to be talking to oneself. But in Browning's dramatic monologue, the speaker does not speak to himself, but to the mock listener in the poem rather than the reader. The mock listener is always the trigger of the monologue, thus creating a kind of hidden dialogue. One can always feel the presence and existence of the mock listener. In this way, the speaker becomes the independent person rather than the poet himself. So Browning's dramatic monologue is an objective form of drama with a purpose of characterisation rather than expressing the poet's feeling or sentiment.

## Selections

### My Last Duchess[1]

(Ferrara)

That's my last Duchess painted on the wall,
Looking as if she were alive. I call
That piece a wonder, now: Frà Pandolf's[2] hands
Worked busily a day, and there she stands.
Will 't please you sit and look at her? I said
"Frà Pandolf" by design, for never read
Strangers like you that pictured countenance,
The depth and passion of its earnest glance,
But to myself they turned (since none puts by
The curtain I have drawn for you, but I)
And seemed as they would ask me, if they durst,
How such a glance came there; so, not the first
Are you to turn and ask thus. Sir, 'twas not
Her husband's presence only, called that spot
Of joy into the Duchess' cheek: perhaps
Frà Pandolf chanced to say "Her mantle laps
Over my lady's wrist too much", or "Paint
Must never hope to reproduce the faint
Half-flush that dies along her throat": such stuff
Was courtesy, she thought, and cause enough
For calling up that spot of joy. She had
A heart—how shall I say?—too soon made glad,
Too easily impressed; she liked whate'er
She looked on, and her looks went everywhere.
Sir, 'twas all one! My favour at her breast,

The dropping of the daylight in the West,
The bough of cherries some officious fool
Broke in the orchard for her, the white mule
She rode with round the terrace—all and each
Would draw from her alike the approving speech,
Or blush, at least. She thanked men—good! but thanked
Somehow—I know not how—as if she ranked
My gift of a nine-hundred-years-old name
With anybody's gift. Who'd stoop to blame
This sort of trifling? Even had you skill
In speech—(which I have not)—to make your will
Quite clear to such an one, and say, "Just this
Or that in you disgusts me; here you miss,
Or there exceed the mark"—and if she let
Herself be lessoned so, nor plainly set
Her wits to yours, forsooth, and made excuse
—E'en then would be some stooping; and I choose
Never to stoop. Oh sir, she smiled, no doubt,
Whene'er I passed her; but who passed without
Much the same smile? This grew; I gave commands;
Then all smiles stopped together. There she stands
As if alive. Will 't please you rise? We'll meet
The company below, then. I repeat,
The Count your master's known munificence
Is ample warrant that no just pretense
Of mine for dowry will be disallowed;
Though his fair daughter's self, as I avowed
At starting, is my object. Nay, we'll go
Together down, sir. Notice Neptune, though,
Taming a sea horse, thought a rarity,
Which Claus of Innsbruck[3] cast in bronze for me!

## Notes

1. The poem is based on incidents in the life of Alfonso II, Duke of Ferrara in Italy, whose first wife, Lucrezia, a young girl, died in 1561 after three years of marriage. Following her death, the Duke negotiated through an agent to marry a niece of the Count of Tyrol. Browning represents the Duke as addressing this agent.
2. Frà Pandolf: an imaginary painter

3. Claus of Innsbruck: an unidentified or imaginary sculptor. The Count of Tyrol had his capital at Innsbruck.

## For Study and Discussion

1. This poem is a typical example of Browning's use of dramatic monologue. Read this poem again and find who the speaker is and to whom the speaker addresses.
2. According to the speaker, what kind of person is the last duchess? Why does the speaker hate her and put her to death?
3. Why does the speaker tell the listener about his first wife?
4. Please comment on the character of the speaker.

### Home-Thoughts, from Abroad

1

Oh, to be in England
Now that April's there,[1]
And whoever wakes in England
Sees, some morning, unaware,
That the lowest boughs and the brush-wood sheaf
Round the elm-tree bole are in tiny leaf,
While the chaffinch sings on the orchard bough
In England—now!

2

And after April, when May follows,
And the whitethroat builds, and all the swallows!
Hark! where my blossomed pear-tree in the hedge
Leans to the field and scatters on the clover
Blossoms and dewdrops—at the bent spray's edge—
That's the wise thrush; he sings each song twice over,
Lest you should think he never could recapture
The first fine careless[2] rapture!
And though the fields look rough with hoary dew,
All will be gay when noontide wakes anew
The buttercups, the little children's dower
—Far brighter than this gaudy melon-flower!

## Notes

1. Oh, to be in England / Now that April's there: Oh, how wonderful it is to be in England now that April is there. This sentence expresses the poet's wish to be back in his home country.
2. careless: carefree; without care; free from care

## For Study and Discussion

1. Why does the speaker want to be in England? What's the April scenery?
2. The whole poem is almost a mere description of the scenes of England in April and May. In what ways does the description of scenery convey a kind of patriotic feeling?
3. Learn the first stanza by heart.

### Meeting at Night

The gray sea and the long black land;
And the yellow half-moon large and low;
And the startled little waves that leap
In fiery ringlets[1] from their sleep,
As I gain the cove with pushing prow,
And quench its speed i'the slushy sand.

Then a mile of warm sea-scented beach,
Three fields to cross till a farm appears;
A tap at the pane, the quick sharp scratch
And blue spurt of a lighted match,
And a voice less loud, thro' its joys and fears[2],
Than the two hearts beating each to each!

## Notes

1. In fiery ringlets: in ringlets like fire, which was caused by the moonlight
2. thro' its joys and fears: The girl speaks in a low voice for fear that her family members might hear them and come to separate them.

## For Study and Discussion

1. What is the setting of this poem? What is the significance of the image of the yellow half-moon?
2. The first stanza contains a description of the speeding boat. Why is the speaker so urgent?
3. What do you think of the rendezvous of the speaker and his lady? Can you find similar poems in classical Chinese poetry? If you can, cite some of them and make a comparison.
4. Learn this poem by heart.

### Parting at Morning[1]

Round the cape of a sudden came the sea,
And the sun looked over the mountain's rim:
And straight was a path of gold for him,
And the need of a world of men for me.

## Notes

1. This is a kind of aubade, describing the unwillingness to separate from one's lover.

## For Study and Discussion

1. What is the rhyme scheme of this poem? Why does the poet use such an envelope form?
2. What is the image of the sun used for in the poem?
3. Learn this poem by heart.

# Chapter 15

# George Eliot

## Life and Works

George Eliot (1819–1880) is the penname of Mary Ann Evans. She was the daughter of a prosperous estate agent at Warbury, Warwickshire. From the age of five to the age of sixteen, Mary Ann (or Marian, as she later signed her name) was educated at boarding schools at Attleborough, Nuneaton and Coventry. She was shy and awkward, plain and a little priggish. Because social exchange or activity was difficult for her, she threw herself into hard and concentrated study. She was interested in music: she played the piano well all her life. She was also interested in religion, in which she was moved gradually away from the conventional Anglicanism of her childhood, through a fervent and emotional evangelicalism, to the rationalism of her adult life.

When she was eighteen, her mother died and her elder sister got married, so she began to take charge of her father's house. At the same time, she kept up a rigorous course of study, reading German, Italian, Greek and Latin. In religion she became more and more intolerant of the exclusive claims of any single sect, and for a time she refused to go to church with her father.

In 1849, after her father's death, she visited the Continent and lived for some months in Geneva. On her return to England she became the assistant editor of the *Westminster Review*, a journal of philosophical liberalism edited by John Chapman. At this time she made friends with many people in the liberal and rationalist intellectual circle of London. Among them was the philosopher Herbert Spencer, who remained her close friend all his life. Through Herbert Spencer she met George Henry Lewes, a journalist and miscellaneous writer who had a broken family because of his wife's infidelity. Miss Evans fell in love with Lewes. But she could not get married to him because he could not divorce on account of strictness of Victorian divorce laws.

In July, 1854, she followed Lewes to travel in Germany, quietly announcing to their friends their intention to live as husband and wife henceforth. In spite of its having no legal status, they always regarded their association as a true marriage. This was against the social rules of Victorian society. She called herself "Mrs. Lewes" and took very good care of Lewes' three sons. They returned to England a year later. But she felt unhappy because the society did not tolerate their relationship. However, she got satisfaction from Lewes' constant encouragement to write fiction. She thus began her writing career with short sketches for a magazine.

In 1856 she read Lewes a sketch of rural life she had written; in spite of his feeling that it was dramatically weak, he admired it greatly and encouraged her to continue her writing. Her first published story, "Amos Barton", appeared in *Blackwood's Magazine*, followed by two other tales, "Mr. Gilfil's Love Story" and "Janet's Repentance", all of which were later collected in *Scenes of Clerical Life* (1858), published under the masculine pseudonym of "George Eliot". The following year she published her first long novel, *Adam Bede*, a rural tragedy played out among the non-conformists in country scenes remembered from her Warwickshire childhood. After the publication of *Adam Bede* the identity of the author leaked out gradually in spite of her efforts to conceal her real name. The first two works of fiction had brought her a critical reputation as one of the most powerful of contemporary writers. Her preoccupation was always with the serious consideration of the moral position of the individual in the universe, but her psychological insight into the development of character, her flair for country scenes and speech, her fine sense of fun, and the narrative interest of her novels gave her a general popularity not common to didactic novelists.

From this time on, the story of her life is chiefly the history of writing. *The Mill on the Floss* tells of the love, estrangement and eventual reconciliation of the daughter and son of a country miller. The early sections of the book are the most clearly autobiographical of all her writing. *Silas Marner*, the last and shortest of the rustic novels, is set in the period before the Industrial Revolution, telling the life story of Marner, a poor hand-loom weaver, who was thrown into despair when young but was given a new life finally.

After the great success of the early novels, she spent a decade in experimentation, not always with happy results. A trip to Italy, where she worked diligently at research in Renaissance politics, preceded the writing of her historical novel, *Romola*, which is set in the time of Savonarola. Her genius for psychological development of character was shown strikingly in the study of progressive degeneration of Romola's husband, Tito. An estimate of her popularity was afforded by a rival publisher's offer of £10,000 for the copyright of the novel, which appeared in *The Cornhill Magazine*. *Felix Holt*, the complicated story of a young radical in the 1830s, was in the tradition of Disraeli's political novels. Her major poetical work, *The Spanish Gypsy*, a blank verse drama, showed that her real talent lay in prose.

A return to scenes she knew more intimately produced the long novel, *Middlemarch: A Study of Provincial Life*, which is set in one of the new towns of the industrial North. This is the book on which her reputation rests with modern readers, and some critics have called it the greatest of Victorian novels. *Daniel Deronda* is a study of Jewish racial consciousness. By this time she had achieved a position of respect never approached by any other English woman writer. Even today, among all the Victorian women novelists, only the Brontë sisters seem to be her equals; in the study of aspiration and nobility in the mind of woman she has no rival.

The great sales of George Eliot's books insured financial security for herself and Lewes, and allowed him the leisure to win a name of his own as a philosophical and scientific writer and critic. Their increasing reputation put them well above mean gossip, so that during the last years of their life together the circle of friends who visited them included many of the most famous and respected of their contemporaries. Lewes' death in 1878 put an end to their long and happy relationship; in her grief Miss Evans leant heavily on John Cross, who was more than twenty years her junior. The friendship deepened, and in May, 1880, they were married. Seven months later she caught a chill at a concert and died after four days of illness, on December 22, 1880.

## Brief Comment

Eliot did not begin to write until she was nearly forty years of age, but she was the most important living English novelist of the decade between 1870 and 1880. She is often called the most intellectual of the English novelists. In her novels, she had a comprehensive study of the village life in the 1830s. She combined a humourous and affectionate treatment of rural and small town characters with a deep analysis of major characters who aspire to more than the mediocre roles that society could offer. Her novels are also called didactic novels. In many of her novels, one can find that she was always concerned with virtue and morality. Her novels are good examples of moral criticism.

Among her many novels, most critics agree that *Middlemarch* is required reading in university English courses, and it is regarded as her greatest novel, probably inspired by her life at Coventry. The story follows the sexual and intellectual frustrations of Dorothea Brooke. Eliot weaves into her story other narrative lines, which offer a sad comment upon human aspirations. A novel of English provincial life in the early 19th century, just before the Reform Bill of 1832, *Middlemarch* was called by the famous American writer Henry James a "treasure-house of detail". Harold Bloom noted in *The Western Canon* the implicit but clear relation of the work to Dante's *Comedy*.

In her novels, especially in *The Mill on the Floss,* there is fusion of traditional tragedy and realism. This fusion was recognised as one of the greatest phenomena in the 19th century. The death of the heroine embodies unity of tragic structure and realism. Eliot developed Aristotle's idea of character flaw in describing common people rather than high-born people. She kept the principles of Aristotelian tragedy in character delineation. In the novel, the heroine was pure, kind, warm-hearted, forming a sharp contrast with indifferent and narrow-minded people, but she was impulsive and irrational, a clear character flaw. So she did things that the society, her family and she herself could not forgive.

## Selections

### Adam Bede

## The Story

In the village of Hayslope at the close of the 18th century, there lived a young carpenter named Adam Bede. Tall and muscular, Adam was respected by everyone as a good workman and an honest and upright man. Even the young squire, Captain Arthur Donnithorne, knew Adam and liked him, and Adam in turn regarded the squire as his best friend.

Adam was, in fact, so good a workman that his employer, Mr. Jonathan Burge, the builder, would have welcomed him as his son-in-law and partner. But Adam had no eyes for Mary Burge; his only thoughts were of distractingly pretty Hetty Sorrell, niece of Mrs. Poyser, whose husband, Martin, ran the Hall Farm. Hetty, however, cared nothing for Adam. She was interested only in Captain Donnithorne, whom she had met one day in her aunt's dairy.

No one in Hayslope thought Hetty would make Adam a good wife, least of all Adam's mother, Lisbeth, who would have disapproved of any girl who threatened to take her favourite son from her. Her feelings of dependence upon Adam were intensified after her husband, Matthias Bede, drowned in Willow Brook while on his way home from the village inn.

In the meantime, Adam's brother Seth had fallen in love with the young Methodist preacher, Dinah Morris. Dinah was another niece of Mrs. Poyser, as unlike her cousin Hetty as Adam was unlike Seth. Hetty resembled nothing so much as a soft, helpless kitten, but Dinah was firm and serious in all things. One evening while she and Seth were walking home together from the village green, he had proposed marriage. Dinah sadly declined, saying she had dedicated her life to preaching the gospel.

When funeral services for Matthias Bede were held in Hayslope Church on the following Sunday, the thoughts of the congregation were on many things other than the solemn occasion they were attending. Adam's thoughts of Hetty blended with memories of his father. Hetty's thoughts were all of Captain Donnithorne, who had promised to make his appearance. She was disappointed, however, for Donnithorne had already departed with his regiment. When he returned on leave, the young squire celebrated his twenty-first birthday with a great feast to which nearly all of Hayslope was invited. Adam was singled out as a special guest to sit at Donnithorne's table. Adam's mother was both proud and jealous lest her son be getting more and more out of her reach.

One August night, exactly three weeks after the Donnithorne party, Adam was returning home from his work on the Donnithorne estate when he saw two figures in close embrace. They were Donnithorne and Hetty Sorrel. When Adam's dog barked, Hetty hurried away. Donnithorne, embarrassed, tried to explain that he had met the girl by chance and had stolen a kiss. Adam called his friend a scoundrel and a coward. They came to blows, and Donnithorne was knocked senseless. Adam, frightened that he might have killed the young squire in his rage, revived him and helped him to a nearby summerhouse. There he demanded that Donnithorne write a letter to Hetty telling her that he would not see her again.

The next day Donnithorne sent the letter to Hetty in Adam's care, thus placing the responsibility for its possible effect upon Adam himself. Adam gave her the letter while they were walking the following Sunday. When, in the privacy of her bedchamber, Hetty read the letter. She was in despair. Her dreams shattered, she thought only of finding some way out of her misery. Then in November Adam was offered a partnership in Mr. Burge's business, and he proposed to Hetty. Mr. and Mrs. Poyser were delighted to find that their niece was to marry the man they so much admired.

But the wedding had to be delayed until two new rooms could be added to the Bede house. In February, Hetty told her aunt she was going to visit Dinah Morris at Snowfield. Actually, however, she was determined to find Donnithorne. When she arrived at Windsor, where he was supposed to be stationed, she found that his regiment had been transferred to Ireland. Now in complete despair Hetty roamed about until in a strange village, and in the house of a widow named Sarah Stone, her child by Donnithorne was born. Frightened, Hetty wandered on, leaving her baby to die in a wood. Later, tortured by her conscience, she returned to find the child gone.

When his grandfather died, Donnithorne returned to Hayslope to discover that Hetty was in prison, charged with the murder of her child. He did everything in his power to free her, and Dinah Morris came to her prison cell and prayed with her to open up her heart and tell the truth. Finally poor Hetty broke down and confessed everything that had happened since she left Hayslope. She had not intended to kill her baby; in fact, she had not actually killed the child. She had considered taking her own life. Two days later, Donnithorne, filled with shame and remorse, brought a reprieve. Hetty's sentence was committed to deportation. A few years later she died on her way home. Donnithorne went to Spain.

Dinah Morris stayed with the Poysers often now, and gradually she and Adam were drawn to each other. But Dinah's heart was still set on her preaching. She left Hall Farm and went back to Snowfield. Adam Bede found his only satisfaction toiling at his workbench. Then one day his mother spoke again of Dinah and her gentle ways. Adam could wait no longer. He went to find her.

## Chapter XXVII
## A Crisis

It was beyond the middle of August—nearly three weeks after the birthday feast. The reaping of the wheat had begun in our north midland county of Loamshire, but the harvest was likely still to be retarded by the heavy rains, which were causing inundations and much damage throughout the country. From this last trouble the Broxton and Hayslope farmers, on their pleasant uplands, and in their brook-watered valleys, had not suffered, and as I cannot pretend that they were such exceptional farmers as to love the general good better than their own, you will infer that they were not in very low spirits about the rapid rise in the price of bread, so long as there was hope of gathering in their own corn undamaged; and occasional days of sunshine and drying winds flattered this hope.

The eighteenth of August was one of these days, when the sunshine looked brighter in all eyes for the gloom that went before. Grand masses of cloud were hurried across the blue, and the great round hills behind the Chase seemed alive with their flying shadows; the sun was hidden for a moment, and then shone out warm again like a recovered joy; the leaves, still green, were tossed off the hedgerow trees by the wind; around the farmhouses there was a sound of clapping doors; the apples fell in the orchards; and the stray horses on the green sides of the lanes and on the common had their manes blown about their faces. And yet the wind seemed only part of the general gladness because the sun was shining. A merry day for the children, who ran and shouted to see if they could top the wind with their voices; and the grown-up people, too, were in good spirits, inclined to believe in yet finer days, when the wind had fallen. If only the corn were not ripe enough to be blown out of the husk and scattered as untimely seed!

And yet a day on which a blighting sorrow may fall upon a man. For if it be true that Nature at certain moments seems charged with a presentiment of one individual lot, must it not also be true that she seems unmindful, unconscious of another? For there is no hour that has not its births of gladness and despair, no morning brightness that does not bring new sickness to desolation as well as new forces to genius and love. There are so many of us, and our lots are so different: what wonder that Nature's mood is often in harsh contrast with the great crisis of our lives? We are children of a large family, and must learn, as such children do, not to expect that our hurts will be made much of—to be content with little nurture and caressing, and help each other the more.

It was a busy day with Adam, who of late had done almost double work; for he was continuing to act as foreman for Jonathan Burge, until some satisfactory person could be found to supply his place, and Jonathan was slow to find that person. But he had done the extra work cheerfully, for his hopes were buoyant again about Hetty. Every time she had seen him since the birthday, she had seemed to make an effort to behave all the more kindly to him, that she might make him understand she had forgiven his silence and coldness during the dance. He had never mentioned the locket to her again; too happy that she smiled at him—still happier because he observed in her a more subdued air, something that he interpreted as the growth of womanly tenderness and seriousness. "Ah!" he thought, again and again, "she's only seventeen; she'll be thoughtful enough after a while. And her aunt always says how clever she is at the work. She'll make a wife as mother'll have no occasion to grumble at, after all." To be sure, he had only seen her at home twice since the birthday; for one Sunday, when he was intending to go from church to the Hall Farm, Hetty had joined the party of upper servants from the Chase, and had gone home with them—almost as if she were inclined to encourage Mr. Craig. "She's takin' too much likin' to them folks i' the housekeeper's room," Mrs. Poyser remarked. "For my part, I was never over-fond o' gentlefolks's servants—they're mostly like the fine ladies' fat dogs, nayther good for barking nor butcher's meat, but on'y for show." And another evening she was gone to Treddleston to buy some things; though, to his great surprise, as he was returning home, he saw her at a distance getting over a stile quite out of the Treddleston road. But when he hastened to her, she was very kind, and asked him to go in again when he had taken her to the yard gate. She had gone a little farther into the fields after coming from Treddleston, because she didn't want to go in, she said: it was so nice to be out of doors, and her aunt always made such a fuss about it if she wanted to go out. "Oh, do come in with me!" she said, as he was going to shake hands with her at the gate, and he could not resist that. So he went in, and Mrs. Poyser was contented with only a slight remark on Hetty's being later than was expected; while Hetty, who had looked out of spirits when he met her, smiled and talked, and waited on them all with unusual promptitude.

That was the last time he had seen her; but he meant to make leisure for going to the Farm tomorrow. Today, he knew, was her day for going to the Chase to sew with the lady's maid, so he would get as much work done as possible this evening, that the next might be clear.

One piece of work that Adam was superintending was some slight repairs at the Chase Farm, which had been hitherto occupied by Satchell, as bailiff, but which it was now rumoured that the old Squire was going to let to a smart man in top-boots, who had been seen to ride over it one day. Nothing but the desire to get a tenant could account for the Squire's undertaking repairs, though the Saturday-evening party at Mr. Casson's agreed over their pipes that no man in his senses would take the Chase Farm unless there was a bit more plough land laid to it. However that might be, the repairs were ordered to be executed with all dispatch; and Adam, acting for Mr. Burge, was carrying out the order with his usual energy. But today, having been occupied elsewhere, he had not been able to arrive at the Chase Farm till late in the afternoon; and he then discovered that some old roofing, which he had calculated on preserving, had given way. There was clearly no good to be done with this part of the building without pulling it all down; and Adam immediately saw in his mind a plan for building it up again, so as to make the most convenient of cow-sheds and calf-pens, with a hovel for implements; and all without any great expense for materials. So, when the workmen were gone, he sat down, took out his pocket-book, and busied himself with sketching a plan, and making a specification of the expenses, that he might show it to Burge the next morning, and set him on persuading the Squire to consent. To "make a good job" of anything, however small, was always a pleasure to Adam; and he sat on a block, with his book resting on a planning-table, whistling low every now and then, and turning his head on one side with a just perceptible smile of gratification—of pride, too, for if Adam loved a bit of good work, he loved also to think, "I did it!" And I believe the only people who are free from that weakness are those who have no work to call their own. It was nearly seven before he had finished and put on his jacket again; and, on giving a last look round, he observed that Seth, who had been working here today, had left his basket of tools behind him.

"Why, th' lad's forgot his tools," thought Adam, "and he's got to work up at the shop tomorrow. There never was such a chap for woolgathering; he'd leave his head behind him, if it was loose. However, it's lucky I've seen 'em; I'll carry 'em home."

The buildings of the Chase Farm lay at one extremity of the Chase, at about ten minutes' walking distance from the Abbey. Adam had come thither on his pony, intending to ride to the stables, and put up his nag on his way home. At the stables he encountered Mr. Craig, who had come to look at the Captain's new horse, on which he was to ride away the day after tomorrow; and Mr. Craig detained him to tell how all the servants were to collect at the gate of the courtyard to wish the young Squire luck as he rode out; so that, by the time Adam had got into the Chase, and was striding along with the basket of tools over his shoulder, the sun was on the point of setting, and was sending level crimson rays among the great trunks of the old oaks, and touching every bare patch of ground with a transient glory, that made it like a jewel dropt upon the grass. The wind had fallen now, and there was only enough breeze to stir the delicate-stemmed leaves. Any one who had been sitting in the house all day would have been glad to walk now; but Adam had been quite enough in the open air to wish to shorten his way home; and he bethought himself that he might do so by striking across the Chase and going through the Grove, where he had never been for years. He hurried on across the Chase, stalking along the narrow paths between the fern, with Gyp at his heels, not lingering to watch the magnificent changes of the light—hardly once thinking of it—yet feeling its presence in a certain calm happy awe which mingled itself with his busy working-day thoughts. How could he help feeling it? The very deer felt it, and were more timid.

Presently Adam's thoughts recurred to what Mr. Craig had said about Arthur Donnithorne, and pictured his going away, and the changes that might take place before he came back; then they travelled back affectionately over the old scenes of boyish companionship, and dwelt on Arthur's good qualities, which Adam had a pride in, as we all have in the virtues of the superior who honours us. A nature like Adam's, with a great need of love and reverence in it, depends for so much of its happiness on what it can believe and feel about others! And he had no ideal world of dead heroes; he knew little of the life of men in the past; he must find the beings to whom he could cling with loving admiration among those who came within speech of him. These pleasant thoughts about Arthur brought a milder expression than usual into his keen rough face: perhaps they were the reason why, when he opened the old green gate leading into the Grove, he paused to pat Gyp, and say a kind word to him.

After that pause, he strode on again along the broad winding path through the Grove. What grand beeches! Adam delighted in a fine tree of all things; as the fisherman's sight is keenest on the sea, so Adam's perceptions were more at home with trees than with other objects. He kept them in his memory, as a painter does, with all the flecks and knots in their bark, all the curves and angles of their boughs; and had often calculated the height and contents of a trunk to a nicety, as he stood looking at it. No wonder that, notwithstanding his desire to get on, he could not help pausing to look at a curious large beech which he had seen standing before him at a turning in the road, and convinced himself that it was not two trees wedded together, but only one. For the rest of his life he remembered that moment when he was calmly examining the beech, as a man remembers his last glimpse of the home where his youth was passed, before the road turned, and he saw it no more. The beech stood at the last turning before the Grove ended in an archway of boughs that let in the eastern light; and as Adam stepped away from the tree to continue his walk, his eyes fell on two figures about twenty yards before him.

He remained as motionless as a statue, and turned almost as pale. The two figures were standing opposite to each other, with clasped hands, about to part; and while they were bending to kiss, Gyp, who had been running among the brushwood, came out, caught sight of them, and gave a sharp bark. They separated with a start—one hurried through the gate out of the Grove, and the other, turning round, walked slowly, with a sort of saunter, towards Adam, who still stood transfixed and pale, clutching tighter the stick with which he held the basket of tools over his shoulder, and looking at the approaching figure with eyes in which amazement was fast turning to fierceness.

Arthur Donnithorne looked flushed and excited; he had tried to make unpleasant feelings more bearable by drinking a little more wine than usual at dinner today, and was still enough under its flattering influence to think more lightly of this unwished-for rencontre with Adam than he would otherwise have done. After all, Adam was the best person who could have happened to see him and Hetty together: he was a sensible fellow, and would not babble about it to other people. Arthur felt confident that he could laugh the thing off, and explain it away. And so he sauntered forward with elaborate carelessness—his flushed face, his evening dress of fine cloth and fine linen, his white jewelled hands half thrust into his waistcoat pockets, all shone upon by the strange evening light which the light clouds had caught up even to the zenith, and were now shedding down between the topmost branches above him.

Adam was still motionless, looking at him as he came up. He understood it all now—the locket, and everything else that had been doubtful to him: a terrible scorching light showed him the hidden letters that changed the meaning of the past. If he had moved a muscle, he must inevitably have sprung upon Arthur like a tiger; and in the conflicting emotions that filled those long moments, he had told himself that he would not give loose to passion, he would only speak the right thing. He stood as if petrified by an unseen force, but the force was his own strong will.

"Well, Adam," said Arthur, "you've been looking at the fine old beeches, eh? They're not to come near by the hatchet, though; this is a sacred grove. I overtook pretty Hetty Sorrel as I was coming to my den—the Hermitage, there. She ought not to come home this way so late. So I took care of her to the gate, and asked for a kiss for my pains. But I must get back now, for this road is confoundedly damp. Good-night, Adam. I shall see you tomorrow—to say good-bye, you know."

Arthur was too much preoccupied with the part he was playing himself to be thoroughly aware of the expression in Adam's face. He did not look directly at Adam, but glanced carelessly round at the trees, and then lifted up one foot to look at the sole of his boot. He cared to say no more; he had thrown quite dust enough into honest Adam's eyes; and as he spoke the last words, he walked on.

"Stop a bit, sir," said Adam, in a hard peremptory voice, without turning round. "I've got a word to say to you."

Arthur paused in surprise. Susceptible persons are more affected by a change of tone than by unexpected words, and Arthur had the susceptibility of a nature at once affectionate and vain. He was still more surprised when he saw that Adam had not moved, but stood with his back to him, as if summoning him to return. What did he mean? He was going to make a serious business of this affair. Confound the fellow! Arthur felt his temper rising. A patronising disposition always has its meaner side, and in the confusion of his irritation and alarm there entered the feeling that a man to whom he had shown so much favour as to Adam, was not in a position to criticise his conduct. And yet he was dominated, as one who feels himself in the wrong always is, by the man whose good opinion he cares for. In spite of pride and temper, there was as much deprecation as anger in his voice when he said,

"What do you mean, Adam?"

"I mean, sir," answered Adam, in the same harsh voice, still without turning round, "I mean, sir, that you don't deceive me by your light words. This is not the first time you've met Hetty Sorrel in this grove, and this is not the first time you've kissed her."

Arthur felt a startled uncertainty how far Adam was speaking from knowledge, and how far from mere inference. And this uncertainty, which prevented him from contriving a prudent answer, heightened his irritation. He said in a high sharp tone,

"Well, sir, what then?"

"Why, then instead of acting like th' upright, honourable man we've all believed you to be, you've been acting the part of a selfish, light-minded scoundrel. You know, as well as I do, what it's to lead to, when a gentleman like you kisses and makes love to a young woman like Hetty, and gives her presents as she's frightened for other folks to see. And I say it again, you're acting the part of a selfish, light-minded scoundrel, though it cuts me to th' heart to say so, and I'd rather ha' lost my right hand."

"Let me tell you, Adam," said Arthur, bridling his growing anger, and trying to recur to his careless tone, "you're not only devilishly impertinent, but you're talking nonsense. Every pretty girl is not such a fool as you, to suppose that when a gentleman admires her beauty, and pays her a little attention, he must mean something particular. Every man likes to flirt with a pretty girl, and every pretty girl likes to be flirted with. The wider the distance between them the less harm there is, for then she's not likely to deceive herself."

"I don't know what you mean by flirting," said Adam, "but if you mean behaving to a woman as if you loved her, and yet not loving her all the while, I say that's not the action of an honest man, and what isn't honest does come t' harm. I'm not a fool, and you're not a fool, and you know better than what you're saying. You know it couldn't be made public as you've behaved to Hetty as y' have done, without her losing her character, and bringing shame and trouble on her and her relations. What if you meant nothing by your kissing and your presents? Other folks won't believe as you've meant nothing; and don't tell me about her not deceiving herself. I tell you as you've filled her mind so with the thought of you as it'll mayhap poison her life; and she'll never love another man as 'ud make her a good husband."

Arthur had felt a sudden relief while Adam was speaking; he perceived that Adam had no positive knowledge of the past, and that there was no irrevocable damage done by this evening's unfortunate rencontre. Adam could still be deceived. The candid Arthur had brought himself into a position in which successful lying was his only hope. The hope allayed his anger a little.

"Well, Adam," he said, in a tone of friendly concession, "you're perhaps right. Perhaps I've gone a little too far in taking notice of the pretty little thing, and stealing a kiss now and then. You're such a grave, steady fellow, you don't understand the temptation to such trifling. I'm sure I wouldn't bring any trouble or annoyance on her and the good Poysers on any account if I could help it. But I think you look a little too seriously at it. You know I'm going away immediately, so I shan't make any more mistakes of the kind. But let us say good-night,"—Arthur here turned round to walk on—"and talk no more about the matter. The whole thing will soon be forgotten."

"No, by God!" Adam burst out with rage that could be controlled no longer, throwing down the basket of tools, and striding forward till he was right in front of Arthur. All his jealousy and sense of personal injury, which he had been hitherto trying to keep under, had leaped up and mastered him. What man of us, in the first moments of a sharp agony, could ever feel that the fellowman who has been the medium of inflicting it, did not mean to hurt us? In our instinctive rebellion against pain, we are children again, and demand an active will to wreak our vengeance on. Adam at this moment could only feel that he had been robbed of Hetty—robbed treacherously by the man in whom he had trusted; and he stood close in front of Arthur, with fierce eyes glaring at him, with pale lips and clenched hands, the hard tones in which he had hitherto been constraining himself to express no more than a just indignation, giving way to a deep agitated voice that seemed to shake him as he spoke.

"No, it'll not be soon forgot, as you've come in between her and me, when she might ha' loved me—it'll not soon be forgot, as you've robbed me o' my happiness, while I thought you was my best friend, and a noble-minded man, as I was proud to work for. And you've been kissing her, and meaning nothing, have you? And I never kissed her i' my life, but I'd ha' worked hard for years for the right to kiss her. And you make light of it. You think little o' doing what may damage other folks, so as you get your bit o' trifling, as means nothing. I throw back your favours, for you're not the man I took you for. I'll never count you my friend any more. I'd rather you'd act as my enemy, and fight me where I stand—it's all th' amends you can make me."

Poor Adam, possessed by rage that could find no other vent, began to throw off his coat and his cap, too blind with passion to notice the change that had taken place in Arthur while he was speaking. Arthur's lips were now as pale as Adam's; his heart was beating violently. The discovery that Adam loved Hetty was a shock which made him for the moment see himself in the light of Adam's indignation, and regard Adam's suffering as not merely a consequence, but an element of his error. The words of hatred and contempt—the first he had ever heard in his life—seemed like scorching missiles that were making ineffaceable scars on him. All screening self-excuse, which rarely falls quite away while others respect us, forsook him for an instant, and he stood face to face with the first great irrevocable evil he had ever committed. He was only twenty-one—and three months ago—nay, much later—he had thought proudly that no man should ever be able to reproach him justly. His first impulse, if there had been time for it, would perhaps have been to utter words of propitiation; but Adam had no sooner thrown off his coat and cap, than he became aware that Arthur was standing pale and motionless, with his hands still thrust in his waistcoat pockets.

"What!" he said, "won't you fight me like a man? You know I won't strike you while you stand so."

"Go away, Adam," said Arthur. "I don't want to fight you."

"No," said Adam, bitterly; "You don't want to fight me—you think I'm a common man, as you can injure without answering for it."

"I never meant to injure you," said Arthur, with returning anger. "I didn't know you loved her."

"But you've made her love you," said Adam. "You're a double-faced man—I'll never believe a word you say again."

"Go away, I tell you," said Arthur, angrily, "or we shall both repent."

"No," said Adam, with a convulsed voice, "I swear I won't go away without fighting you. Do you want provoking any more? I tell you you're a coward and a scoundrel, and I despise you."

The colour had all rushed back to Arthur's face; in a moment his white right hand was clenched, and dealt a blow like lightning, which sent Adam staggering backward. His blood was as thoroughly up as Adam's now, and the two men, forgetting the emotions that had gone before, fought with the instinctive fierceness of panthers in the deepening twilight darkened by the trees. The delicate-handed gentleman was a match for the workman in everything but strength, and Arthur's skill in parrying enabled him to protract the struggle for some long moments. But between unarmed men, the battle is to the strong, where the strong is no blunderer, and Arthur must sink under a well-planted blow of Adam's, as a steel rod is broken by an iron bar. The blow soon came, and Arthur fell, his head lying concealed in a tuft of fern, so that Adam could only discern his darkly-clad body.

He stood still in the dim light waiting for Arthur to rise. The blow had been given now, towards which he had been straining all the force of nerve and muscle—and what was the good of it? What had he done by fighting? Only satisfied his own passion, only wreaked his own vengeance. He had not rescued Hetty, nor changed the past—there it was, just as it had been; and he sickened at the vanity of his own rage.

But why did not Arthur rise? He was perfectly motionless, and the time seemed long to Adam. Good God! Had the blow been too much for him? Adam shuddered at the thought of his own strength, as with the oncoming of this dread he knelt down by Arthur's side and lifted his head from among the fern. There was no sign of life: the eyes and teeth were set. The horror that rushed over Adam completely mastered him, and forced upon him its own belief. He could feel nothing but that death was in Arthur's face, and that he was helpless before it. He made not a single movement, but knelt like an image of despair gazing at an image of death.

## For Study and Discussion

1. Adam was really very busy, but yet he was happy. Why? What did he think about Hetty?
2. Describe the crisis of this chapter in your own words. What is the climax of this crisis? How is it ended?
3. Give your comment on the three characters, Adam, Arthur and Hetty.

# Chapter 16

# Charlotte Brontë and Emily Brontë

## Life and Works

Charlotte Brontë (1816–1855) and Emily Brontë (1818–1848) were born in Thornton, Yorkshire, but they were undoubtedly of Celtic blood, for their mother came from Cornwall and their father was born in Ireland. Mr. Brontë, an eccentric and domineering clergyman, wrote and published several volumes of undistinguished religious verse and prose. In 1820 he moved his wife and six children to Haworth, a remote and gloomy village on the Yorkshire moors, where Mrs. Brontë died soon after. Her sister came to live at the parsonage to care for the children, but she was no substitute for their mother, and they grew up wild, independent children, devoted to each other and suspicious of outsiders.

Emily and Charlotte and their two elder sisters were sent in 1824 to the Clergy Daughters' School at Cowan Bridge; bad food and poor living conditions aggravated the ill health of the two elder girls, who were sent home in 1825 and died there. Charlotte used, and perhaps exaggerated, the horrors of Cowan Bridge in *Jane Eyre*. Emily and Charlotte were removed from school, and their lessons were resumed at Haworth in the company of their brother Branwell, an intelligent and promising boy a year younger than Charlotte, and their sister Anne, two years younger than Emily. The home teaching was sketchy, but the children read widely and wrote cycles of stories set in lands of their imagination.

In 1831 Charlotte went away once more to school, to Roe Head, where she stayed for a year. She returned to the school again in 1835 as an assistant teacher, taking Emily with her, but Emily's health declined as she silently and rebelliously yearned for the freedom of the moors of Haworth, and at last she had to be sent home. After a little more than two years Charlotte left Roe Head, and for the next three years she and Emily worked intermittently as teachers and governesses, the only occupations open to ladies of the time. In 1842 their aunt provided them with money to go to Brussels for nine months to study French in a fashionable school for young ladies, the Pensionnat Heger. Emily hated being away from home and returned to Haworth with joy at the end of their stay, but Charlotte consented to return to Brussels as a teacher the following year, 1843. Without Emily she was lonely, and after falling unhappily in love with her married employer, she left at the end of the year for which she had contracted.

All the Brontës scribbled poetry secretly, and in 1845 Charlotte found and read Emily's manuscripts. To judge by her later emendations of her sister's poems, Charlotte never completely understood them any more than she understood Emily herself, but she at least realised in them the presence of untrammelled, mystical lyricism which she knew neither she nor Anne possessed. The poems were intensely personal, and Emily was furious at having them read, but after much persuasion she agreed to let Charlotte publish them. To Emily's poems Charlotte added some of her own and Anne's, and in May 1846 *Poems, by Currer, Ellis, and Acton Bell* (the pseudonyms they chose preserved their own initials) was published at the expense of the sisters. Only two copies were sold, and there were but three reviews of the little collection. After this each of the sisters began a novel. Charlotte's book, *The Professor*, based on her Brussels experiences, was refused by a publisher and was not published until after her death. Undiscouraged, she set to work on a new novel, *Jane Eyre*, which was published in October, 1847. This poetic, imaginative story of the love of a young governess for her married employer also has undoubted connections with Charlotte's experiences in Brussels. It was an immediate success with both readers and most of the critics. Emily and Anne had been more successful in getting their first novels accepted, and in December, 1847, a joint book appeared, containing Anne's *Agnes Grey* and Emily's only novel, *Wuthering Heights*; neither work attracted much attention. Like *Jane Eyre*, they were published under the sisters' pseudonyms. As inspiration in her masterpiece, one of the great works of genius in English fiction, Emily drew equally on her own emotional, introverted nature and on the wild and mysterious moorland around her for the story of the passionate Cathy and her savage lover Heathcliff, whose love lasts through their lives and beyond their death and burial in the quiet churchyard on the moors. Both *Jane Eyre* and the still greater *Wuthering Heights* brought to the novel an introspection and an intense concentration on the inner life of emotion which before them had been the province of poetry alone.

In September, 1848, Branwell, whose early promise had degenerated into drunkenness and sloth, died, and in December Emily died of inflammation of the lungs. Anne, who had published a second novel, *The Tenant of Wildfell Hall*, in 1848, failed rapidly after Emily's death, and six months later she died of tuberculosis.

For some years Charlotte continued to live with her father at Haworth, working at her writing. *Shirley* was begun before the death of Emily, whose unconventional personality furnished Charlotte with the character for whom the book was named. The story was concerned with the Luddite mill riots in Yorkshire in 1807–1812, the setting for which Charlotte knew from her schooldays at Roe Head. For *Villette* she returned to her own sad days in Brussels for the tale of a beautifully passionate and tender affection between a plain schoolmistress and an irascible middle-aged professor.

All Charlotte's novels were successful, and she occasionally broke her Yorkshire seclusion for a visit to London, where she was something of a celebrity, once her real identity was known. Among the friendships she formed there was one with Thackeray, to whom she had dedicated *Jane Eyre*. She had several proposals of marriage but she rejected them until the summer of 1854, when she married her father's curate, Arthur Bell Nicholls. Her health was already poor, and after a few months of marriage a cold which she caught during pregnancy brought about her death on March 31, 1855, at thirty-nine.

## Selections

### *Jane Eyre*

### The Story

Jane Eyre was an orphan. Both her father and mother had died when Jane was a baby, and the little girl passed into the care of Mrs. Reed of Gateshead Hall. Mrs. Reed's husband, now dead, had been the brother of Jane Eyre's mother, and on his deathbed he had directed Mrs. Reed to look after the orphan as she would her own three children. At Gateshead Hall Jane knew ten years of neglect and abuse. One day a cousin knocked her to the floor. When she fought back, Mrs. Reed punished her by sending her to the gloomy room where Mr. Reed had died. There Jane lost consciousness. Furthermore, the experience caused a dangerous illness from which she was nursed slowly back to health by sympathetic Bessie Leaven, the Gateshead Hall nurse.

Feeling that she could no longer keep her unwanted charge in the house, Mrs. Reed made arrangements for Jane's admission to Lowood School. Early one morning, without farewells, Jane left Gateshead Hall and rode fifty miles by stage to Lowood, her humble possessions in a trunk beside her.

At Lowood, Jane was a diligent student, well liked by her superiors, especially by Miss Temple, the mistress, who refused to accept without proof Mrs. Reed's low estimate of Jane's character. During the period of Jane's schooldays at Lowood an epidemic of fever caused many deaths among the girls. It resulted, too, in an investigation which caused improvements at the institution. At the end of her studies Jane was retained as a teacher. When Jane grew weary of her life at Lowood, she advertised for a position as governess. She was engaged by Mrs. Fairfax, housekeeper at Thornfield, near Millcote.

At Thornfield the new governess had only one pupil, Adele Varens, a ward of Jane's employer, Mr. Edward Rochester. From Mrs. Fairfax, Jane learnt that Mr. Rochester travelled much and seldom came to Thornfield. Jane was pleased with the quiet country life with the beautiful old house and gardens, the book-filled library, and her own comfortable room.

Jane met Mr. Rochester for the first time while she was out walking, going to his aid after his horse had thrown him. She found her employer a somber, moody man, quick to change in his manner towards her, brusque in his speech. He commended her work with Adele, however, and confided that the girl was the daughter of a French dancer who had deceived him and deserted her daughter. Jane felt that this experience alone could not account for Mr. Rochester's moody nature.

Mysterious happenings occurred at Thornfield. One night Jane, alarmed by a strange noise, found Mr. Rochester's door open and his bed on fire. When she attempted to arouse the household, he commanded her to keep quiet about the whole affair. She also learnt that Thornfield had a strange tenant, a woman who laughed like a maniac and who stayed in rooms on the third floor of the house. Jane believed that this woman was Grace Poole, a seamstress employed by Mr. Rochester.

Mr. Rochester attended numerous parties at which he was obviously paying court to Blanche Ingram, daughter of Lady Ingram. One day the inhabitants of Thornfield were informed that Mr. Rochester was bringing a party of house guests home with him. In the party was the fashionable Miss Ingram. During the house party Mr. Rochester called Jane to the drawing room, where the guests treated her with the disdain which they thought her humble position deserved. To herself Jane had already confessed her interest in her employer, but it seemed to her that he was interested only in Blanche Ingram. One evening while Mr. Rochester was away from home the guests played charades. At the conclusion of the game a gipsy fortune teller appeared to read the palms of the lady guests. Jane, during her interview with the gipsy, discovered that the so-called fortune teller was Mr. Rochester in disguise.

While the guests were still at Thornfield, a stranger named Mason arrived to see Mr. Rochester on business. That night Mason was mysteriously wounded by the strange inhabitant of the third floor. The injured man was taken away secretly before daylight.

One day Bessie Leaven came from Gateshead to tell Jane that Mrs. Reed, now on her deathbed, had asked to see her former ward. Jane returned to her aunt's home. The dying woman gave Jane a letter, dated three years before, from John Eyre in Madeira, who asked that his niece be sent to him for adoption. Mrs. Reed confessed that she had let him believe that Jane had died in the epidemic at Lowood. The sin of keeping from Jane the news had become a heavy burden on the conscience of the dying woman.

Jane went back to Thornfield, which she now looked upon as her home. One night in the garden Edward Rochester embraced her and proposed marriage. Jane accepted and made plans for a quiet ceremony in the village church. She wrote also to her uncle in Madeira, explaining Mrs. Reed's deception and telling him she was to marry Mr. Rochester.

Shortly before the date set for the wedding Jane had a harrowing experience. She awakened to find a strange, repulsive-looking woman in her room. The intruder tried on Jane's wedding veil and then ripped it to shreds. Mr. Rochester tried to persuade Jane that the whole incident was only her imagination, but in the morning she found the torn veil in her room. At the church, as the vows were being said, a stranger spoke up declaring existence of an impediment to the marriage. He presented an affirmation, signed by Mr. Mason who had been wounded during his visit to Thornfield. The document stated that Edward Rochester had married Bertha Mason, Mr. Mason's sister, in Spanish Town, Jamaica, fifteen years before. Mr. Rochester admitted this fact; then he conducted the party to the third-storey chamber at Thornfield. There they found the attendant Grace Poole and her charge, Bertha Rochester, a raving maniac. Mrs. Rochester was the woman Jane had seen in her room.

Jane felt that she must leave Thornfield at once. She notified Mr. Rochester and left quietly early the next morning, using all her small store of money for the coach fare. Two days later she was set down on the moors of a north midland shire. Starving, she actually begged for food. Finally she was befriended by the Reverend St John Rivers and his sisters, Mary and Diana, who took Jane in and nursed her back to health. Assuming the name of Jane Elliot, she refused to divulge anything of her history except her connection with the Lowood institution. The Reverend Rivers eventually found place for her as the mistress in a girl's school.

Shortly afterwards St John Rivers received from his family solicitor word that John Eyre had died in Madeira, leaving Jane Eyre a fortune of twenty thousand pounds. Because Jane had disappeared under mysterious circumstances, the lawyer was trying to locate her through the next of kin, St John Rivers. Jane's identity was now revealed through her connection with Lowood School, and she learnt, to her surprise, that St John Rivers and his sisters were really her own cousins. She then insisted on sharing her inheritance with them.

When St John Rivers decided to go to India as a missionary, he asked Jane to go with him as his wife—not because he loved her, as he frankly admitted, but because he admired her and wanted her services as his assistant. Jane felt indebted to him for his kindness and aid, but she hesitated to accept his proposal.

One night, while St John Rivers was awaiting decision, she dreamed that Mr. Rochester was calling her name. The next day she returned to Thornfield by coach. Arriving there, she found the mansion gutted—a burnt and blackened ruin. Neighbours told her that the fire had broken out one stormy night, set by the mad woman, who died while Mr. Rochester was trying to rescue her from the roof of the blazing house.

Mr. Rochester, blinded during the fire, was living at Ferndean, a lonely farm some miles away. Jane Eyre went to him at once, and there they were married. For both, their story had an even happier ending. After two years Mr. Rochester regained the sight of one eye, so that he was able to see his first child when it was put in his arms.

## Brief Comment on the Novel

*Jane Eyre* has a very good ending: though the house of Rochester was destroyed by fire and he himself became disabled, Jane Eyre, overcoming the contradiction between dignity and love, married Rochester. This is quite a moving ending.

People like the character of Jane Eyre for the following reasons. She is plain-looking and ordinary, but she has a good personality, a sense of dignity and real love. She would rather go away than remain as a mistress. But when obstacle was removed after Mrs. Rochester died, she resolutely married the disabled Rochester. So she is noble. She is true to her own emotion, faithful to her feeling, constant in her love, resolute in her decision. To her, love, dignity and virtue are the utmost importance. If she had married Rochester regardless of the fact that Rochester's wife was still alive though mad, her image would have been greatly harmed. If she had followed St. John Rivers to India, she would never have been so praised for her pure love of Rochester. She never based her decisions on economic status. She was not poor in her later life because she inherited a fortune big enough for her, but she was always generous enough to share her inheritance. This was hard enough for a poor girl to choose and pursue.

The reason *Jane Eyre* has great appeal to readers is that it successfully created the first woman character who takes an independent and freedom-seeking attitude towards love, life and society. This novel took the world by storm and is still exerting great influence on the contemporary readers. From the details of the novel, one can see that the author was quite familiar with life. It was written with love, soul and experience of life.

### Chapter V

Lulled by the sound, I at last dropped asleep. I had not long slumbered when the sudden cessation of motion awoke me; the coach-door was open, and a person like a servant was standing at it; I saw her face and dress by the light of the lamps.

"Is there a little girl called Jane Eyre here?" she asked. I answered "Yes," and was then lifted out; my trunk was handed down, and the coach instantly drove away.

I was stiff with long sitting, and bewildered with the noise and motion of the coach; gathering my faculties, I looked about me. Rain, wind, and darkness filled the air; nevertheless, I dimly discerned a wall before me and a door open in it; through this door I passed with my new guide; she shut and locked it behind her. There was now visible a house or houses—for the building spread far—with many windows, and lights burning in some; we went up a broad pebbly path, splashing wet, and were admitted at a door; then the servant led me through a passage into a room with a fire, where she left me alone.

I stood and warmed my numbed fingers over the blaze, then I looked round; there was no candle, but the uncertain light from the hearth showed by intervals, papered walls, carpet, curtains, shining mahogany furniture; it was a parlour, not so spacious or splendid as the drawing-room at Gateshead, but comfortable enough. I was puzzling to make out the subject of a picture on the wall, when the door opened, and an individual carrying a light entered; another followed close behind.

The first was a tall lady with dark hair, dark eyes, and a pale and large forehead; her figure was partly enveloped in a shawl, her countenance was grave, her bearing erect.

"The child is very young to be sent alone," said she, putting her candle down on the table. She considered me attentively for a minute or two, then further added:

"She had better be put to bed soon; she looks tired. Are you tired?" she asked, placing her hand on my shoulder.

"A little, Ma'am."

"And hungry too, no doubt; let her have some supper before she goes to bed, Miss Miller. Is this the first time you have left your parents to come to school, my little girl?"

I explained to her that I had no parents. She inquired how long they had been dead; then how old I was, what was my name, whether I could read, write, and sew a little; then she touched my cheek gently with her forefinger, and saying, "She hoped I should be a good child," dismissed me along with Miss Miller.

The lady I had left might be about twenty-nine; the one who went with me appeared some years younger; the first impressed me by her voice, look, and air. Miss Miller was more ordinary; ruddy in complexion, though of a care-worn countenance; hurried in gait and action, like one who had always a multiplicity of tasks on hand; she looked, indeed, what I afterwards found she really was, an under-teacher. Led by her, I passed from compartment to compartment, from passage to passage of a large and irregular building; till, emerging from the total and somewhat dreary silence pervading that portion of the house we had traversed, we came upon the hum of many voices, and presently entered a wide, long room, with great deal tables, two at each end, on each of which burnt a pair of candles, and seated all round on benches, a congregation of girls of every age, from nine or ten to twenty. Seen by the dim light of the dips, their number to me appeared countless, though not in reality exceeding eighty; they were uniformly dressed in brown stuff frocks of quaint fashion, and long Holland pinafores. It was the hour of study; they were engaged in conning over their tomorrow's task, and the hum I had heard was the combined result of their whispered repetitions.

Miss Miller signed to me to sit on a bench, near the door, then walking up to the top of the long room, she cried out:

"Monitors, collect the lesson-books and put them away!"

Four tall girls arose from different tables, and going round gathered the books and removed them, Miss Miller again gave the word of command:

"Monitors, fetch the supper trays!"

The tall girls went out and returned presently, each bearing a tray, with portions of something, I knew not what, arranged thereon, and a pitcher of water and mug in the middle of each tray. The portions were handed round; those who liked took a draught of the water, the mug being common to all. When it came to my turn, I drank, for I was thirsty, but did not touch the food; excitement and fatigue rendering me incapable of eating; I now saw, however, that it was a thin oaten cake, shared into fragments.

The meal over, prayers were read by Miss Miller, and the classes filed off—two and two upstairs. Overpowered by this time with weariness, I scarcely noticed what sort of a place the bedroom was; except that, like the school-room, I saw it was very long. Tonight I was to be Miss Miller's bed-fellow; she helped me to undress. When laid down I glanced at the long rows of beds, each of which was quickly filled with two occupants; in ten minutes the single light was extinguished; amidst silence and complete darkness, I fell asleep.

The night passed rapidly; I was too tired even to dream; I only once awoke to hear the wind rave in furious gusts, and the rain fall in torrents, and to be sensible that Miss Miller had taken her place by my side. When I again unclosed my eyes, a loud bell was ringing, the girls were up and dressing, day had not yet begun to dawn, and a rushlight or two burnt in the room. I, too, rose reluctantly; it was bitter cold, and I dressed as well as I could for shivering, and washed, when there was a basin at liberty, which did not occur soon, as there was but one basin to six girls, on the stands down the middle of the room. Again the bell rang; all formed in file, two and two, and in that order descended the stairs and entered the cold and dimly lit school-room; here prayers were read by Miss Miller; afterwards she called out:

"Form classes!"

A great tumult succeeded for some minutes, during which Miss Miller repeatedly exclaimed, "Silence!" and "Order!" When it subsided, I saw them all drawn up in four semicircles, before four chairs, placed at the four tables; all held books in their hands, and a great book, like a Bible, lay on each table, before the vacant seat. A pause of some seconds succeeded, filled up by the low, vague hum of numbers; Miss Miller walked from class to class, hushing this indefinite sound.

A distant bell tinkled. Immediately three ladies entered the room, each walked to a table and took her seat; Miss Miller assumed the fourth vacant chair, which was that nearest the door, and around which the smallest of the children were assembled; to this inferior class I was called, and placed at the bottom of it.

Business now began. The day's collect was repeated, then certain texts of Scripture were said, and to these succeeded a protracted reading of chapters in the Bible, which lasted an hour. By the time that exercise was terminated, day had fully dawned. The indefatigable bell now sounded for the fourth time; the classes were marshalled and marched into another room to breakfast. How glad I was to behold a prospect of getting something to eat! I was now nearly sick from inanition, having taken so little the day before.

The refectory was a great, low-ceiled, gloomy room; on two long tables smoked basins of something hot, which, however, to my dismay, sent forth an odour far from inviting. I saw a universal manifestation of discontent when the fumes of the repast met the nostrils of those destined to swallow it. From the van of the procession, the tall girls of the first class, rose the whispered words:

"Disgusting! The porridge is burnt again!"

"Silence!" ejaculated a voice—not that of Miss Miller, but one of the upper teachers, a little and dark personage, smartly dressed, but of somewhat morose aspect, who installed herself at the top of one table, while a more buxom lady presided at the other. I looked in vain for her I had first seen the night before—she was not visible. Miss Miller occupied the foot of the table, where I sat, and a strange, foreign-looking, elderly lady, the French teacher, as I afterwards found, took the corresponding seat at the other board. A long grace was said and a hymn sung; then a servant brought in some tea for the teachers, and the meal began.

Ravenous, and now very faint, I devoured a spoonful or two of my portion without thinking of its taste; but the first edge of hunger blunted, I perceived I had got in hand a nauseous mess. Burnt porridge is almost as bad as rotten potatoes; famine itself soon sickens over it. The spoons were moved slowly; I saw each girl taste her food and try to swallow it, but in most cases the effort was soon relinquished. Breakfast was over, and none had breakfasted. Thanks being returned for what we had not got, and a second hymn chanted, the refectory was evacuated for the school-room. I was one of the last to go out; and, in passing the tables, I saw one teacher take a basin of the porridge and taste it. She looked at the others; all their countenances expressed displeasure, and one of them, the stout one, whispered:

"Abominable stuff! How shameful!"

A quarter of an hour passed before lessons again began, during which the school-room was in a glorious tumult. For that space of time, it seemed to be permitted to talk loud and more freely, and they used their privilege. The whole conversation ran on the breakfast, which one and all abused roundly. Poor things! It was the sole consolation they had. Miss Miller was now the only teacher in the room; a group of great girls standing about her, spoke with serious and sullen gestures. I heard the name of Mr. Brocklehurst pronounced by some lips; at which Miss Miller shook her head disapprovingly; but she made no great effort to check the general wrath, doubtless she shared in it.

A clock in the school-room struck nine; Miss Miller left her circle, and, standing in the middle of the room, cried:

"Silence! To you seats!"

Discipline prevailed: in five minutes the confused throng was resolved into order, and comparative silence quelled the Babel clamour of tongues. The upper teachers now punctually resumed their posts; but still, all seemed to wait. Ranged on benches down the sides of the room, the eighty girls sat motionless and erect; a quaint assemblage they appeared, all with plain locks combed from their faces, not a curl visible; in brown dresses, made high and surrounded by a narrow tucker about the throat, with little pockets of Holland (shaped something like a Highlander's purse) tied in front of their frocks, and destined to serve the purpose of a work-bag; all, too, wearing woollen stockings and country-made shoes fastened with brass buckles. Above twenty of those clad in this costume were full-grown girls, or rather, young women; it suited them ill, and gave an air of oddity even to the prettiest.

I was still looking at them, and also at intervals examining the teachers—none of whom precisely pleased me; for the stout one was a little coarse, the dark one not a little fierce, the foreigner harsh and grotesque, and Miss Miller, poor thing! Looked purple, weather-beaten, and overworked—when, as my eye wandered from face to face, the whole school rose simultaneously, as if moved by a common spring.

What was the matter? I had heard no order given; I was puzzled. Ere I had gathered my wits, the classes were again seated; but all eyes were now turned to one point, mine followed the general direction, and encountered the personage who had received me last night. She stood at the bottom of the long room, on the hearth; for there was a fire at each end; she surveyed the two rows of girls silently and gravely. Miss Miller approaching, seemed to ask her a question, and, having received her answer, went back to her place, and said aloud,

"Monitor of the first class, fetch the globes!"

While the direction was being executed, the lady consulted moved slowly up the room. I suppose I have a considerable organ of veneration, for I retain yet the sense of admiring awe with which my eyes traced her steps. Seen now, in broad daylight, she looked tall, fair, and shapely; brown eyes, with a benignant light in their irises, and a fine pencilling of long lashes round, relieved the whiteness of her large front; on each of her temples her hair, of a very dark brown, was clustered in round curls, according to the fashion of those times, when neither smooth bands nor long ringlets were in vogue; her dress, also in the mode of the day, was of purple cloth, relieved by a sort of a Spanish trimming of black velvet; a gold watch (watches were not so common then as now) shone at her girdle. Let the reader add, to complete the picture, refined features; a complexion if pale, clear; and a stately air and carriage, and he will have, at least, as clearly as words can give it, a correct idea of the exterior of Miss Temple—Maria Temple, as I afterwards saw the name written in a prayer book entrusted to me to carry to church.

The superintendent of Lowood (for such was this lady) having taken her seat before a pair of globes placed on one of the tables, summoned the first class round her, and commenced giving a lesson in geography; the lower classes were called by the teachers; repetitions in history, grammar, etc., went on for an hour; writing and arithmetic succeeded, and music lessons were given by Miss Temple to some of the elder girls. The duration of each lesson was measured by the clock, which at last struck twelve. The superintendent rose:

"I have a word to address to the pupils," said she.

The tumult of cessation from lessons was already breaking forth, but it sank at her voice. She went on:

"You had this morning a breakfast which you could not eat; you must be hungry; I have ordered that a lunch of bread and cheese shall be served to all."

The teachers looked at her with a sort of surprise.

"It is to be done on my responsibility," she added, in an explanatory tone to them, and immediately afterwards left the room.

The bread and cheese was presently brought in and distributed, to the high delight and refreshment of the whole school. The order was now given, "To the garden!" Each put on a coarse straw bonnet, with strings of coloured calico, and a cloak of grey frieze. I was similarly equipped, and, following the stream, I made my way into the open air.

The garden was a wide inclosure, surrounded with walls so high as to exclude every glimpse of prospect; a covered verandah ran down one side, and broad walks bordered a middle space divided into scores of little beds; these beds were assigned as gardens for the pupils to cultivate, and each bed had an owner. When full of flowers they would, doubtless, look pretty; but now, at the latter end of January, all was wintry blight and brown decay. I shuddered as I stood and looked round me: it was an inclement day for outdoor exercise—not positively rainy, but darkened by a drizzling yellow fog; all underfoot was still soaking wet with the floods of yesterday. The stronger among the girls ran about and engaged in active games, but sundry pale and thin ones herded together for shelter and warmth in the verandah; and amongst these, as the dense mist penetrated to their shivering frames, I heard frequently the sound of a hollow cough.

As yet I had spoken to no one, nor did anybody seem to take notice of me; I stood lonely enough: but to that feeling of isolation I was accustomed, it did not oppress me much. I leant against a pillar of the verandah, drew my grey mantle close about me, and trying to forget the cold which nipped me without, and the unsatisfied hunger which gnawed me within, delivered myself up to the employment of watching and thinking. My reflections were too undefined and fragmentary to merit record; I hardly yet knew where I was. Gateshead and my past life seemed floated away to an immeasurable distance; the present was vague and strange, and of the future, I could form no conjecture. I looked round the convent-like garden, and then, up at the house, a large building, half of which seemed grey and old, the other half quite new. The new part, containing the school-room and dormitory was lit by mullioned and latticed windows, which gave it a church-like aspect; a stone tablet over the door bore this inscription:

"Lowood Institution. This portion was rebuilt, AD[1]—, by Naomi Brocklehurst, of Brocklehurst Hall, in this county. 'Let your light so shine before men that they may see your good works, and glorify your Father which is in heaven.'—St Matt. v., 16.[2]"

I read these words over and over again. I felt that an explanation belonged to them, and was unable fully to penetrate their import. I was still pondering the signification of "Institution", and endeavouring to make out a connection between the first words and the verse of Scripture, when the sound of a cough, close behind me, made me turn my head. I saw a girl sitting on a stone bench near; she was bent over a book, on the perusal of which she seemed intent; from where I stood I could see the title—it was "Rasselas"[3], a name that struck me as strange, and consequently attractive. In turning a leaf she happened to look up, and I said to her directly,

"Is your book interesting?" I had already formed the intention of asking her to lend it to me some day.

"I like it," she answered, after a pause of a second or two, during which she examined me.

"What is it about?" I continued. I hardly know where I found the hardihood thus to open a conversation with a stranger; the step was contrary to my nature and habits: but I think her occupation touched a cord of sympathy somewhere; for I, too, liked reading, though of a frivolous and childish kind; I could not digest or comprehend the serious or substantial.

"You may look at it," replied the girl, offering me the book.

I did so; a brief examination convinced me that the contents were less taking than the title: "Rasselas" looked dull to my trifling taste; I saw nothing about fairies, nothing about genii; no bright variety seemed spread over the closely-printed pages. I returned it to her; she received it quietly, and without saying anything, she was about to relapse into her former studious mood: again I ventured to disturb her—

"Can you tell me what the writing on that stone over the door means? What is Lowood Institution?"

"This house where you are come to live."

"And why do they call it Institution? Is it in any way different from other schools?"

"It is partly a charity-school: you and I, and all the rest of us are charity-children. I suppose you are an orphan: are not either your father or your mother dead?"

"Both died before I can remember."

"Well, all the girls here have lost either one or both parents, and this is called an institution for educating orphans."

"Do we pay no money? Do they keep us for nothing?"

"We pay, or our friends pay, fifteen pounds a year for each."

"Then why do they call us charity-children?"

"Because fifteen pounds is not enough for board and teaching, and the deficiency is supplied by subscription."

"Who subscribes?"

"Different benevolent-minded ladies and gentlemen in this neighbourhood and in London."

"Who was Naomi Brocklehurst?"

"The lady who built the new part of this house, as that tablet records, and whose son overlooks and directs everything here."

"Why?"

"Because he is treasurer and manager of the establishment."

"Then this house does not belong to that tall lady who wears a watch, and who said we were to have some bread and cheese?"

"To Miss Temple? Oh, no! I wish it did. She has to answer to Mr. Brocklehurst for all she does. Mr. Brocklehurst buys all our food and all our clothes."

"Does he live here?"

"No—two miles off, at a large hall."

"Is he a good man?"

"He is a clergyman, and is said to do a great deal of good."

"Did you say that tall lady was called Miss Temple?"

"Yes."

"And what are the other teachers called?"

"The one with red cheeks is called Miss Smith; she attends to the work, and cuts out—for we make our own clothes, our frocks, and pelisses, and everything; the little one with black hair is Miss Scatcherd; she teaches history and grammar, and hears the second class repetitions; and the one who wears a shawl, and has a pocket handkerchief tied to her side with a yellow ribbon, is Madame Pierrot; she comes from Lisle, in France, and teaches French."

"Do you like the teachers?"

"Well enough."

"Do you like the little black one, and the Madame—?—I cannot pronounce her name as you do."

"Miss Scatcherd is hasty—you must take care not to offend her; Madame Pierrot is not a bad sort of person."

"But Miss Temple is the best—isn't she?"

"Miss Temple is very good, and very clever; she is above the rest, because she knows far more than they do."

"Have you been long here?"

"Two years."

"Are you an orphan?"

"My mother is dead."

"Are you happy here?"

"You ask rather too many questions. I have given you answers enough for the present; now I want to read."

But at the moment the summons sounded for dinner; all reentered the house. The odour which now filled the refectory was scarcely more appetising than that which had regaled our nostrils at breakfast; the dinner was served in two huge tin-plated vessels, whence rose a strong steam redolent of rancid fat. I found the mess to consist of indifferent potatoes and strange shreds of rusty meat, mixed and cooked together. Of this preparation a tolerably abundant plateful was apportioned to each pupil. I ate what I could, and wondered within myself whether every day's fare would be like this.

After dinner, we immediately adjourned to the school-room: lessons recommenced, and were continued till five o'clock.

The only marked event of the afternoon was, that I saw the girl with whom I had conversed in the verandah dismissed in disgrace, by Miss Scatcherd, from a history class, and sent to stand in the middle of the large school-room. The punishment seemed to me in a high degree ignominious, especially for so great a girl—she looked thirteen or upward. I expected she would show signs of great distress and shame; but, to my surprise, she neither wept nor blushed: composed, though grave, she stood, the central mark of all eyes. "How can she bear it so quietly—so firmly?" I asked of myself. "Were I in her place, it seems to me I should wish the earth to open and swallow me up. She looks as if she were thinking of something beyond her punishment—beyond her situation: of something not round her nor before her. I have heard of daydreams—is she in a daydream now? Her eyes are fixed on the floor, but I am sure they do not see it—her sight seems turned in, gone down into her heart: she is looking at what she can remember, I believe; not at what is really present. I wonder what sort of a girl she is—whether good or naughty."

Soon after five pm we had another meal, consisting of a small mug of coffee, and half a slice of brown bread. I devoured my bread and drank my coffee with relish; but I should have been glad of as much more—I was still hungry. Half an hour's recreation succeeded, then study; then the glass of water and the piece of oat-cake, prayers, and bed. Such was my first day at Lowood.

## For Study and Discussion

1. What is Jane Eyre's first impression of the ladies she first see?
2. What is the class like? How is the class organised?
3. What subjects are studied by the students?
4. Who is Miss Temple? What does she teach? What does she do to surprise the other teachers?
5. From whom does Jane know a lot about the school? What do you know about this charity school through the dialogue?

### *Wuthering Heights*

## The Story

Mr. Lockwood, the new tenant at Thrushcross Grange, met a surly reception from servants, dogs, and the landlord himself, Mr. Heathcliff, when he paid his first call. Mr. Heathcliff looked like a dark-skinned gypsy, but had the dress and manners of a country squire. Erect and handsome in figure, he was extremely morose and reserved.

Wuthering Heights, the landlord's home, was a well-built, battered old farmhouse, its name descriptive of the atmospheric tumult to which its exposed position subjected it in stormy weather.

The tenant, his interest aroused, called again next day and was forced by a snowstorm to remain overnight. He met the rest of this strange household—Heathcliff's widowed daughter-in-law, pretty and scarcely past girlhood, but silent and scornful; and a clumsy youth named Hareton Earnshaw, which was the same name as that carved over the door of the Heights along with the date "1500".

Put into a disused bedroom for the night, Mr. Lockwood found scratched in the wall the names "Catherine Earnshaw", "Catherine Heathcliff" and "Catherine Linton". And on the blank leaves of books in the room he found a scrawled diary with such entries as: "Hindley is a detestable substitute—his conduct to Heathcliff is atrocious—H. and I are going to rebel… Poor Heathcliff! Hindley calls him a vagabond, and won't let him sit with us." Nightmares beset Mr. Lockwood, and he woke after dreaming that a pale child who called herself Catherine Linton stood outside the window and wailed to be let in, crying: "I've been a waif for twenty years."

Back at the Grange, Mr. Lockwood was told this story by Mrs. Nelly Dean, his housekeeper, who had long been a servant at the Heights and the Grange.

Old Mr. Earnshaw, Hareton's grandfather, brought back with him from a trip to Liverpool, a dirty, ragged, black-haired boy that he had found homeless in the streets there. They washed the child, gave it the single name of Heathcliff, and Earnshaw took a liking to this hard, silent boy who could absorb a blow without shedding a tear. Earnshaw's daughter Catherine (Cathy) soon became a constant play-mate of Heathcliff, but her brother Hindley hated him for usurping his father's affections.

Earnshaw died, and Hindley returned from college with a wife who disliked Heathcliff and drove him to the company of the servants. Cathy clung to the youth and they promised to grow up together as rude as savages. One night the pair were locked out for the night and Cathy took refuge with the Lintons at Thrushcross Grange—they wouldn't admit Heathcliff. She stayed there five weeks, becoming friendly with the Linton children, Edgar and Isabella.

Hindley's wife died in giving birth to Hareton, and the sorrowing husband abandoned himself to dissipation and fiendish torment of Heathcliff, who grew more savage as Catherine, now fifteen, developed into a headstrong beauty.

One day Cathy told Nelly that Edgar had proposed to her and that she loved him, despite his placid temperament. But Cathy added that Heathcliff was "more myself than I am", though brought so low by Hindley that it would degrade her to marry him.

Heathcliff overheard, and bolted before Catherine, who added that she wouldn't have given Edgar a second thought except that this marriage would enable her to help Heathcliff.

That night she and Nelly searched the moors fruitlessly for Heathcliff, and next day Cathy went to bed with a dangerous fever. She recovered slowly, but not for three years did she marry Edgar.

After the marriage Heathcliff reappeared, tall, well-dressed and with ample money—where he got it and where he had been were never explained. Cathy welcomed him despite Edgar's frowns, and his old enemy Hindley was pleased to let him pay for lodging at Wuthering Heights.

Now came stories of gambling and drinking at the Heights, with Hindley going deeply into debt, while Heathcliff visited the Grange regularly. Unexpectedly, defying all warnings that he was no man for her, Isabella Linton became infatuated with Heathcliff. One day Edgar ordered Heathcliff ejected bodily from the Grange, and Heathcliff took revenge by eloping with Isabella.

Eight weeks later the unhappy Isabella wrote to Nelly, now at the Grange, asking whether her husband was man or devil. Nelly went to see her and was induced by Heathcliff to arrange a meeting between him and Cathy, who had been ill in bed since the men had quarrelled.

Heathcliff saw that she was dying. "You and Edgar have killed me," she told him, then sobbingly admitted that she had done wrong, after Heathcliff asked by what right she had left him when she loved him. That night she died in giving birth to her child, Catherine Linton.

Heathcliff dashed his head against a tree, calling on Cathy's ghost to haunt him and crying: "Only do not leave me in this abyss, where I cannot find you!"

Soon afterwards Isabella fled to London, where her son Linton, a sickly creature, was born, and where she died a dozen years later. Linton was brought to Thrushcross Grange, about the time that Hindley Earnshaw finished drinking himself to death after mortgaging all his property to Heathcliff.

Now Heathcliff's purpose became apparent—to destroy the Earnshaw family and unite the Heights and Grange estates. He kept Hareton as a bemused dependent, ignorant that Heathcliff was his father's enemy. Heathcliff brought his son Linton home from the Grange, terrorised him into slavery, and arranged a marriage between him and young Catherine. Shortly came the deaths of young Catherine's husband and her father, who had been led to bequeath all his property to Heathcliff.

Thus came about the situation which Mr. Lockwood had found some time later, on a trip north, when he revisited the Heights. He found that Heathcliff had died. Catherine Linton had won over the untutored Hareton, and they planned to wed. Heathcliff had at first been angry at their friendship, then calmed down. "Nelly, there is a strange change approaching; I'm in its shadow," he said. And soon after he was found dead in bed.

## Brief Comment on the Novel

*Wuthering Heights* is written as a series of diary entries by Lockwood, who writes down what he learns from Nelly Dean. He also inserts several narrations within the main narrations, made of as-told-tos and letters. The characters in the novel speak according to their social class. It is Emily Brontë's only novel while this novel alone has attracted one generation of readers after another because it touched upon the utmost intensity of human feeling and sentiment.

*Wuthering Heights* is a symbolic novel combining the techniques of realism, romanticism and symbolism. Through a series of vivid plots and symbolic descriptions, the novel has created a lot of peculiar characters and detailed the daily life, love and marriage in the English countryside. The description of nature is very important in this novel in that the exterior nature expressed the inner nature of humanity. The moody nature and climate of the moorlands portrays and mirrors the inner turmoil of the characters, who, in turn, are associated with elements of nature themselves.

A meditation on the nature of love is at the center of the novel. The relationship between Cathy and Heathcliff, which is all-consuming and brings Cathy to fully identify with Heathcliff, guides the novel, while the other types of love are portrayed as either ephemeral (Cathy and Edgar) or self-serving (Heathcliff and Isabella). The novel's tragic turn comes because of the class differences between Cathy (middle class) and Heathcliff (an orphan, the ultimate outcast), as she is bound to marry an equal. Hate is another theme of the novel. Heathcliff's hate parallels, in fierceness, his love for Cathy. When he finds out he can't have her, he starts a revenge plan to settle the score with all of those who wronged him, and morphs from a Byronic hero into a Gothic villain.

## Chapter XV

Another week over—and I am so many days nearer health, and spring! I have now heard all my neighbour's history, at different sittings, as the housekeeper could spare time from more important occupations. I'll continue it in her own words, only a little condensed. She is, on the whole, a very fair narrator, and I don't think I could improve her style.

In the evening, she said, the evening of my visit to the Heights, I knew, as well as if I saw him, that Mr. Heathcliff was about the place; and I shunned going out, because I still carried his letter in my pocket, and didn't want to be threatened or teased any more. I had made up my mind not to give it till my master went somewhere, as I could not guess how its receipt would affect Catherine. The consequence was, that it did not reach her before the lapse of three days. The fourth was Sunday, and I brought it into her room after the family were gone to church. There was a man-servant left to keep the house with me, and we generally made a practice of locking the doors during the hours of service; but on that occasion the weather was so warm and pleasant that I set them wide open, and, to fulfil my engagement, as I knew who would be coming, I told my companion that the mistress wished very much for some oranges, and he must run over to the village and get a few, to be paid for on the morrow. He departed, and I went upstairs.

Mrs. Linton[1] sat in a loose, white dress, with a light shawl over her shoulders, in the recess of the open window, as usual. Her thick, long hair had been partly removed at the beginning of her illness, and now she wore it simply combed in its natural tresses over her temples and neck. Her appearance was altered, as I had told Heathcliff; but when she was calm, there seemed unearthly beauty in the change. The flash of her eyes had been succeeded by a dreamy and melancholy softness; they no longer gave the impression of looking at the objects around her: they appeared always to gaze beyond, and far beyond—you would have said out of this world. Then the paleness of her face—its haggard aspect having vanished as she recovered flesh—and the peculiar expression arising from her mental state, though painfully suggestive of their causes, added to the touching interest which she awakened; and—invariably to me, I know, and to any person who saw her, I should think—refuted more tangible proofs of convalescence, and stamped her as one doomed to decay.

A book lay spread on the sill before her, and the scarcely perceptible wind fluttered its leaves at intervals. I believe Linton had laid it there: for she never endeavoured to divert herself with reading, or occupation of any kind, and he would spend many an hour in trying to entice her attention to some subject which had formerly been her amusement. She was conscious of his aim, and in her better moods endured his efforts placidly, only showing their uselessness by now and then suppressing a wearied sigh, and checking him at last with the saddest of smiles and kisses. At other times, she would turn petulantly away, and hide her face in her hands, or even push him off angrily; and then he took care to let her alone, for he was certain of doing no good.

Gimmerton chapel bells were still ringing; and the full, mellow flow of the beck in the valley came soothingly on the ear. It was a sweet substitute for the yet absent murmur of the summer foliage, which drowned that music about the Grange when the trees were in leaf. At Wuthering Heights it always sounded on quiet days following a great thaw or a season of steady rain. And of Wuthering Heights Catherine was thinking as she listened: that is, if she thought or listened at all; but she had the vague, distant look I mentioned before, which expressed no recognition of material things either by ear or eye.

"There's a letter for you, Mrs. Linton," I said[2], gently inserting it in one hand that rested on her knee. "You must read it immediately, because it wants an answer. Shall I break the seal?" "Yes," she answered, without altering the direction of her eyes. I opened it—it was very short. "Now," I continued, "read it."

She drew away her hand, and let it fall. I replaced it in her lap, and stood waiting till it should please her to glance down; but that movement was so long delayed that at last I resumed—

"Must I read it, ma'am? It is from Mr. Heathcliff."

There was a start and a troubled gleam of recollection, and a struggle to arrange her ideas. She lifted the letter, and seemed to peruse it; and when she came to the signature she sighed; yet still I found she had not gathered its import, for, upon my desiring to hear her reply, she merely pointed to the name, and gazed at me with mournful and questioning eagerness.

"Well, he wishes to see you," said I, guessing her need of an interpreter. "He's in the garden by this time, and impatient to know what answer I shall bring."

As I spoke, I observed a large dog lying on the sunny grass beneath raise its ears as if about to bark, and then smoothing them back, announce, by a way of the tail, that someone approached whom it did not consider a stranger. Mrs. Linton bent forward, and listened breathlessly. The minute after a step traversed the hall; the open house was too tempting for Heathcliff to resist walking in: most likely he supposed that I was inclined to shirk my promise, and so resolved to trust to his own audacity. With straining eagerness Catherine gazed towards the entrance of her chamber. He did not hit the right room[3] directly, she motioned me to admit him; but he found it out, ere I could reach the door, and in a stride or two was at her side, and had her grasped in his arms.

He neither spoke nor loosed his hold for some five minutes, during which period he bestowed more kisses than ever he gave in his life before, I dare say: but then my mistress had kissed him first, and I plainly saw that he could hardly bear, for downright agony, to look into her face! The same conviction had stricken him as me, from the instant he beheld her, that there was no prospect of ultimate recovery there—she was fated, sure to die.

"Oh, Cathy! Oh, my life! How can I bear it?" was the first sentence he uttered, in a tone that did not seek to disguise his despair. And now he stared at her so earnestly that I thought the very intensity of his gaze would bring tears into his eyes; but they burnt with anguish; they did not melt[4].

"What now?" said Catherine, leaning back, and returning his look with a suddenly clouded brow[5]: her humour was a mere vane for constantly varying caprices. "You and Edgar[6] have broken my heart, Heathcliff! And you both come to bewail the deed to me, as if you were the people to be pitied! I shall not pity you, not I. You have killed me—and thriven on it, I think. How strong you are! How many years do you mean to live after I am gone?"

Heathcliff had knelt on one knee to embrace her; he attempted to rise, but she seized his hair, and kept him down.

"I wish I could hold you," she continued bitterly, "till we were both dead! I shouldn't care what you suffered. I care nothing for your sufferings. Why shouldn't you suffer? I do! Will you forget me? Will you be happy when I am in the earth? Will you say twenty years hence, 'that's the grave of Catherine Earnshaw? I loved her long ago, and was wretched to lose her; but it is past. I've loved many others since: my children are dearer to me than she was; and at death, I shall not rejoice that I am going to her; I shall be sorry that I must leave them!' Will you say so, Heathcliff?"

"Don't torture me till I am as mad as yourself," cried he, wrenching his head free, and grinding his teeth.

The two, to a cool spectator, made a strange and fearful picture. Well might Catherine deem that heaven would be a land of exile to her, unless with her mortal body she cast away her mortal character also. Her present countenance had a wild vindictiveness in its white cheek, and a bloodless lip and scintillating eye; and she retained in her closed fingers a portion of the locks she had been grasping. As to her companion, while raising himself with one hand, he had taken her arm with the other; and so inadequate was his stock of gentleness to the requirements of her condition, that on his letting go I saw four distinct impressions left blue in the colourless skin.

"Are you possessed with a devil," he pursued, savagely, "to talk in that manner to me when you are dying? Do you reflect that all those words will be branded in my memory, and eating deeper eternally after you have left me? You know you lie to say I have killed you: and, Catherine, you know that I could as soon forget you as my existence! Is it not sufficient for your infernal selfishness, that while you are at peace I shall writhe in the torments of hell?"

"I shall not be at peace," moaned Catherine, recalled to a sense of physical weakness by the violent, unequal throbbing of her heart, which beat visibly and audibly under this excess of agitation. She said nothing further till the paroxysm was over; then she continued, more kindly—

"I'm not wishing you greater torment than I have, Heathcliff. I only wish us never to be parted: and should a word of mine distress you hereafter, think I feel the same distress underground, and for my own sake, forgive me! Come here and kneel down again! You never harmed me in your life. Nay, if you nurse anger[7], that will be worse to remember than my harsh words! Won't you come here again? Do!"

Heathcliff went to the back of her chair, and leant over, but not so far as to let her see his face, which was livid with emotion. She bent round to look at him; he would not permit it: turning abruptly, he walked to the fireplace, where he stood, silent, with his back towards us. Mrs. Linton's glance followed him suspiciously: every movement woke a new sentiment in her. After a pause and a prolonged gaze, she resumed; addressing me in accents of indignant disappointment—

"Oh, you see, Nelly, he would not relent a moment to keep me out of the grave. *That* is how I'm loved! Well, never mind. That is not *my* Heathcliff. I shall love mine yet; and take him with me: he's in my soul. And," added she, musingly, "the thing that irks me most is this shattered prison, after all. I'm tired of being enclosed here. I'm wearying to escape into that glorious world, and to be always there: not seeing it dimly through tears, and yearning for it through the walls of an aching heart; but really with it, and in it. Nelly, you think you are better and more fortunate than I; in full health and strength: you are sorry for me—very soon that will be altered. I shall be sorry for *you*. I shall be incomparably beyond and above you all. I *wonder* he won't be near me!" She went on to herself. "I thought he wished it. Heathcliff, dear! You should not be sullen now. Do come to me, Heathcliff."

In her eagerness she rose and supported herself on the arm of the chair. At that earnest appeal he turned to her, looking absolutely desperate. His eyes, wide and wet, at last flashed fiercely on her; his breast heaved convulsively. An instant they held asunder, and then how they met I hardly saw, but Catherine made a spring, and he caught her, and they were locked in an embrace from which I thought my mistress would never be released alive: in fact, to my eyes, she seemed directly insensible. He flung himself into the nearest seat, and on my approaching hurriedly to ascertain if she had fainted, he gnashed at me, and foamed like a mad dog, and gathered her to him[8] with greedy jealousy. I did not feel as if I were in the company of a creature of my own species: it appeared that he would not understand, though I spoke to him; so I stood off, and held my tongue, in great perplexity.

A movement of Catherine's relieved me a little presently: she put up her hand to clasp his neck, and bring her cheek to his as he held her; while he, in return, covering her with frantic caresses, said wildly—

"You teach me now how cruel you've been—cruel and false. *Why* did you despise me? *Why* did you betray your own heart, Cathy? I have not one word of comfort. You deserve this. You have killed yourself. Yes, you may kiss me, and cry; and wring out my kisses and tears: they'll blight you—they'll damn you. You loved me—then what *right* had you to leave me? What right—answer me—for the poor fancy you felt for Linton? Because misery and degradation, and death, and nothing that God or Satan could inflict would have parted us, *you*, of your own will, did it. I have not broken your heart—*you* have broken it; and in breaking it, you have broken mine. So much the worse for me, that I am strong. Do I want to live? What kind of living will it be when you—oh, God! Would *you* like to live with your soul in the grave?"

"Let me alone. Let me alone," sobbed Catherine. "If I have done wrong, I'm dying for it. It is enough! You left me too: but I won't upbraid you! I forgive you. Forgive me!"

"It is hard to forgive, and to look at those eyes, and feel those wasted hands," he answered. "Kiss me again; and don't let me see your eyes! I forgive what you have done to me. I love *my* murderer—but *yours*! How can I?"

They were silent—their faces hid against each other, and washed by each other's tears. At least, I suppose the weeping was on both sides; as it seemed Heathcliff *could* weep on a great occasion like this.

I grew very uncomfortable, meanwhile; for the afternoon wore fast away, the man whom I had sent off returned from his errand, and I could distinguish, by the shine of the westering sun up the valley, a concourse thickening outside Gimmerton chapel porch.

"Service is over," I announced. "My master will be here in half an hour."

Heathcliff groaned a curse, and strained Catherine closer; she never moved.

Ere long I perceived a group of the servants passing up the road towards the kitchen wing. Mr. Linton was not far behind; he opened the gate himself and sauntered slowly up, probably enjoying the lovely afternoon that breathed as soft as summer.

"Now he is here," I exclaimed. "For Heaven's sake, hurry down! You'll not meet any one on the front stairs. Do be quick; and stay among the trees till he is fairly in."

"I must go, Cathy," said Heathcliff, seeking to extricate himself from his companion's arms. "But, if I live, I'll see you again before you are asleep. I won't stray five yards from your window."

"You must not go!" she answered, holding him as firmly as her strength allowed. "You shall not, I tell you."

"For one hour," he pleaded, earnestly.

"Not for one minute," she replied.

"I *must*—Linton will be up immediately," persisted the alarmed intruder.

He would have risen, and unfixed her fingers by the act—she clung fast, grasping: there was mad resolution in her face.

"No!" she shrieked. "Oh, don't, don't go. It is the last time! Edgar will not hurt us.

Heathcliff, I shall die! I shall die!"

"Damn the fool! There he is," cried Heathcliff, sinking back into his seat. "Hush, my darling! Hush, hush, Catherine! I'll stay. If he shot me so, I'd expire with a blessing on my lips."

And there they were fast again. I heard my master mounting the stairs—the cold sweat ran from my forehead: I was horrified.

"Are you going to listen to her ravings?" I said passionately. "She does not know what she says. Will you ruin her, because she has not wit to help herself? Get up! You could be free instantly. That is the most diabolical deed that ever you did. We are all done for—master, mistress, and servant."

I wrung my hands, and cried out; and Mr. Linton hastened his step at the noise. In the midst of my agitation, I was sincerely glad to observe that Catherine's arms had fallen relaxed, and her head hung down.

"She's fainted or dead," I thought: "so much the better. Far better that she should be dead, than lingering a burden and a misery-maker to all about her."

Edgar sprang to his unbidded guest, blanched with astonishment and rage. What he meant to do, I cannot tell; however, the other stopped all demonstrations, at once, by placing the lifeless-looking form in his arms.

"Look there!" he said. "Unless you be a fiend, help her first—then you shall speak to me!"

He walked into the parlour, and sat down. Mr. Linton summoned me, and with great difficulty, and after resorting to many means, we managed to restore her to sensation; but she was all bewildered; she sighed, and moaned, and knew nobody. Edgar, in his anxiety for her, forgot her hated friend. I did not. I went, at the earliest opportunity, and besought him to depart; affirming that Catherine was better, and he should hear from me in the morning how she passed the night.

"I shall not refuse to go out of doors," he answered; "but I shall stay in the garden; and, Nelly, mind you keep your word tomorrow. I shall be under those larch trees. Mind! Or I pay another visit, whether Linton be in or not."

He sent a rapid glance through the half-open door of the chamber, and, ascertaining that what I stated was apparently true, delivered the house of his luckless presence.

## Notes

1. Mrs. Linton: Catherine
2. I said: This episode is supposed to be related by Nelly Dean, Catherine's maid.
3. hit the right room: find the room in which Catherine was reclining
4. they did not melt: It implies that his eyes did not shed any tears.
5. clouded brow: gloomy and sorrowful expression
6. Edgar: Edgar Linton, Catherine's husband

7. nurse anger: be angry all the time
8. gathered her to him: embraced her

## For Study and Discussion

1. What is the mood of Catherine at the beginning of this selection? Who put a book on the sill? Why is it opened?
2. What is Catherine's response to the letter brought to her? What is the difference before and after she read it?
3. Describe how Heathcliff enters Catherine's room and how they meet each other. What impresses you the most about their meeting?
4. Why does Catherine say "You and Edgar have broken my heart, Heathcliff!"? Is she right to say so? What are her fears and hopes when she talks with Heathcliff?
5. How does Heathcliff criticise Catherine about her deserting him? What does Catherine say? Why does Heathcliff say that he loves his murderer Catherine? Why is she a murderer to him?
6. It is said that this chapter is the most touching, exciting and adventurous meeting in all episodes of love. What is your comment? What is your opinion of Heathcliff and Catherine?

## Chapter 17

# Matthew Arnold

### Life and Works

Matthew Arnold (1822–1888) was born in Middlesex, southeast England. His father, Dr. Thomas Arnold, was an important religious and educational reformer who became headmaster of the Rugby School, one of the most prestigious private schools in England. Arnold was deeply influenced by his father's ideas, but he also showed a certain rebellious defiance of his father's rigorous principles. When Arnold left Rugby to attend Oxford University in 1841, he assumed the style of an aristocratic wit and dandy famous for his elegant, colourful clothes and flippant manner. He did not work particularly hard at Oxford, and only by desperate last-minute cramming did he manage a respectable performance on his final examinations. But underneath the casual manner that Arnold cultivated as a young man were a wide-ranging intellect and a sensitive, brooding imagination. Even before he abandoned his youthful dandyism, Arnold was beginning to write poems that would surprise his closest friends and family with their meditative intensity and their power of symbolic suggestion. In 1851 Arnold became a government inspector of schools, a position he held for over thirty years. The job was a demanding one and left him with less free time for his own writing than was enjoyed by other major Victorian writers. Yet Arnold wrote continually throughout these years.

Arnold's career as a writer may be divided roughly into four phases. Most of his poems appeared during the 1850s: a volume entitled *The Strayed Reveller and Other Poems* was followed by additional volumes in 1852 and 1853. During the 1860s the focus of his writing shifted from poetry to literary and social criticism. In 1865 the first series of his *Essays in Criticism* was published, and in 1869, *Culture and Anarchy*, a fierce attack on middle-class materialism and narrow-mindedness, considered by many to be his finest work. In the 1870s Arnold devoted himself mainly to writing about education and religion. Finally, in the 1880s he returned to literary criticism and wrote the second series of his *Essays in Criticism,* published soon after his death in 1888.

## Brief Comment

Matthew Arnold is important both as a poet and as a critic. In his poetry, Arnold confronted more directly than either Tennyson or Browning the central Victorian problems in the dehumanising atmosphere of a modern industrial society. In his critical essays, Arnold tried to provide answers to the questions about modern life that he posed but left for the most part unanswered in his poems.

Many of his best poems convey a melancholy, pessimistic sense of the dilemmas of modern life, without offering any secure source of hope, joy and permanent value. Today his poetry seems distinctively expressive of mid-Victorian anxiety because it avoids offering optimistic answers to the doubtful questions it has raised.

## Selections

### Dover Beach[1]

The sea is calm tonight.
The tide is full, the moon lies fair
Upon the straits[2]; on the French coast the light
Gleams and is gone; the cliffs of England[3] stand,
Glimmering and vast, out in the tranquil bay.
Come to the window, sweet is the night air![4]
Only, from the long line of spray
Where the sea meets the moon-blanched land[5],
Listen! you hear the grating[6] roar
Of pebbles which the waves draw back, and fling,
At their return, up the high strand,
Begin, and cease, and then again begin,
With tremulous cadence slow[7], and bring
The eternal note of sadness[8] in.

Sophocles[9] long ago
Heard it[10] on the Aegean[11], and it brought
Into his mind the turbid[12] ebb and flow
Of human misery[13]; we
Find also in the sound a thought,
Hearing it by this distant[14] northern sea.

The Sea of Faith[15]

Was once, too, at the full, and round earth's shore
Lay like the folds of a bright girdle furled.[16]
But now I only hear
Its melancholy, long, withdrawing roar,
Retreating, to the breath
Of the night wind, down the vast edges drear[17]
And naked shingles[18] of the world.

Ah, love, let us be true
To one another! for the world, which seems
To lie before us like a land of dreams,
So various, so beautiful, so new,
Hath really neither joy, nor love, nor light,
Nor certitude, nor peace, nor help for pain;[19]
And we are here as on a darkling plain
Swept with confused alarms of struggle and flight,
Where ignorant armies clash by night.

## Notes

1. The poem is written in four stanzas of irregular lengths and rhythms.
2. straits: the Straits of Dover, a crossing between England and France
3. the cliffs of England: referring to the white steep cliffs on the bank of the Straits of Dover
4. sweet is the night air: cf. John Keats' "Ode to the Nightingale": "tender is the night..."
5. the moon-blanched land: land that is made white by the moonlight
6. grating: making harshly sound
7. tremulous cadence slow: tremulous slow cadence. This *adj.* +*n.* +*adj.* structure is know as Miltonic structure in which the two adjectives before and after both modify the noun.
8. The eternal note of sadness: the basic tone of the poem. Here the change from the calm, beautiful night scene to the sorrow and anxiety of the poet's inner world is made.
9. Sophocles: a famous Athenian tragedian (496 BC–406 BC) in the golden age of Greek drama
10. it: referring to the eternal note of sadness
11. Aegean: Aegean Sea, an arm of the Mediterranean Sea
12. turbid: not clear
13. human misery: the central idea of the poem
14. distant: far away (from the Aegean Sea)
15. The Sea of Faith: here faith is compared to the ebb and flow of the sea tide

16. Lay like the folds of a bright girdle furled: lay furled like the folds of a bright girdle. It means at high tide the sea envelops the land closely; at ebb tide, as the sea retreats, it is unfurled and spread out.
17. the vast edges drear: another Miltonic structure, the vast drear edges
18. naked shingles: referring to the barren state of modern culture. shingles: beaches covered with pebbles
19. Hath really neither joy, nor love, nor light, /Nor certitude, nor peace, nor help for pain: The poet thinks that the Industrial Revolution has taken away the religious spirit of England and made it a wasteland of spirit.

## *For Study and Discussion*

1. What is the basic tone of the whole poem? Try to find out some key words that help create the tone.
2. What do you think of the sound pattern of this poem? What's the significance of this pattern?
3. Why does the poet mention Sophocles in his poem?
4. In what way does the sea resemble Faith?
5. Study carefully the image that the poet places at the end of the poem. Why does the poet think of himself and the person he loves as being situated "on a darkling plain"? What is suggested by the idea of "ignorant armies" clashing "by night"?

# Chapter 18

# Christina Rossetti

## Life and Works

Christina Rossetti (1830–1894) was born in London, the youngest child of Gabriel Rossetti, an Italian patriot who fled to England for refuge in 1824. Like her brothers and sister, she was educated mostly at home where she met politicians, artists and writers, many of whom, like her parents, were exiles from Italy. She was the model for many paintings by her brother Dante Gabriel Rossetti, an artist and the founder of the Pre-Raphaelite Brotherhood, and his artist friends. Her first verses, written when she was 12, were printed by her grandfather. At 19 some of her poems were printed by her brothers in *The Germ*, the magazine of the Pre-Raphaelite Brotherhood.

Her collection *Goblin Market and Other Poems*, illustrated by her brother Dante, received public recognisation. *The Prince's Progress and Other Poems* was published four years later. The collection of her earlier writings for children, *Sing-Song, a Nursery Rhyme Book*, appeared in 1872, and *A Pageant and Other Poems* in 1881. Her later works in prose and verse were mostly religious. She died in London on December 29, 1894.

## Brief Comment

Christina Rossetti's work ranges from poems for children to love lyrics, sonnets and religious poetry. Her poetry is remarkable for its simplicity and singing quality. The recurring theme in her love poems is the unhappy or frustrated love. Her religious poetry often shows a strong sense of duty. Frequently suffering from ill health, Christina wrote poetry that was often melancholy and concerned with thoughts of death. However, she could also be sprightly and fanciful in her writing.

## Selections

### Remember[1]

Remember me when I am gone away,
Gone far away into the silent land;[2]
When you can no more hold me by the hand,
Nor I half turn to go yet turning stay.[3]
Remember me when no more day by day
You tell me of our future that you plann'd:
Only remember me; you understand
It will be late to counsel[4] then or pray.
Yet if you should forget me for a while
And afterwards remember, do not grieve:
For if the darkness and corruption[5] leave
A vestige of the thoughts that once I had,
Better by far[6] you should forget and smile
Than that you should remember and be sad.

## Notes

1. It is written in Italian sonnet rhyming abba abba cdd ece.
2. Gone far away into the silent land: (Euphemism) dead
3. Nor I half turn to go yet turning stay: referring to her reluctance to part with her love and die
4. counsel: give advice
5. corruption: putrescence of the body
6. Better by far: I shall think it better.

## For Study and Discussion

1. What does "the silent land" symbolise?
2. Explain the structure of this sonnet. How does it serve the development of the theme?
3. How do you understand the contradictory ideas expressed in the poem? Is this contradiction reasonable? Why or why not?
4. Interpret the last two lines.

# Chapter 19

# Gerard Manley Hopkins

## Life and Works

Gerard Manley Hopkins (1844–1889) was born in Stratford, Essex in 1844. He was the eldest child of a large and very religious English family. He attended Highgate School in northwest London, where he showed academic and artistic promise. In 1863 he went to study classics at Oxford University, and there his brilliant intellect and imagination began to flower. He was a student of Walter Pater, the eloquent late-Victorian spokesman for artistic experience as the only stable source of value in the modern world. And he was influenced by the Oxford movement, which sought to revive the ritualistic and dogmatic traditions of the Church of England. The original leader of the Oxford movement, John Henry Newman, had left the Church of England in 1845 to become a Roman Catholic. After a period of deep religious turmoil, Hopkins himself, under Newman's sponsorship, joined the Catholic Church in 1866.

In 1868 he entered the Society of Jesus, one of the most intellectually demanding and disciplined orders of the Church. Before becoming a Jesuit, Hopkins burned all the poems he had written up to that time, feeling that his artistic interests were incompatible with strict devotion to his religious obligation. He did not begin to write poetry again until 1875 or 1876, and even then he resisted his friend's suggestion that he publish at least some of his works. In 1877 he became an ordained priest and served in a number of parishes, including one in a depressing working class district of Liverpool. In 1884 he was appointed Professor of Classics at University College, Dublin. Hopkins died in Dublin of typhoid fever in 1889, when he was only 45. His poems were finally published in 1918 by his close friend, the poet Robert Bridges.

## Brief Comment

Although not widely read or appreciated until thc 20th century, Hopkins is in many respects a deeply characteristic Victorian writer. He is, to be sure, a remarkable experimenter and innovator in the rhythm, vocabulary and formal arrangements of English verse. As much as any other Victorian poet, including Browning, Hopkins has influenced the direction of modern English and American poetry. Yet in his expressions of intense spiritual anxiety and in his passionate devotion to the unique particularised beauty of the natural world, he is very much a 19th-century poet. To read Hopkins well, we must learn to value the Victorian dimension of his writing as well as its advanced, forward-looking modernity.

## Selections

### Pied Beauty[1]

Glory be to God for dappled things—
    For skies of couple-colour as a brinded[2] cow;
        For rose-moles all in stipple[3] upon trout that swim;
Fresh-firecoal chestnut-falls,[4] finches' wings;
    Landscape plotted and pieced—fold, fallow, and plough;[5]
        And all trades, their gear and tackle and trim.[6]

All things counter[7], original, spare[8], strange;
    Whatever is fickle, freckled (who knows how?)
With swift, slow; sweet, sour; adazzle, dim;[9]
He fathers-forth [10] whose beauty is past change:
                                        Praise him.

## Notes

1. It is written in two stanzas with the first stanza of six lines rhyming abcabc, the second of five lines rhyming decdc. pied: of two or more colours in blotches, variegated
2. brinded: streaked with dark, brownish orange in colour with streaks of gray
3. stipple: dots or small spots
4. Fresh-firecoal chestnut-falls: freshly fallen chestnuts, bright as coals
5. Landscape plotted and pieced—fold, fallow, and plough: the fields either lying fallow or plowed for cultivation, thus looking like patches of different colours
6. their gear and tackle and trim: their equipment
7. counter: contrary.
8. spare: rare
9. With swift, slow; sweet, sour; adazzle, dim: with slow (countering with) swift; sweet (countering with) sour; adazzle (countering with) dim. adazzle: dazzling
10. fathers-forth: creates everything

## For Study and Discussion

1. What kind of beauty in the natural world is the poet celebrating in this poem? What specific examples are given to show the beauty?
2. The look and sound of individual words in "Pied Beauty" are important aspects of the poem's meaning. What do "dappled" (Line 1) "couple-colour" (Line 2) and "stipple" (Line 3) have in common? What other words in the poem can you relate to these through their look and sound? (Notice "plotted" in Line 5, for example.)
3. In what sense is the poet imitating in language the "pied beauty" he celebrates in nature?
4. What does the poet mean by "All things counter"? Why are they part of the "pied beauty"?

# Part IX

# The 20th Century from 1900 to 1945: Modern Literature

# Introduction

## Background of History

The long and progressive reign of Queen Victoria came to a climax in the Diamond Jubilee Year (1897), a time of peace and plenty when the British Empire seemed to be at the summit of its power and security. Of the discord that soon followed there were two factors that had great influence on contemporary English literature.

The first disturbing factor was imperialism, the reawakening of a dominating spirit which had seemingly been put to sleep by the proclamation of an Imperial Federation. Its coming was heralded by the Boer War (1899–1902) in South Africa, through which Britain blundered to what was hoped to be an era of peace and good will. Other nations promptly made such hope a vain whistling in the wind. Germany demanded her larger "place in the sun" and began warlike preparation for a future "push to the East". France enlarged her huge empire in Africa and Indo-China. Italy began a career of disaster by her first attack on Abyssinia. Japanese War Lords, inflated by victory over Russia, aimed to make Japan the master of Asia. Pacific islands that had for ages slept peacefully were turned into frowning naval stations. All these nations began to dismember China by seizing treaty ports and claiming special concessions in trade. Even the United States, aroused by an easy triumph in the Spanish War, started on an imperialistic adventure by taking control of the Philippines, thus making an implacable enemy of Japan, which had covetous eyes on the same prize.

Only a nation that enters on a dangerous course with eyes wide open has any chance of a safe way out, and the imperialistic nations were all alike blind. An inevitable result was the First World War and the greater horror of the Second World War, the two calamities being different acts of the same tragedy of imperialism, separated only by a breathing spell.

Another factor that influenced literature for the worse was a widespread demand for social reform of every kind; not slow and orderly reform, which could be progress, but immediate and intemperate reform, which bred a spirit of rebellion and despair. Before the Victorian age had come to an end, English literature appeared to have lost touch with healthy English life. Many writers, as if alternating between chills and fever, echoed the sorrowful cry of James Thomson in his long poem *The City of Dreadful Night*, or babbled of "art for art's sake" with Oscar Wilde, Aubrey Beardsley, and other decadents in *The Yellow Book*, a quarterly literary periodical. Groom, in his survey of the period, noted that writers had mostly a critical attitude towards morals and religion, Church and State, considered as relics from "the dead hand of Puritan beliefs". It was small wonder that German and Japanese warmongers regarded Englishmen as a decadent race when the same or a worse opinion was daily read in the novels of Samuel Butler and nightly heard in the plays of George Bernard Shaw.

## Literary Reactions

Imperialism had its outstanding advocate in Rudyard Kipling, who with drum and trumpet called upon England to "take up the White Man's burden" by dominating all "lesser breeds without the law". No other prominent writer of his day was ever quite so dogmatic; no other so cocksure that his was the only message worthy of attention.

Social reform had its advocates by the score, not in censorious essays only, following the example of Thomas Carlyle, but also in fiction, in verse, and especially in drama. One unexpected literary feature of the age was the enthusiasm for plays that rolled like a tide over the whole English-speaking world. In the Elizabethan age, also called "the age of drama", London had five playhouses, and there was not another in the kingdom. Early in the 20th century new stages appeared like mushrooms after a warm rain; nearly every city had its provincial theatre, as well as a number of regular playhouses, and there was hardly a town in England or America without its "drama-study group" or a college without its "drama workshop". Nearly all successful novelists wrote plays also, and most of them used the stage as an instrument of social reform.

On the surface, at least, the contrast between Victorian and post-Victorian literature was rather startling. Tennyson and Kipling served as excellent examples, since they were in turn acclaimed wherever English is spoken, one for his idealism, the other for his intolerance of everything outside the British pale. Dickens, the outstanding Victorian novelist, was a man of colossal optimism; and Thomas Hardy, the most "finished" novelist of the age following, was sunk to the deep of pessimism. Poets of the Victorian age, as reflected in Stedman's *A Victorian Anthology*, left a general impression of beauty, of faith, and therefore of cheerfulness.

The end of the 19th century was a period of struggle between realistic and anti-realistic trends in art and literature. While such writers as George Meredith, Samuel Butler, Thomas Hardy and later on George Bernard Shaw, H. G. Wells and John Galsworthy created a truthful picture of contemporary England, others, like Robert Louis Stevenson and Oscar Wilde, led the readers away from the burning issues of social reality.

The growth of anti-realistic art and literature reflected the crisis of bourgeois culture at the period of imperialism. The chief aim of R. L. Stevenson was to entertain his readers. His masterly written stories and novels abound in interesting adventures, fantastical situations and vivid descriptions. But even in his best books he avoided touching upon the social contradictions of his time.

Oscar Wilde was the most conspicuous writer of the English decadence. In his critical essays Wilde expounded the theory of "art for art's sake". Though in many of his brilliant plays and fairy tales he criticised the cynicism and bigotry of the bourgeois-aristocratic world of his days, he, for all that, remained a sceptic and pessimist.

In his short stories, poems and novels, Kipling, the bard of imperialism, glorified the colonial expansion of Great Britain. Describing the everyday life of ordinary British officials and military men in India and other colonial and semi-colonial countries, he never raised his voice in protest against the oppression of the natives. His picture of India, though exceedingly vivid and fascinating, presented a perverted view of the country and its glorious people.

The English realists of the end of the 19th and the beginning of the 20th centuries continued and developed the traditions of their predecessors, like Dickens, Thackeray and Charlotte Brontë. They sought for new ways and means of revealing the truth of life. In their works criticism of the bourgeois world reached considerable depth and poignancy. The narrow-mindedness, hypocrisy and avidity of the propertied classes were mercilessly scourged in the works of Samuel Butler and his follower George Bernard Shaw.

The later realists excelled in revealing the characters from a psychological point of view. The novels of G. Meredith, Thomas Hardy and J. Galsworthy were masterpieces of satirical portrayal and psychological analysis.

Of great interest were the works of H. G. Wells. His social and fantastic novels also brought out the crying contradictions of bourgeois civilisation. In an attempt at solving social problems, Wells devised a number of projects, but none of them had anything in common with scientific socialism.

With all their merits and achievements, however, the later realists were inferior to their great predecessors in the scope and breadth of their portrayal of social phenomena.

The works of Samuel Butler, Thomas Hardy and H. G. Wells were imbued with pessimism often bordering on despair. Condemning the existing order of things, the later English realists failed to see the forces at work in society which were bound to change it. The greatest books of the period were cries of suffering and protest.

## Modernist Breakthrough

In the 1920s, the modernist breakthrough made by Joyce, Lawrence, Woolf and others in fiction writing obviously affected poetry writing. For example, Yeats' dreamily aesthetic style of the late 19th century began to shift to a more lean and conversational style. The voice of the poem within the character as used in dramatic monologues began to be reinforced under the influence of the Freudian psychology. The mind's distorted and fragmented perception, explored by the "stream of consciousness" technique in the hands of the fictional writers, also became the poets' dominant focus. T. S. Eliot wrote about the wasteland scenes and the impotence of the modern man. He and other poets of the 1920s and 1930s presented poetry hard and obscure to understand. They used new expressions and new images to depict the fatigue and disillusionment of the modern individuals. But each of these writers had his own aim of modernism in a different way. They experimented and departed from the demands of formal realism, interested in how the mind and emotion work in private realm of thought, memory and desire.

The poets of the generation following T. S. Eliot, namely in the 1930s and 1940s, had two lines of development. One was influenced by politics of the 1930s and was liberal in their sympathies. For example, Auden became a voice of protest against exploitation and suffering. The other line was more personal, left politics behind and focused on the intensity of private experience, indulged in the rich play of language, and used energetic and suggestive but obscure and seemingly carefree flow of words. Dylan Thomas was a painstaking craftsman, but the lively and vigorous tone in his poems concealed this effort. In the poems of this period, the speaking voice was often tough and cynical, never sentimental. And in their use of imagery, they became more allusive, private and idiosyncratic. They were often accused of being obscure or difficult because they threw the readers into strange, illogical realm with no familiar landmarks or narrative line.

In the field of drama, early in the 20th century, Shaw attempted to turn the English theatre into an arena for the play of ideas. Social and political plays were unable to hold a mainstream audience. Radical and experimental drama remained on the fringe. The commercial plays were successful. Comedies were popular with the middle-class audience. There also appeared a group of experimental playwrights, such as Samuel Beckett, Harold Pinter and Tom Stoppard. They were influenced by existentialism and the concept of life as absurd. They wrote plays to dramatise the elemental psychological forces and absurd situations of modern life. Mere entertainment gave way to a more forceful, ironic and provocative drama. Among them, Samuel Beckett is worth mentioning. Beckett's *Waiting for Godot* revolutionised the expectations of the British theatre audience.

# Chapter 20

# Thomas Hardy

## Life and Works

Thomas Hardy (1840–1928), last and one of the greatest of Victorian novelists, was born in Dorset on June 2, 1840, in the centre of the Wessex country which later figured in his works. Both his mother and his father, a builder, came of Dorset stock.

Thomas Hardy early learned to love the rustic ways and speech around him. He was a precocious boy but reserved. His health was delicate, so he was educated at home until he was eight, and then in the village schools and in the nearby town of Dorchester. At sixteen he was apprenticed to a local architect. In 1862 he left for London to continue his work as an architect, an occupation he practised until his marriage.

In the meantime he had found poetry as the chief love for the rest of his life. He tried to publish his poems, but failed. Yet even after they were rejected he continued writing poetry. In 1867 he, because of poor health, returned to Dorset, where his work as an architect supported him so that he could write in his leisure. He turned to write fiction, and after his return to Dorset he began his first novel, *The Poor Man and the Lady*. He submitted it to George Meredith, then a reader for *Chapman and Hall*, who advised him to concentrate on plot. Hardy, completely humble about his own talents, promptly and regrettably destroyed the manuscript. *Desperate Remedies*, his first published novel, is a contrived, melodramatic murder story, the result of following Meredith's advice. It had bad reviews and failed to earn its publication costs. The first of his many novels of country life, *Under the Greenwood Tree*, shows in a pleasant little idyll how deeply Hardy understood rustic ways. *A Pair of Blue Eyes*, is a romantic tragedy which alternates between Cornwall and London, between peasantry and upper-class society, and once more it is in the rustic scenes that the real interest lies. The success of these last two novels brought a commission to write a serial for the *Cornbill Magazine*. *Far from the Madding Crowd*, published anonymously in 1874, is Hardy's first masterpiece, a story of fortitude and of suffering brought about by the capriciousness of a country girl. After this, most of his novels made their first appearance in periodicals.

Hardy still preferred poetry to fiction, but he felt compelled to write stories to support himself, for he had married and given up architecture in 1874, encouraged by his success with *Far from the Madding Crowd*. His next work, *The Hand of Etbelberta* is a "society" novel in which the reader misses the elemental strength of the Wessex tales. In *The Return of the Native* he looked again to the land as a source of his power; the two major "characters" are Eustacia Vye, who broods with a tragic passion over the heath on which she lives, and the heath itself, which symbolises the blind forces of nature against which she rebels.

*The Trumpet-Major* is a light-hearted love story of the period of the Napoleonic Wars, written with little of Hardy's characteristic irony. *Two on a Tower* shocked his audience with the frankness of its treatment of sexual passion in a woman. Over the pages of *The Mayor of Casterbridge* hangs the shadow of an inexorable fate hounding a man to miserable death by means of the flaws in his own character, but for all its gloom it is one of Hardy's most powerful novels. *The Woodlanders*, is the quietly beautiful story of a simple countryman, unable to marry the girl he loves, who has risen above him socially.

At the same time Hardy was writing short stories, and, although they were hardly so successful, many of them are worth ranking beside his longer works. *Wessex Tales*, *A Group of Noble Dames* and *Life's Little Ironies* are the major collections.

His novels culminated with the two greatest, *Tess of the D'Urbervilles* and *Jude the Obscure*. The second part of the title of *Tess of the D'Urbervilles* is *A Pure Woman*, showing what Hardy thought of his heroine, who is seduced, abandoned, and finally driven to murder for which she is hanged. Through it all she remains his most lovable woman character, cruelly tormented by fate and innocent of any intention to sin. Jude in *Jude the Obscure* shows the horrible decline of a man and a woman drawn together by sexual desire and torn apart by the disaster it entails. Both novels were badly bowdlerised for serial publication, but even so, they shocked British society and Hardy was terribly abused for being "filthy".

Partly because of the reception of *Tess* and *Jude*, partly because of his preference for poetry, Hardy announced in 1896 that *Jude* was his last novel, and turned with relief to the writing of vigorously intellectual and experimental lyrical poetry considered by many critics at least as great as his novels. His career is thus divided sharply between his Victorian novels and his post-Victorian poetry. One poetic work, requires attention, his gigantic epic drama, *The Dynasts*, published in three parts in 1903, 1906 and 1908. This tremendous work, set in the Napoleonic Wars, is the capstone of his career and shows most clearly his idea of the Immanent Will working itself out in human affairs.

In 1914, two years after the death of his first wife, he remarried, this time to a woman much younger than himself with whom he spent a happy old age. The public had long since stopped calling his last novel *Jude the Obscene* "filthy" and his final years were full of honours: he succeeded Tennyson and Meredith as president of the Society of Authors. He died of a cold on January 11, 1928, and his ashes were placed in Westminster Abbey, but his heart was buried with his first wife in Dorset.

## Selections

### *Tess of the D'Urbervilles*

## The Story

It was a proud day when Jack Durbeyfield learnt that he was descended from the famous D'Urberville family. Durbeyfield had never done more work than was necessary to keep his family supplied with meager food and himself with beer, but from that day on he ceased doing even that small amount of work. His wife joined him in thinking that such a high family should live better with less effort, and she persuaded their oldest daughter, Tess, to visit the Stoke-D'Urbervilles, a wealthy family who had assumed the D'Urbervilles name because no one else claimed it. It was her mother's hope that Tess would make a good impression on the rich D'Urbervilles and perhaps a good marriage with one of the sons.

When Tess met her supposed relatives, however, she found only a blind mother and a dapper son who made Tess uncomfortable by his improper remarks to her. The son, Alec, tricked the innocent young Tess into working as a poultry maid, not letting her know that his mother was unaware of Tess' identity. After a short time Tess decided to look for work elsewhere to support her parents and her numerous brothers and sisters. She was innocent, but she knew that Alec meant her no good. Alec, cleverer than she, at last managed to get her alone and possessed her.

When Tess returned to her home and told her mother of her terrible experience, her mother's only worry was that Alec was not going to marry Tess. The poor girl worked in the fields, facing the slander of her associates bravely. Her trouble was made worse by the fact that Alec followed her from place to place, trying to possess her again. By going about to different farms during the harvest season, Tess managed to elude Alec long enough to give birth to her baby without his knowledge. The baby did not live long, however, and a few months after its death, Tess went to a dairy farm far to the south and worked there as a dairymaid.

At the dairy farm Tess was liked and well treated. Also at the farm was Angel Clare, a pastor's son who had rejected the ministry to study farming. It was his wish to own a farm some day, and he was working on different kinds of farms, so that he could learn something of the many kinds of work required of a general farmer. Although all the dairymaids were attracted to Angel, Tess interested him the most. He thought her a beautiful and innocent young maiden, as she was, for it was her innocence that had caused her trouble with Alec.

Tess felt that she herself was wicked, however, and rejected the attentions Angel paid to her. She urged him to turn to one of the other girls for companionship. It was unthinkable that the son of a minister would marry a dairymaid, but Angel did not care much about family tradition. In spite of her pleas, he continued to pay court to Tess. At last, against the wishes of his parents, Angel asked Tess to be his wife. Not only did he love her, but also he realised that a farm girl would be a help to him on his own land. Although Tess was in love with Angel by this time, the memory of her night with Alec made her refuse Angel again and again. At last his insistence, coupled with the written pleas of her parents to marry someone who could help the family financially, won her over, and she agreed to marry him.

On the night before the wedding, which Tess had postponed many times because she felt unworthy, she wrote Angel a letter, telling everything about herself and Alec. She slipped the letter under his door, sure that when he read it he would renounce her forever. But in the morning Angel acted as tenderly as before and Tess loved him more than ever for his forgiving nature. When she realised that Angel had not found the letter, she attempted to tell him about her past. Angel only teased her about wanting to confess, thinking that such a pure girl could have no black sins in her history. They were married without Angel's learning about Alec and her dead baby.

On their wedding night Angel told Tess about an evening of debauchery in his own past. Tess forgave him and then told about her past with Alec, thinking that he would forgive her as she had him. But such was not the case. Angel was at first stunned, and then so hurt that he could not even speak to Tess. Finally he told her that she was not the woman he loved, the one he had married, but a stranger with whom he could not live, at least for the present. He took her to her home and left her there. Then he went to his home and on to Brazil, where he planned to buy a farm. At first neither Tess nor Angel told their parents the reason for their separation. When Tess finally told her mother, that ignorant woman blamed Tess for losing her husband by confessing something he need never have known.

Angel had left Tess some money and some jewels which had been given to him by his godmother. The jewels Tess put in a bank; the money she spent on her parents. When it was gone, her family went hungry once more, for her father still thought himself too high-born to work for a living. Tess again went from farm to farm, doing hard labour in the fields in order to get enough food to keep herself and her family alive.

While she was working in the fields, she met Alec again. He had met Angel's minister father and, repenting his evil ways, had become an itinerant preacher. The sight of Tess, for whom he had always lusted, caused a lapse in his new religious fervour, and he began to pursue her once more. Frightened, Tess wrote to Angel, sending the letter to his parents to forward to him. She told Angel that she loved him and needed him, that an enemy was pursuing her. She begged him to forgive her and to return to her.

The letter took several months to reach Angel. Meanwhile Alec was so kind to Tess and so generous to her family that she began to relent in her feelings towards him. At last, when she did not receive a reply from Angel, she wrote him a note saying that he was cruel not to forgive her and that now she would not forgive his treatment of her. Then she went to Alec again, living with him as his mistress.

It was thus that Angel found her. He had come to tell her that he had forgiven her and that he still loved her. But when he found her with Alec, he turned away, more hurt than before.

Tess, too, was bitterly unhappy. She now hated Alec because once again he had been the cause of her husband's repudiation of her. Feeling that she could find happiness only if Alec were dead, she stabbed him as he slept. Then she ran out of the house and followed Angel, who was aimlessly walking down a road leading out of the town. When they met and Tess told him what she had done, Angel forgave her everything, even the murder of Alec, and they went on together. They were happy with one another for a few days, even though Angel knew that the authorities would soon find Tess.

When the officers finally found them, Tess was asleep. Angel asked the officers to wait until she awoke. As soon as she opened her eyes, Tess saw the strangers and knew that they had come for her and that she would be hanged, but she was not unhappy. She had had a few days with the husband she truly loved, and now she was ready for her punishment. She stood up bravely and faced her captors. She was not afraid.

## Brief Comment on the Novel

Hardy's *Tess of the D'Urbervilles* is a novel worth reading several times. Each time one reads, he can find something new.

First, one can find Hardy's sympathy for Tess. In his description, Tess was an innocent and pure girl. She was also industrious, working from one place to another. She was considerate, always trying to help her parents to feed the whole family. Throughout the book, Tess is portrayed as a symbol of rural innocence and closeness to nature.

Second, one can find that Tess was firmly controlled by fate. No matter how she tried to gain happiness, she could not get it. No matter how she tried to get away from Alec, she could not free herself. No matter how she tried to prove that she loved Angel Clare, she could not make him understand her. Though Angel Clare returned to her, she could not really enjoy the love. Her misfortunes are hardly ever of her own doing.

Third, this novel is somewhat modernistic. The phenomenon Hardy described was much ahead of his time, quite similar to that of today. In some sense, in the eyes of some people, Tess was not moral when she killed Alec. As a matter of fact, she became Alec's mistress for the sake of money. So in this sense, Tess was not pure and innocent. In light of this view Tess' chastity was also questionable. One can doubt Hardy's motive when he added the subtitle of this novel as *A Pure Woman*.

### Chapter XIV
### Maiden No More

It was a hazy sunrise in August. The denser nocturnal vapours, attacked by the warm beams, were dividing and shrinking into isolated fleeces[1] within hollows and coverts[2], where they waited till they should be dried away to nothing.

The sun, on account of the mist, had a curious sentient, personal look, demanding the masculine pronoun for its adequate expression. His present aspect, coupled with the lack of all human forms in the scene, explained the old-time heliolatries[3] in a moment. One could feel that a saner religion had never prevailed under the sky. The luminary[4] was a golden-haired, beaming, mild-eyed, God-like creature, gazing down in the vigour and intentness of youth upon an earth that was brimming with interest for him.

His light, a little later, broke through chinks of cottage shutters, throwing stripes like red-hot pokers upon cupboards, chests of drawers, and other furniture within; and awakening harvesters who were not already astir.

But of all ruddy things that morning the brightest were two broad arms of painted wood, which rose from the margin of a yellow cornfield hard by Marlott village. They, with two others below, formed the revolving Maltess cross[5] of the reaping-machine, which had been brought to the field on the previous evening to be ready for operations this day. The paint with which they were smeared, intensified in hue by the sunlight, imparted to them a look of having been dipped in liquid fire.

The field had already been "opened", that is to say, a lane a few feet wide had been hand-cut through the wheat along the whole circumference of the field, for the first passage of the horses and machine.

Two groups, one of men and lads, the other of women, had come down the lane just at the hour when the shadows of the eastern hedge-top struck the west hedge midway, so that the heads of the groups were enjoying sunrise while their feet were still in the dawn. They disappeared from the lane between the two stone posts which flanked the nearest field-gate.

Presently there arose from within a ticking like the love-making of the grasshopper. The machine had begun, and a moving concatenation of three horses and the aforesaid long rickety machine was visible over the gate, a driver sitting upon one of the hauling horses, and an attendant on the seat of the implement. Along one side of the field the whole wain[6] went, the arms of the mechanical reaper revolving slowly, till it passed down the hill quite out of sight. In a minute it came up on the other side of the field at the same equable pace; the glistening brass star in the forehead of the fore horse first catching the eye as it rose into view over the stubble, then the bright arms, and then the whole machine.

The narrow lane of stubble encompassing the field grew wider with each circuit, and the standing corn was reduced to a smaller area as the morning wore on. Rabbits, hares, snakes, rats, mice, retreated inwards as into a fastness[7], unaware of the ephemeral nature of their refuge, and of the doom that awaited them later in the day when, their covert shrinking to a more and more horrible narrowness, they were huddled together, friends and foes, till the last few yards of upright wheat fell also under the teeth of the unerring reaper, and they were every one put to death by the sticks and stones of the harvesters.

The reaping-machine left the fallen corn behind it in little heaps, each heap being of the quantity for a sheaf; and upon these the active binders in the rear laid their hands—mainly women, but some of them men in print shirts and trousers supported round their waists by leather straps, rendering useless the two buttons behind, which twinkled and bristled with sunbeams at every movement of each wearer, as if they were a pair of eyes in the small of his back.

But those of the other sex were the most interesting of this company of binders, by reason of the charm which is acquired by woman when she becomes part and parcel of outdoor nature, and is not merely an object set down therein as at ordinary times. A field-man is a personality afield; a field-woman is a portion of the field; she had somehow lost her own margin, imbibed the essence of her surrounding and assimilated herself with it.

The women—or rather girls, for they were mostly young—wore drawn cotton bonnets with great flapping curtains to keep off the sun, and gloves to prevent their hands being wounded by the stubble. There was one wearing a pale pink jacket, another in a cream-coloured tight-sleeved gown, another in a petticoat as red as the arms of the reaping-machine; and others, older, in the brown-rough "wropper" or over-all—the old-established and most appropriate dress of the field-woman, which the young ones were abandoning. This morning the eye returns involuntarily to the girl in the pink cotton jacket, she being the most flexuous and finely-drawn figure of them all. But her bonnet is pulled so far over her brow that none of her face is disclosed while she binds, though her complexion may be guessed from a stray twine or two of dark brown hair which extends below the curtain of her bonnet. Perhaps one reason why she seduces casual attention is that she never courts it, though the other women often gaze around them.

Her binding proceeds with clock-like monotony. From the sheaf last finished she draws a handful of ears, patting their tips with her left palm to bring them even. Then stooping low she moves forward, gathering the corn with both hands against her knees, and pushing her left gloved hand under the bundle to meet the right on the other side, holding the corn in an embrace like that of a lover. She brings the ends of the bond together, and kneels on the sheaf while she ties it, beating back her skirts now and then when lifted by the breeze. A bit of her naked arm is visible between the buff leather of the gauntlet and the sleeve of her gown; and as the day wears on its feminine smoothness becomes scarified by the stubble, and bleeds.

At intervals she stands up to rest, and to retie her disarranged apron, or to pull her bonnet straight. Then one can see the oval face of a handsome young woman with deep dark eyes and long heavy clinging tresses, which seem to clasp in a beseeching way anything they fall against. The cheeks are paler, the teeth more regular, the red lips thinner than is usual in a country-bred girl.

It is Tess Durbeyfield, otherwise D'Urberville, somewhat changed—the same, but not the same; at the present stage of her existence living as a stranger and an alien here, though it was no strange land that she was in. After a long seclusion she had come to a resolve to undertake outdoor work in her native village, the busiest season of the year in the agricultural world having arrived, and nothing that she could do within the house being so remunerative for the time as harvesting in the fields.

## Notes

1. fleeces: coats of wool covering sheep, here used to describe the white patch of mist
2. coverts: covered places
3. heliolatry: worship of the sun
4. luminary: a source of light, here referring to the sun
5. Maltess cross: the badge of the Knights of Malta, a cross with two-pointed expanding broad limbs
6. wain: a team and implements used in cultivation of land, a wagon for hay or other agricultural produce
7. fastness: fortress

## For Study and Discussion

1. This selection opens with a minute description of the sun. How do you like this description? Why is it important here?
2. The author is a master hand in describing farm work. He seems to know so well about the details of field work. What kind of feeling does his description arouse in you?
3. Give a description of what Tess is like in your own words. If you are asked to choose one paragraph describing her work in the field, which paragraph would you choose? Why?

### Chapter XXXV
### The Woman Pays

Her narrative ended; even its reassertions and secondary explanations were done. Tess' voice throughout had hardly risen higher than its opening tone; there had been no exculpatory phrase of any kind, and she had not wept.

…

Clare performed the irrelevant act of stirring the fire; the intelligence had not even yet got to the bottom of him. After stirring the embers he rose to his feet; all the force of her disclosure had imparted itself now. His face had withered. In the strenuousness of his concentration he treadled fitfully on the floor. He could not, by any contrivance, think closely enough; that was the meaning of his vague movement. When he spoke it was in the most inadequate, commonplace voice of the many varied tones she had heard from him.

"Tess!"

"Yes, dearest."

"Am I to believe this? From your manner I am to take it as true. O you cannot be out of your mind! You ought to be! Yet you are not…My wife, my Tess—nothing in you warrants such a supposition as that?"

"I am not out of my mind," she said.

"And yet—" He looked vacantly at her, to resume with dazed senses: "Why didn't you tell me before? Ah, yes, you would have told me, in a way—but I hindered you, I remember!"

These and other of his words were nothing but the perfunctory babble of the surface while the depths remained paralysed. He turned away, and bent over a chair. Tess followed him to the middle of the room, where he was, and stood there staring at him with eyes that did not weep. Presently she slid down upon her knees beside his foot, and from this position she crouched in a heap.

"In the name of our love, forgive me!" she whispered with a dry mouth. "I have forgiven you for the same!"

And, as he did not answer, she said again—

"Forgive me as you are forgiven! *I* forgive *you*, Angel."

"You—yes, you do."

"But you do not forgive me?"

"O, Tess, forgiveness does not apply to the case! You were one person; now you are another. My God—how can forgiveness meet such a grotesque—prestidigitation as that!"

He paused, contemplating this definition; then suddenly broke into horrible laughter—as unnatural and ghastly as a laugh in hell.

"Don't—don't! It kills me quite, that!" she shrieked. "O have mercy upon me—have mercy!"

He did not answer; and, sickly white, she jumped up.

"Angel, Angel! What do you mean by that laugh?" she cried out. "Do you know what this is to me?"

He shook his head.

"I have been hoping, longing, praying, to make you happy! I have thought what joy it will be to do it, what an unworthy wife I shall be if I do not! That's what I have felt, Angel!"

"I know that."

"I thought, Angel, that you loved me—me, my very self! If it is I you do love, O how can it be that you look and speak so? It frightens me! Having begun to love you, I love you forever—in all changes, in all disgraces, because you are yourself. I ask no more. Then how can you, O my own husband, stop loving me?"

"I repeat, the woman I have been loving is not you."

"But who?"

"Another woman in your shape."

She perceived in his words the realisation of her own apprehensive foreboding in former times. He looked upon her as a species of impostor; a guilty woman in the guise of an innocent one. Terror was upon her white face as she saw it; her cheek was flaccid, and her mouth had almost the aspect of a round little hole. The horrible sense of his view of her so deadened her that she staggered, and he stepped forward, thinking she was going to fall.

"Sit down, sit down," he said gently. "You are ill; and it is natural that you should be."

She did sit down, without knowing where she was, that strained look still upon her face, and her eyes such as to make his flesh creep.

"I don't belong to you any more, then; do I, Angel?" she asked helplessly. "It is not me, but another woman like me that he loved, he says."

The image raised caused her to take pity upon herself as one who was ill-used. Her eyes filled as she regarded her position further; she turned round and burst into a flood of self-sympathetic tears.

Clare was relieved at this change, for the effect on her of what had happened was beginning to be a trouble to him only less than the woe of the disclosure itself. He waited patiently, apathetically, till the violence of her grief had worn itself out, and her rush of weeping had lessened to a catching gasp at internals.

"Angel," she said suddenly in her natural tones, the insane, dry voice of terror having left her now. "Angel, am I too wicked for you and me to live together?"

"I have not been able to think what we can do."

"I shan't ask you to let me live with you, Angel, because I have no right to! I shall not write to mother and sisters to say we be married, as I said I would do; and I shan't finish the good-hussif[1] I cut out and meant to make while we were in lodgings."

"Shan't you?"

"No, I shan't do anything, unless you order me to; and if you go away from me I shall not follow 'ee; and if you never speak to me any more I shall not ask why, unless you tell me I may."

"And if I do order you to do anything?"

"I will obey you like your wretched slave, even if it is to lie down and die."

"You are very good. But it strikes me that there is a want of harmony between your present mood of self-sacrifice and your past mood of self-preservation."

These were the first words of antagonism. To fling elaborate sarcasms at Tess, however, was much like flinging them at a dog or cat. The charms of their subtlety passed by her unappreciated, and she only received them as inimical sounds which meant that anger ruled. She remained mute, not knowing that he was smothering his affection for her. She hardly observed that a tear descended slowly upon his cheek, a tear so large that it magnified the pores of the skin over which it rolled, like the object lens of a microscope. Meanwhile reillumination as to the terrible and total change that her confession had wrought in his life, in his universe, returned to him, and he tried desperately to advance among the new conditions in which he stood. Some consequent action was necessary; yet what?

"Tess," he said, as gently as he could speak, "I cannot stay—in this room—just now. I will walk out a little way."

He quietly left the room, and the two glasses of wine that he had poured out for their supper—one for her, one for him—remained on the table untasted. This was what their Agape[2] had come to. At tea, two or three hours earlier, they had, in the freakishness of affection, drunk from one cup.

The closing of the door behind him, gently as it had been pulled to, roused Tess from her stupor. He was gone; she could not stay. Hastily flinging her cloak around her she opened the door and followed, putting out the candles as if she were never coming back. The rain was over and the night was now clear.

She was soon close at his heels, for Clare walked slowly and without purpose. His form beside her light gray figure looked black, sinister, and forbidding, and she felt as sarcasm the touch of the jewels of which she had been momentarily so proud. Clare turned at hearing her footsteps, but his recognition of her presence seemed to make no difference in him, and he went on over the five yawning arches of the great bridge in front of the house.

The place to which they had travelled today was in the same valley as Talbothays, but some miles lower down the river; and the surroundings being open, she kept easily in sight of him. Away from the house the road wound through the meads, and along these she followed Clare without any attempt to come up with him or to attract him, but with dumb and vacant fidelity.

At last, however, her listless walk brought her up alongside him, and still he said nothing. The cruelty of fooled honesty is often great after enlightenment, and it was mighty in Clare now. The outdoor air had apparently taken away from him all tendency to act on impulse; she knew that he saw her without irradiation—in all her bareness.

He was still intently thinking, and her companionship had now insufficient power to break or divert the strain of thought. What a weak thing her presence must have become to him! She could not help addressing Clare.

"What have I done—what *have* I done! I have not told of anything that interferes with or belies my love for you. You don't think I planned it, do you? It is in your own mind what you are angry at. Angel; it is not in me. O, it is not in me, and I am not that deceitful woman you think me!"

"H'm—well. Not deceitful, my wife; but not the same. No, not the same. But do not make me reproach you. I have sworn that I will not; and I will do everything to avoid it."

But she went on pleading in her distraction; and perhaps said things that would have been better left to silence.

"Angel!—Angel! I was a child—a child when it happened! I knew nothing of men."

"You were more sinned against than sinning[3], that I admit."

"Then will you not forgive me?"

"I do forgive you, but forgiveness is not all."

"And love me?"

To this qucstion hc did not answcr.

"O Angel—my mother says that it sometimes happens so—she knows several cases where they were worse than I, and the husband had not minded it much—has got over it at least. And yet the woman has not loved him as I do you!"

"Don't, Tess; don't argue. Different societies, different manners. You almost make me say you are an unapprehending peasant woman, who have never been initiated into the proportions of social things. You don't know what you say."

"I am only a peasant by position, not by nature!"

She spoke with an impulse to anger, but it went as it came.

"So much the worse for you. I think that parson who unearthed your pedigree would have done better if he had held his tongue. I cannot help associating your decline as a family with this other fact—of your want of firmness. Decrepit families imply decrepit wills, decrepit conduct. Heaven, why did you give me a handle for despising you more by informing me of your descend! Here was I thinking you a new-sprung child of nature; there were you, the belated seedling of an effete aristocracy!"

"Lots of families are as bad as mine in that! Retty's family were once large landowners, and so were Dairyman Billett's. And the Debbyhouses, who now are carters, were once the De Bayeux family. You find such as I everywhere; 'tis a feature of our county, and I can't help it."

"So much the worse for the county."

She took these reproaches in their bulk simply, not in their particulars; he did not love her as he had loved her hitherto, and to all else she was indifferent.

## Notes

1. good-hussif: (dialect) a bag holding needle and thread
2. Agape: (Greek) love-feast, as held by the early Christians
3. more sinned against than sinning: cf Shakespeare's *King Lear*, Act III, Scene II: "A man more sinned against than sinning."

## For Study and Discussion

1. In this selection, Tess is confessing to Angel what she suffered from and asks to be forgiven. What is Angel's view of chastity? What do you think of him? If you were Angel, what would you do? What is the author's view of chastity?
2. What does Angel mean by saying that Tess changed from self-preservation to self-sacrifice? What of Tess' words make him say so?
3. In this selection, there is an episode talking about the difference between Angel's class and Tess' class. On this question, what is Angel's viewpoint? What is Tess'? What does it mean when Tess says "I am only a peasant by position, not by nature!"?
4. The title of this chapter is "The Woman Pays". How do you understand it? Do you think it fair in such a case?

## The Darkling Thrush[1]

I leant upon a coppice gate[2]
When Frost was spectre-gray[3],
And Winter's dregs[4] made desolate
The weakening eye of day.[5]
The tangled bine-stems[6] scored the sky[7]
Like strings of broken lyres,
And all mankind that haunted nigh[8]
Had sought their household fires.

The land's sharp features seemed to be
The Century's corpse[9] outleant[10],
His crypt[11] the cloudy canopy[12],
The wind his death-lament[13].
The ancient pulse of germ[14] and birth
Was shrunken hard and dry,
And every spirit[15] upon earth
Seemed fervourless as I.

At once a voice arose among
The bleak twigs overhead
In a full-hearted evensong[16]
Of joy illimited;
An aged thrush, frail, gaunt, and small,
In blast-beruffled plume,[17]
Had chosen thus to fling his soul[18]
Upon the growing gloom.

So little cause for carolings[19]
Of such ecstatic sound
Was written[20] on terrestrial[21] things
Afar or nigh[22] around,
That I could think there trembled through
His happy good-night air[23]
Some blessed[24] Hope, whereof he knew
And I was unaware.

## Notes

1. This poem is chosen from *Poems of the Past and Present* (1902). It was written in four 8-line stanzas rhyming ababcdcd with the odd lines in iambic tetrameter, while the even lines in iambic trimeter.
2. coppice gate: the gate leading to a small wood or thicket
3. spectre-gray: gray or white as a ghost. spectre: ghost
4. dregs: last remains
5. The weakening eye of day: the dimming sun. Here "eye of day" referring to the sun.
6. tangled bine-stems: twining stems of shrubs
7. scored the sky: marked the sky with lines
8. nigh: near
9. Century's corpse: The century was compared to a corpse for the poem was written on December 31, 1900, the last day of the 19th century.
10. outleant: leaning out (of its coffin)
11. crypt: the underground chamber or vault under a church, used as a burial place
12. canopy: referring to the sky
13. death-lament: dirge
14. germ: the seed or bud
15. every spirit: every breath of life
16. evensong: evening song
17. In blast-beruffled plume: with his feathers ruffled by the wind
18. fling his soul: pour out all his emotional energy
19. carolings: singing joyously
20. written: marked
21. terrestrial: earthly
22. Afar or nigh: far or near
23. air: music, melody
24. blessed: blissful

## For Study and Discussion

1. What is the setting of the poem?
2. Discuss the imagery of this poem.
3. There is a mental change in this poem. Where does it happen? Why?
4. What's the poet's attitude towards the past century? And what's the poet's attitude towards the coming century?

# Chapter 21

# Oscar Wilde

## Life and Works

Oscar Wilde (1854–1900) was born in Dublin and attended Trinity College in Dublin. His full name is Oscar Fingal O'Flahertie Wills Wilde. His father was a distinguished surgeon in Dublin. After majoring in classical studies at Trinity College, Oscar Wilde won a scholarship to Oxford where he established a brilliant academic record. At Oxford he received the influence of the aesthetic theories of John Ruskin (Professor of Fine Arts then) and Walter Pater, under whose influence the "art for art's sake" movement became the foundation of Wilde's literary creation and of his flamboyant and hedonistic lifestyle and costume style.

After graduation in 1878, Wilde settled down in London, where his fellow Irishmen, George Bernard Shaw and William Butler Yeats, were also to settle. Here Wilde quickly established himself both as a writer and as a spokesman for the school of "art for art's sake". In Wilde's view, this school included not only French poets and critics but also a line of English poets going back through Rossetti and the Pre-Raphaelites to Keats. In 1882 he visited America for a long and successful lecture tour during which he startled audiences by airing the gospel of the "aesthetic movement".

As a spokesman for aestheticism, Wilde had many gifts. He was an eloquent conversationalist and a master of paradoxical utterance, for example, "I can resist anything except temptation." Yeats thus talked of him after first listening to him, "I never before heard a man talking with perfect sentences, as if he had written them all overnight with labour and yet all spontaneous."

In addition to his witty conversation, Wilde had the gifts of an actor who delighted in gaining attention. He had discovered, early, that a flamboyant style of dress was one of the most effective means of gaining attention. Like the dandies of the earlier decades of the 19th century, Wilde favoured colourful costumes in marked contrast to the sober black suits of the late-Victorian middle class. A green carnation in his buttonhole and velvet knee breeches became for Wilde badges of his youthful iconoclasm, and even when he approached middle age, he continued to emphasise the gap between generations.

Wilde's success for 17 years in England and America were of course not limited to his self-advertising stunts as a dandy. In his writings he excelled in a variety of genres: as a critic of literature and of society ("The Decay of Lying" and "The Soul of Man Under Socialism"), and also as a novelist, poet and dramatist. His novel, *The Picture of Dorian Gray*, a Gothic tale that makes one's hair stand on end, created a sensation when it was published in 1891. In the preface to this novel he set out his artistic principle: "There is no such a thing as a moral or an immoral book. Books are well written or badly written. That is all." It is a strikingly ingenious story of a handsome young man and his selfish pursuit of sensual pleasures. Until the end of the novel he himself remains fresh and healthy in appearance while his portrait mysteriously changes into a horrible image of his corrupted soul. Although the preface to the novel emphasises that art and morality are totally separate, in the novel itself, at least in its later chapters, Wilde seemed to be expounding a moral lesson on the evils of self-regarding hedonism.

As a poet Wilde felt overshadowed by the Victorian predecessors whom he admired: Browning, Rossetti and Swinburne. He had trouble finding his own voice in poetry. He also wrote fairy tales for children and other stories. His best years of creation were the 1890s, especially in drama. His most outstanding achievements were his comedies, which were performed in London and New York from 1892 to 1895, including *Lady Windermere's Fan*, *A Woman of No Importance*, *An Ideal Husband* and *The Importance of Being Earnest*.

But at the same time a disaster was brewing. By the spring of 1895 his triumphant success suddenly came to an end when Wilde was accused, arrested and sentenced to jail for two years. Wilde had been married for several years and was the father of two children at the time of his meeting, in 1891, with a handsome young poet, Lord Alfred Douglas, with whom he established a relationship, which turned out to be a disaster for him. In 1895, Lord Alfred's father, the Marquis of Queensberry, accused Wilde of homosexuality. Though he recklessly sued for libel, Wilde lost the case and was thereupon arrested and convicted for what was then on the statute books a serious criminal offense. The revulsion of feeling against him was violent in both England and America. The aesthetic movement itself suffered a severe setback not only with the public but among writers as well.

His two years in jail led Wilde to write two sober and emotionally high-pitched works, his poem, *The Ballad of Reading Gaol*, and his prose confession, *De Profoundis* (meaning *From the Depth* in English), a defense and confession of himself.

After he was released, he divorced and went bankrupt. He went into exile in France and died three years later in a Paris hotel.

Wilde was buried in Paris in the same cemetery as the poet, Charles Baudelaire, whose *Fleurs du Mal* had profoundly affected his attitude towards life and literature.

## Brief Comment

No one can really escape from life and social reality. They just reflect it from different angles and by different means. If one reads the works carefully, one might finally find that Oscar Wilde was as a matter of fact making his criticism of the society in his own way, a way different from that of Dickens and other writers. Oscar voiced his reaction against the high-minded, serious preoccupations of the middle class in Victorian England in the form of search for beauty. Oscar's satiric weapons were aimed against the aristocracy, a class on the verge of ruin, clinging, absurdly, to his artistic form and standards. He did not try to probe the economic and political problems. Though his irony did not bring about any change, he, as well as others, was preparing the way for new directions in literature at the turn of the century.

## The School of Aestheticism and "Art for Art's Sake"

The school of aestheticism in the last decades of the 19th century in England stemmed from the Pre-Raphaelites and Keats. The foreign influences include French poets such as Theophile Gautier who created the term "art for art's sake" and Paul Verlaine, a poet of French symbolism.

The main figures of the school of aestheticism in England include Walter Pater, Oscar Wilde, Arthur Symons, Earnest Dowson, John Davidson and Aubrey Beardsley.

They had much in common. According to them, literature and art does not reflect life and social reality. They escaped from life and reality because they were disgusted with society and tried to protest against the sordid life. The result of this escapism was that they cried out "art for art's sake". By this they meant a divorce of literature and art from morality, paying attention to only artistic form, neglecting content and thought of a work. One can find and summarise some ideas about this school after he reads the preface to *The Picture of Dorian Gray.*

## Selections

### *The Picture of Dorian Gray*

## The Story

One day, in his London studio, Basil Hallward was putting a few last finishing touches on a portrait of his handsome young friend, Dorian Gray. Lord Henry Wotton, a caller, indolently watched the painter at work. In reply to his friend's admiration for the painting, the artist explained that Dorian was his ideal of youth. For this reason he asked Lord Henry never to meet Dorian because the older man's influence on the boy would be absolute and evil.

While they were talking, Dorian himself came to the studio, and he and Lord Henry met, much against Hallward's wishes. Half seriously, half jokingly, Lord Henry began to exert his influence on Dorian. Hallward signed the portrait and announced it was finished. When Lord Henry offered to buy the picture, the painter said it was not his property, and it belonged to Dorian, to whom he was presenting it. Looking at his portrait, after listening to Lord Henry's witty conversation, Dorian grew sad. He would become old and wrinkled, he said, while the picture would remain the same. He wished, instead, that the portrait might grow old while he remained forever young. He said he would give his soul to keep his youth.

Dorian and Lord Henry became close friends. One of the gifts Lord Henry gave the boy was a book about a young man who attempted to realise in his brief lifetime all the passions of man's history. Dorian made the book a pattern for his own life, and the first lesson from its pages was the lesson of love. In a third-rate theatre he saw Sibyl Vane, a young actress who played the role of Juliet with such sincerity and charm that he fell in love with her on the spot. After he had met her, Dorian dreamed of taking her away from the cheap theatrical troupe and making her a great actress who would thrill the world. One night he took Lord Henry to watch her performance. That night Sibyl was listless and wooden, so uninspired in her acting that the audience hissed her. When Dorian went to her dressing room after the final curtain, she explained that before meeting him she had considered acting her only reality. Now she said, Dorian's love had taught her what reality actually was, and she could no longer act. Dorian coldly and cruelly told her she had killed his love and he never intended to see her again.

In the meantime, Hallward had delivered the painting to Dorian. When the young man returned to his home after the theatre that night he saw that the appearance of his portrait had changed. There was a new, faint line of cruelty about the mouth. Looking at his own features in a mirror, he found no such line on his own lips. His wish had evidently been granted. He would remain young and untouched—the portrait would take on an appearance of experience and age.

Disturbed, he resolved to reform, to see no more of Lord Henry, to ask Sibyl Vane's forgiveness and marry her. Accordingly, he wrote her a passionate letter declaring his love. The next morning, however, Lord Henry visited him before he could post the letter, bringing the news that Sibyl had killed herself in her dressing room the night before.

After his friend had gone, forgetting all his good resolutions Dorian decided on a life of sensation and pleasure. The portrait only was to bear the burden of his shame. That night he attended the opera with Lord Henry. The next day, when Basil Hallward attempted to reason with him over scandalous reports beginning to circulate, Dorian refused to show any emotion over Sibyl's suicide. His part in her tragic story would never be revealed, for she had known him only as Prince Charming. Before he left, Hallward asked to see his painting. Dorian refused to show it. In sudden rage, he shouted that he never wished to see Hallward again. Later he hung the portrait in an old schoolroom upstairs, locked the door, and put the key where only he could find it.

London continued to gossip about the friendship of Lord Henry and Dorian Gray. The young man was suspected of strange vices, and gentlemen walked out of their club rooms when he entered them. He was invited to fewer balls and parties at country houses. Many of his former friends refused to recognise him when they met. It was reported he had been seen in low dives with drunken sailors and thieves. Meanwhile Dorian's features did not change; only the portrait reflected his life of crime and debauchery. Dorian's life, like that of the hero in the book Lord Henry had given him, became a frenzied quest for fresh experiences and new sensations. In turn, he became interested in religious rituals, perfumes, music, jewels. He frequented opium dens. He had sordid affairs with women. His features in the portrait became the terrible record of his life.

On the eve of Dorian's thirty-eighth birthday, Basil Hallward visited him again. Though the two had been estranged for years, Hallward came in a last attempt to persuade Dorian to change his dissolute ways. He was still unable to believe many of the stories he had heard about Dorian. With a bitter laugh, Dorian said that Hallward should see what he had truly become. He took Hallward to the schoolroom and unveiled the portrait. The artist was horrified, for only by signature could he identify his own handiwork. In anger that he had betrayed his true self to his former friend, Dorian seized a knife which lay nearby and stabbed Hallward in the neck and back.

Dorian relocked the door and went down to the drawing room. Because Hallward had intended to leave for Paris that night, Dorian knew the painter would not be missed for some time. Removal of the body, he decided, was not enough. He wanted it completely destroyed. Suddenly he thought of Alan Campbell, a young chemist who had once been his intimate. By threatening the young scientist with exposure for some secret crime, Dorian forced Campbell to destroy the body with fire and chemicals. After that night, the hands of the portrait were smeared with blood.

Late one night, commonly dressed, Dorian visited an opium den. As he was leaving the place, a drunken woman addressed him as Prince Charming. A sailor followed him out. The sailor was James Vane, Sibyl's brother, who had sworn revenge on his sister's betrayer. The sailor would have killed Dorian but for the fact that he looked so young. Sibyl had committed suicide eighteen years before, and Dorian seemed no more than twenty years old. When Vane, convinced that Dorian could not have known his sister, returned to the den, the woman told him that Dorian Gray had ruined her many years before, and that he had not changed in appearance since then.

Some time later, at his country home, Dorian saw James Vane watching him outside a window. During a hunt on the estate Vane was accidentally shot and killed. In the meantime, Alan Campbell had committed suicide under strange circumstances, and Basil Hallward's disappearance was being investigated.

Back in London, Dorian, having decided to destroy the picture which stood as an awful record of his guilt, went to the old schoolroom. The portrait now had an appearance of cunning and triumph. Using the knife with which he had murdered Basil Hallward, Dorian stabbed the frightful portrait. The servants in the house heard a horrible cry of agony. When they forced open the locked door of the room, they found, hanging on the wall, a fine portrait of their master as he had always looked. On the floor was a dead body, withered, wrinkled, in evening dress, with a knife in its breast. Only by his jewelry did they recognise Dorian Gray, who, in his desperate attempt to kill his conscience, had killed himself.

## The Preface

The artist is the creator of beautiful things. To reveal art and conceal the artist is art's aim.

The critic is he who can translate into another manner or a new material his impression of beautiful things. The highest, as the lowest, form of criticism is a mode of autobiography.

Those who find ugly meaning in beautiful things are corrupt without being charming. This is a fault. Those who find beautiful meanings in beautiful things are the cultivated. For these there is hope. They are the elect to whom beautiful things mean only Beauty.

There is no such thing as a moral or an immoral book. Books are well written, or badly written. That is all.

The nineteenth-century dislike of Realism is the rage of Caliban[1] seeing his own face in a glass. The nineteenth-century dislike of Romanticism is the rage of Caliban not seeing his own face in a glass.

The moral life of man forms part of the subject matter of the artist, but the morality of art consists in the perfect use of an imperfect medium.

No artist desires to prove anything. Even things that are true can be proved. No artist has ethical sympathies. An ethical sympathy in an artist is an unpardonable mannerism of style.

No artist is ever morbid. The artist can express everything.

Thought and language are to the artist instruments of an art.

Vice and virtue are to the artist materials for an art. From the point of view of form, the type of all the arts is the art of the musician. From the point of view of feeling, the actor's craft is the type.

All art is at once surface and symbol.

Those who go beneath the surface do so at their peril.

Those who read the symbol do so at their peril. It is the spectator, and not life, that art really mirrors.

Diversity of opinion about a work of art shows that the work is new, complex and vital.

When critics disagree the artist is in accord with himself.

We can forgive a man for making a useful thing as long as he does not admire it. The only excuse for making a useless thing is that one admires it intensely.

All art is quite useless.

## Chapter X

He sighed, and, having poured himself out some tea, opened Lord Henry's note. It was simply to say that he sent him round the evening paper, and a book that might interest him, and that he would be at the club at eight-fifteen. He opened *The St. James's*[2] languidly, and looked through it. A red pencil-mark on the fifth page caught his eye. It drew attention to the following paragraph:

> INQUEST ON AN ACTRESS.—An inquest was held this morning at the Bell Tavern, Hoxton Road, by Mr. Danby, the District Coroner, on the body of Sibyl Vane, a young actress recently engaged at the Royal Theatre, Holborn. A verdict of death by misadventure was returned. Considerable sympathy was expressed for the mother of the deceased, who was greatly affected during the giving of her own evidence, and that of Dr. Birrell, who had made the post-mortem examination of the deceased.

He frowned, and, tearing the paper in two, went across the room and flung the pieces away. How ugly it all was! And how horribly real ugliness made things! He felt a little annoyed with Lord Henry for having marked it with red pencil. Victor[3] might have read it. The man knew more than enough English for that.

Perhaps he had read it, and had begun to suspect something. And yet, what did it matter? What had Dorian Gray to do with Sibyl Vane's death? There was nothing to fear. Dorian Gray had not killed her.

His eye fell on the yellow book that Lord Henry had sent him. What was it, he wondered. He went towards the little pearl-coloured octagonal stand, that had always looked to him like the work of some strange Egyptian bees that wrought in silver, and taking up the volume, flung himself into an armchair, and began to turn over the leaves. After a few minutes he became absorbed. It was the strangest book that he had ever read. It seemed to him that in exquisite raiment, and to the delicate sound of flutes, the sins of the world were passing in dumb show before him. Things that he had dimly dreamed of were suddenly made real to him. Things of which he had never dreamed were gradually revealed.

It was a novel without a plot, and with only one character, being, indeed, simply a psychological study of a certain young Parisian, who spent his life trying to realise in the nineteenth century all the passions and modes of thought that belonged to every century except his own, and to sum up, as it were, in himself the various moods through which the world-spirit had ever passed, loving for their mere artificiality those renunciations that men have unwisely called virtue, as much as those natural rebellions that wise men still call sin. The style in which it was written was that curious jewelled style, vivid and obscure at once, full of argot[4] and of archaisms, of technical expressions and of elaborate paraphrases, that characterises the work of some of the finest artists of the French school of symbolists[5]: There were in it metaphors as monstrous as orchids, and as subtle in colour. The life of the senses was described in the terms of mystical philosophy. One hardly knew at times whether one was reading the spiritual ecstasies of some medieval saint or the morbid confessions of a modern sinner. It was a poisonous book. The heavy odour of incense seemed to cling about its pages and to trouble the brain. The mere cadence of the sentences, the subtle monotony of their music, so full as it was of complex refrains and movements elaborately repeated, produced in the mind of the lad, as he passed from chapter to chapter, a form of reverie, a malady of dreaming, that made him unconscious of the falling day and creeping shadows.

Cloudless, and pierced by one solitary star, a copper-green sky gleamed through the windows. He read on by its wan light till he could read no more. Then, after his valet had reminded him several times of the lateness of the hour, he got up, and, going into the next room, placed the book on the little Florentine table that always stood at his bedside, and began to dress for dinner.

It was almost nine o'clock before he reached the club, where he found Lord Henry sitting alone, in the morning-room, looking very much bored.

"I am so sorry, Harry," he cried, "but really it is entirely your fault. That book you sent me so fascinated me that I forgot how the time was going."

"Yes. I thought you would like it," replied his host, rising from his chair.

"I didn't say I liked it, Harry. I said it fascinated me. There is a great difference."

"Ah, you have discovered that?" murmured Lord Henry. And they passed into the dining-room.

## Notes

1. Caliban: Caliban is a character in Shakespeare's *The Tempest*, who is half man and half monster.
2. *The St. James's*: a London newspaper
3. Victor: Dorian Gray's manservant
4. argot: (from French) slang
5. symbolists: representatives of a literary trend in the last decades of the 19th century

## For Study and Discussion

1. Lord Henry has sent Dorian Gray a book in which the red pencil-mark draws Dorian's attention. What is his response to this note? Why does he respond in this way?
2. Dorian is absorbed in the book. What has fascinated him? Why is he late for his appointment with Lord Henry?
3. Keats wrote in *Endymion*, "A thing of beauty is a joy for ever." Wilde wrote in the preface to *The Picture of Dorian Gray*, "The artist is the creator of beautiful things." Can you identify the closeness in their ideas?

# Chapter 22

# George Bernard Shaw

## Life and Works

George Bernard Shaw (1856–1950) is an important figure in the transition from late-Victorian to modern times. He was born in Dublin in 1856, but his family had been English. In 1876, his mother, a musician and music teacher, moved to London to better her teaching career. He followed his mother to London. His family was not rich enough, so he left school and began to work at fourteen. He taught himself through reading. He received influence in music from his mother, so he found employment in writing music reviews in his early career.

He began his career as a novelist, but not successful. He became interested in socialist ideas; in 1884, he even became one of the founders of the Fabian Society which spread the socialist ideas, through peaceful means and gradual reform of the inadequate and unjust social and economic institutions and laws.

Since his novels did not sell and he could find no commercial producer for his early plays, he earned his living as a critic of music, art and the theatre.

He began to write plays in the 1890s, with his own understanding of the function of drama. He was interested in the social problem plays of Henrik Ibsen. In 1891, he showed his alertness to the influences by writing "The Quintessence of Ibsenism". His foreign influence can also be felt in "The Perfect Wagnerite" written in 1898.

In his eyes, the theatre could be used to shake up the middle class and make them reexamine their assumptions about the right and wrong. Plays could contain discussions in which the characters speak on behalf of the playwright and reflect on the false ideas of the majority. So familiar with the theatre conventions, he used clever plotting and theatrical surprises to keep the audience's attention as well as to stress his ideas. He was a master of paradox. He often took a familiar assumption and seemed to stand it on its head so that the good was seen as bad and the bad as, if not good, at least less bad than it at first appeared. His main characters, those who embodied the life force, dazzled the audience with wit and shocked them by taking radical positions.

His first play, *Widowers' Houses*, about the slum landlords, was written in 1885, but not produced until 1892, with scant success. He followed this with *The Philanderer*, a satire on the emancipated woman, and *Mrs. Warren's Profession* (written in 1893 but published in 1898), a treatment of commercialised vice. This play was banned to be performed for its bold treatment of its theme. In order to have a larger readership and audience, he published these and other plays in the book called *Plays Pleasant and Unpleasant* in 1898. In his later published plays, he included long prefaces to talk about his characters, their social background and the problems they had.

His dramatic production was the greatest in the first two decades of the 20th century. He reached dramatic maturity in *Arms and the Man*, a brilliant satire on military glory and antiwar statement, *Candida*, a resolution of a triangular situation by Shaw's ideal woman, *The Man of Destiny*, a mock-heroic skit on Napoleon, and *You Never Can Tell*, a farcical treatment of the new woman. His *Man and Superman* is a depiction of his ideas of the life force. In this play he represented courtship as a war of the sexes and man as the victim of woman, who was the incarnation of nature's purpose and the will to live. *Major Barbara* is an attack on charity as a social good. His *Pygmalion* is a treatment of language and social-class barriers, later adapted into musical comedy entitled *My Fair Lady*. In 1923, he even wrote about Joan of Arc in the play *Saint Joan*.

These plays were all distinguished by their attack upon some time-honoured sham, their juxtaposition of reality and some pretentiously false view. Perhaps because of their slight success on the stage Shaw published them in two series. In the elaborate prefaces to these volumes he commented on the technical and social qualities of the plays, and, further to guide his readers, expanded the stage directions into full descriptions, character sketches and analysis. By this campaign on behalf of the printed play he helped to raise prose drama again to the status of literature.

Shaw continued to publish his plays in book form, and by the aid of prefaces to make them effective propaganda for his views on the art of the theatre and on society. He attacked the illusions of history in *Caesar and Cleopatra*, and of romantic morality in *The Devil's Disciple*. In *John Bull's Other Island* he invented the usual conceptions of Englishman and Irishman, depicting the former as a soft-headed sentimentalist, the latter as a type of practical sense. His arraignment of the British atrocities in Egypt, which occurs in the preface to this play, is one of the most powerful polemical passages in modern English. In *The Doctor's Dilemma* he tilted against the professional humbug that surrounded medical practice and in *Getting Married* against the prudery which concealed the true relation of the sexes.

## Brief Comment

As a playwright, Bernard Shaw created a way to make his plays more popular by publishing them in the form of books. He endowed them with the function of social criticism and reform. He raised the questions for his characters to talk about on the stage and for the audiences to think about, thus causing public attention. He served to contradict the idea that the playwright should merely aim to amuse and entertain. His audiences expected to hear ideas and issues discussed on the stage and thus he opened the way for other less conventional forms of drama.

He was not merely the best comic dramatist of his time but also one of the most significant playwrights in the English language since the 17th century. Some of his greatest works for the stage have a high seriousness and prose beauty that were unmatched by his stage contemporaries. His development of a drama of moral passion and of intellectual conflict and debate, his revivifying of the comedy of manners, and his ventures into symbolic farce and into a theatre of disbelief helped shape the theatre of his time and after. His vast contributions to dramas to English literature made him win the Nobel Prize in Literature in 1925(he refused the award).

## Selections

**_Mrs. Warren's Profession_**

### The Story

The play *Mrs. Warren's Profession*, written in 1893, was forbidden to be performed because of the frank discussion of prostitution. It was privately performed in London and publicly performed in New York in 1905, though it was soon closed. It was published in 1898, together with two other plays, all of which were called by the writer himself "plays unpleasant". Unpleasant they were to the bourgeois public, because Shaw attacked in them the vices of capitalist society. The play shows that under the guise of bourgeois respectability horrible crimes and corruption are concealed. Mrs. Warren's profession is keeping brothels. Mr. Crofts is her partner in this business. Vivie, Mrs. Warren's daughter, is educated in a very moral atmosphere at a boarding school. On graduating, she returns home and by accident discovers the source of her mother's income. Her conversations with Mrs. Warren and Mr. Crofts reveal the cynicism of these members of the ruling class. It must be noted however, that while protesting strongly against bourgeois exploitation and the immorality of the ruling classes of England, Shaw did not point a way out. His heroine Vivie simply leaves her mother and, living independently, tries to earn her bread by honest work. Like Shaw, she is under the delusion that petty and gradual reforms will eventually do away with the evils of capitalism.

This play is a comedy for its witty dialogue and surprising turns of plot, but it does not have thc conventional comic ending, for example, the marriage of the lovers and the reconciliation between generations. Its "happy" ending is more modern. Vivie embodies the idea of reforming of Shaw. She finds happiness in not being married and in being free of the duties of a daughter.

## Act II

*Inside the cottage after nightfall.*

*Looking eastward from within instead of westward from without, the latticed window, with its curtains drawn, is now seen in the middle of the front wall of the cottage, with the porch door to the left of it. In the left-hand side wall is the door leading to the kitchen. Farther back against the same wall is a dresser with a candle and matches on it, and Frank's rifle standing beside them, with the barrel resting in the plate-rack. In the centre a table stands with a lighted lamp on it. Vivie's books and writing materials are on a table to the right of the window, against the wall. The fireplace is on the right, with a settle: there is no fire. Two of the chairs are set right and left of the table.*

*The cottage door opens, showing a fine starlit night without; and Mrs. Warren, her shoulders wrapped in a shawl borrowed from Vivie, enters, followed by Frank, who throws his cap on the window seat. She has had enough of walking, and gives a gasp of relief as she unpins her hat; takes it off; sticks the pin through the crown; and puts it on the table.*

Mrs. Warren: O Lord! I don't know which is the worst of the country, the walking or the sitting at home with nothing to do. I could do with a whisky and soda now very well, if only they had such a thing in this place.

Frank: Perhaps Vivie's got some.

Mrs. Warren: Nonsense! What would a young girl like her be doing with such things! Never mind: it don't matter. I wonder how she passes her time here. I'd a good deal rather be in Vienna.

Frank: Let me take you there. [*He helps her to take off her shawl, gallantly giving her shoulders a very perceptible squeeze as he does so.*]

Mrs. Warren: Ah! Would you? I'm beginning to think you're a chip of the old block.

Frank: Like the gov'nor, eh? [*He hangs the shawl on the nearest chair, and sits down.*]

Mrs. Warren: Never you mind. What do you know about such things? You're only a boy. [*She goes to the hearth, to be farther from temptation.*]

Frank: Do come to Vienna with me? It'd be ever such larks.

Mrs. Warren: No, thank you. Vienna is no place for you—at least not until you're a little older. [*She nods at him to emphasise this piece of advice. He makes a mock-piteous face, belied by his laughing eyes. She looks at him; then comes back to him.*] Now, look here, little boy [*taking his face in her hands and turning it up to her*]. I know you through and through by your likeness to your father, better than you know yourself. Don't you go taking any silly ideas into your head about me. Do you hear?

Frank: [*gallantly wooing her with his voice*] Can't help it, my dear Mrs. Warren. It runs in the family.

[*She pretends to box his ears; then looks at the pretty laughing upturned face for a moment, tempted. At last she kisses him, and immediately turns away, out of patience with herself.*]

Mrs. Warren: There! I shouldn't have done that. I *am* wicked. Never you mind, my dear. It's only a motherly kiss. Go and make love to Vivie.

Frank: So I have.

Mrs. Warren: [*turning on him with a sharp note of alarm in her voice*] What!

Frank: Vivie and I are ever such chums.

Mrs. Warren: What do you mean? Now see here. I won't have any young scamp tampering with my little girl. Do you hear? I won't have it.

Frank: [*quite unabashed*] My dear Mrs. Warren, don't you be alarmed. My intentions are honourable, ever so honourable; and your little girl is jolly well able to take care of herself. She don't need looking after half so much as her mother. She ain't so handsome, you know.

Mrs. Warren: [*taken aback by his assurance*] Well, you have got a nice healthy two inches thick of cheek all over you. I don't know where you got it. Not from your father, anyhow.

Crofts: [*in the garden*] The gipsies, I suppose?

Rev Samuel: [*replying*] The broomsquires[1] are far worse.

Mrs. Warren: [*to Frank*] S-sh! Remember! You've had your warning.

[*Crofts and the Reverend Samuel come in from the garden, the clergyman continuing his conversation as he enters.*]

Rev Samuel: The perjury at the Winchester assizes[2] is deplorable.

Mrs. Warren: Well? What became of you two? And where's Praddy and Vivie?

Crofts: [*putting his hat on the settle and his stick in the chimney corner*] They went up the hill. We went to the village. I wanted a drink. [*He sits down on the settle, putting his legs up along the seat.*]

Mrs. Warren: Well, she oughtn't to go off like that without telling me. [*to Frank*] Get your father a chair, Frank. Where are your manners? [*Frank springs up and gracefully offers his father his chair; and then takes another from the wall and sits down at the table, in the middle, with his father on his right and Mrs. Warren on his left.*] George, where are you going to stay tonight? You can't stay here. And what's Praddy going to do?

Crofts: Gardner'll put me up.

Mrs. Warren: Oh no doubt you've taken care of yourself! But what about Praddy?

Crofts: Don't know. I suppose he can sleep at the inn.

Mrs. Warren: Haven't you room for him, Sam?

Rev Samuel: Well-er-you see, as rector here, I am not free to do as I like. Er—what is Mr. Praed's social position?

Mrs. Warren: Oh, he's all right. He's an architect. What an old stick-in-the-mud you are, Sam!

Frank: Yes, it's all right, gov'nor. He built that place down in Wales for the Duke. Caernarvon Castle they call it. You must have heard of it. [*He winks with lightning smartness at Mrs. Warren, and regards his father blandly.*]

Rev Samuel: Oh, in that case, of course we shall only be too happy. I suppose he knows the Duke personally.

Frank: Oh, ever so intimately! We can stick him in Georgina's old room.

Mrs. Warren: Well, that's settled. Now if those two would only come in and let us have supper. They've no right to stay out after dark like this.

Crofts: [*aggressively*] What harm are they doing you?

Mrs. Warren: Well, harm or not, I don't like it.

Frank: Better not wait for them, Mrs. Warren. Praed will stay out as long as possible. He has never known before what it is to stray over the heath on a summer night with my Vivie.

Crofts: [*sitting up in some consternation*] I say, you know! Come!

Rev Samuel: [*rising, startled out of his professional manner into real force and sincerity*] Frank, once for all, it's out of the question. Mrs. Warren will tell you that it's not to be thought of.

Crofts: Of course not.

Frank: [*with enchanting placidity*] Is that so, Mrs. Warren?

Mrs. Warren: [*reflectively*] Well, Sam, I don't know. If the girl wants to get married, no good can come of keeping her unmarried.

Rev Samuel: [*astounded*] But married to him!—your daughter to my son! Only think. It's impossible.

Crofts: Of course it's impossible. Don't be a fool, Kitty.

Mrs. Warren: [*nettled*] Why not? Isn't my daughter good enough for your son?

Rev Samuel: But surely, my dear Mrs. Warren, you know the reasons—

Mrs. Warren: [*defiantly*] I know no reasons. If you know any, you can tell them to the lad or to the girl, or to your congregation, if you like.

Rev Samuel: [*collapsing helplessly into his chair*] You know very well that I couldn't tell anyone the reasons. But my boy will believe me when I tell him there are reasons.

Frank: Quite right, Dad, he will. But has your boy's conduct ever been influenced by your reasons?

Crofts: You can't marry her, and that's all about it. [*He gets up and stands on the hearth, with his back to the fireplace, frowning determinedly.*]

Mrs. Warren: [*turning on him sharply*] What have you got to do with it, pray?

Frank: [*with his prettiest lyrical cadence*] Precisely what I was going to ask, myself, in my own graceful fashion.

Crofts: [*to Mrs. Warren*] I suppose you don't want to marry the girl to man younger than herself and without either a profession or two pence to keep her on. Ask Sam, if you don't believe me. [*to the parson*] How much more money are you going to give him?

Rev Samuel: Not another penny. He has had his patrimony; and he spent the last of it in July.

[*Mrs. Warren's face falls.*]

Crofts: [*watching her*] There! I told you. [*He resumes his place on the settle and puts up his legs on the seat again, as if the matter were finally disposed of.*]

Frank: [*plaintively*] This is ever so mercenary. Do you suppose Miss Warren's going to marry for money? If we love one another—

Mrs. Warren: Thank you. Your love's a pretty cheap commodity, my lad. If you have no means of keeping a wife, that settles it: you can't have Vivie.

Frank: [*much amused*] What do you say, gov'nor, eh?

Rev Samuel: I agree with Mrs. Warren.

Frank: And good old Crofts has already expressed his opinion.

Crofts: [*turning angrily on his elbow*] Look here. I want none of your cheek.

Frank: [*pointedly*] I'm ever so sorry to surprise you, Crofts, but you allowed yourself the liberty of speaking to me like a father a moment ago. One father is enough, thank you.

Crofts: [*contemptuously*] Yah! [*He turns away again.*]

Frank: [*rising*] Mrs. Warren, I cannot give my Vivie up, even for your sake.

Mrs. Warren: [*muttering*] Young scamp!

Frank: [*continuing*] And as you no doubt intend to hold out other prospects to her, I shall lose no time in placing my case before her. [*They stare at him; and he begins to declaim gracefully.*]

Frank: He either fears his fate too much,
Or his deserts are small,
That dares not put it to the touch
To gain or lose it all.[3]

[*The cottage door opens whilst he is reciting; and Vivie and Praed come in. He breaks off. Praed put his hat on the dresser. There is an immediate improvement in the company's behaviour. Crofts takes down his legs from the settle and pulls himself together as Praed joins him at the fireplace. Mrs. Warren loses her ease of manner and takes refuge in querulousness.*]

Mrs. Warren: Wherever have you been, Vivie?

Vivie: [*taking off her hat and throwing it carelessly on the table*] On the hill.

Mrs. Warren: Well, you shouldn't go off like that without letting me know. How could I tell what had become of you? And night coming on too!

Vivie: [*going to the door of the kitchen and opening it, ignoring her mother*] Now, about supper? [*All rise except Mrs. Warren.*] We shall be rather crowded in here, I'm afraid.

Mrs. Warren: Did you hear what I said, Vivie?

Vivie: [*quietly*] Yes, mother. [*reverting to the supper difficulty*] How many are we? [*counting*] One, two, three, four, five, six. Well, two will have to wait until the rest are done: Mrs. Alison has only plates and knives for four.

Praed: Oh, it doesn't matter about me. I—

Vivie: You have had a long walk and are hungry, Mr. Praed. You shall have your supper at once. I can wait myself. I want one person to wait with me. Frank, are you hungry?

Frank: Not the least in the world. Completely off my peck, in fact.

Mrs. Warren: [*to Crofts*] Neither are you, George. You can wait.

Crofts: Oh, hang it. I've eaten nothing since teatime. Can't Sam do it?

Frank: Would you starve my poor father?

Rev Samuel: [*testily*] Allow me to speak for myself, sir. I am perfectly willing to wait.

Vivie: [*decisively*] There's no need. Only two are wanted. [*She opens the door of the kitchen.*] Will you take my mother in, Mr. Gardner.

[*The parson takes Mrs. Warren; and they pass into the kitchen. Praed and Crofts follow. All except Praed clearly disapprove of the arrangement, but do not know how to resist it. Vivie stands at the door looking in at them.*]

Vivie: Can you squeeze past to that corner, Mr. Praed? It's rather a tight fit. Take care of your coat against the white-wash. That's right. Now, are you all comfortable?

Praed: [*within*] Quite, thank you.

Mrs. Warren: [*within*] Leave the door open, dearie. [*Vivie frowns; but Frank checks her with a gesture, and steals to the cottage door, which he softly sets wide open.*] Oh Lor, what a draught! You'd better shut it, dear.

[*Vivie shuts it with a slam, and then, noting with disgust that her mother's hat and shawl are lying about, takes them tidily to the window seat, whilst Frank noiselessly shuts the cottage door.*]

Frank: [*exulting*] Aha! Got rid of 'em. Well, Vivvums, what do you think of my governor?

Vivie: [*preoccupied and serious*] I've hardly spoken to him. He doesn't strike me as being a particularly able person.

Frank: Well, you know, the old man is not altogether such a fool as he looks. You see, he was shoved into the Church rather; and in trying to live to it he makes much bigger ass of himself than he really is. I don't dislike him as much as you might expect. He means well. How do you think you'll get on with him?

Vivie: [*rather grimly*] I don't think my future life will be much concerned with him, or with any of that old circle of my mother's, except perhaps Praed. [*She sits down on the settle.*] What do you think of my mother?

Frank: Really and truly?

Vivie: Yes, really and truly.

Frank: Well, she's ever so jolly. But she's rather a caution, isn't she? And Crofts! Oh my eye, Crofts! [*He sits beside her.*]

Vivie: What a lot, Frank!

Frank: What a crew!

Vivie: [*with intense contempt for them*] If I thought that *I* was like that—that I was going to be a waster, shifting along from one meal to another with no purpose, and no character, and no grit in me, I'd open an artery and bleed to death without one moment's hesitation.

Frank: Oh no, you wouldn't. Why should they take any grind when they can afford not to? I wish I had their luck. No, what I object to is their form. It isn't the thing: It's slovenly, ever so slovenly.

Vivie: Do you think your form will be any better when you're as old as Crofts, if you don't work?

Frank: Of course I do. Ever so much better. Vivvums mustn't lecture: her little boy's incorrigible. [*He attempts to take her face caressingly in his hands.*]

Vivie: [*striking his hands down sharply*] Off with you. Vivvums is not in a humour for petting her little boy this evening. [*She rises and comes forward to the other side of the room.*]

Frank: [*following her*] How unkind!

Vivie: [*stamping at him*] Be serious. I'm serious.

Frank: Good. Let us talk learnedly. Miss Warren, do you know that all the most advanced thinkers are agreed that half the diseases of modern civilisation are due to starvation of the affections in the young. Now, *I*—

Vivie: [*cutting him short*] You are very tiresome. [*She opens the inner door.*] Have you room for Frank there? He's complaining of starvation.

Mrs. Warren: [*within*] Of course there is. [*clatter of knives and glasses as she moves the things on the table*] Here! There's room now beside me. Come along, Mr. Frank.

Frank: Her little boy will be ever so even with his Vivvums for this. [*He passes into the kitchen.*]

Mrs. Warren: [*within*] Here, Vivie, come on you too, child. You must be famished. [*She enters, followed by Crofts, who holds the door open for Vivie with marked deference. She goes out without looking at him; and he shuts the door after her.*] Why, George, you can't be done. You've eaten nothing. Is there anything wrong with you?

Crofts: Oh, all I wanted was a drink. [*He thrusts his hands in his pockets, and begins prowling about the room, restless and sulky.*]

Mrs. Warren: Well, I like enough to eat. But a little of that cold beef and cheese and lettuce goes a long way. [*With a sigh of only half repletion she sits down lazily on the settle.*]

Crofts: What do you go encouraging that young pup for?

Mrs. Warren: [*on the alert at once*] Now see here, George, what are you up to about that girl? I've been watching your way of looking at her. Remember, I know you and what your looks mean.

Crofts: There's no harm in looking at her, is there?

Mrs. Warren: I'd put you out and pack you back to London pretty soon if I saw any of your nonsense. My girl's little finger is more to me than your whole body and soul. [*Crofts receives this with a sneering grin. Mrs. Warren, flushing a little at her failure to impose on him in the character of a theatrically devoted mother, adds in a lower key.*] Make your mind easy: the young pup has no more chance than you have.

Crofts: Mayn't a man take an interest in a girl!

Mrs. Warren: Not a man like you.

Crofts: How old is she?

Mrs. Warren: Never you mind how old she is.

Crofts: Why do you make such a secret of it?

Mrs. Warren: Because I choose.

Crofts: Well, I'm not fifty yet, and my property is as good as ever it was—

Mrs. Warren: [*interrupting him*] Yes. Because you're as stingy as you're vicious.

Crofts: [*continuing*] And a baronet isn't to be picked up every day. No other man in my position would put up with you for a mother-in-law. Why shouldn't she marry me?

Mrs. Warren: You!

Crofts: We three could live together quite comfortably. I'd die before her and leave a bouncing widow with plenty of money. Why not? It's been growing in my mind all the time I've been walking with that fool inside there.

Mrs. Warren: [*revolted*] Yes. It's the sort of thing that would grow in your mind.

[*He halts in his prowling; and the two look at one another, she steadfastly, with a sort of awe behind her contemptuous disgust; he stealthily, with a carnal gleam in his eye and a loose grin.*]

Crofts: [*suddenly becoming anxious and urgent as he sees no sign of sympathy in her*] Look here, Kitty. You're a sensible woman: you needn't put on any moral airs. I'll ask no more questions; and you need answer none. I'll settle the whole property on her; and if you want a cheque for yourself on the wedding day, you can name any figure you like—in reason.

Mrs. Warren: So it's come to that with you, George, like all the other worn-out old creatures!

Crofts: [*savagely*] Damn you!

[*Before she can retort, the door of the kitchen is opened; and the voices of the others are heard returning. Crofts, unable to recover his presence of mind, hurries out of the cottage. The clergyman appears at the kitchen door.*]

Rev Samuel: [*looking around*] Where is Sir George?

Mrs. Warren: Gone out to have a pipe.

[*The clergyman takes his hat from the table, and joins Mrs. Warren at the fireside. Meanwhile, Vivie comes in, followed by Frank, who collapses into the nearest chair with an air of extreme exhaustion.*]

Mrs. Warren: [*looking round at Vivie and saying with her affectation of maternal patronage even more forced than usual*] Well, dearie, have you had a good supper?

Vivie: You know what Mrs. Alison's suppers are. [*She turns to Frank and pets him.*] Poor Frank! Was all the beef gone? Did it get nothing but bread and cheese and ginger beer? [*Seriously, as if she had done quite enough trifling for one evening.*] Her butter is really awful. I must get some down from the stores.

Frank: Do, in Heaven's name!

[*Vivie goes to the writing-table and makes a memorandum to order the butter. Praed comes in from the kitchen, putting up his handkerchief, which he has been using as a napkin.*]

Rev Samuel: Frank, my boy, it is time for us to be thinking of home. Your mother does not know yet that we have visitors.

Praed: I'm afraid we're giving trouble.

Frank: [*rising*] Not the least in the world; my mother will be delighted to see you. She's a genuinely intellectual artistic woman; and she sees nobody here from one year's end to another except the gov'nor; so you can imagine how jolly dull it pans out for her.

[*to his father*] You're not intellectual or artistic. Are you, pater? So take Praed home at once; and I'll stay here and entertain Mrs. Warren. You'll pick up Crofts in the garden. He'll be excellent company for the bull-pup.

Praed: [*taking his hat from the dresser, and coming close to Frank*] Come with us, Frank. Mrs. Warren has not seen Miss Vivie for a long time; and we have prevented them from having a moment together yet.

Frank: [*quite softened, and looking at Praed with romantic admiration*] Of course. I forgot. Ever so thanks for reminding me. Perfect gentleman, Praddy. Always were. My ideal through life. [*He rises to go, but pauses a moment between the two older men, and puts his hand on Praed's shoulder.*] Ah, if you had only been my father instead of this unworthy old man! [*He puts his other hand on his father's shoulder.*]

Rev Samuel: [*blustering*] Silence, sir, silence. You are profane.

Mrs. Warren: [*laughing heartily*] You should keep him in better order, Sam. Good night. Here, take George his hat and stick with my compliments.

Rev Samuel: [*taking them*] Good night. [*They shake hands. As he passes Vivie he shakes hands with her also and bids her good night. Then, in booming command, to Frank*] Come along, sir, at once. [*He goes out.*]

Mrs. Warren: Byebye, Praddy.

Praed: Byebye, Kitty.

[*They shake hands affectionately and go out together, she accompanying him to the garden gate.*]

Frank: [*to Vivie*] Kissums?

Vivie: [*fiercely*] No. I hate you. [*She takes a couple of books and some paper from the writing-table, and sits down with them at the middle table, at the end next the fireplace.*]

Frank: [*grimacing*] Sorry. [*He goes for his cap and rifle. Mrs. Warren returns. He takes her hand.*] Good night, dear Mrs. Warren.

[*He kisses her hand. She snatches it away, her lips tightening, and looks more than half disposed to box his ears. He laughs mischievously and runs off, clapping to the door behind him.*]

Mrs. Warren: [*resigning herself to an evening of boredom now that the men are gone*] Did you ever in your life hear anyone rattle on so? Isn't he a tease? [*She sits at the table.*] Now that I think of it, dearie, don't you go on encouraging him. I'm sure he's a regular good-for-nothing.

Vivie: [*rising to fetch more books*] I'm afraid so. Poor Frank! I shall have to get rid of him; but I shall feel sorry for him, though he's not worth it. That man Crofts does not seem to me to be good for much either: is he? [*She throws the books on the table rather roughly.*]

Mrs. Warren: [*galled by Vivie's indifference*] What do you know of men, child, to talk that way about them? You'll have to make up your mind to see a good deal of Sir George Crofts, as he's a friend of mine.

Vivie: [*quite unmoved*] Why? [*She sits down and opens a book*]. Do you expect that we shall be much together? You and I, I mean?

Mrs. Warren: [*staring at her*] Of course, until you're married. You're not going back to college again.

Vivie: Do you think my way of life would suit you? I doubt it.

Mrs. Warren: Your way of life! What do you mean?

Vivie: [*cutting a page of her book with the paper knife on her chatelaine*] Has it really never occurred to you, mother, that I have a way of life like other people?

Mrs. Warren: What nonsense is this you're trying to talk? Do you want to show your independence, now that you're a great little person at school? Don't be a fool, child.

Vivie: [*indulgently*] That's all you have to say on the subject, is it, mother?

Mrs. Warren: [*puzzled, then angry*] Don't you keep on asking me questions like that. [*violently*]

Hold your tongue. [*Vivie works on, losing no time, and saying nothing.*] You and your way of life, indeed! What next? [*She looks at Vivie again. No reply.*] Your way of life will be what I please, so it will. [*another pause*] I've been noticing these airs in you ever since you got that tripos or whatever you call it. If you think I'm going to put up with them you're mistaken; and the sooner you find it out, the better. [*muttering*] All I have to say on the subject, indeed! [*again raising her voice angrily*] Do you know who you're speaking to, Miss?

Vivie: [*looking across at her without raising her head from her book*] No. Who are you? What are you?

Mrs. Warren: [*rising breathless*] You young imp!

Vivie: Everybody knows my reputation, my social standing, and the profession I intend to pursue. I know nothing about you. What is that way of life which you invite me to share with you and Sir George Crofts, pray?

Mrs. Warren: Take care. I shall do something I'll be sorry for after, and you too.

Vivie: [*putting aside her books with cool decision*] Well, let us drop the subject until you are better able to face it. [*looking critically at her mother*] You want some good walks and a little lawn tennis to set you up. You are shockingly out of condition: you were not able to manage twenty yards uphill today without stopping to pant; and your wrists are mere rolls of fat. Look at mine. [*She holds out her wrists.*]

Mrs. Warren: [*after looking at her helplessly, begins to whimper*] Vivie—

Vivie: [*springing up sharply*] Now pray don't begin to cry. Anything but that. I really cannot stand whimpering. I will go out of the room if you do.

Mrs. Warren: [*piteously*] Oh, my darling, how can you be so hard on me? Have I no rights over you as your mother?

Vivie: Are you my mother?

Mrs. Warren: [*appalled*] *Am* I your mother? Oh, Vivie!

Vivie: Then where are our relatives? My father? Our family friends? You claim the rights of a mother; the right to call me fool and child; to speak to me as no woman in authority over me at college dare speak to me; to dictate my way of life; and to force on me the acquaintance of a brute whom anyone can see to be the most vicious sort of London man about town. Before I give myself the trouble to resist such claims. I may as well find out whether they have any real existence.

Mrs. Warren: [*distracted, throwing herself on her knees*] Oh no, no. Stop, stop. I *am* your mother; I swear it. Oh, you can't mean to turn on me—my own child! It's not natural. You believe me, don't you? Say you believe me.

Vivie: Who was my father?

Mrs. Warren: You don't know what you're asking. I can't tell you.

Vivie: [*determinedly*] Oh yes you can, if you like. I have a right to know; and you know very well that I have that right. You can refuse to tell me, if you please; but if you do, will see the last of me tomorrow morning.

Mrs. Warren: Oh, it's too horrible to hear you talk like that. You wouldn't—you *couldn't* leave me.

Vivie: [*ruthlessly*] Yes, without a moment's hesitation, if you trifle with me about this. [*shivering with disgust*] How can I feel sure that I may not have the contaminated blood of that brutal waster in my veins?

Mrs. Warren: No, no. On my oath it's not he, nor any of the rest that you have ever met. I'm certain of that, at least.

[*Vivie's eyes fasten sternly on her mother as the significance of this flashes on her.*]

Vivie: [*slowly*] You are certain of that, at last. Ah! You mean that that is all you are certain of. [*thoughtfully*] I see. [*Mrs. Warren buries her face in her hands.*] Don't do that, mother. You know you don't feel it a bit. [*Mrs. Warren takes down her hands and looks up deplorably at Vivie, who takes out her watch and says*] Well, that is enough for tonight. At what hour would you like breakfast? Is half-past eight too early for you?

Mrs. Warren: [*wildly*] My God, what sort of woman are you?

Vivie: [*coolly*] The sort the world is mostly made of, I should hope. Otherwise I don't understand how it gets its business done. Come [*taking her mother by the wrist, and pulling her up pretty resolutely*], pull yourself together. That's right.

Mrs. Warren: [*querulously*] You're very rough with me, Vivie.

Vivie: Nonsense. What about bed? It's past ten.

Mrs. Warren: [*passionately*] What's the use of my going to bed? Do you think I could sleep?

Vivie: Why not? I shall.

Mrs. Warren: You! You've no heart. [*She suddenly breaks out vehemently in her natural tongue—the dialect of a woman of the people—with all her affectations of maternal authority and—conventional manners gone, and an overwhelming inspiration of true conviction and scorn in her.*] Oh, I won't bear it. I won't put up with the injustice of it. What right have you to set yourself up above me like this? You boast of what you are to me—to *me*, who gave you the chance of being what you are. What chance had I? Shame on you for a bad daughter and a stuck-up prude!

Vivie: [*sitting down with a shrug, no longer confident; for her replies, which have sounded sensible and strong to her so far, now begin to ring rather woodenly and even priggishly against the new tone of her mother*] Don't think for a moment I set myself above you in any way. You attacked me with the conventional authority of a mother; I defended myself with the conventional superiority of a respectable woman. Frankly, I am not going to stand any of your nonsense; and when you drop it I shall not expect you to stand any of mine. I shall always respect your right to your own opinions and your own way of life.

Mrs. Warren: My own opinions and my own way of life! Listen to her talking! Do you think I was brought up like you? Able to pick and choose my own way of life? Do you think I did what I did because I liked it, or thought it right, or wouldn't rather have gone to college and been a lady if I'd had the chance?

Vivie: Everybody has some choice, mother. The poorest girl alive may not be able to choose between being Queen of England or Principal of Newnham; but she can choose between rag-picking and flower-selling, according to her taste. People are always blaming their circumstances for what they are. I don't believe in circumstances. The people who get on in this world are the people who get up and look for the circumstances they want, and, if they can't find them, make them.

Mrs. Warren: Oh, it's easy to talk, very easy, isn't it? Here! Would you like to know what my circumstances were?

Vivie: Yes. You had better tell me. Won't you sit down?

Mrs. Warren: Oh, I'll sit down; don't you be afraid. [*She plants her chair farther forward with brazen energy, and sits down. Vivie is impressed in spite of herself.*] D'you know what your gran'mother was?

Vivie: No.

Mrs. Warren: No, you don't. I do. She called herself a widow and had a fried-fish shop down by the Mint, and kept herself and four daughters out of it. Two of us were sisters: that was me and Liz; and we were both good-looking and well made. I suppose our father was a well-fed man; mother pretended he was a gentleman; but I don't know. The other two were only half sisters: undersized, ugly, starved looking, hardworking, honest poor creatures. Liz and I would have half-murdered them if mother hadn't half-murdered us to keep our hands off them. They were the respectable ones. Well, what did they get by their respectability? I'll tell you. One of them worked in a white lead factory twelve hours a day for nine shillings a week until she died of lead poisoning. She only expected to get her hands a little paralysed; but she died. The other was always held up to us as a model because she married a Government labourer in the Deptford victualling yard, and kept his room and the three children neat and tidy on eighteen shillings a week—until he took to drink. That was worth being respectable for, wasn't it?

Vivie: [*now thoughtfully attentive*] Did you and your sister think so?

Mrs. Warren: Liz didn't, I can tell you. She had more spirit. We both went to a church school—that was part of the ladylike airs we gave ourselves to be superior to the children that knew nothing and went nowhere—and we stayed there until Liz went out one night and never came back. I know the school-mistress thought I'd soon follow her example; for the clergyman was always warning me that Lizzie'd end by jumping off Waterloo Bridge. Poor fool! That was all he knew about it! But I was more afraid of the white lead factory than I was of the river; and so would you have been in my place. That clergyman got me a situation as a scullery maid in a temperance restaurant where they sent out for anything you liked. Then I was waitress; and then I went to the bar at Waterloo station: fourteen hours a day serving drinks and washing glasses for four shillings a week and my board. That was considered a great promotion for me. Well, one cold, wretched night, when I was so tired I could hardly keep myself awake, who should come up for a half of Scotch but Lizzie, in a long fur cloak, elegant and comfortable, with a lot of sovereigns in her purse.

Vivie: [*grimly*] My aunt Lizzie!

Mrs. Warren: Yes; and a very good aunt to have, too. She's living down at Winchester now, close to the cathedral, one of the most respectable ladies there. Chaperones girls at the county ball, if you please. No river for Liz, thank you! You remind me of Liz a little: she was a first-rate business woman—saved money from the beginning—never let herself look too like what she was—never lost her head or threw away a chance. When she saw I'd grown up good-looking she said to me across the bar "What are you doing there, you little fool? Wearing out your health and your appearance for other people's profit!" Liz was saving money then to take a house for herself in Brussels; and she thought we two could save faster than one. So she lent me some money and gave me a start; and I saved steadily and first paid her back, and then went into business with her as her partner. Why shouldn't I have done it? The house in Brussels was real high class, a much better place for a woman to be in than the factory where Anne Jane got poisoned. None of our girls were ever treated as I was treated in the scullery of that temperance place, or at the Waterloo bar, or at home. Would you have had me stay in them and become a worn out old drudge before I was forty?

Vivie: [*intensely interested by this time*] No; but why did you choose that business? Saving money and good management will succeed in any business.

Mrs. Warren: Yes, saving money. But where can a woman get the money to save in any other business? Could you save out of four shillings a week and keep yourself dressed as well? Not you. Of course, if you're a plain woman and can't earn anything more; or if you have a turn for music, or the stage, or newspaper-writing: that's different. But neither Liz nor I had any turn for such things at all: all we had was our appearance and our turn for pleasing men. Do you think we were such fools as to let other people trade in our good looks by employing us as shop girls, or barmaids, or waitresses, when we could trade in them ourselves and get all the profits instead of starvation wages? Not likely.

Vivie: You were certainly quite justified—from the business point of view.

Mrs. Warren: Yes; or any other point of view. What is any respectable girl brought up to do but to catch some rich man's fancy and get the benefit of his money by marrying him?—as if a marriage ceremony could make any difference in the right or wrong of the thing! Oh, the hypocrisy of the world makes me sick! Liz and I had to work and save and calculate just like other people; elseways we should be as poor as any good-for-nothing drunken waster of a woman that thinks her luck will last for ever. [*with great energy*] I despise such people: they've no character; and if there's a thing I hate in a woman, it's want of character.

Vivie: Come now, mother; frankly! Isn't it part of what you call character in a woman that she should greatly dislike such a way of making money?

Mrs. Warren: Why, of course. Everybody dislikes having to work and make money; but they have to do it all the same. I'm sure I've often pitied poor girl, tired out and in low spirits, having to try to please some man that she doesn't care two straws for—some half-drunken fool that thinks he's making himself agreeable when he's teasing and worrying and disgusting a woman so that hardly any money could pay her for putting up with it. But she has to bear with disagreeables and take the rough with the smooth, just like a nurse in a hospital or anyone else. It's not work that any woman would do for pleasure, goodness knows; though to hear the pious people talk you would suppose it was a bed of roses.

Vivie: Still, you consider it worthwhile. It pays.

Mrs. Warren: Of course it's worthwhile to a poor girl, if she can resist temptation and is good-looking and well conducted and sensible. It's far better than any other employment open to her. I always thought that oughtn't to be. It *can't* be right, Vivie, that there shouldn't be better opportunities for women. I stick to that: it's wrong. But it's so, right or wrong; and a girl must make the best of it. But of course it's not worthwhile for a lady. If you took to it you'd be a fool; but I should have been a fool if I'd taken to anything else.

Vivie: [*more and more deeply moved*] Mother, suppose we were both as poor as you were in those wretched old days, are you quite sure that you wouldn't advise me to try the Waterloo bar, or marry a labourer, or even go into the factory?

Mrs. Warren: [*indignantly*] Of course not. What sort of mother do you take me for! How could you keep your self-respect in such starvation and slavery? And what's a woman worth? What's life worth? Without self-respect! Why am I independent and able to give my daughter a first-rate education, when other women that had just as good opportunities are in the gutter? Because I always knew how to respect myself and control myself. Why is Liz looked up to in a cathedral town? The same reason. Where would we be now if we'd minded the clergyman's foolishness? Scrubbing floors for one and sixpence a day and nothing to look forward to but the workhouse infirmary. Don't you be led astray by people who don't know the world, my girl. The only way for a woman to provide for herself decently is for her to be good to some man that can afford to be good to her. If she's in his own station of life, let her make him marry her; but if she's far beneath him she can't expect it: why should she? It wouldn't be for her own happiness. Ask any lady in London society that has daughters; and she'll tell you the same, except that I tell you straight and she'll tell you crooked. That's all the difference.

Vivie: [*fascinated, gazing at her*] My dear mother, you are a wonderful woman; you are stronger than all England. And are you really and truly not one wee bit doubtful—or—or—ashamed?

Mrs. Warren: Well, of course, dearie, it's only good manners to be ashamed of it: it's expected from a woman. Women have to pretend to feel a great deal that they don't feel. Liz used to be angry with me for plumping out the truth about it. She used to say that when every woman could learn enough from what was going on in the world before her eyes, there was no need to talk about it to her. But then Liz was such a perfect lady! She had the true instinct of it; while I was always a bit of a vulgarian. I used to be so pleased when you sent me your photos to see that you were growing up like Liz: you've just her ladylike, determined way. But I can't stand saying one thing when everyone knows I mean another. What's the use in such hypocrisy? If people arrange the world that way for women, there's no good pretending it's arranged the other way. No, I never was a bit ashamed really. I consider I had a right to be proud of how we managed everything so respectably, and never had a word against us, and how the girls were so well taken care of. Some of them did very well: one of them married an ambassador. But of course now I daren't talk about such things: whatever would they think of us! [*She yawns.*] Oh dear! I do believe I'm getting sleepy after all. [*She stretches herself lazily, thoroughly relieved by her explosion, and placidly ready for her night's rest.*]

Vivie: I believe it is I who will not be able to sleep now. [*She goes to the dresser and lights the candle. Then she extinguishes the lamp, darkening the room a good deal.*] Better let in some fresh air before locking up. [*She opens the cottage door, and finds that it is broad moonlight.*] What a beautiful night! Look! [*She draws aside the curtains of the window. The landscape is seen bathed in the radiance of the harvest moon rising over Blackdown.*]

Mrs. Warren: [*with a perfunctory glance at the scene*] Yes, dear. But take care you don't catch your death of cold from the night air.

Vivie: [*contemptuously*] Nonsense.

Mrs. Warren: [*querulously*] Oh yes. Everything I say is nonsense, according to you.

Vivie: [*turning to her quickly*] No. Really that is not so, mother. You have got completely the better of me tonight, though I intended it to be the other way. Let us be good friends now.

Mrs. Warren: [*shaking her head a little ruefully*] So it has been the other way. But I suppose I must give in to it. I always got the worst of it from Liz; and now I suppose it'll be the same with you.

Vivie: Well, never mind. Come. Good night, dear old mother. [*She takes her mother in her arms.*]

Mrs. Warren: [*fondly*] I brought you up well, didn't I, dearie?

Vivie: You did.

Mrs. Warren: And you'll be good to your poor old mother for it, won't you?

Vivie: I will, dear. [*kissing her*] Good night.

Mrs. Warren: [*with unction*] Blessings on my own dearie darling! A mother's blessing! [*She embraces her daughter protectingly, instinctively looking upward for divine sanction.*]

## Notes

1. broomsquires: small country landowners
2. assizes: law courts
3. These lines are from the poem "My Dear and Only Love" written by the Marquis of Montrose (1612–1650).

## For Study and Discussion

1. Both the visitors, namely, Crofts and Reverend Samuel, object to their own sons to marry Vivie. Why?
2. After the visitors left, Vivie had a sort of quarrel with her mother. How do they reach peace? Why is Vivie first angry and then happy and even moved?
3. Change this act of the play into a story told in the third person. Write your story and enjoy the fun of being a novelist.

# Chapter 23

# William Butler Yeats

## Life and Works

William Butler Yeats (1865–1939), early in his life, resolved to become a great literary artist, and by the end of his life he was judged by many to be among the greatest poets who had ever lived. The British poet Edwin Muir has defined the source of Yeats' poetry as "a magnificent temperament associated with a magnificent style".

Yeats was born to an Anglo-Irish family in Dublin. He spent part of his childhood with his mother's family in Sligo, an underdeveloped area on the northwest coast of Ireland. There he became acquainted with traditional Irish legends and lore. It was there that he found a rich tradition of the Celtic folklore back to the heroic era of Ireland's past. His father, a painter, moved the family between Dublin and London, where Yeats attended school and spent much time reading. In Dublin, where he was born, he was involved in the politics of the Irish movement for independence from England. In London, he was associated with the younger poets of the Pre-Raphaelite movement. All these gave him great influence. He pursued his interests in Irish legend and romantic idealism and occult philosophies. Mixed into his thought were the mysticism of Blake, the romantic idealism of Shelley, and the aesthetic ideas of the Pre-Raphaelites.

By the time he moved to London in 1887, his goals as an artist were fixed. He was particularly interested in making the Irish people conscious of their past and in resurrecting a heroic ideal by which they could live. His first book of poetry, published in 1889, and *The Celtic Twilight,* published in 1893, drew on ancient Irish legend.

In 1889 Yeats met the beautiful actress and Irish nationalist Maud Gonne, with whom he was desperately in love for many years, but who persistently refused to marry him. She became the subject of his early love poems. Maud Gonne's marriage to John MacBride in 1903 marked an important change in Yeats' life. Disappointed in love, he was resolved to make great poetry out of his experience, seeking perfection "of the work" instead of perfection "of 1ife", as he put it in a late poem. Yeats was working to toughen his poetry and to bring it more into touch with the language and preoccupations of the modern world. He was working to simplify his style, to rid it of romantic vagueness, and to bring it close to the rhythm of everyday speech. His aim was to write poems "as cold and passionate as the dawn". In his aim and practice, and rejection of late Victorian poetic modes, Yeats gave impetus to the modernist movement in poetry, in which Ezra Pound, T. S. Eliot, Edith Sitwell and others sought a fresh language, new rhythm and an extension of poetic subjects.

Throughout his poetic career, Yeats sought to unify his experience of the world and to gain for his poems a central illuminating vision comparable to that of Dante and Shelley, one that would pull together the thousand separate fragments of everyday life. He sought that vision in the mysticism of Blake and occult philosophies, drawing these various ideas together in his philosophical and historical book, *A Vision,* published in 1925. He saturated his poetry with these ideas, constructing in various volumes of poetry a composite portrait of a complex modern being. No single poem revealed Yeats' personality completely: each poem provided some insight into a moment of thought or feeling. At the same time, these poems took the pulse of current thought and feeling.

In 1917 Yeats married the English woman Georgie Hyde-Lees, and his two children were born in 1919 and 1921. He became a senator in the Irish Free State founded in 1921. In 1923, he was awarded the Nobel Prize. By the time of his death in 1939, Yeats had become the leading poet of his age, who had taught "the free man how to praise". W. H. Auden wrote of him in his great elegiac poem, "In Memory of W. B. Yeats".

## Brief Comment

Yeats is a poet of Ireland, of England, and of the world. He is first of all Irish, a sort of nationalist. He devoted all his life to the freedom of Ireland and much of his literary activity was likewise linked with Irish national movement. He is English in that England is one of the places that helped make him a celebrity. As a poet of the world, he has influenced many writers with his practice and ideas.

Yeats is a critical figure in the history of poetry. He is a transitional figure, inheriting the past and leading the future. He is both traditional and modernistic. With his art he satisfied those who were conservative enough to cherish the old and those who wished for a change in taste.

## Selections

### When You Are Old

When you are old and grey and full of sleep,
And nodding by the fire, take down this book,

And slowly read, and dream of the soft look
Your eyes had once, and of their shadows deep;

How many loved your moments of glad grace,
And loved your beauty with love false or true,
But one man loved the pilgrim soul in you,
And loved the sorrows of your changing face;

And bending down beside the glowing bars
Murmur, a little sadly, how Love fled
And paced upon the mountains overhead
And hid his face amid a crowd of stars.

## For Study and Discussion

1. What book do you think the woman is reading?
2. What does the phrase "pilgrim soul" tell you about the woman? How does the poet contrast his love for her with the love of others?
3. What evidence can you find to show that the poet's love is not reciprocated and is finally withdrawn?

### The Lake Isle of Innisfree[1]

I will arise and go now, and go to Innisfree
And a small cabin build there, of clay and wattles made:
Nine bean-rows will I have there, a hive for the honeybee,
And live alone in the bee-loud glade[2].

And I shall have some peace there, for peace comes dropping slow,
Dropping from the veils of the morning to where the cricket sings;
There midnight's all a glimmer, and noon a purple glow,
And evening full of the linnet's wings[3].

I will arise and go now, for always night and day
I hear lake water lapping with low sounds by the shore[4];
While I stand on the roadway, or on the pavements grey
I heard it in the deep heart's core[5].

## Notes

1. The poem is one of Yeats' best known lyrics. Innisfree is an islet in the lake in Irish legends. Here the poet was referring to a place for hermitage. Written in 1893, it is one of the poet's early works under the influence of the Pre-Raphaelites in late 19th-century England. Tired of the life of his day, Yeats sought to escape into an ideal "fairy land" where he could live calmly as a hermit and enjoy the beauty of nature. The poem is closely-woven, subtle and musical, consisting of three quatrains of iambic pentametre, with each stanza rhymed abab.
2. the bee-loud glade: an open place in the wood where bees buzz loudly
3. full of the linnet's wings: here referring to the fact that lots of linnets (红雀) flying here and there
4. lapping…by the shore: flowing against the shore
5. in the deep heart's core: at the bottom of my heart

## For Study and Discussion

1. What is the poet's attitude towards life in this poem?
2. Discuss the images used in this poem.
3. In his love for nature and hermitage as expressed in this poem, the poet was quite like Tao Yuanming (陶渊明), a poet of the Jin Dynasty in China. Find some poems of such sort written by Tao Yuanming and make a comparison of them.

# Chapter 24

# John Galsworthy

## Life and Works

John Galsworthy (1867–1933), one of the most prominent writers of 20th-century England, was born in a well-to-do bourgeois family. He studied law at Oxford University and was called to the bar in 1890, but practised only for a short time. He travelled widely when he was young and became acquainted with Joseph Conrad, the ship's officer on one of the voyages. In 1905 Galsworthy married the divorced wife of his cousin, their association having begun some years earlier when her first marriage proved unhappy. These experiences were reflected in *The Man of Property* and the later novels which were to constitute *The Forsyte Saga*.

Adopting the pseudonym John Sinjohn, Galsworthy began his writing career with *From the Four Winds*, followed by *Jocelyn*, *The Villa Rubein*, and *A Man of Devon*. *The Island Pharisees* and all its successors were published under his own name. In addition to *The Forsyte Chronicles*, which embraces the *Saga* and some dozen or so other novels and shorter stories, Galsworthy's prose fiction includes *The Country House*, *The Patrician*, *The Dark Flower*, *The Freelands*, and the collection of his short stories *Caravan*.

He was equally prolific as a dramatist who for many years rivalled Bernard Shaw and J. M. Barrie in popularity and shared with them the attentive notice of dramatic and literary critics. *The Silver Box*, *Strife*, *Justice*, and *The Skin Game* are in lasting interest of subject matter and in technical skill the best of his many plays.

Fickleness of literary fashion led to the rapid decline of Galsworthy's reputation in the decades following his death, though it seems improbable that the plays named above will remain permanently neglected; and in spite of critical and academic disfavour, *The Forsyte Saga* continued to be widely read, even before it became in the late 1960s the most popular and lengthiest of all television serials, causing some clergy to change their service times so that the congregation should not miss any of the twenty-six Sunday evening instalments. Independent of its literary merits or demerits, this sequence of novels preserves a view of the Edwardian upper middle class which social historians will not undervalue.

## Brief Comment

Galsworthy's novels, by their abstention from complicated psychology and their greatly simplified social viewpoint, became accepted as faithful patterns of English life for a time. Galsworthy is remembered for this evocation of Victorian and Edwardian upper-middle-class life and for his creation of Soames Forsyte, a dislikable character who nevertheless compels the reader's sympathy. Galsworthy was moved throughout life by an acute sense of social justice, and though he aimed to hold the balance fairly between the rich and the poor, between the powerful and the helpless, and his emotions were always engaged on the side of the poor and the loser. He saw human existence in terms of the hunters and the hunted: with varying emphasis and in a variety of guises. This is the theme of the majority of his novels and plays. He won the Nobel Prize in 1932 "for his distinguished art of narration which takes its highest form in *The Forsyte Saga*".

## Selections

### *The Forsyte Saga*

### The Story

In 1886 all the Forsytes gathered at Old Jolyon's house to celebrate the engagement of his granddaughter, June, to Philip Bosinney, a young architect. Young Jolyon Forsyte, June's father, was estranged from his family because he had run away with a governess, whom he had married after June's mother died.

Old Jolyon complained that he saw little of June. Lonely, he called on Young Jolyon, whom he had not seen in many years. He found his son working as an underwriter for Lloyd's and painting watercolours. By his second wife he had two children, Holly (son) and Jolly (daughter).

The family knew that Soames had been having trouble with his lovely wife, Irene. She had a profound aversion for Soames, and had recently reminded him of her premarital stipulation that she should have her freedom if the marriage were not a success. In his efforts to please her, Soames planned to build a large country place. Deciding that June's fiance would be a good choice for an architect, he bought an estate at Robin Hill and hired Bosinney to build the house.

When Soames made suggestions about the plans, Bosinney appeared offended, and in the end the plans were drawn as Bosinney wished. As the work proceeded, Soames and Bosinney argued over costs that exceeded the original estimate.

One day Swithin Forsyte, Soames' uncle, took Irene to see the house. Bosinney met them, and while Swithin dozed the architect talked to Irene alone. That day Irene and Bosinney fell hopelessly in love with one another. Irene's already unbearable life with Soames became impossible. She asked for a separate room.

There were new troubles over the house. Bosinney had agreed to decorate it, but only if he could have a free hand. Soames finally agreed. Irene and Bosinney began to meet secretly. As their affair progressed, June became more unhappy and self-centred. Finally Old Jolyon took June away for a holiday. He wrote to Young Jolyon, asking him to see Bosinney and learn his intentions toward June. Young Jolyon talked to Bosinney, but the report he made to his father was vague.

When the house was completed, Soames sued Bosinney for exceeding his highest estimate and Irene refused to move to Robin Hill. When the lawsuit over the house came to trial, Soames won his case without difficulty. That same night Bosinney, after spending the afternoon with Irene and learning that Soames had forced himself on her, was accidentally run over. Irene left her husband on the day of the trial, but that night she returned to his house because there was now no place else for her to go. June persuaded her grandfather to buy Robin Hill for Jolyon's family.

A short time after Bosinney's death Irene left Soames permanently, settled in a small flat, and gave music lessons to support herself. Several years later, she visited Robin Hill secretly and there met Old Jolyon. She won him by her gentleness and charm, and during that summer she made his days happy for him. Late in the summer he died quietly while waiting for her.

After his separation from Irene, Soames devoted himself to making money. Then, still hoping to have an heir, he began to court a French girl, Annette Lamotte. At the same time his sister Winifred was in difficulties. Her husband, Monty Dartie, stole her pearls and ran away to South America with a Spanish dancer. When he decided to marry Annette, Soames went to Irene to see if she would provide grounds for his suit. He found that she had lived a model life. While visiting her, Soames realised that he still loved her and he tried to persuade her to come back to him. When she refused, he hired a detective to get the evidence he needed.

Old Jolyon had willed a legacy to Irene, with Young Jolyon, now a widower, as trustee. When Soames annoyed Irene, she appealed to Young Jolyon for protection. Irene went to Paris to avoid Soames and shortly afterwards Young Jolyon joined her. His visit was cut short by Jolly, who announced that he had joined the yeomanry to fight in the Boer War. Holly had in the meantime fallen in love with Val Dartie, her cousin. When Val proposed to Holly, he was overheard by Jolly, who dared Val to join the yeomanry with him. Val accepted. June then decided to become a Red Cross nurse, and Holly went with her. Monty Dartie reappeared unexpectedly. To avoid further scandal, Winifred decided to take him back.

Soames went to Paris in a last effort to persuade Irene. Frightened, Irene returned to Young Jolyon. Before they became lovers indeed, they were presented with papers by Soames' lawyer. They decided to go abroad together. Before their departure Young Jolyon received word that Jolly had died of enteric fever during the African campaign. Later Soames secured his divorce and married Annette. Val married Holly, to the discomfiture of both branches of the family.

Irene presented Young Jolyon with a son, Jon. When Annette was about to give birth to a child, Soames had to choose between saving the mother or the child. Wishing an heir, Soames chose to save the child. Fortunately both Annette and the baby lived.

Little Jon grew up under the adoring eyes of his parents. Fleur, Soames' daughter, grew up spoiled by her doting father.

Years passed. Monty Dartie was dead. Val and Holly were training race horses. One day in a picture gallery Soames impulsively invited a young man, Michael Mont, to see his collection of pictures. That same afternoon he saw Irene and her son Jon for the first time in twenty years. By chance Fleur and Jon met. Having decided that he wanted to try farming, Jon went to stay with Val Dartie. Fleur also appeared to spend the week with Holly. Jon and Fleur fell deeply in love.

They had only vague ideas regarding the cause of the feud between their respective branches of the family. Later Fleur learnt all the details from Prosper Profond, with whom Annette was having an affair, and from Winifred Dartie. She was still determined to marry Jon. Meanwhile Michael Mont had Soames' permission to court Fleur. When Soames heard of the affair between Annette and Prosper, she did not deny it, but she promised there would be no scandal.

Fleur tried to persuade Jon into a hasty marriage. She failed because Young Jolyon reluctantly gave his son a letter revealing the story of Soames and Irene. Reading it, Jon realised that he could never marry Fleur. His decision became irrevocable when his father died. He left England at once and went to America, where Irene joined him. Fleur, disappointed, married Michael Mont.

When Timothy, the last of the old Forsytes, died, Soames realised that the Forsyte age had passed. Its way of life was like an empty house—to let. He felt lonely and old.

## About the Selection

*The Man of Property*, the first novel of *The Forsyte Saga*, was the highest point of social criticism ever attained by Galsworthy. In the chapter presented here, the definition of "Forsytism" could be found, that is, the specifically English type of bourgeois morality and social attitudes. To understand the various allusions to persons and events, it is necessary to recall some facts about the characters: Philip Bosinney, an architect, is engaged to June Forsyte, the daughter of Young Jolyon Forsyte. Young Jolyon has broken away from the Forsytes owing to his marriage with a former governess, which is considered by the Forsytes a misalliance. June lives with her grandfather, Old Jolyon Forsyte. Another Forsyte, Soames, invites Bosinney, June's fiance, to build a house for him. Bosinney falls in love with Soames' wife, Irene, and is loved by her. June is too proud to interfere, but Old Jolyon thinks it necessary to take some measures. At this point begins the following passage.

## *The Man of Property*
## Part II, Chapter X
## Diagnosis of a Forsyte

It is in the nature of a Forsyte to be ignorant that he is a Forsyte; but Young Jolyon was well aware of being one. He had not known it till after the decisive step which had made him an outcast; since then the knowledge had been with him continually. He felt it throughout his alliance, throughout all his dealings with his second wife, who was emphatically not a Forsyte.

He knew that if he had not possessed in great measure the eye for what he wanted, the tenacity to hold on to it, the sense of the folly of wasting that for which he had given so big a price—in other words, the "sense of property" he could never have retained her (perhaps never would have desired to retain her) with him through all the financial troubles, slights, and misconstructions of those fifteen years; never have induced her to marry him on the death of his first wife; never have lived it all through, and come up, as it were, thin, but smiling.

He was one of those men who, seated cross-legged like a miniature Chinese idol in the cages of their own hearts, are ever smiling at themselves a doubting smile. Nor that this smile, so intimate and eternal, interfered with his actions, which, like his chin and his temperament, were quite a peculiar blend of softness and determination.

He was conscious, too, of being a Forsyte in his work, that painting of watercolours to which he devoted so much energy, always with an eye on himself, as though he could not take so unpractical a pursuit quite seriously, and always with a certain queer uneasiness that he did not make more money at it. It was, then, this consciousness of what it meant to be a Forsyte, that made him receive the following letter from Old Jolyon, with a mixture of sympathy and disgust:

Sheldrake House,<br>Broadstairs,<br>July 1

My Dear Jo,

(*The Dad's handwriting had altered very little in the thirty odd years that he remembered it.*)

We have been here now a fortnight, and have had good weather on the whole. The air is bracing, but my liver is out of order, and I shall be glad enough to get back to town. I cannot say much for June, her health and spirits are very indifferent, and I don't see what is to come of it. She says nothing, but it is clear that she is harping on this engagement, which is an engagement and no engagement, and—goodness knows what. I have grave doubts whether she ought to be allowed to return to London in the present state of affairs, but she is so self-willed that she might take it into her head to come up at any moment. The fact is someone ought to speak to Bosinney and ascertain what he means. I'm afraid of this myself, for I should certainly rap him over the knuckles, but I thought that you, knowing him at the Club, might put in a word, and get to ascertain what the fellow is about. You will of course in no way commit June. I shall be glad to hear from you in the course of a few days whether you have succeeded in gaining any information. The situation is very distressing to me, I worry about it at night.

With my love to Jolly and Holly.

I am,<br>Your affect. father,<br>Jolyon Forsyte

Young Jolyon pondered this letter so long and seriously that his wife noticed his preoccupation, and asked him what was the matter. He replied: "Nothing."

It was a fixed principle with him never to allude to June. She might take alarm, he did not know what she might think; he hastened, therefore, to banish from his manner all traces of absorption, but in this he was about as successful as his father would have been, for he had inherited all Old Jolyon's transparency in matters of domestic finesse; and Young Mrs. Jolyon, busying herself over the affairs of the house, went about with tightened lips, stealing at him unfathomable looks.

He started for the Club in the afternoon with the letter in his pocket, and without having made up his mind.

To sound a man as to "his intentions" was peculiarly unpleasant to him; nor did his own anomalous position diminish this unpleasantness. It was so like his family, so like all the people they knew and mixed with, to enforce what they called their rights over a man, to bring him up to the mark; so like them to carry their business principles into their private relations!

And how that phrase in the letter—"you will, of course, in no way commit June"—gave the whole thing away.

Yet the letter, with the personal grievance, the concern for June, the "rap over the knuckles", was all so natural. No wonder his father wanted to know what Bosinney meant, no wonder he was angry.

It was difficult to refuse! But why give the thing to him to do? That was surely quite unbecoming; but so long as a Forsyte got what he was after, he was not too particular about the means, provided appearances were saved.

How should he set about it, or how to refuse? Both seemed impossible to Young Jolyon!

He arrived at the Club at three o'clock, and the first person he saw was Bosinney himself, seated in a corner, staring out of the window.

Young Jolyon sat down not far off, and began nervously to reconsider his position. He looked covertly at Bosinney sitting there unconscious. He did not know him very well, and studied him attentively for perhaps the first time; and unusual-looking man, unlike in dress, face, and manner to most of the other members of the Club—Young Jolyon himself, however different he had become in mood and temper, had always retained the neat reticence of Forsyte appearance. He alone among Forsytes was ignorant of Bosinney's nickname[1]. The man was unusual, not eccentric, but unusual; he looked worn, too, haggard, hollow in the cheeks beneath those broad, high cheekbones, though without any appearance of ill-health, for he was strongly built, with curly hair that seemed to show all the vitality of a fine constitution.

Something in his face and attitude touched Young Jolyon. He knew what suffering was like, and this man looked as if he were suffering.

He got up and touched his arm.

Bosinney started, but exhibited no sign of embarrassment on seeing who it was.

Young Jolyon sat down.

"I haven't seen you for a long time," he said. "How are you getting on with my cousin's house?"

"It'll be finished in about a week."

"I congratulate you!"

"Thanks—I don't know that it's much of a subject for congratulation."

"No?" queried Young Jolyon. "I should have thought you'd be glad to get a long job like that off your hands; but I suppose you feel it much as I do when I part with a picture—a sort of child?"

He looked kindly at Bosinney.

"Yes," said the latter more cordially, "it goes out from you and there's an end of it. I didn't know you painted."

"Only watercolours; I can't say I believe in my work."

"Don't believe in it? Then how can you do it? Work's no use unless you believe in it!"

"Good," said Young Jolyon, "it's exactly what I've always said. By-the-bye, have you noticed that whenever one says 'Good', one always adds 'it's exactly what I've always said!' But if you ask me how I do it, I answer, because I'm a Forsyte."

"A Forsyte! I never thought of you as one!"

"A Forsyte," replied Young Jolyon, "is not an uncommon animal. There are hundreds among the members of this Club. Hundreds out there in the streets; you meet them wherever you go!"

"And how do you tell them, may I ask?" said Bosinney.

"By their sense of property. A Forsyte takes a practical—one might say a commonsense—view of things, and a practical view of things is based fundamentally on a sense of property. A Forsyte, you will notice, never gives himself away."

"Joking?"

Young Jolyon's eye twinkled.

"Not much. As a Forsyte myself, I have no business to talk. But I'm a kind of thoroughbred mongrel; now, there's no mistaking you. You're as different from me as I am from my Uncle James, who is the perfect specimen of a Forsyte. His sense of property is extreme, while you have practically none. Without me in between, you would seem like a different species. I'm the missing link. We are, of course, all of us the slaves of property, and I admit that it's a question of degree, but what I call a 'Forsyte' is a man who is decidedly more than less a slave of property. He knows a good thing, he knows a safe thing, and his grip on property—it doesn't matter whether it be wives, houses, money, or reputation—is his hall-mark."

"Ah," murmured Bosinney. "You should patent the word."

"I should like," said Young Jolyon, "to lecture on it: 'Properties and quality of a Forsyte. This little animal, disturbed by the ridicule of his own sort, is unaffected in his motions by the laughter of strange creatures (you or I). Hereditarily disposed to myopia, he recognises only the persons and habitats of his own species, amongst which he passes an existence of competitive tranquility.'"

"You talk of them," said Bosinney, "as if they were half England."

"They are," repeated Young Jolyon, "half England and the better half, too, the safe half, the three per cent half[2], the half that counts. It's their wealth and security that makes everything possible; makes your art possible, makes literature, science, even religion, possible. Without Forsytes, who believe in none of these things, but turn them all to use, where should we be? My dear sir, the Forsytes are the middlemen, the commercials, the pillars of society, the cornerstones of convention; everything that is admirable!"

"I don't know whether I catch your drift," said Bosinney, "but I fancy there are plenty of Forsytes, as you call them, in my profession."

"Certainly," replied Young Jolyon. "The great majority of architects, painters, or writers have no principles, like any other Forsytes. Art, literature, religion, survive by virtue of the few cranks who really believe in such things, and the many Forsytes who make a commercial use of them. At a low estimate, three-fourths of our Royal Academicians are Forsytes, seven-eights of our novelists, a large proportion of the press. Of science I can't speak; they are magnificently represented in religion; in the House of Commons perhaps more numerous than anywhere; the aristocracy speaks for itself. But I'm not laughing. It is dangerous to go against the majority—and what a majority?" He fixed his eyes on Bosinney: "It's dangerous to let anything carry you away—a house, a picture, a—woman!"

They looked at each other. And, as though he had done that which no Forsyte did—given himself away, Young Jolyon drew into his shell. Bosinney broke the silence.

"Why do you take your own people as the type?" said he.

"My people," replied Young Jolyon, "are not very extreme, and they have their own private peculiarities, like every other family, but they possess in a remarkable degree those two qualities which are the real tests of a Forsyte—the power of never being able to give yourself up to anything soul and body, and the 'sense of property'."

Bosinney smiled: "How about the big one, for instance?"

"Do you mean Swithin?" asked Young Jolyon. "Ah! in Swithin there's something primeval still. The town and middle-class life haven't digested him yet. All the old centuries of farmwork and brute force have settled in him, and there they've stuck, for all he's so distinguished."

Bosinney seemed to ponder. "Well, you've hit your cousin Soames off to the life[3]," he said suddenly. "He'll never blow his brains out."

Young Jolyon shot at him a penetrating glance.

"No," he said, "he won't. That's why he's to be reckoned with. Look out for their grip! It's easy to laugh, but don't mistake me. It doesn't do to despise a Forsyte; it doesn't do to disregard them!"

"Yet you've done it yourself!"

Young Jolyon acknowledged the hit by losing his smile.

"You forget," he said with a queer pride, "I can hold on, too—I'm a Forsyte myself. We're all in the path of great forces. The man who leaves the shelter of the wall—well—you know what I mean. I don't," he added very low, as though uttering a threat, "recommend every man to—go—my—way. It depends."

The colour rushed into Bosinney's face, but soon receded, leaving it sallow-brown as before. He gave a short laugh, that left his lips fixed in a queer, fierce smile; his eyes mocked Young Jolyon.

"Thanks," he said. "It's deuced kind of you. But you're not the only chap that can hold on." He rose.

Young Jolyon looked after him as he walked away, and, resting his head on his hand, sighed.

## Notes

1. Bosinney's nickname: Bosinney was nicknamed "Buccaneer" by George Forsyte, Soames' cousin.
2. the three per cent half: people who invest their money in government securities and bonds
3. you've hit…the life: you have drawn Soames' portrait with great precision

## For Study and Discussion

1. Old Jolyon wrote a letter to his son, Young Jolyon. What is it about? Why does he conceal it from his young wife?
2. What is a Forsyte? What is the difference between a Forsyte and others?

# Chapter 25

# Virginia Woolf

## Life and Works

Virginia Woolf (1882–1941), one of the most innovative writers of the 20th century, originally Virginia Stephen, was born in London. Her father, Leslie Stephen, was a well-known Victorian critic, philosopher, biographer and scholar. She grew up as a member of a large and talented family, educating herself in her father's library, meeting even in childhood many eminent Victorians, learning Greek from Walter Pater's sister. After her father's death in 1904 she settled with her sister and two brothers in Bloomsbury, a residential section of London near the British Museum.

Bloomsbury became the centre of a coterie of writers, painters and intellectuals in the early 20th century. They were united by the belief that the greatest goals of life are the pleasures of friendship and the enjoyment of art. They rejected the restraints of propriety and the sexual prudery of Victorian society. They were avant garde in art and literature, and were free in their interlocking personal lives. The Bloomsbury group included Lyttom Strachey, a writer and biographer, J. Maynard Keynes, an eminent economist, Roger Fry, a playwright and art critic, and E. M. Forster.

When her sister Vanessa married Clive Bell, an art critic, in 1907, Virginia and her brother took together another house in Bloomsbury, and there they entertained their literary and artistic friends at evening gatherings.

In 1912 she married Leonard Woolf, a journalist, essayist and political thinker. Together they founded the Hogarth Press in 1917—a press which made a contribution to world literature. It published some of the most interesting literature of the time, including an early volume of T. S. Eliot's *Poems* (1919) and his *Homage to John Dryden* (1924). It also published the translations of such great writers on the Continent as Chekhov, Dostoevsky, Rilke and others. The most important of all, this press presented the new, experimental works that would be refused by other publishing houscs.

Virginia Woolf suffered from and died of bouts of mental depression. Her suicide in

March, 1941, resulting from her fear that she was about to lose her mind and become a burden on her husband, first revealed to the public that she had been subject to periods of nervous depression, particularly after finishing a book, and that underneath the liveliness and wit so well-known among the Bloomsbury group lay disturbing psychological tensions.

Living in a world of the middle-class and upper middle-class London intelligentsia, Woolf came naturally into the profession of writing. She rebelled against what she called the "materialism" of such novelists as Arnold Bennett and John Galsworthy, and sought a more delicate rendering of those aspects of consciousness in which she felt that the truth of human experience really lay. After two novels cast in traditional form, she developed her own style, which handled the "stream of consciousness" with a carefully modulated poetic flow and brought into prose fiction something of the rhythms and the imagery of lyric poetry. The sketches in which she explored the possibilities of moving between action and contemplation, between specific external events in time and delicate tracings of the flow of consciousness where the mind moved between retrospect and anticipation, were collected in *Monday or Tuesday*. The "stream of consciousness" technique is a means of exploring the inner lives of her characters. These were technical experiments, and they made possible those later novels where her characteristic method was fully developed—*Jacob's Room*, an impressionistic and poetic treatment of the death of a young man during the First World War, *Mrs. Dalloway*, the first completely successful novel in her "new" style, *To the Lighthouse*, *The Waves*, the most stylised of her novels, which established her as a major innovative novelist.

## Brief Comment

Woolf was a skilled exponent of the "stream of consciousness" technique in her novels, exploring with great subtlety problems of personal identity and personal relationships as well as the significance of time, change and memory for human personality. The delicate lyrical prose of her finest novels was remarkable achievement.

She also wrote a great many reviews and critical essays, collected in *The Common Reader* and *The Second Common Reader*. Informal and personal in tone, her criticism was suggestive rather than authoritative and had an engaging air of spontaneity. She was equally concerned with her own craft as a writer and with what it was like to be a quite different person living in a different age.

Woolf was much concerned with the position of women, especially professional women, and the constrictions they suffered under. She wrote several essays on the subject, and women's social subjection also arises in her fiction. Her novel *The Years* (1937) was originally to have included reflections on the position of women interspersed amid the action, but she later decided to publish them as a separate book, *Three Guineas*. In *A Room of One's Own* she discussed various male institutions that historically either were denied to or oppressed women. As one of

Woolf's most influential works, it is widely recognized for its extraordinary contribution to the women's movement.

## A Room of One's Own

In the autumn of 1928, Woolf, on invitation, made two lectures on the subject of women and fiction. They were expanded and published as *A Room of One's Own.* In Woolf's opinion, to have a private room to think and write was a basic requirement for literary creation, a requirement that, along with economic independence, few women had ever enjoyed in history. After raising the question why women had not written first-class works, Woolf described poverty, social pressures, family demands, and lack of education that prevented women from writing.

In this work, Woolf created an imaginary figure, Judith Shakespeare, sister of the playwright Shakespeare, in order to make a comparison. Judith followed the steps of Shakespeare's career. Woolf tried to show how a woman with similar talents would have still been thwarted and opposed. Judith, though mentally powerful, would not have been sent to school. Instead, she would have been kept at home and betrothed to someone against her own will. If she had run away to avoid the marriage, she would still be in great difficulties and could not have possibly found a job in the theatre in which there were no actresses then. Unable to survive alone, she would have to degrade herself by doing different things, good and bad, moral and immoral, including death. Woolf supposed that women of unusual talents ended up isolated and despised. Even if a woman had been allowed to write, her imagination would have been distorted and made morbid by the difficulties of keeping an independent existence.

# Selections

### *Mrs. Dalloway*

## The Story

Mrs. Clarissa Dalloway went to make last-minute preparations for an evening party. During her day in the city she enjoyed the summer air, the many sights and people, the general bustle of London. She met Hugh Whitbread, now a court official, a handsome and sophisticated man. She had known Hugh since her youth, and she knew his wife, Evelyn, as well, but she did not particularly care for Evelyn. Other people came down to London to see paintings, to hear music, or to shop. The Whitbreads came down to consult doctors, for Evelyn was always ailing.

Mrs. Dalloway went about her shopping. While she was in a flower shop, a luxurious limousine pulled up outside. Everyone speculated on the occupant behind the drawn curtains of the car. Everywhere the limousine went, it was followed by curious eyes. Mrs. Dalloway, who had thought that the queen was inside, felt that she was right when the car drove into the Buckingham Palace grounds.

The sights and sounds of London reminded Mrs. Dalloway of many things. She thought back to her youth, to the days before her marriage, to her husband, to her daughter Elizabeth. Her daughter was indeed a problem and all because of that horrid Miss Kilman who was her friend. Miss Kilman was something of a religious fanatic, who scoffed at the luxurious living of the Dalloways and felt sorry for Mrs. Dalloway. Mrs. Dalloway hated her. Miss Kilman was not at all like the friend of her own girlhood. Sally Seton had been different. Mrs. Dalloway had really loved Sally.

Mrs. Dalloway wondered what love really was. She had loved Sally, but she had loved Richard Dalloway and Peter Walsh, too. She had married Richard, and then Peter had left for India. Later she learnt that he had married someone he met on shipboard. She had heard little about his wife since his marriage. But the day was wonderful and life itself was wonderful. The war was over and she was giving a party.

While Mrs. Dalloway was shopping, Septimus Smith and his wife were sitting in the park. Septimus had married Lucrezia while he was serving in Italy and she had given up her family and her country for him. Now he frightened her because he acted so queerly and talked of committing suicide. The doctor said that there was nothing wrong with him, nothing wrong physically. Septimus, one of the first to volunteer for war duty, had gone to war to save his country, the England of Shakespeare. When he got back, he was a war hero and he was given a good job at the office. They had nice lodgings and Lucrezia was happy. Septimus began reading Shakespeare again. He was unhappy; he brooded. He and Lucrezia had no children. To Septimus the world was in such a horrible condition that it was unjust to bring children into it.

When Septimus began to have visitations from Evans, a comrade who had been killed in the war, Lucrezia became even more frightened and she called in Dr. Holmes. Septimus felt almost completely abandoned by that time. Lucrezia could not understand why her husband did not like Dr. Holmes, for he was so kind, so interested in Septimus. Finally she took her husband to Sir William Bradshaw, a wealthy and noted psychiatrist. Septimus had had a brilliant career ahead of him. His employer spoke highly of his work. No one knew why he wanted to kill himself. Septimus said that he committed a crime, but his wife said that he was guilty of absolutely nothing. Sir William suggested a place in the country, where Septimus would be by himself, without his wife. It was not, Sir William said, a question of preference. Since he had threatened suicide, it was a question of law.

In the meantime Mrs. Dalloway returned home. Lady Bruton had invited Richard Dalloway to lunch. Mrs. Dalloway had never liked Millicent Bruton; she was far too clever. Then Peter Walsh came to call, and Mrs. Dalloway was surprised and happy to see him again. She introduced him to her Elizabeth. He asked Mrs. Dalloway if she were happy; she wondered why. When he left, she called out to him not to forget her party. Peter thought, Clarissa Dalloway and her parties! That was all life meant to her. He had been divorced from his wife and had come to England. For him, life was far more complicated. He had fallen in love with another woman, one who had two children, and he had come to London to arrange for her divorce and to get some sort of a job. He hoped Hugh Whitbread would find him one, something in the government.

That night Clarissa Dalloway's party was a great success. At first she was afraid that it would fail. But at last the prime minister arrived and her evening was complete. Peter was there, and Peter met Lady Rossetter. Lady Rossetter turned out to be Sally Seton. She had not been invited, but had just dropped in. She had five sons, she told Peter. They chatted. Then Elizabeth came in and Peter noticed how beautiful she was. Later, Sir William Bradshaw and his wife entered. They were late, they explained, because one of Sir William's patients had committed suicide. For Septimus Smith, feeling altogether abandoned, had jumped out of a window before they could take him into the country. Clarissa was upset. Here was death, she thought. Although the suicide was completely unknown to her, she somehow felt it was her own disaster, her own disgrace. The poor young man had thrown away his life when it became useless. Clarissa had never thrown away anything more valuable than a shilling into the Serpentine. Yes, once she had stood beside a fountain while Peter Walsh, angry and humiliated, had asked her whether she intended to marry Richard. And Richard had never been prime minister. Instead, the prime minister came to her parties. Now she was growing old. Clarissa Dalloway knew herself at last for the beautiful, charming, inconsequential person she was.

Sally and Peter talked on. They thought idly of Clarissa and Richard, and wondered whether they were happy together. Sally agreed that Richard had improved. She left Peter and went to talk with Richard. Peter was feeling strange. A sort of terror and ecstasy took hold of him, and he could not be certain what it was that excited him so suddenly. It was Clarissa, he thought. Even after all these years, it must be Clarissa.

## Chapter I

She had reached the Park gates[1]. She stood for a moment, looking at the omnibuses in Piccadilly[2].

She would not say of any one in the world now that they were this or were that. She felt very young; at the same time unspeakably aged. She sliced like a knife through everything; at the same time was outside, looking on. She had a perpetual sense, as she watched the taxi cabs, of being out, out, far out to sea and alone; she always had the feeling that it was very, very dangerous to live even one day. Not that she thought herself clever, or much out of the ordinary. How she had got through life on the few twigs of knowledge Fraulein Daniels[3] gave them she could not think. She knew nothing; no language, no history; she scarcely read a book now, except memoirs in bed; and yet to her it was absolutely absorbing; all this; the cabs passing; and she would not say of Peter[4], she would not say of herself, I am this, I am that.

Her only gift was knowing people almost by instinct, she thought, walking on. If you put her in a room with someone, up went her back like a cat's; or she purred. Devonshire House, Bath House[5], the house with the china cockatoo[6], she had seen them all lit up once; and remembered Sylvia, Fred Sally Seton—Such hosts of people; and dancing all night; and the waggons plodding past to market; and driving home across the Park. She remembered once throwing a shilling into the Serpentine[7]. But every one remembered; what she loved was this, here, now, in front of her; the fat lady in the cab. Did it matter then, she asked herself, walking towards Bond Street[8], did it matter that she must inevitably cease completely; all this must go on without her; did she resent it; or did it not become consoling to believe that death ended absolutely? but that somehow in the streets of London, on the ebb and flow of things, here, there, she survived, Peter survived, lived in each other, she being part, she was positive, of the trees at home; of the house there, ugly, rambling all to bits and pieces as it was[9]; part of people she had never met; being laid out like a mist between the people she knew best, who lifted her on their branches as she had seen the trees lift the mist, but it spread ever so far, her life, herself. But what was she dreaming as she looked into Hatchard's shop window[10]? What was she trying to recover? What image of white dawn in the country, as she read in the book spread open:

Fear no more the heat o' the sun
Nor the furious winter's rages.[11]

This late age of the world's experience had bred in them all, all men and women, a well of tears. Tears and sorrows; courage and endurance; a perfectly upright and stoical bearing. Think, for example, of the woman she admired most, Lady Bexborough[12], opening the bazaar.

There were *Jorrocks' Jaunts and Jollities*; there were *Soapy Sponge* and Mrs. Asquith's *Memoirs* and *Big Game Shooting in Nigeria*[13], all spread open. Ever so many books there were; but none that seemed exactly right to take to Evelyn Whitbread[14] in her nursing home. Nothing that would serve to amuse her and make that indescribably dried-up little woman look, as Clarissa came in, just for a moment cordial; before they settled down for the usual interminable talk of women's ailments. How much she wanted it—that people should look pleased as she came in, Clarissa thought and turned and walked back towards Bond Street, annoyed, because it was silly to have other reasons for doing things. Much rather would she have been one of those people like Richard who did things for themselves, whereas, she thought, waiting to cross, half the time she did things not simply, not for themselves; but to make people think this or that; perfect idiocy she knew (and now the policeman held up his hand) for no one was ever for a second taken in. Oh if she could have had her life over again! she thought, stepping on to the pavement, could have looked even differently!

She would have been, in the first place, dark like Lady Bexborough, with a skin of crumpled leather and beautiful eyes. She would have been, like Lady Bexborough, slow and stately; rather large; interested in politics like a man; with a country house; very dignified, very sincere. Instead of which she had a narrow pea-stick figure; a ridiculous little face, beaked like a bird's. That she held herself well was true; and had nice hands and feet; and dressed well, considering that she spent little. But often now this body she wore (she stopped to look at a Dutch picture), this body, with all its capacities, seemed nothing—nothing at all. She had the oddest sense of being herself invisible; unseen; unknown; there being no more marrying, no more having of children now, but only this astonishing and rather solemn progress with the rest of them, up Bond Street, this being Mrs. Dalloway; not even Clarissa any more; this being Mrs. Richard Dalloway.

Bond Street fascinated her; Bond Street early in the morning in the season; its flags flying; its shops; no splash; no glitter; one roll of tweed in the shop where her father had bought his suits for fifty years; a few pearls; salmon on an ice block.

"That is all," she said, looking at the fishmonger's. "That is all," she repeated, pausing for a moment at the window of a glove shop where, before the War[15], you could buy almost perfect gloves. And her old Uncle William used to say a lady is known by her shoes and her gloves. He had turned on his bed one morning in the middle of the War. He had said, "I have had enough." Gloves and shoes, she had a passion for gloves; but her own daughter, her Elizabeth, cared not a straw for either of them.

Not a straw, she thought, going on up Bond Street to a shop where they kept flowers for her when she gave a party. Elizabeth really cared for her dog most of all. The whole house this morning smelt of tar. Still, better poor Grizzle[16] than Miss Kilman[17]; better distemper and tar and all the rest of it than sitting mewed in a stuffy bedroom with a prayer book! Better anything, she was inclined to say. But it might be only a phase, as Richard said, such as all girls go through. It might be falling in love. But why with Miss Kilman? who had been badly treated of course; one must make allowances for that, and Richard said, she was very able, had a really historical mind. Anyhow they were inseparable, and Elizabeth, her own daughter, went to Communion; and how she dressed, how she treated people who came to lunch she did not care a bit, it being her experience that the religious ecstasy made people callous (so did causes); dulled their feelings, for Miss Kilman would do anything for the Russians, starved herself for the Austrians, but in private inflicted positive torture, so insensitive was she, dressed in a green mackintosh coat. Year in year out she wore that coat; she perspired; she was never in the room five minutes without making you feel her superiority, your inferiority; how poor she was; how rich you were; how she lived in a slum without a cushion or a bed or a rug or whatever it might be, all her soul rusted with that grievance sticking in it, her dismissal from school during the War—poor embittered unfortunate creature! For it was not her one hated but the idea of her, which undoubtedly had gathered into itself a great deal that was not Miss Kilman; had become one of those spectres with which one battles in the night; one of those spectres who stand astride us and suck up half our life-blood, dominators and tyrants; for no doubt with another throw of the dice, had the black been uppermost and not the white, she would have loved Miss Kilman! But not in this world. No.

It rasped her, though, to have stirring about in her this brutal monster! to hear twigs cracking and feel hooves planted down in the depths of that leaf-encumbered forest, the soul; never to be content quite, or quite secure, for at any moment the brute would be stirring, this hatred, which, especially since her illness, had power to make her feel scraped, hurt in her spine; gave her physical pain, and made all pleasure in beauty, in friendship, in being well, in being loved and making her home delightful rock, quiver, and bend as if indeed there were a monster grubbing at the roots, as if the whole panoply of content were nothing but self love! this hatred!

Nonsense, nonsense! she cried to herself, pushing through the swing doors of Mulberry's the florists.

She advanced, light, tall, very upright, to be greeted at once by button-faced Miss Pym, whose hands were always bright red, as if they had been stood in cold water with the flowers.

There were flowers: delphiniums, sweet peas, bunches of lilac; and carnations, masses of carnations. There were roses; there were irises. Ah yes—so she breathed in the earthy garden sweet smell as she stood talking to Miss Pym who owed her help, and thought her kind, for kind she had been years ago; very kind, but she looked older, this year, turning her head from side to side among the irises and roses and nodding tufts of lilac with her eyes half closed, snuffing in, after the street uproar, the delicious scent, the exquisite coolness. And then, opening her eyes, how fresh like frilled linen clean from a laundry laid in wicker trays the roses looked; and dark and prim the red carnations, holding their heads up; and all the sweet peas spreading in their bowls, tinged violet, snow white, pale—as if it were the evening and girls in muslin frocks came out to pick sweet peas and roses after the superb summer's day, with its almost blue-black sky, its delphiniums, its carnation, its arum lilies was over; and it was the moment between six and seven when every flower—roses, carnations, irises, lilac—glows; white, violet, red, deep orange; every flower seems to burn by itself, softly, purely in the misty beds; and how she loved the grey-white moths spinning in and out, over the cherry pie, over the evening primroses!

And as she began to go with Miss Pym from jar to jar, choosing, nonsense, nonsense, she said to herself, more and more gently, as if this beauty, this scent, this colour, and Miss Pym liking her, trusting her, were a wave which she let flow over her and surmount that hatred, that monster, surmount it all; and it lifted her up and up when—oh! a pistol shot in the street outside!

"Dear, those motor cars," said Miss Pym, going to the window to look, and coming back and smiling apologetically with her hands full of sweet peas, as if those motor cars, those tyres of motor cars, were all her fault.

## Notes

1. Park gates: the gates of St James' Park in London
2. Piccadilly: a street in London, the traditional centre of fashionable shops, clubs and hotels

3. Fraulein Daniels: the German governess who taught Mrs. Dalloway in her childhood
   Fraulein: (German) Miss
4. Peter: Peter Walsh, Mrs. Dalloway's former lover
5. Devonshire House, Bath House: the buildings she remembered she had seen some time in the past
6. china cockatoo: a large crested parrot made of porcelain
7. the Serpentine: ornamental water in Hyde Park, London
8. Bond Street: a street in the West End of London
9. ugly, rambling all to bits and pieces as it was: the ugly house, big but somewhat old and dilapidated, where she lived
10. Hatchard's shop window: shop window of Hatchard's (name of the shop)
11. They are the first two lines of the dirge on Imogen in Shakespeare's *Cymbeline* which Mrs. Dalloway remembered to have read.
12. Lady Bexborough: an aristocratic lady Mrs. Dalloway knew and admired, who was asked to open the bazaar (somewhere some time ago)
13. These are books for popular reading in the 1920s that came to Mrs. Dalloway's mind at the moment. Mrs. Margot Asquith (1864–1945) was the wife of Herbert Henry Asquith (1852–1928), a well-known English statesman.
14. Evelyn Whitbread: Mrs. Dalloway's friend, wife of Hugh Whitbread, a coal merchant
15. the War: the First World War
16. Grizzle: the dog at the Dalloways'
17. Miss Kilman: the servant at the Dalloways'

## For Study and Discussion

1. What feeling do you get when you read this selection? What impression does Mrs. Dalloway give you?
2. Do you like the "stream of consciousness" technique? Why?
3. Read the introduction about Virginia Woolf in this chapter carefully and find more materials and other sources. Then make a summary of the "stream of consciousness" technique and discuss how this technique is used in the selection.

# Chapter 26

# James Joyce

## Life and Works

James Joyce (1882–1941) was born in Dublin. His father was a talented but feckless person, a failed businessman but skillful storyteller, who drifted steadily down the financial and social scale, moving his family from house to house, each one less genteel and more shabby than the previous.

James Joyce's education was Catholic, from the age of six to the age of nine at Clongowes Wood College, and from eleven to sixteen at Belvedere College, Dublin. Both were Jesuit institutions, and were normal roads to the priesthood. He then studied modern languages at University College Dublin.

In the meantime, he felt repelled by the narrow life of the middle-class Dubliners. He found such an existence too commercial in its values and its sentiment highly hypocritical. These narrow-minded Dubliners became the main characters in Joyce's writing, as objects either to be exposed or to be ridiculed.

From a comparatively early age Joyce regarded himself as a rebel against the shabbiness and philistinism of Dublin. In his early youth he was very religious, but in his last year at Belvedere he began to reject his Catholic faith in favour of a literary mission which he saw as involving rebellion and exile. He refused to play any part in the nationalist or other popular activities of his fellow students, and created some stir by his outspoken articles, one of which, on the Norwegian playwright Henrik Ibsen, appeared in *The Fortnightly Review* for April, 1900. He taught himself Norwegian to be able to read Ibsen and to write to him. When an article by Joyce significantly entitled "The Day of the Rabblement", was refused, on instructions of the faculty adviser, by the student magazine that had commissioned it, he had it printed privately. By 1902, when he received his BA degree, he was already committed to a career as an exile and a writer.

Joyce went to Paris after graduation, was recalled to Dublin by his mother's fatal illness, had a short spell there as a schoolteacher, and then returned to the Continent in 1904 to teach

English at Trieste and then at Zurich. He took with him Nora Barnacle, an uneducated Galway girl with no interest in literature; her native vivacity and peasant wit charmed Joyce, and the two lived in devoted companionship until Joyce's death, though they were not married until 1931. In 1920 Joyce settled in Paris, where he lived until December, 1940, when the war forced him to take refuge in Switzerland; he died in Zurich a few weeks later.

Proud, obstinate, absolutely convinced of his genius, given to fits of sudden gaiety and of sudden silence, Joyce was not always an easy person to get on with, yet he never lacked friends and throughout his thirty-six years on the Continent was always the centre of a literary circle. Life was hard at first. At Trieste he had very little money, and he did not improve matters by drinking heavily, a habit checked somewhat by his brother Stanislaus who came out from Dublin to act (as Stanislaus put it much later) as his "brother's keeper". His financial position was much improved by the patronage of Mrs. McCormick (Edith Rockefeller), who provided him with a monthly stipend from March, 1917, until September, 1919, when they quarrelled, apparently because Joyce refused to submit to the psychoanalysis by Carl Jung, who had been heavily endowed by Mrs. McCormick. The New York lawyer and art patron John Quinn, steered in Joyce's direction by Ezra Pound, also helped Joyce financially in 1917. A more permanent benefactor was the English feminist and editor Harriet Shaw Weaver, who not only subsidised Joyce generously from 1917 to the end of his life, but occupied herself indefatigably with arrangements for publishing his work.

Joyce's almost life-long exile from his native Ireland had something paradoxical about it. No writer had ever been more soaked in Dublin, its atmosphere, its history, its topography; in spite of doing most of his writing in Trieste, Zurich and Paris, he wrote only and always about Dublin. He devised ways of expanding his accounts of Dublin, however, so that they became microcosms, small-scale models, of all human life, of all history and all geography. Indeed that was his life's work: to write about Dublin in such a way that he was writing about all of human experience.

Joyce began his career by writing a series of stories depicting aspects of Dublin life with extraordinary clarity. But these stories—published as *Dubliners* in 1914—are more than sharp realistic sketches. In each, the detail is so chosen and organised that carefully interacting symbolic meanings are set up, and as a result *Dubliners* is a book about man's fate as well as a series of sketches of Dublin. Publication of *Dubliners* was held up for many years while he fought with both English and Irish publishers about certain words and phrases which they wished to eliminate. (It was the former who finally published the book.)

*A Portrait of the Artist as a Young Man* (1916) is an example showing how carefully Joyce reworked and compressed his material for maximum effect. *The Portrait* is not literally true as an autobiography, though it has many autobiographical elements. It is representatively true not only of Joyce but of the relation between the artist and society in the modern world.

The book's narrative style changes to evoke developments of the artist's consciousness. He used childish language and limited concepts of a teenager in the first episodes. The later episodes are articulated in the sophisticated and abstract vocabulary of a young scholar. In this novel, Joyce developed a literary form that moves from simple, direct expression of emotion in lyric form, to the less personal forms of narrative, to the drama, which is the most objective and in which the author's own speaking voice is completely removed, and the characters speak on their own.

His masterpiece *Ulysses* was banned in both Britain and America on its first appearance in 1922. Its earlier serialisation in *The Little Review* had to stop abruptly when the US Post Office brought a charge of obscenity against it. Fortunately, Judge Woolsey's history-making decision in favour of *Ulysses* in the United States district court on December 6, 1933, resulted in the lifting of the ban and the free circulation of the work first in America and soon afterwards in Britain.

*Ulysses* broke entirely with traditional forms of the realistic novel. Joyce introduced and extended the "stream of consciousness" technique, in which a character presents an unbroken stream of thoughts, feelings, memories and reactions to the current action, with no description or explanation by a separate narrator.

## Brief Comment

The innovative Joyce displayed the liberating effect of modernism. His innovations in organisation, style and narrative technique have influenced countless other writers. They gave the readers a maze of conflicting and sometimes incoherent thoughts in a character's mind and consciousness. The narration is freed from traditional ordinary chronological sequence to accommodate the movements of memory and mental pattern of association. The focus of the novel shifted from character's efforts to find their proper roles in society towards an illustration and an examination of states, for example, of doubt, isolation and self-absorption. The freedom of form in the new novel was so extended that they even included a more frank way of presenting sex, which became intolerable to the public. So, more often than not, such writers chose to leave their own country and sought lodging in other countries, living in exile in order to continue their special way of writing. As outsiders, they enjoyed the freedom of writing and they could look back and created powerful images of the fears and dilemmas of men and women that lived in the complex modern world.

## Selections

### *Dubliners*

### Araby[1]

North Richmond Street, being blind, was a quiet street except at the hour when the Christian Brothers' School[2] set the boys free. An uninhabited house of two storeys stood at the blind end, detached from its neighbours in a square ground. The other houses of the street, conscious of decent lives within them, gazed at one another with brown imperturbable faces.

The former tenant of our house, a priest, had died in the back drawing-room. Air, musty from having been long enclosed, hung in all the rooms, and the waste room behind the kitchen was littered with old useless papers. Among these I found a few paper-covered books, the pages of which were curled and damp: *The Abbot* by Walter Scott, *The Devout Communicant* and *The Memoirs of Vidocq*[3]. I liked the last best because its leaves were yellow. The wild garden behind the house contained a central apple-tree and a few straggling bushes under one of which I found the late tenant's rusty bicycle-pump. He had been a very charitable priest; in his will he had left all his money to institutions and the furniture of his house to his sister.

When the short days of winter came dusk fell before we had well eaten our dinners. When we met in the street the houses had grown sombre. The space of sky above us was the colour of ever-changing violet and towards it the lamps of the street lifted their feeble lanterns. The cold air stung us and we played till our bodies glowed. Our shouts echoed in the silent street. The career of our play brought us through the dark muddy lanes behind the houses where we ran the gantlet of the rough tribes from the cottages, to the back doors of the dark dripping gardens where odours arose from the ash pits, to the dark odorous stables where a coachman smoothed and combed the horse or shook music from the buckled harness. When we returned to the street light from the kitchen window had filled the areas. If my uncle was seen turning the corner we hid in the shadow until we had seen him safely housed. Or if Mangan's sister came out on the doorstep to call her brother in to his tea we watched her from our shadow peer up and down the street. We waited to see whether she would remain or go in and, if she remained, we left our shadow and walked up to Mangan's steps resignedly. She was waiting for us, her figure defined by the light from the half-opened door. Her brother always teased her before he obeyed and I stood by the railings looking at her. Her dress swung as she moved her body and the soft rope of her hair tossed from side to side.

Every morning I lay on the floor in the front parlour watching her door. The blind was pulled down to within an inch of the sash so that I could not be seen. When she came out on the doorstep my heart leaped. I ran to the hall, seized my books and followed her. I kept her brown figure always in my eye and, when we came near the point at which our ways diverged. I quickened my pace and passed her. This happened morning after morning. I had never spoken to her, except for a few casual words, and yet her name was like a summons to all my foolish blood.

Her image accompanied me even in places the most hostile to romance. On Saturday evenings when my aunt went marketing I had to go to carry some of the parcels. We walked through the flaring streets, jostled by drunken men and bargaining women, amid the curses of labourers, the shrill litanies of shop-boys who stood on guard by the barrels of pigs' cheeks, the nasal chanting of street-singers, who sang a *come-all-you*[4] about O'Donovan Rossa, or a ballad about the troubles in our native land. These noises converged in a single sensation of life for me: I imagined that I bore my chalice safely through a throng of foes. Her name sprang to my lips at movement in strange prayers and praises which I myself did not understand. My eyes were often full of tears (I could not tell why) and at times a flood from my heart seemed to pour itself out into my bosom. I thought little of the future. I did not know whether I would ever speak to her or not or, if I spoke to her, how I could tell her of my confused adoration. But my body was like a harp and her words and gestures were like fingers running upon the wires.

One evening I went into the back drawing-room in which the priest had died. It was a dark rainy evening and there was no sound in the house. Through one of the broken panes I heard the rain impinge upon the earth, the fine incessant needles of water playing in the sodden beds. Some distant lamp or lighted window gleamed below me. I was thankful that I could see so little. All my senses seemed to desire to veil themselves and, feeling that I was about to slip from them, I pressed the palms of my hands together until they trembled, murmuring: O love! O love! many times.

At last she spoke to me. When she addressed the first words to me I was so confused that I did not know what to answer. She asked me was I going to Araby[5]. I forget whether I answered yes or no. It would be a splendid bazaar, she said; she would love to go.

—And why can't you? I asked.

While she spoke she turned a silver bracelet round and round her wrist. She could not go, she said, because there would be a retreat that week in her convent[6]. Her brother and two other boys were fighting for their caps and I was alone at the railings. She held one of the spikes, bowing her head towards me. The light from the lamp opposite our door caught the white curve of her neck, lit up her hair that rested there and, falling, lit up the hand upon the railing. It fell over one side of her dress and caught the white border of a petticoat, just visible as she stood at ease.

—It's well for you, she said.

—If I go, I said, I will bring you something.

What innumerable follies laid waste my waking and sleeping thoughts after that evening! I wished to annihilate the tedious intervening days. I chafed against the work of school. At night in my bedroom and by day in the classroom her image came between me and the page I strove to read. The syllables of the word *Araby* were called to me through the silence in which my soul luxuriated and cast an Eastern enchantment over me. I asked for leave to go to the bazaar Saturday night. My aunt was surprised and hoped it was not some Freemason affair.[7] I answered few questions in class. I watched my master's face pass from amiability to sternness; he hoped I was not beginning to idle. I could not call my wandering thoughts together. I had hardly any patience with the serious work of life which, now that it stood between me and my desire, seemed to me child's play, ugly monotonous child's play.

On Saturday morning I reminded my uncle that I wished to go to the bazaar in the evening. He was fussing at the hallstand, looking for the hat-brush, and answered me curtly:

—Yes, boy, I know.

As he was in the hall I could not go into the front parlour and lie at the window. I left the house in bad humour and walked slowly towards the school. The air was pitilessly raw and already my heart misgave me.

When I came home to dinner my uncle had not yet been home. Still it was early. I sat staring at the clock for some time and, when its ticking began to irritate me, I left the room, I mounted the staircase and gained the upper of the house. The high cold empty gloomy rooms liberated me and I went from room to room singing. From the front window I saw my companions playing below in the street. Their cries reached me weakened and indistinct and, leaning my forehead against the cool glass, I looked over at the dark house where she lived. I may have stood there for an hour, seeing nothing but the brown-clad figure cast by my imagination, touched discreetly by the lamplight at the curved neck, at the hand upon the railings and at the border below the dress.

When I came downstairs again I found Mrs. Mercer sitting at the fire. She was an old garrulous woman, a pawnbroker's widow, who collected used stamps for some pious purpose. I had to endure the gossip of the tea-table. The meal was prolonged beyond an hour and still my uncle did not come. Mrs. Mercer stood up to go: she was sorry she couldn't wait any longer, but it was after eight o'clock and she did not like to be out late, as the night air was bad for her. When she had gone I began to walk up and down the room, clenching my fists. My aunt said:

—I'm afraid you may put off your bazaar for this night of Our Lord.

At nine o'clock I heard my uncle's latchkey in the hall-door. I heard him talking to himself and heard the hall-stand rocking when it had received the weight of his overcoat. I could interpret these signs. When he was midway through his dinner I asked him to give me the money to go to the bazaar. He had forgotten.

—The people are in bed and after their first sleep now, he said.

I did not smile. My aunt said to him energetically:

—Can't you give him the money and let him go? You've kept him late enough as it is.

My uncle said he was very sorry he had forgotten. He said he believed in the old saying: All work and no play makes Jack a dull boy. He asked me where I was going and, when I had told him a second time he asked me did I know "The Arab's Farewell to His Steed"[8]. When I left the kitchen, he was about to recite the opening lines of the piece to my aunt.

I held a florin tightly in my hand as I strode down Buckingham Street towards the station.

The sight of the streets thronged with buyers and glaring with gas recalled to me the purpose of my journey. I took my seat in a third-class carriage of a deserted train. After an intolerable delay the train moved out of the station slowly. It crept onward among ruinous houses and over the twinkling river. At Westland Row Station a crowd of people pressed to the carriage doors; but the porters moved them back, saying that it was a special train for the bazaar. I remained alone in the bare carriage. In a few minutes the train drew up beside an improvised wooden platform. I passed out on to the road and saw by the lighted dial of a clock that it was ten minutes to ten. In front of me was a large building which displayed the magical name.

I could not find any sixpenny entrance and, fearing that the bazaar would be closed, I passed in quickly through a turnstile, handing a shilling to a weary-looking man. I found myself in a big hall girdled at half its height by a gallery. Nearly all the stalls were closed and the greater part of the hall was in darkness. I recognised a silence like that which pervades a church after a service. I walked into the centre of the bazaar timidly. A few people were gathered about the stalls which were still open. Before a curtain, over which the words Cafe Chantant[9] were written in coloured lamps, two men were counting money on a salver. I listened to the fall of the coins.

Remembering with difficulty why I had come I went over to one of the stalls and examined porcelain vases and flowered tea-sets. At the door of the stall a young lady was talking and laughing with two young gentlemen. I remarked their English accents and listened vaguely to their conversation.

—Oh, I never said such a thing!

—O, but you did!

—O, but I didn't

—Didn't she say that?

—Yes, I heard her.

—O, there's a…fib!

Observing me the young lady came over and asked me did I wish to buy anything. The tone of her voice was not encouraging; she seemed to have spoken to me out of a sense of duty. I looked humbly at the great jars that stood like eastern guards at either side of the dark entrance to the stall and murmured:

—No, thank you.

The young lady changed the position of one of the vases and went back to the two young men. They began to talk of the same subject. Once or twice the young lady glanced at me over her shoulder.

I lingered before her stall, though I knew my stay was useless, to make my interest in her wares seem the more real. Then I turned away slowly and walked down the middle of the bazaar. I allowed the two pennies to fall against the sixpence in my pocket. I heard a voice call from one end of the gallery that the light was out. The upper part of the hall was now completely dark.

Gazing up into the darkness I saw myself as a creature driven and derided by vanity; and my eyes burnt with anguish and anger.

## Notes

1. This is the third of the fifteen stories in *Dubliners*. This tale of the frustrated quest for beauty in the midst of drabness is both meticulously realistic in its handling of details of Dublin life and scene and highly symbolic in that almost every image and incident suggests some particular aspect of the theme (e.g., the suggestion of the Holy Grail in the image of the chalice, mentioned in the fifth paragraph). Joyce was drawing on his own childhood recollections, and the uncle in the story is a reminiscence of Joyce's father. In all the stories in *Dubliners* dealing with childhood, that a child lives not with his parents but with an uncle and aunt—a symbol of isolation and lack of proper relation between "consubstantial" ("in the flesh") parents and children—is a major theme.
2. North Richmond Street: The Joyce family moved to 17 North Richmond Street, Dublin, in 1894, and Joyce had earlier briefly attended the Christian Brothers school a few doors away (the Christian Brothers were a Catholic religious community). The details of the house described here correspond exactly to those of No. 17.
3. *The Abbot*, is a historical novel dealing with Mary Queen of Scots by Walter Scott; *The Devout Communicant* is a Catholic religious manual. *The Memoirs* of Vidocq: Francois Eugene Vidocq (1775–1857) was a legendary figure in history, known as the first detective and an inspiration to great writers such as Balzac and Hugo. In December 1828, Vidocq published his memoirs, with the help of some ghostwriters.
4. *come-all-you*: a street ballad, so called from its opening words. It was about the 19th-century Irish nationalist Jeremiah Donovan, popularly known as O'Donovan Rossa.
5. Araby: the bazaar, described by its "official catalogue" as a "Grand Oriental Fete"
6. there would be a retreat that week in her convent: retreat is a period of seclusion from ordinary activities devoted to religious exercises. "her convent" meaning her convent school
7. hoped it was not some Freemason affair: His aunt shared her church's distrust of the Freemasons, an old European secret society, reputedly anti-Catholic.
8. The Arab's Farewell to His Steed: once-popular sentimental poem by Caroline Norton
9. Cafe Chantant: literally "singing cafe" (cafe providing musical entertainment)

## For Study and Discussion

1. What is North Richmond Street like? What is the significance of the first paragraph?
2. What kind of person is the former tenant of the narrator's house?
3. In the third paragraph, the narrator describes what they would do in the street on a winter evening. Some people suggest that the way of telling the story is quite similar to the way

Charles Lamb does in his familiar essays. Some other readers even find familiarity like that presented by Zhu Ziqing in some paragraphs of his "Lotus Pool by Moonlight" (朱自清《荷塘月色》). What is your opinion?

4. What is the narrator's feeling towards Mangan's sister? Why does he behave that way in front of Mangan's sister?
5. Why does Araby the eastern bazaar appeal so much to the narrator?
6. Why does the narrator insist on going to the bazaar even when it is late at night? What does he see? Here is the last paragraph: "Gazing up into the darkness I saw myself as a creature driven and derided by vanity; and my eyes burned with anguish and anger." Why do his eyes burn with anguish and anger?

# Chapter 27

# David Herbert Lawrence

## Life and Works

David Herbert Lawrence (1885–1930) was born in the Midland mining village of Eastwood, Nottinghamshire. His father was a miner. His mother was better educated than his father and self-consciously genteel, fighting all her married life to lift her children out of the working class. D. H. Lawrence was aware from an early age of the struggle between his parents. He was very much on his mother's side during his childhood, resenting his father's coarse and drunken behaviour and allying himself with his mother's delicacy and refinement. After the death of an elder brother he became the centre of his mother's emotional life and played a loving and protective role in his own relation to her. His mother's claims on him kept frustrating his relationships with girls, and the personal problems and conflicts resulted were presented in *Sons and Lovers* (1913), his first really distinguished novel, where, against a background of paternal coarseness and vitality conflicting with maternal refinement and gentility, he set the theme of the demanding mother who had given up the prospect of achieving a true emotional life with her husband and turned to her sons with a dull and possessive love. This is an autobiographical novel reflecting his close relationship with his mother and describing the encouragement of his friend Jessie Chambers, who appears as Miriam in the novel. The theme of *Sons and Lover*s is usually said to concern the effect of mother-love upon the development of a son.

Spurred on and encouraged by his mother, Lawrence escaped through education from the mining world of his father. He won a scholarship to Nottingham High School and later, after working first as a clerk and then as an elementary school teacher, studied for two years at Nottingham University College, where he obtained his teacher's certificate in 1908. His first published work was a group of poems which appeared in the *English Review* for November, 1909. The following February the same periodical published his first short story. He was now regarded in London literary circles as a promising young writer.

His first novel, *The White Peacock*, was received with respect. From 1908 to 1912 he taught in Croydon, a southern suburb of London, but he gave this up after falling in love with Frieda von Richthofen, the wife of a professor of French at Nottingham. They went to Germany, the country of Frieda, and married after her divorce in 1914. The war brought them back to England but Frieda's German nationality made their life in England uncomfortable. Also, Lawrence found his novel *The Rainbow* banned for its frank description of sexual life. Lawrence came to feel that the forces of modern civilisation were arrayed against him. He was disgusted with the English society and decided to exile himself from England. After the war he sought refuge in Italy, Australia, Mexico, the United States, then again in Italy, and finally in the south of France, often desperately ill, restlessly searching for an ideal, or at least a tolerable community in which to live. It is an interesting phenomenon that almost all writers who wrote boldly about sexual relationships in their works had to choose to exile themselves in other countries for the freedom of writing.

After *The Rainbow*, his next novel was a sequel, *Women in Love*. In these two novels, he developed a new style, breaking away from the conventional realism he used in *Sons and Lovers*. He created an intense and symbolic prose in the rest of his novels. *Lady Chatterley's Lover* (written in 1928 and published in 1959) made him notorious for his bold sexual descriptions. Lawrence was also a poet. His poems are worth reading, presenting his ideas on many things. He died of tuberculosis in the south of France in March, 1930, at the early age of 45.

## Brief Comment

In his poetry and fiction, Lawrence sought to express the deep-rooted, the elemental, the instinctual in people and nature. He was at constant war with the mechanical and artificial, with the constraints and hypocrisies that civilisation imposes. Because he had new things to say and a new way of saying them, he was not easily or quickly appreciated. Although his early novels are more conventional in style and treatment, from the publication of *The Rainbow* the critics turned away in bewilderment and condemnation. The rest of his life, during which he produced a dozen more novels and poems, short stories, sketches and miscellaneous articles, was, in his own words, "a savage enough pilgrimage" marked by incessant struggle and by periods of frustration and despair. Phrases such as "supreme impulse" and "quickening spontaneous emotion" were characteristic of Lawrence's in intuition, in the dark forces of the inner self that must not be allowed to be swamped by the rational faculties but must be brought into a harmonious relation with them. A restless pilgrim, Lawrence had uncanny perceptions into the depths of physical things and an uncompromising honesty in his view of human beings and the world.

## Selections

### Sons and Lovers

## The Story

Walter Morel, a collier, had been a handsome, dashing young man when Gertrude had married him. But after a few years of marriage he proved to be an irresponsible breadwinner and a drunkard, and his wife hated him for what he had once meant to her and for what he now was. Her only solace lay in her children, William, Annie, Paul and Arthur, for she leant heavily upon them for companionship and lived in their happiness. She was a good parent; her children loved her. The oldest son, William, was successful in his work but he longed to go to London, where he had promise of a better job. After he had gone, Mrs. Morel turned to Paul for the companionship and love she had found in William.

Paul liked to paint. More sensitive than his brothers and sister, he was closer to Mrs. Morel than any of the others. William brought a girl named Lily home to visit, but it was apparent that she was not the right kind of girl for him; she was too shallow and self-centred. Before long, William himself became aware of that fact, but he resigned himself to keeping the promise he had made to his fiancee.

When William became ill, Mrs. Morel went to London to nurse her son and was with him there when he died. Returning home once more after she had buried her first son, Mrs. Morel could not bring herself out of her sorrow. Not until Paul became sick did she realise that her duty lay with the living rather than with the dead. After that she centred all her attention upon Paul. The two other children were capable of carrying on their affairs without the consistent attention that Paul demanded.

At sixteen Paul went to visit some friends of Mrs. Morel. The Leivers were a warm-hearted family, and Paul easily gained the friendship of the Leivers children. Fifteen-year-old Miriam Leivers was a strange girl, but her inner charm attracted Paul. Mrs. Morel, like many others, did not care for Miriam. Paul went to work at a stocking mill, where he was successful in his social relationships and in his work. He continued to draw. Miriam watched over his work and with quiet understanding offered judgment concerning his success or failure. Mrs. Morel sensed that some day her son would become famous for his art.

By the time Miriam and Paul had grown into their twenties, Paul realised that Miriam loved him deeply and that he loved her. But for some reason he could not bring himself to touch her. Then through Miriam he met Clara Dawes. For a long while Mrs. Morel had been urging him to give up Miriam, and now Paul tried to tell Miriam that it was all over between them. He did not want to marry her, but he felt that he did belong to her. He could not make up his own mind.

Clara Dawes was separated from her husband, Baxter Dawes. She was five years Paul's senior, but a beautiful woman whose loveliness charmed him. Although Clara became his mistress, she refused to divorce her husband and marry Paul. Sometimes Paul wondered whether he could bring himself to marry Clara if she was free. She was not what he wanted. His mother was the only woman to whom he could turn for complete understanding and love, for Miriam had tried to possess him and Clara maintained a barrier against him. Paul continued to devote much of his time and attention to making his mother happy. Annie had married and gone to live with her husband near the Morel home, and Arthur had married a childhood friend who bore him a son six months after the wedding.

Baxter Dawes resented Paul's relationship with his wife. Once he accosted Paul in a tavern and threatened him. Paul knew that he could not fight with Baxter, but he continued to see Clara.

Paul had entered pictures in local exhibits and had won four prizes. With encouragement from Mrs. Morel, he continued to paint. He wanted to go abroad, but he could not leave his mother. He began to see Miriam again. When she yielded herself to him, his passion was ruthless and savage. But their relationship was still unsatisfactory. He turned again to Clara.

Miriam knew about his love affair with Clara, but the girl felt that Paul would tire of his mistress and come back to her. Paul stayed with Clara, however, because he found in her an outlet for his unknown desires. His life was a great conflict. Meanwhile Paul was earning enough money to give his mother the things her husband had failed to provide. Mr. Morel stayed on with his wife and son, but he was no longer accepted as a father or a husband.

One day it was revealed that Mrs. Morel had cancer and was beyond any help except that of morphine and then death. During the following months Mrs. Morel declined rapidly. Paul was tortured by his mother's pain. Annie and Paul marvelled at her resistance to death, wishing that it would come to end her suffering. Paul dreaded such a catastrophe in his life, although he knew it must come eventually. He turned to Clara for comfort, but she failed to make him forget his misery. Then, visiting his mother at the hospital, Paul found Baxter Dawes recovering from an attack of typhoid fever. For a long time Paul had sensed that Clara wanted to return to Dawes, and now, out of pity for Dawes, he brought about reconciliation between the husband and wife.

When Mrs. Morel's suffering had mounted to a torturing degree, Annie and Paul decided that anything would be better than to let her live in agony. One night Paul gave her an overdose of morphine, and Mrs. Morel died the next day.

Left alone, Paul was lost. He felt that his own life had ended with the death of his mother. Clara, to whom he had turned before, was now back with Dawes. Because they could not bear to stay in the house without Mrs. Morel, Paul and his father parted, each taking different lodgings.

For a while Paul wandered helplessly trying to find some purpose in his life. Then he thought of Miriam, to whom he had once belonged. He returned to her, but with the renewed association he realised more than ever that she was not what he wanted. Once he had thought of going abroad. Now he wanted to join his mother in death. Leaving Miriam for the last time, he felt trapped and lost in his own indecision. But he also felt that he was free from Miriam after many years of passion and regret.

His mother's death was too great a sorrow for Paul to cast off immediately. Finally, after a lengthy inner struggle, he was able to see that she would always be with him and that he did not need to die to join her. With his new-found courage he set out to make his own life anew.

## Chapter X
## Clara

He soon made occasion to call again on Clara.

"Would you," he said, "care to come back to Jordan's?"

She put down her work, laid her beautiful arms on the table, and looked at him for some moments without answering. Gradually the flush mounted her cheek.

"Why?" she asked.

Paul felt rather awkward.

"Well, because Susan is thinking of leaving," he said.

Clara went on with her jennying. The white lace leaped in little jumps and bounds on to the card. He waited for her. Without raising her head, she said at last, in a peculiar low voice:

"Have you said anything about it?"

"Except to you, not a word."

There was again a long silence. "I will apply when the advertisement is out," she said.

"You will apply before that. I will let you know exactly when."

She went on spinning her little machine, and did not contradict him.

Clara came to Jordan's. Some of the older hands, Fanny among them, remembered her earlier rule, and cordially disliked the memory. Clara had always been "ikey[1]," reserved, and superior. She had never mixed with the girls as one of themselves. If she had occasion to find fault, she did it coolly and with perfect politeness, which the defaulter felt to be a bigger insult than crossness. Towards Fanny, the poor, overstrung hunchback, Clara was unfailingly compassionate and gentle, as a result of which Fanny shed more bitter tears than ever the rough tongues of the other overseers had caused her.

There was something in Clara that Paul disliked, and much that piqued him. If she were about, he always watched her strong throat or her neck, upon which the blonde hair grew low and fluffy. There was a fine down, almost invisible, upon the skin of her face and arms, and when once he had perceived it, he saw it always.

When he was at his work, painting in the afternoon, she would come and stand near to him, perfectly motionless. Then he felt her, though she neither spoke nor touched him. Although she stood a yard away he felt as if he were in contact with her. Then he could paint no more. He flung down the brushes, and turned to talk to her.

Sometimes she praised his work; sometimes she was critical and cold.

"You are affected in that piece," she would say; and, as there was an element of truth in her condemnation, his blood boiled with anger.

Again: "What of this?" he would ask enthusiastically.

"H'm!" she made a small doubtful sound. "It doesn't interest me much."

"Because you don't understand it," he retorted.

"Then why ask me about it?"

"Because I thought you would understand."

She would shrug her shoulders in scorn of his work. She maddened him. He was furious. Then he abused her, and went into passionate exposition of his stuff. This amused and stimulated her. But she never owned that she had been wrong.

During the ten years that she had belonged to the women's movement she had acquired a fair amount of education, and, having had some of Miriam's passion to be instructed, had taught herself French, and could read in that language with a struggle. She considered herself as a woman apart, and particularly apart, from her class. The girls in the spiral department were all of good homes. It was a small, special industry, and had a certain distinction. There was an air of refinement in both rooms. But Clara was aloof also from her fellow-workers.

None of these things, however, did she reveal to Paul. She was not the one to give herself away. There was a sense of mystery about her. She was so reserved, he felt she had much to reserve. Her history was open on the surface, but its inner meaning was hidden from everybody. It was exciting. And then sometimes he caught her looking at him from under her brows with an almost furtive, sullen scrutiny, which made him move quickly. Often she met his eyes. But then her own were, as it were, covered over, revealing nothing. She gave him a little, lenient smile. She was to him extraordinarily provocative, because of the knowledge she seemed to possess, and gathered fruit of experience he could not attain.

One day he picked up a copy of *Lettres de Mon Moulin*[2] from her work-bench.

"You read French, do you?" he cried.

Clara glanced round negligently. She was making an elastic stocking of heliotrope silk, turning the spiral machine with slow balanced regularity, occasionally bending down to see her work or to adjust the needles; then her magnificent neck, with its down and fine pencils of hair, shone white against the lavender[3], lustrous silk. She turned a few more rounds, and stopped.

"What did you say?" she asked, smiling sweetly.

Paul's eyes glittered at her insolent indifference to him.

"I did not know you read French," he said, very polite.

"Did you not?" she replied, with a faint, sarcastic smile.

"Rotten swank!" he said, but scarcely loud enough to be heard.

He shut his mouth angrily as he watched her. She seemed to scorn the work she mechanically produced; yet the hose she made were as nearly perfect as possible.

"You don't like spiral work," he said.

"Oh, well, all work is work," she answered, as if she knew all about it.

He marvelled at her coldness. He had to do everything hotly. She must be something special.

"What would you prefer to do?" he asked.

She laughed at him indulgently, as she said:

"There is so little likelihood of my ever being given a choice, that I haven't wasted time considering."

"Pah!" he said, contemptuous on his side now. "You only say that because you are too proud to own up what you want and can't get."

"You know me very well," she replied coldly.

"I know you think you're terrific great shakes, and that you live under the eternal insult of working in a factory."

He was very angry and very rude. She merely turned away from him in disdain. He walked whistling down the room, flirted and laughed with Hilda.

Later on he said to himself:

"What was I so impudent to Clara for?" He was rather annoyed with himself, at the same time glad. "Serve her right; she stinks with silent pride," he said to himself angrily.

In the afternoon he came down. There was a certain weight on his heart which he wanted to remove. He thought to do it by offering her chocolates.

"Have one?" he said. "I bought a handful to sweeten me up."

To his great relief, she accepted. He sat on the workbench beside her machine, twisting a piece of silk round his finger. She loved him for his quick, unexpected movements, like a young animal. His feet swung as he pondered. The sweets lay strewn on the bench. She bent over her machine, grinding rhythmically, then stooping to see the stocking that hung beneath, pulled down by the weight. He watched the handsome crouching of her back, and the apron-strings curling on the floor.

"There is always about you," he said, "a sort of waiting. Whatever I see you doing, you're not really there: you are waiting—like Penelope[4] when she did her weaving." He could not help a spurt of wickedness. "I'll call you Penelope," he said.

"Would it make any difference?" she said, carefully removing one of her needles.

"That doesn't matter, so long as it pleases me. Here, I say, you seem to forget I'm your boss. It just occurs to me."

"And what does that mean?" she asked coolly.

"It means I've got a right to boss you."

"Is there anything you want to complain about?"

"Oh I say, you needn't be nasty," he said angrily.

"I don't know what you want," she said, continuing her task.

"I want you to treat me nicely and respectfully."

"Call you 'sir', perhaps?" she asked quietly.

"Yes, call me 'sir'. I should love it."

"Then I wish you would go upstairs, sir."

His mouth closed, and a frown came on his face. He jumped suddenly down.

"You're too blessed superior for anything," he said.

And he went away to the other girls. He felt he was being angrier than he had any need to be. In fact, he doubted slightly that he was showing off. But if he were, then he would. Clara heard him laughing, in a way she hated, with the girls down the next room.

When at evening he went through the department after the girls had gone, he saw his chocolates lying untouched in front of Clara's machine. He left them. In the morning they were still there, and Clara was at work. Later on Minnie, a little brunette they called Pussy, called to him:

"Hey, haven't you got a chocolate for anybody?"

"Sorry, Pussy," he replied. "I meant to have offered them; then I went and forgot 'em."

"I think you did," she answered.

"I'll bring you some this afternoon. You don't want them after they've been lying about, do you? "

"Oh, I'm not particular," smiled Pussy.

"Oh no," he said. "They'll be dusty."

He went up to Clara's bench.

"Sorry I left these things littering about," he said.

She flushed scarlet. He gathered them together in his fist.

"They'll be dirty now," he said. "You should have taken them. I wonder why you didn't. I meant to have told you I wanted you to."

He flung them out of the window into the yard below. He just glanced at her. She winced from his eyes.

In the afternoon he brought another packet.

"Will you take some?" he said, offering them first to Clara. "These are fresh."

She accepted one, and put it onto the bench.

"Oh, take several—for luck," he said.

She took a couple more, and put them on the bench also. Then she turned in confusion to her work. He went on up the room.

"Here you are, Pussy," he said. "Don't be greedy!"

"Are they all for her?" cried the others, rushing up.

"Of course they're not," he said.

The girls clamoured around. Pussy drew back from her mates.

"Come out!" she cried. "I can have first pick, can't I, Paul?"

"Be nice with 'em," he said, and went away.

"You are a dear," the girls cried.

"Tenpence," he answered.

He went past Clara without speaking. She felt the three chocolate creams would burn her if she touched them. It needed all her courage to slip them into the pocket of her apron.

...

That day he met Clara as he ran downstairs to wash his hands at dinner-time.

"You have stayed to dinner!" he exclaimed. It was unusual for her.

"Yes; and I seem to have dined on old surgical-appliance stock. I must go out now, or I shall feel stale India-rubber right through."

She lingered. He instantly caught at her wish.

"You are going anywhere?" he asked.

They went together up to the Castle. Outdoors she dressed very plainly, down to ugliness; indoors she always looked nice. She walked with hesitating steps alongside Paul, bowing and turning away from him. Dowdy in dress, and drooping, she showed to great disadvantage. He could scarcely recognise her strong form, that seemed to slumber with power. She appeared almost insignificant, drowning her stature in her stoop, as she shrank from the public gaze.

The Castle grounds were very green and fresh. Climbing the precipitous ascent, he laughed and chattered, but she was silent, seeming to brood over something. There was scarcely time to go inside the squat, square building that crowns the bluff of rock. They leant upon the wall where the cliff runs sheer down to the Park. Below them, in their holes in the sandstone, pigeons preened themselves and cooed softly. Away down upon the boulevard at the foot of the rock, tiny trees stood in their own pools of shadow, and tiny people went scurrying about in almost ludicrous importance.

"You feel as if you could scoop up the folk like tadpoles, and have a handful of them," he said.

She laughed, answering:

"Yes; it is not necessary to get far off in order to see us proportionately. The trees are much more significant."

"Bulk only," he said.

She laughed cynically.

Away beyond the boulevard the thin stripes of the metals showed upon the railways track, whose margin was crowded with little stacks of timber, beside which smoking toy engines fussed. Then the silver string of the canal lay at random among the black heaps. Beyond, the dwellings, very dense on the river flat, looked like black, poisonous herbage, in thick rows and crowded beds, stretching right away, broken now and then by taller plants, right to where the river glistened in a hieroglyph across the country. The steep scarp cliffs across the river looked puny. Great stretches of country darkened with trees and faintly brightened with cornland, spread towards the haze, where the hills rose blue beyond grey.

"It is comforting," said Mrs. Dawes, "to think the town goes no farther. It is only a little sore upon the country yet."

"A little scab," Paul said.

She shivered. She loathed the town. Looking drearily across at the country which was forbidden her, her impassive face pale and hostile, she reminded Paul of one of the bitter, remorseful angels.

"But the town's all right," he said. "It's only temporary. This is the crude, clumsy makeshift we've practised on, till we find out what the idea is. The town will come all right."

The pigeons in the pockets of rock, among the perched bushes, cooed comfortably. To the left the large church of St Mary rose into space, to keep close company with the Castle, above the heaped rubble of the town. Mrs. Dawes smiled brightly as she looked across the country.

"I feel better," she said.

"Thank you," he replied. "Great compliment!"

"Oh, my brother!" she laughed.

"H'm! That's snatching back with the left hand what you gave with the right, and no mistake," he said.

She laughed in amusement at him.

"But what was the matter with you?" he asked. "I know you were brooding something special. I can see the stamp of it on your face yet."

"I think I will not tell you," she said.

"All right, hug it," he answered.

She flushed and bit her lip.

"No," she said, "it was the girls."

"What about 'em?" Paul asked.

"They have been plotting something for a week now, and today they seem particularly full of it. All alike; they insult me with their secrecy."

"Do they?" he asked in concern.

"I should not mind," she went on, in the metallic, angry tone, "if they did not thrust it into my face—the fact that they have a secret."

"Just like women," said he.

"It is hateful, their mean gloating," she said intensely.

Paul was silent. He knew what the girls gloated over. He was sorry to be the cause of this new dissension.

"They can have all the secrets in the world," she went on, brooding bitterly; "but they might refrain from glorying in them, and making me feel more out of it than ever. It is—it is almost unbearable."

Paul thought for a few minutes. He was much perturbed.

"I will tell you what it's all about," he said, pale and nervous. "It's my birthday, and they've bought me a fine lot of paints, all the girls. They're jealous of you"—he felt her stiffen coldly at the word "jealous"—"merely because I sometimes bring you a book," he added slowly. "But, you see, it's only a trifle. Don't bother about it, will you—because"—he laughed quickly—"well, what would they say if they saw us here now, in spite of their victory?"

She was angry with him for his clumsy reference to their present intimacy. It was almost insolent of him. Yet he was so quiet, she forgave him, although it cost her an effort.

Their two hands lay on the rough stone parapet of the Castle wall. He had inherited from his mother a fineness of mould, so that his hands were small and vigorous. Hers were large, to match her large limbs, but white and powerful looking. As Paul looked at them he knew her. "She is wanting somebody to take her hands—for all she is so contemptuous of us," he said to himself. And she saw nothing but his two hands, so warm and alive, which seemed to live for her. He was brooding now, staring out over the country from under sullen brows. The little, interesting diversity of shapes had vanished from the scene; all that remained was a vast, dark matrix of sorrow and tragedy, the same in all the houses and the river-flats and the people and the birds; they were only shapen differently. And now that the forms seemed to have melted away, there remained the mass from which all the landscape was composed, a dark mass of struggle and pain. The factory, the girls, his mother, the large, uplifted church, the thicket of the town, merged into one atmosphere—dark, brooding, and sorrowful, every bit.

"Is that two o'clock striking?" Mrs. Dawes said in surprise.

Paul started, and everything sprang into form, regained its individuality, its forgetfulness, and its cheerfulness.

They hurried back to work.

When he was in the rush of preparing for the night's post, examining the work up from Fanny's room, which smelt of ironing, the evening postman came in.

"Mr. Paul Morel," he said smiling, handing Paul a package. "A lady's handwriting! Don't let the girls see it."

The postman, himself a favourite, was pleased to make fun of the girls' affection for Paul.

It was a volume of verse with a brief note: "You will allow me to send you this, and so spare me my isolation. I also sympathise and wish you well.—C. D." Paul flushed hot.

"Good Lord! Mrs. Dawes. She can't afford it. Good Lord, who ever'd have thought it!"

He was suddenly intensely moved. He was filled with the warmth of her. In the glow he could almost feel her as if she were present—her arms, her shoulders, her bosom, see them, feel them, almost contain them.

This move on the part of Clara brought them into closer intimacy. The other girls noticed that when Paul met Mrs. Dawes his eyes lifted and gave that peculiar bright greeting which they could interpret. Knowing he was unaware, Clara made no sign, save that occasionally she turned aside her face from him when he came upon her.

They walked out together very often at dinner-time; it was quite open, quite frank. Everybody seemed to feel that he was quite unaware of the state of his own feeling, and that nothing was wrong. He talked to her now with some of the old fervour with which he had talked to Miriam, but he cared less about the talk; he did not bother about his conclusions.

One day in October they went out to Lambley for tea. Suddenly they came to a halt on top of the hill. He climbed and sat on a gate, she sat on the stile. The afternoon was perfectly still, with a dim haze, and yellow sheaves glowing through. They were quiet.

"How old were you when you married?" he asked quietly.

"Twenty-two."

Her voice was subdued, almost submissive. She would tell him now.

"It is eight years ago."

"Yes."

"And when did you leave him?"

"Three years ago."

"Five years! Did you love him when you married him?"

She was silent for some time; then she said slowly, "I thought I did—more or less. I didn't think much about it. And he wanted me. I was very prudish then."

"And you sort of walked into it without thinking?"

"Yes. I seemed to have been asleep nearly all my life."

"Somnambule[5]? But—when did you wake up?"

"I don't know that I ever did, or ever have—since I was a child."

"You went to sleep as you grew to be a woman? How queer! And he didn't wake you?"

"No; he never got there," she replied, in a monotone.

The brown birds dashed over the hedges where the rose-hips stood naked and scarlet.

"Got where?" he asked.

"At me. He never really mattered to me."

The afternoon was so gently warm and dim. Red roofs of the cottages burnt among the blue haze. He loved the day. He could feel, but he could not understand, what Clara was saying.

"But why did you leave him? Was he horrid to you?"

She shuddered lightly.

"He—he sort of degraded me. He wanted to bully me because he hadn't got me. And then I felt as if I wanted to run, as if I was fastened and bound up. And he seemed dirty."

"I see."

He did not at all see.

"And was he always dirty?" he asked.

"A bit," she replied slowly. "And then he seemed as if he couldn't get at me, really. And then he got brutal—he was brutal!"

"And why did you leave him finally?"

"Because—because he was unfaithful to me—"

They were both silent for some time. Her hand lay on the gatepost as she balanced. He put his own over it. His heart beat thickly.

"But did you—were you ever—did you ever give him a chance?"

"Chance? How?"

"To come near to you."

"I married him—and I was willing—"

They both strove to keep their voices steady.

"I believe he loves you," he said.

"It looks like it," she replied.

He wanted to take his hand away, and could not. She saved him by removing her own. After a silence, he began again:

"Did you leave him out of count all along?"

"He left me," she said.

"And I suppose he couldn't make himself mean everything to you?"

"He tried to bully me into it."

But the conversation had got them both out of their depth. Suddenly Paul jumped down.

"Come on," he said. "Let's go and get some tea."

They found a cottage, where they sat in the cold parlour. She poured out his tea. She was very quiet. He felt she had withdrawn again from him. After tea, she stared broodingly into her teacup, twisting her wedding ring all the time. In her abstraction she took the ring off her finger, stood it up, and spun it upon the table. The gold became a diaphanous, glittering globe. It fell, and the ring was quivering upon the table. She spun it again and again. Paul watched, fascinated.

But she was a married woman, and he believed in simple friendship. And he considered that he was perfectly honourable with regard to her. It was only a friendship between man and woman, such as any civilised persons might have.

He was like so many young men of his own age. Sex had become so complicated in him that he would have denied that he ever could want Clara or Miriam or any woman whom he knew. Sex desire was a sort of detached thing, that did not belong to a woman. He loved Miriam with his soul. He grew warm at the thought of Clara, he battled with her, he knew the curves of her breast and shoulders as if they had been moulded inside him; and yet he did not positively desire her. He would have denied it for ever. He believed himself really bound to Miriam. If ever he should marry, some time in the far future, it would be his duty to marry Miriam. That he gave Clara to understand, and she said nothing, but left him to his courses. He came to her, Mrs. Dawes, whenever he could. Then he wrote frequently to Miriam, and visited the girl occasionally. So he went on through the winter; but he seemed not so fretted. His mother was easier about him. She thought he was getting away from Miriam.

Miriam knew now how strong was the attraction of Clara for him; but still she was certain that the best in him would triumph. His feeling for Mrs. Dawes—who, moreover, was a married woman—was shallow and temporal, compared with his love for herself. He would come back to her, she was sure; with some of his young freshness gone, perhaps, but cured of his desire for the lesser things which other women than herself could give him. She could bear all if he were inwardly true to her and must come back.

He saw none of the anomaly of his position. Miriam was his old friend, lover, and she belonged to Bestwood and home and his youth. Clara was a newer friend, and she belonged to Nottingham, to life, to the world. It seemed to him quite plain.

Mrs. Dawes and he had many periods of coolness, when they saw little of each other; but they always came together again.

"Were you horrid with Baxter Dawes?" he asked her. It was a thing that seemed to trouble him.

"In what way?"

"Oh, I don't know. But weren't you horrid with him? Didn't you do something that knocked him to pieces?"

"What, pray?"

"Making him feel as if he were nothing—I know," Paul declared.

"You are so clever, my friend," she said coolly.

The conversation broke off there. But it made her cool with him for some time.

She very rarely saw Miriam now. The friendship between the two women was not broken off, but considerably weakened.

"Will you come in to the concert on Sunday afternoon?" Clara asked him just after Christmas.

"I promised to go up to Willey Farm," he replied.

"Oh, very well."

"You don't mind, do you?" he asked.

"Why should I?" she answered.

Which almost annoyed him.

"You know," he said, "Miriam and I have been a lot to each other ever since I was sixteen—that's seven years now."

"It's a long time," Clara replied.

"Yes; but somehow she—it doesn't go right—"

"How?" asked Clara.

"She seems to draw me and draw me, and she wouldn't leave a single hair of me free to fall out blow away—she'd keep it."

"But you like to be kept."

"No," he said, "I don't. I wish it could be normal, give and take—like me and you. I want a woman to keep me, but not in her pocket."

"But if you love her, it couldn't be normal, like me and you."

"Yes; I should love her better then. She sort of wants me so much that I can't give myself."

"Wants you how?"

"Wants the soul out of my body. I can't help shrinking back from her."

"And yet you love her!"

"No, I don't love her. I never even kiss her."

"Why not?" Clara asked.

"I don't know."

"I suppose you're afraid," she said.

"I'm not. Something in me shrinks from her like hell—she's so good, when I'm not good."

"How do you know what she is?"

"I do! I know she wants a sort of soul union."

"But how do you know what she wants?"

"I've been with her for seven years."

"And you haven't found out the very first thing about her."

"What's that?"

"That she doesn't want any of your soul communion. That's your own imagination. She wants you."

He pondered over this. Perhaps he was wrong.

"But she seems—" he began.

"You've never tried," she answered.

## Notes

1. ikey: mispronunciation of "iconic", meaning having the nature of a sacred image
2. *Lettres de Mon Moulin*: (French) *Letters from My Mill*, a well-known book by the French novelist Alphonse Daudet (1840–1897)
3. lavender: a labiate plant with fragrant pale-lilac flowers. Here, it refers to its pale purple colour.
4. Penelope: Penelope was wife of Odysseus and mother of Telemachus in Homeric legend. She was a model of all the domestic virtues.
5. somnambule: a sleep walker

## For Study and Discussion

1. What kind of woman is Clara? Talk about her appearance and character.
2. Why is always Paul angry with Clara in the early part of this selection? What does he usually do when he is angry with her? What is Clara's reaction?
3. In this selection, chocolates are used as an image to reveal the character of Paul and Clara. What interesting episodes do you find about chocolates?
4. How do Paul and Clara talk about the town?
5. Why is Clara unhappy with the other girls?
6. Why does Paul feel the day is warm after he has talked with Clara about her marriage and her feeling?
7. What does Paul think about his relationship with Miriam and Clara? What do they mean to him?
8. How does Clara teach Paul to love Miriam? What does she encourage him to do?

# Chapter 28

# Rupert Brooke

## Life and Works

Rupert Brooke (1887–1915), the full name being Rupert Chawner Brooke, was the son of the Rugby School's housemaster. He fell in love with poetry at nine and attended his father's school at fourteen. He attended King's College, Cambridge, where he was known for his charm and intellect. While at Cambridge, he became interested in acting and was president of the Fabian Society.

He was early identified with the Georgian poets, who wrote in an anti-Victorian style, and whose themes were usually friendship and love. Some critics considered Brooke's poetry too sentimental and lacking depth, but they also considered his work a reflection of the mood in England during the years leading up to World War I. Much of his verse also reflected his interest in John Donne and the early 17th-century dramatist John Webster, on whom he wrote a dissertation at Cambridge University. He was an English poet best known for his idealistic war sonnets written during the War, especially "The Soldier".

He made friends with Winston Churchill and Henry James. He also made friends with the Bloomsbury group of writers. Some of them admired his talent while others were more impressed by his good looks. Virginia Woolf boasted of once going skinny-dipping with Brooke in a moonlit pool when they were at Cambridge together. William Butler Yeats described him as "the handsomest young man in England".

In 1913 he travelled in the United States, Canada and the South Pacific region, spending several months in Tahiti, where he wrote some of his most famous poems and where he might have fathered a daughter with a woman named Taatamata, with whom he seemed to have enjoyed his most complete emotional relationship. Following his enlistment in the navy and brief service in Belgium, he wrote his war sonnets, among them "The Soldier". Traditional not only in form, these poems were the last of that period to express idealistic patriotism in the face of war. Unlike Siegfried Sassoon and Wilfred Owen, Brooke did not live to witness the horror of trench warfare, for he died of blood poisoning on the way to the Dardanelles with the British army.

## Brief Comment

Handsome, charming and talented, a symbol in England of the tragic loss of talented youth during the war, Brooke was a national hero even before his death in 1915 at the age of twenty-eight. His poetry, with its unabashed patriotism and graceful lyricism, was revered in a country that was yet to feel the devastating effects of two world wars. In the decades after World War I, however, critics reacted against the Brooke legend by calling his verse foolishly naive and sentimental. Despite such extreme opinions, most contemporary observers agree that Brooke—though only a minor poet—occupies a secure place in English literature as a representative of the mood and character of England before World War I.

## Selections

### The Soldier

If I should die, think only this of me:
  That there's some corner of a foreign field
That is forever England. There shall be
  In that rich earth a richer dust concealed;
A dust whom England bore, shaped, made aware,
  Gave, once, her flowers to love, her ways to roam;
A body of England's, breathing English air,
  Washed by the rivers, blest by suns of home.

And think, this heart, all evil shed away,
  A pulse in the Eternal mind, no less
  Gives somewhere back the thoughts by England given,
Her sights and sounds; dreams happy as her day;
  And laughter, learnt of friends; and gentleness,
  In hearts at peace, under an English heaven.

## For Study and Discussion

1. What are the poet's feelings towards England and the cause for which he may die? What traditional English qualities does he stress?

2. The poet expresses an ideal of happiness, not the actual reality of his life. What statements in the poem show his awareness of the courage and hope needed to achieve that ideal?
3. T. S. Eliot characterised Georgian poetry in these words: "…the Georgian poets insist upon the English countryside, and are even positively patriotic…" To what extent does this poem fit this characterisation?

# Chapter 29

# Thomas Stearns Eliot

## Life and Works

Thomas Stearns Eliot (1888–1965) was the leading writer in the English world in the first half of the 20th century. He was not only a great poet, an insightful critic, a fine playwright, but also he sought to become the conscience of his generation, deliberately fitting himself for this role, which he summed up in a celebrated phrase when he defined his beliefs as "classicist in literature, royalist in politics, and Anglo-Catholic in religion".

When Eliot began to publish verse at the age of twenty-six, his very few readers were shocked by his poems. They thought his poems were dry, over-clever, revolutionary in the use of language and syntax. Fifty years later, when his name was surrounded by an air of majesty unique in his time, that same verse still had a contemporary ring to it. Today he seems to have been a representative of an age in which many people, feeling themselves barren because of their doubt, searched for an experience of faith.

Eliot was born and raised in St. Louis, Missouri, the United States. He attended Harvard University where he studied philosophy and literature, and subsequently the Sorbonne in Paris and Oxford University in England. World War I caught him in England, where he worked for a time in Lloyd's Bank, married Vivienne Haight-Wood, and finally settled for good by 1915. In the 1920s he joined the London publishing house that later became Faber & Faber, and in 1927 he became a British subject. In the years following, he avoided publicity and deliberately cultivated a shy aloofness, lightened by an almost youthful sense of humour.

After the unquenchable optimism of the Victorian Age had burned itself out in World War I, a period of intense questioning began. A society that had appeared both stable and progressive for over a century broke into fragments. Eliot's classic expression of the temper of his age is *The Waste Land* (1922), published in *The Criterion*, his own quarterly journal. This poem, despite its extreme difficulty, brought him immediate fame.

With 433 lines long, *The Waste Land* itself is a desolate and sterile country ruled by an impotent king. The whole poem is divided into five parts: I. "The Burial of the Dead", representing the stirring life in the land after the barren winter; II. "The Game of Chess", contrasting the splendours of the past represented by Cleopatra with uneasiness and despair of modern life; III. "The Fire Sermon", making an imaginative silhouette sketch of the ugliness of cities and the mechanisation of modern life and emotion; IV. "Death by Water", presumptively proving by the vision of a drowned Phoenician sailor that water is not only the constructive source of life but also the destructive source of death because of drowning and also its absence as well, which causes drought； and V. "What the Thunder Said", presenting a picture through symbols of the Grail legend, of the drought, the decay and emptiness of modern life.

The theme of the poem is modern spiritual barrenness, the despair and depression that followed World War I, the sterility and turbulence of the modern world, and the decline and break-down of Western culture. The poem's noticeable characteristics are varied length and rhythm to harmonise with the changing subject matter, the unrhymed lines, lots of borrowings from some thirty-five different writers, the employment of materials such as the legends of the Holly Grail, Frazer's anthropological work *The Golden Bough*, several popular songs, and passages in six foreign languages, including Sanskrit. The poem, therefore, is obscure and hard to understand, needless to say its absence of logical continuity. The poem, nevertheless, is broadly acknowledged as one of the most recognisable landmarks of modernism.

*The Hallow Men*, published two years after *The Waste Land*, was almost as powerful an expression of an age of doubt that longed in despair for belief. He cultivated an ironic, detached, corrosive manner in his poetry, and when he wrote prose, it was with the didactic purpose of turning his readers away from what he considered the self-indulgence of the romantics and towards the sterner splendours of Elizabethan drama and 17th-century metaphysical poetry. He wished to discourage the easy acceptance of popular favourites like Milton or Shelley in order to make room for neglected masters like John Donne. In this field, he made the greatest contribution to rediscovering the charm of the metaphysical poetry and the drama of the early 17th century. His essay entitled "Metaphysical Poets" is worth reading. His own journal *The Criterion* made a great contribution to publishing literary essays and new poems and stories.

Close study of Dante brought Eliot to consider traditional Christianity as the one chance of finding a still centre in the midst of chaos. His poem "Ash Wednesday" (1930), written following his confirmation in 1927 in the Church of England, was a significant step in this direction. But the final expression of a long process of thought took place nine years later when he wrote the first *Four Quartets*. These poems were published in 1943 and concluded his major work as a poet with a new serenity of outlook.

In the latter part of his life, Eliot turned more and more to playwriting and to the writing of essays and books discussing social and religious themes, notably *Notes Towards the Definition of Culture* and *The Aims of Education*. It was his aim to revitalise poetic drama, to write plays that would seem perfectly natural to audiences although the characters were speaking poetic language. One of his modern plays, *The Cocktail Party*, had a long run in both London and New York, but his earlier play, *Murder in the Cathedral*, is closest to the traditional poetic drama.

## Brief Comment

As a poet, Eliot was above all an intellectual who had put much hard thinking into his verse and who demanded an equal amount of thought from the reader. He could encompass poignant feeling when he chose, but his habitual choice was to establish an exact equation between feeling and thought. Some of his poems are difficult because the links between the ideas have been suppressed. Consequently, the reader must study these poems carefully to piece together the seemingly isolated statements into a logical sequence.

As a critic, he advocated new ideas. He was against the romantic poetry, and turned to Renaissance poetry and drama for proper technique. It is he who helped to bring metaphysical poetry to intense public attention. He also learned a lot from John Donne, John Keats, Samuel Taylor Coleridge, William Butler Yeats, Ezra Pound and others in developing his theory.

It can be said that Eliot has changed the direction of modern writing more sharply than did any of his contemporaries. He changed it in the direction of precision and complexity, and of wide-ranging reference, so that all of history was brought into his poetry. And he moved it towards deep but highly controlled emotion—emotion, as some of his poems imply, that was much too serious to be stated in consciously "poetic" language. In 1948 he was awarded the Nobel Prize in literature.

## Selections

### The Love Song of J. Alfred Prufrock

### About the Poem

"The Love Song of J. Alfred Prufrock", one of the earliest poems to earn fame for Eliot, was begun in 1910 when the poet was still a student at Harvard University. It was finished in 1911 when he was in Munich in Germany. It first appeared in the magazine *Poetry* in Chicago in 1915 and was the titular poem of Eliot's first book of poetry published in England in 1917, *Prufrock and Other Observations*, which was followed by an American edition in 1920.

The poem is a sort of dramatic monologue in lines of varying lengths and occasional rhymes. It falls under the influence of the French symbolists of the late 19th century and of the imagists of early 20th-century American poetry. Here Eliot was partly following the aim of the imagists to restore to poetry the precise use of visual images and to avoid all looseness of expression and sentiment, and was partly trying to convey the spontaneity of the ideas and feelings welling up his mind, by resorting to the psychological principle of the association of ideas, and to the use more or less of the "stream of consciousness" technique. So in the poem there is no sequence of events, nor passage of time. There are random transitions from certain thoughts and feelings of the speaker of the monologue to certain others, interrupted by descriptive passages of the external elements of the fog, the women in the room, etc.

In spite of its title, the poem is not a love song in the normal sense. Or one can say that it is not a love song at all. It contains references to the speaker Prufrock's love affairs, which is true, but the theme of the poem is a much broader one: "it deals with the thoughts of the central figure Prufrock intermixed with random descriptions of his environment." "The Love Song of J. Alfred Prufrock" is actually the confession of Prufrock, a middle-aged man and a romantic aesthete who is bored with his ineffectual life and is faced with despair because he wishes but is unable to break away from his meaningless existence or to find the right answers to "the overwhelming question" always occurring to him. In this sense, the poem is a mild satire on the decadence and futility of life in modern society.

The images of the opening lines describe a lifeless and dirty neighbourhood of cheap hotels and restaurants, where Prufrock lives a solitary and gloomy life. He suggests making a visit, and his mind soon forms an image of the place he and the reader (the "you") will go—perhaps an afternoon tea where women drop in and talk ostensibly about Michelangelo, a man of great creative energy, the opposite of Prufrock himself.

In the rest of the poem, Prufrock imagines his arrival, his attempt to approach the woman he seeks and his failure to make himself understood by her. He has attended parties many times and knows how it will be. This makes him hesitate out of fear that any attempt to push beyond mere polite conversation, to make some claim on the woman's affections, will meet with a frustratingly polite refusal. So he plans his approach and tells himself that he can put off action. He knows that they do not expect much from him. He tries to rehearse a speech he might make to one particular woman, but he gives up almost as soon as he has started. Deciding not to try, he questions whether his efforts would have been worthwhile. He excuses his fear by rationalising that his speaking to the woman would not have received any real response. Then he contrasts himself to Hamlet, a hero who hesitated but finally acted decisively and bravely. But Prufrock sees himself as more like Polonius, the old fool from the same play. Prufrock will retreat into a solitary and dignified old age. He has gone past dreams of romance into the sobre but empty existence of a passionless old man, and has decided not to disturb the world by a love song.

## The Love Song of J. Alfred Prufrock[1]

*S'io credesse che mia risposta fosse*
*a persona che mai tornasse al mondo,*
*questa fiamma staria senza piu scosse.*
*Ma per cio cche giammai di questo fondo*
*non torno vivo alcun, s'I'odo il vero,*
*Senza tema d'infamia ti rispondo.*[2]

Let us go then, you and I,
When the evening is spread out against the sky
Like a patient etherised[3] upon a table;
Let us go, through certain half-deserted streets,
The muttering retreats
Of restless nights in one-night cheap hotels
And sawdust restaurants with oyster-shells:
Streets that follow like a tedious argument
Of insidious intent[4]
To lead you to an overwhelming question…
Oh, do not ask, "What is it?"
Let us go and make our visit.

In the room the women come and go
Talking of Michelangelo[5].

The yellow fog that rubs its back upon the window-panes,
The yellow smoke that rubs its muzzle on the window-panes
Licked its tongue into the corners of the evening,
Lingered upon the pools that stand in drains,
Let fall upon its back the soot that falls from chimneys,
Slipped by the terrace, made a sudden leap,
And seeing that it was a soft October night,
Curled once about the house, and fell asleep.

And indeed there will be time[6]
For the yellow smoke that slides along the street,
Rubbing its back upon the window-panes;
There will be time, there will be time
To prepare a face[7] to meet the faces that you meet;

There will be time to murder and create,
And time for all the works and days of hands[8]
That lift and drop a question on your plate;
Time for you and time for me,
And time yet for a hundred indecisions,
And for a hundred visions and revisions,
Before the taking of a toast and tea.[9]

In the room the women come and go
Talking of Michelangelo.

And indeed there will be time
To wonder, "Do I dare?" and, "Do I dare?"
Time to turn back and descend the stair,
With a bald spot in the middle of my hair[10]—
(They will say: "How his hair is growing thin!")[11]
My morning coat, my collar mounting firmly to the chin,
My necktie rich and modest, but asserted by a simple pin —
(They will say: "But how his arms and legs are thin!")
Do I dare
Disturb the universe?[12]
In a minute there is time
For decisions and revisions which a minute will reverse.

For I have known them all already, known them all—
Have known the evenings, mornings, afternoons,
I have measured out my life with coffee spoons;
I know the voices dying with a dying fall[13]
Beneath the music from a farther room.
  So how should I presume?

And I have known the eyes already, known them all—
The eyes that fix you in a formulated phrase,[14]
And when I am formulated,[15] sprawling on a pin,
When I am pinned and wriggling on the wall,
Then how should I begin
To spit out all the butt-ends of my days and ways?[16]
  And how should I presume?

And I have known the arms already, known them all—
Arms that are braceleted and white and bare
(But in the lamplight, downed with light brown hair!)
Is it perfume from a dress
That makes me so digress?
Arms that lie along a table, or wrap about a shawl.
And should I then presume?
And how should I begin?
* * * * * * * * * *
Shall I say, I have gone at dusk through narrow streets
And watched the smoke that rises from the pipes
Of lonely men in shirt-sleeves, leaning out of windows?...

I should have been a pair of ragged claws[17]
Scuttling across the floors of silent seas.
* * * * * * * * * *
And the afternoon, the evening, sleeps so peacefully!
Smoothed by long fingers,
Asleep ... tired ... or it malingers[18],
Stretched on the floor, here beside you and me.
Should I, after tea and cakes and ices,
Have the strength to force the moment to its crisis?
But though I have wept and fasted, wept and prayed,
Though I have seen my head (grown slightly bald) brought in upon a platter,
I am no prophet[19]—and here's no great matter;
I have seen the moment of my greatness flicker,
And I have seen the eternal Footman hold my coat, and snicker,[20]
And in short, I was afraid.

And would it have been worth it, after all,
After the cups, the marmalade, the tea,
Among the porcelain, among some talk of you and me,
Would it have been worth while,
To have bitten off the matter with a smile,[21]
To have squeezed the universe into a ball
To roll it towards some overwhelming question,[22]
To say: "I am Lazarus[23], come from the dead,
Come back to tell you all, I shall tell you all" —

If one, settling a pillow by her head
  Should say: "That is not what I meant at all.
  That is not it, at all."

And would it have been worth it, after all,
Would it have been worth while,
After the sunsets and the dooryards and the sprinkled streets,
After the novels, after the teacups, after the skirts that trail along the floor —
And this, and so much more?—
It is impossible to say just what I mean!
But as if a magic lantern threw the nerves in patterns on a screen:[24]
Would it have been worth while
If one, settling a pillow or throwing off a shawl,
And turning toward the window, should say:
  "That is not it at all,
  That is not what I meant, at all."
* * * * * * *
No! I am not Prince Hamlet, nor was meant to be;[25]
Am an attendant lord, one that will do
To swell a progress,[26] start a scene or two,
Advise the prince; no doubt, an easy tool,
Deferential, glad to be of use,
Politic, cautious, and meticulous;
Full of high sentence, [27] but a bit obtuse;
At times, indeed, almost ridiculous—
Almost, at times, the Fool[28].

I grow old ... I grow old...
I shall wear the bottoms of my trousers rolled.[29]

Shall I part my hair behind?[30] Do I dare to eat a peach?
I shall wear white flannel trousers, and walk upon the beach.
I have heard the mermaids singing,[31] each to each.
I do not think that they will sing to me.

I have seen them riding seaward on the waves
Combing the white hair of the waves blown back
When the wind blows the water white and black.

We have lingered in the chambers of the sea
By sea-girls wreathed with seaweed red and brown
Till human voices wake us, and we drown.[32]

## Notes

1. J. Alfred Prufrock: obviously a fictitious name whose confession of his life and love, thoughts and feelings, makes up the poem
2. *S'io credesse che mia risposta fosse... senza tema d'infamia ti rispondo*: a quotation from Dante's *Inferno*, *Canto* XXXVII, Lines 61–66. The passage may be rendered into English as follows: " If I thought that my answer were being made to someone who would ever return to earth, this flame would remain without further movement; but since no one has ever returned alive from this depth, if what I hear is true, I answer you without fear of infamy." The speaker of these lines is Guido de Montefeltro who is placed in the eighth circle of hell for giving evil counsel to a pope and, wrapped in a flame, is speaking from its trembling tip. This quotation suggests that the poem that follows is likewise a confession and that the speaker assumes the reader to be in the same hell where he himself is.
3. etherised: anaesthetised, with the application of ether on a patient, for a major surgical operation. The simile of an etherised patient conveys the stillness of the evening.
4. Streets that follow like a tedious argument / Of insidious intent: Note the curious comparison of " streets" to "a tedious argument of insidious intent..."
5. Michelangelo: Michelangelo Buonarroti (1475–1564), the great Italian sculptor, painter and poet of the Renaissance
6. there will be time: Here and in the subsequent uses of the word "time", the speaker is making an allusion to a passage in *Ecclesiastes*: "To everything there is a season, and a time to every purpose under heaven. A time to be born, a time to die, a time to plant, and a time to pluck that which is planted, a time to kill, and a time to heal, ..."
7. To prepare a face: to do one's facial make-up before going to meet friends
8. all the works and days of hands: Here is an allusion to "Works and Days", the title of a didactic poem concerning rural labour, written by the early Greek poet Hesiod ( 8th century BC)
9. Before the taking of a toast and tea: Here "the taking of a toast and tea" brings the speaker back from his wandering thoughts given above to his trivial realities of life.
10. Time to turn back and descend the stair, / With a bald spot in the middle of my hair: Here again the speaker comes down to earth, so to speak.
11. (They will say: "How his hair is growing thin!"): "They" refers to the women the speaker is familiar with; "his" refers to the speaker.
12. Do I dare / Disturb the universe: "Disturb the universe" is obviously an ironical overstatement.
13. a dying fall: See Shakespeare's play *Twelfth Night*, I, 1, 4: "That strain again! It had a dying fall." There the lovesick Duke is commending the music he hears; here the speaker uses the

expression to refer to affected upper-class speech accents.

14. The eyes that fix you in a formulated phrase: the eyes that reduce you to a formula, the eyes that make an estimate of you with a phrase or a formula
15. And when I am formulated: when I am estimated with a specific phrase or formula
16. To spit out all the butt-ends of my days and ways: to utter vehemently all the deeply-embedded thoughts reflecting my life and ways of living
17. a pair of ragged claws: a crab. Here the speaker means that it would be a relief to lead a merely instinctual life (such as that of a crab) that involves no moral decisions and revisions.
18. malingers: pretends to be sick
19. Though I have seen my head (grown slightly bald) brought in upon a platter, / I am no prophet: an allusion taken from the Bible. The speaker here suggests that he has visualised himself to be a great man ready for the sacrifice of his life, but then he realises that he is not a prophet, so he needs not be afraid of having to make the sacrifice of a prophet like John the Baptist ( see the words following: "and here's no great matter").
20. I have seen the eternal Footman hold my coat, and snicker: The speaker here visualises himself in his customary social environment in which a footman (a man-servant who admits visitors and takes their coats) usually takes his coat. "Footman" is capitalised because it is used here as a symbol of death.
21. To have bitten off the matter with a smile: to break off his old way of life and to do or say something of importance ("with a smile" indicates doing or saying the thing in a light, off-handed manner).
22. To have squeezed the universe into a ball / To roll it towards some overwhelming question: See the English poet Andrew Marvell's "To His Coy Mistress": "Let us roll all our strength and all / Our sweetness up into one ball." ("some overwhelming question" meaning some question of great importance)
23. Lazarus: the sick and poor beggar in Jesus' parable of the rich man and the beggar. Lazarus returns from the dead, according to the Bible. Here the speaker refers to himself making a confession, like Guido de Montefeltro in Dante's *Inferno*.
24. But as if a magic lantern threw the nerves in patterns on a screen: an image equivalent to "impossible to say just what I mean"
25. I am not Prince Hamlet, nor was meant to be: Here the speaker suggests that he is not and cannot hope to be a great man.
26. To swell a progress (跑龙套): a progress was a ceremonial royal journey; here the speaker thinks of himself as an "extra" or an actor of no importance, a minor actor participating in a progress in a play.
27. Full of high sentence: expressing worthy sentiments (See Chaucer's *The Canterbury Tales*, the General Prologue, Line 306.)
28. the Fool: referring to the fool as a character in Elizabethan drama, who is given the permission not only to do the clowning but also to quibble with his superiors.

29. I shall wear the bottoms of my trousers rolled: Presumably here the speaker is referring to the adoption of the new fashion of trousers cuffs.
30. Shall I part my hair behind: Here the speaker is referring to a daring new hair style. He seems to contemplate a series of faintly daring gestures in defiance of advanced age.
31. I have heard the mermaids singing: See John Donne's poem "Go and Catch a Falling Star". "Mermaids singing" is something considered to be an impossibility. Here the speaker is visualising something impossible in his life experience.
32. Till human voices wake us, and we drown: Here the speaker suggests that he is brought back to reality from his wandering thoughts and visions. So he ends his monologue.

## For Study and Discussion

1. Is the poem a love song in the strict sense of the term?
2. What is the function of the quotation from Dante's *Inferno* that is immediately following the title of the poem?
3. Do you think the poem is a mild satire?
4. Quote two lines which present the most vivid image.
5. Why does the speaker repeatedly say "there is time"?

# Chapter 30

# Robert Graves

## Life and Works

Robert Graves (1895–1985) served in the British army during World War I. When still in service, he wrote his first poems. He joined the army in 1914 and left in 1917. He was wounded and later suffered shell shock. He refused to glorify the war. He then attended Oxford University which he left without taking a degree. In 1925, he was given a degree because of his contribution in critical writings.

After World War I, he taught English in Cairo, Egypt. The publishing and success of his novel about war, *Goodbye to All That*, enabled him to quit teaching. Then writing became his career. For the rest of his life, he wrote large numbers of essays, poems, novels and stories.

After his marriage ended, he settled in Majorca, an island in the Mediterranean near Spain, with Laura Riding, an American poet. They co-worked until World War II when Graves returned to England and Riding went back to the United States. In 1946, with his second wife, he returned to Majorca, and lived there until his death.

Graves' novel *I, Claudius* is an engaging first-person narrative written in the voice of the Roman emperor Claudius, chronicling the personalities and machinations of the Julio-Claudian line during the reigns of Augustus, Tiberius and Caligula. This work was followed by other historical novels dealing with ancient Mediterranean civilisations and including *Claudius the God*, which extends Claudius' narrative to his own reign as emperor; *Count Belisarius*, a sympathetic study of the great and martyred general of the Byzantine Empire; and *The Golden Fleece*. Graves' researches for *The Golden Fleece* led him into a wide-ranging study of myths and to what was his most controversial scholarly work, *The White Goddess: A Historical Grammar of Poetic Myth* (1948). In it he argued the existence of an all-important religion, rooted in the remote past but continuing into the Christian Era, based on the worship of a goddess.

## Brief Comment

Graves began before 1914 as a typical Georgian poet, but his war experiences and the difficulties of his personal life gave his later poetry a much deeper and more painful note. He remained a traditionalist rather than a modernist, however, in his emphasis on metre and clear meaning in his verse. Graves' sad love poems are regarded as the finest produced in the English language during the 20th century, along with those of W. B. Yeats.

In poetry writing, he experimented with many verse forms, including folksongs, ballads and poems in the metaphysical vein—using highly subtle and complex metaphors. In *A Survey of Modernist Poetry*, Graves, along with his co-author Laura Riding, defined what he felt poetry was now to be engaged in: "The ideal modernist poem is its own clearest, fullest, and most accurate meaning...the poem does not give a rendering of a poetical picture or idea existing outside the poem, but...the poem has the character of a creature by itself." "His poems," declared Richard Wilbur, "...have the air of being spontaneous answers to actual experience."

He has published over 15 volumes of poetry, of which *Collected Poems* represents most of what he wants to preserve, and this volume well represents the range and quality of his genius. Its publication was the sign for clear critical affirmation, on both sides of the Atlantic, that Graves was a major English poet of the 20th century. He won the Queen's Gold Medal for Poetry in 1968.

## Selections

### She Tells Her Love While Half Asleep

She tells her love while half asleep
  In the dark hours,
  With half-words whispered low:
As Earth stirs in her winter sleep
  And puts out grass and flowers
  Despite the snow,
  Despite the falling snow.

## For Study and Discussion

1. What is the function of the repetition of the last two lines?
2. What's the meaning of the phrasal verb "put out" in Line 5?
3. Who is in half sleep? Who is in full sleep? What is happening in winter sleep? Why does the poet use sleep as a central image?
4. Learn this poem by heart.

# Chapter 31

# Samuel Barclay Beckett

## Life and Works

Samuel Barclay Beckett (1906–1989) was born on April 13, 1906 in Foxrock, south of Dublin, into a prosperous Jewish family. His father was a quantity surveyor and his mother was a pious believer and nurse. Beckett attended Portora Royal School in Enniskillen and later studied French and Italian at Trinity College, Dublin, where he took a BA. He then worked as a teacher in Belfast and lecturer in English in Paris in 1926. In 1928, he went to teach in France and got acquaintance with James Joyce who was now blind and served him with his manuscripts. He published some works here. In 1931, Beckett returned to Dublin and received his MA, and taught French at Trinity College. In 1932, he roamed over Europe. In 1938, he settled down in Paris and published his first novel *Murphy* in London (a novel in English, rejected by forty-two publishers before acceptance by Routledge).

When World War II broke out, Beckett was in Ireland, but he hastened to Paris and joined a resistance network. Pursued by the Nazis, he fled to Southern France and hid in a village until 1945 after Paris was liberated from the Germans. In 1945, Beckett returned to Ireland for a short time and worked briefly with the Irish Red Cross in Saint-Lô in Normandy. After the war he returned to Paris and became a professional writer. He became interested in painting and wrote criticisms and essays on painting. Between 1946 and 1949 he produced the major prose narrative trilogy, *Molloy*, *Malone Dies* and *The Unnamable*, which are not, strictly speaking, novels as usually understood. Samuel Beckett's first publication *Molloy* enjoyed modest sales, but more importantly it won praise from French critics. In the fifties, he turned to writing drama. In 1953, he took the world by storm with his play *Waiting for Godot* which achieved quick success. The play ran for 400 performances and enjoyed critical praise.

In 1969 Samuel Beckett received the Nobel Prize for "his writing, which—in new forms for the novel and drama—in the destitution of modern man acquires its elevation". He continued to write until his death in 1989, but towards the end he remarked that each word seemed to him "an unnecessary stain on silence and nothingness".

## Brief Comment

Samuel Beckett wrote in both French and English, but his most well-known works were written in French. His writings were based on his own thoughts and experiences, and were filled with allusions to other writers such as Dante, René Descartes and James Joyce. Beckett's plays were not written along traditional lines with conventional plot and time and place references. Instead, he focused on essential elements of the human condition in dark humorous ways. This style of writing has been called "Theatre of the Absurd" in which the plays focus on human despair and the will to survive in a hopeless world.

Samuel Beckett is generally considered as one of the first absurdist playwrights to win international fame. His work has an acute awareness of the absurdity of human existence, for example, human being's desperate search for meaning, individual isolation and the gulf between human desires and the language in which they find expression. Many of Beckett's works have been intensely and internationally studied by critics, produced on stage and TV, and continue to be greeted with more or less equal proportions of fascination, devotion and horror.

## Selections

### *Waiting for Godot*

### The Story

*Waiting for Godot* is a two-act play that consists of five characters: Estragon, Vladimir, Lucky, Pozzo and a boy. Estragon and Vladimir are two tramps; Lucky is the servant of Pozzo; the boy is the servant of Mr. Godot. The play tells about two tramps Vladimir and Estragon, who are waiting in the evening on a country road by a tree for the arrival of a mysterious man named Godot. It appears they do not remember Godot very well, but they think he is going to give them an answer. They cannot remember the question. They are homeless and penniless, travelling from one place to another. Now they simply wait for Godot. The sun sets and the moon rises. They get the message that Godot will not come today, but will try to come tomorrow. They decide to move on, but they do not move.

Act 1 begins with the repeated dialogue in the play, in which Estragon wants to go and Vladimir tells him that they are waiting for Godot. They wonder out loud why they did not kill themselves years ago; they consider the possibility of doing it today. They are waiting for someone they call "Godot". While they wait, they share conversation, food and memories. Two other elderly men, Pozzo and Lucky, arrive on the scene. Pozzo is the master, and Lucky is his servant. Upon command, Lucky dances and thinks out loud for the entertainment of the others, until he is forcibly silenced. After Lucky and Pozzo depart, a boy arrives. He tells

Estragon and Vladimir that Godot will not be there today, but will be there tomorrow. He leaves, and they continue to wait.

The second act is almost the same as the first. The tree has sprouted leaves, Estragon and Vladimir chat while they wait for Godot, and Pozzo and Lucky arrive again. This time, Pozzo is blind and helpless, and Lucky is mute. After some interaction, Pozzo and Lucky leave, and the boy arrives. He has the same message as before. Godot will be there tomorrow. Estragon and Vladimir are left to wait as before.

Often perceived as being tramps, Vladimir and Estragon are a pair of human beings who do not know why they are put on earth; they make the tenuous assumption that there must be some point to their existence, and they look to Godot for enlightenment. Because they hold out hope for meaning and direction, they acquire a kind of nobility that enables them to rise above their futile existence.

## Act I

*A country road. A tree.*

*Evening.*

*Estragon, sitting on a low mound, is trying to take off his boot. He pulls at it with both hands, panting. He gives up, exhausted, rests, tries again as before. Enter Vladimir.*

Estragon: [*giving up again*]. Nothing to be done.

Vladimir: [*advancing with short, stiff strides, legs wide apart*]. I'm beginning to come round to that opinion. All my life I've tried to put it from me, saying Vladimir, be reasonable, you haven't yet tried everything. And I resumed the struggle. [*He broods, musing on the struggle. Turning to Estragon.*] So there you are again.

Estragon: Am I?

Vladimir: I'm glad to see you back. I thought you were gone forever.

Estragon: Me too.

Vladimir: Together again at last! We'll have to celebrate this. But how? [*He reflects.*] Get up till I embrace you.

Estragon: [*irritably*]. Not now, not now.

Vladimir: [*hurt, coldly*]. May one inquire where His Highness spent the night?

Estragon: In a ditch.

Vladimir: [*admiringly*]. A ditch! Where?

Estragon: [*without gesture*]. Over there.

Vladimir: And they didn't beat you?

Estragon: Beat me? Certainly they beat me.

Vladimir: The same lot as usual?

Estragon: The same? I don't know.

Vladimir: When I think of it... all these years... but for me... where would you be...

[*Decisively.*] You'd be nothing more than a little heap of bones at the present minute, no doubt about it.

Estragon: And what of it?

Vladimir: [*gloomily*]. It's too much for one man. [*Pause. Cheerfully.*] On the other hand what's the good of losing heart now, that's what I say. We should have thought of it a million years ago, in the nineties.[1]

Estragon: Ah stop blathering[2] and help me off with this bloody thing.

Vladimir: Hand in hand from the top of the Eiffel Tower, among the first. We were respectable in those days. Now it's too late. They wouldn't even let us up. [*Estragon tears at his boot.*] What are you doing?

Estragon: Taking off my boot. Did that never happen to you?

Vladimir: Boots must be taken off every day, I'm tired telling you that. Why don't you listen to me?

Estragon: [*feebly*]. Help me!

Vladimir: It hurts?

Estragon: [*angrily*]. Hurts! He wants to know if it hurts!

Vladimir: [*angrily*]. No one ever suffers but you. I don't count. I'd like to hear what you'd say if you had what I have.

Estragon: It hurts?

Vladimir: [*angrily*]. Hurts! He wants to know if it hurts!

Estragon: [*pointing*]. You might button it all the same.

Vladimir: [*stooping*]. True. [*He buttons his fly.*] Never neglect the little things of life.

Estragon: What do you expect, you always wait till the last moment.

Vladimir: [*musingly*]. The last moment...[*He meditates.*] Hope deferred[3] maketh the something sick, who said that?

Estragon: Why don't you help me?

Vladimir: Sometimes I feel it coming all the same. Then I go all queer. [*He takes off his hat, peers inside it, feels about inside it, shakes it, puts it on again.*] How shall I say? Relieved and at the same time...[*he searches for the word*]...appalled. [*With emphasis.*] AP-PALLED. [*He takes off his hat again, peers inside it.*] Funny. [*He knocks on the crown as though to dislodge a foreign body, peers into it again, puts it on again.*] Nothing to be done. [*Estragon with a supreme effort succeeds in pulling off his boot. He peers inside it, feels about inside it, turns it upside down, shakes it, looks on the ground to see if anything has fallen out, finds nothing, feels inside it again, staring sightlessly before him.*] Well?

Estragon: Nothing.

Vladimir: Show me.

Estragon: There's nothing to show.

Vladimir: Try and put it on again.

Estragon: [*examining his foot*]. I'll air it for a bit.

Vladimir: There's man all over for you, blaming on his boots the faults of his feet. [*He takes off his hat again, peers inside it, feels about inside it, knocks on the crown, blows into it, puts it on again.*] This is getting alarming. [*Silence. Vladimir deep in thought, Estragon pulling at his toes.*] One of the thieves was saved. [*Pause.*] It's a reasonable percentage. [*Pause.*] Gogo.

Estragon: What?

Vladimir: Suppose we repented.

Estragon: Repented what?

Vladimir: Oh... [*He reflects.*] We wouldn't have to go into the details.

Estragon: Our being born?

[*Vladimir breaks into a hearty laugh which he immediately stifles, his hand pressed to his pubis, his face contorted.*]

Vladimir: One daren't even laugh any more.

Estragon: Dreadful privation.

Vladimir: Merely smile. [*He smiles suddenly from ear to ear, keeps smiling, ceases as suddenly.*] It's not the same thing. Nothing to be done. [*Pause.*] Gogo.

Estragon: [*irritably*]. What is it?

Vladimir: Did you ever read the Bible?

Estragon: The Bible... [*He reflects.*] I must have taken a look at it.

Vladimir: Do you remember the Gospels?

Estragon: I remember the maps of the Holy Land. Coloured they were. Very pretty. The Dead Sea was pale blue. The very look of it made me thirsty. That's where we'll go, I used to say, that's where we'll go for our honeymoon. We'll swim. We'll be happy.

Vladimir: You should have been a poet.

Estragon: I was. [*Gesture towards his rags.*] Isn't that obvious?

[*Silence.*]

Vladimir: Where was I... How's your foot?

Estragon: Swelling visibly.

Vladimir: Ah yes, the two thieves. Do you remember the story?

Estragon: No.

Vladimir: Shall I tell it to you?

Estragon: No.

Vladimir: It'll pass the time. [*Pause.*] Two thieves, crucified at the same time as our Saviour. One—

Estragon: Our what?

Vladimir: Our Saviour. Two thieves. One is supposed to have been saved and the other... [*he searches for the contrary of saved*]... damned.

Estragon: Saved from what?

Vladimir: Hell.

Estragon: I'm going.

He does not move.

Vladimir: And yet...[*pause*]...how is it–this is not boring you I hope–how is it that of the four Evangelists only one speaks of a thief being saved. The four of them were there—or thereabouts—and only one speaks of a thief being saved. [*Pause.*] Come on, Gogo, return the ball, can't you, once in a way?

Estragon: [*With exaggerated enthusiasm*]. I find this really most extraordinarily interesting.

Vladimir: One out of four. Of the other three, two don't mention any thieves at all and the third says that both of them abused him.

Estragon: Who?

Vladimir: What?

Estragon: What's all this about? Abused who?

Vladimir: The Saviour.

Estragon: Why?

Vladimir: Because he wouldn't save them.

Estragon: From hell?

Vladimir: Imbecile[4]! From death.

Estragon: I thought you said hell.

Vladimir: From death, from death.

Estragon: Well what of it?

Vladimir: Then the two of them must have been damned.

Estragon: And why not?

Vladimir: But one of the four says that one of the two was saved.

Estragon: Well? They don't agree and that's all there is to it.

Vladimir: But all four were there. And only one speaks of a thief being saved. Why believe him rather than the others?

Estragon: Who believes him?

Vladimir: Everybody. It's the only version they know.

Estragon: People are bloody ignorant apes.

[*He rises painfully, goes limping to extreme left, halts, gazes into distance off with his hand screening his eyes, turns, goes to extreme right, gazes into distance. Vladimir watches him, then goes and picks up the boot, peers into it, drops it hastily.*]

Vladimir: Pah! [*He spits. Estragon moves to center, halts with his back to auditorium.*]

Estragon: Charming spot. [*He turns, advances to front, halts facing auditorium.*] Inspiring prospects. [*He turns to Vladimir.*] Let's go.

Vladimir: We can't.

Estragon: Why not?

Vladimir: We're waiting for Godot.

Estragon: [*despairingly*]. Ah! [*Pause.*] You're sure it was here?

Vladimir: What?
Estragon: That we were to wait.
Vladimir: He said by the tree. [*They look at the tree.*] Do you see any others?
Estragon: What is it?
Vladimir: I don't know. A willow.
Estragon: Where are the leaves?
Vladimir: It must be dead.
Estragon: No more weeping.
Vladimir: Or perhaps it's not the season.
Estragon: Looks to me more like a bush.
Vladimir: A shrub.
Estragon: A bush.
Vladimir: A—. What are you insinuating? That we've come to the wrong place?
Estragon: He should be here.
Vladimir: He didn't say for sure he'd come.
Estragon: And if he doesn't come?
Vladimir: We'll come back tomorrow.
Estragon: And then the day after tomorrow.
Vladimir: Possibly.
Estragon: And so on.
Vladimir: The point is—
Estragon: Until he comes.
Vladimir: You're merciless.
Estragon: We came here yesterday.
Vladimir: Ah no, there you're mistaken.
Estragon: What did we do yesterday?
Vladimir: What did we do yesterday?
Estragon: Yes.
Vladimir: Why... [*Angrily.*] Nothing is certain when you're about.
Estragon: In my opinion we were here.
Vladimir: [*looking round*]. You recognize the place?
Estragon: I didn't say that.
Vladimir: Well?
Estragon: That makes no difference.
Vladimir: All the same...that tree...[*turning towards auditorium*] that bog...
Estragon: You're sure it was this evening?
Vladimir: What?
Estragon: That we were to wait.
Vladimir: He said Saturday. [*Pause.*] I think.

Estragon: You think.

Vladimir: I must have made a note of it. [*He fumbles in his pockets, bursting with miscellaneous rubbish.*]

Estragon: [*very insidious*]. But what Saturday? And is it Saturday? Is it not rather Sunday? [*Pause.*] Or Monday? [*Pause.*] Or Friday?

Vladimir: [*looking wildly about him, as though the date was inscribed in the landscape*]. It's not possible!

Estragon: Or Thursday?

Vladimir: What'll we do?

Estragon: If he came yesterday and we weren't here you may be sure he won't come again today.

Vladimir: But you say we were here yesterday.

Estragon: I may be mistaken. [*Pause.*] Let's stop talking for a minute, do you mind?

Vladimir: [*feebly*]. All right. [*Estragon sits down on the mound. Vladimir paces agitatedly to and fro, halting from time to time to gaze into distance off. Estragon falls asleep. Vladimir halts finally before Estragon.*] Gogo!... Gogo!... GOGO! [*Estragon wakes with a start.*]

Estragon: [*restored to the horror of his situation*]. I was asleep! [*Despairingly.*] Why will you never let me sleep?

Vladimir: I felt lonely.

Estragon: I had a dream.

Vladimir: Don't tell me!

Estragon: I dreamt that—

Vladimir: DON'T TELL ME!

Estragon: [*gesture toward the universe*]. This one is enough for you? [*Silence.*] It's not nice of you, Didi. Who am I to tell my private nightmares to if I can't tell them to you?

Vladimir: Let them remain private. You know I can't bear that.

Estragon: [*coldly.*] There are times when I wonder if it wouldn't be better for us to part.

Vladimir: You wouldn't go far.

Estragon: That would be too bad, really too bad. [*Pause.*] Wouldn't it, Didi, be really too bad? [*Pause.*] When you think of the beauty of the way. [*Pause.*] And the goodness of the wayfarers[5]. [*Pause. Wheedling.*] Wouldn't it, Didi?

Vladimir: Calm yourself.

Estragon: [*voluptuously.*] Calm...calm...The English say cawm. [*Pause.*] You know the story of the Englishman in the brothel?

Vladimir: Yes.

Estragon: Tell it to me.

Vladimir: Ah stop it!

Estragon: An Englishman having drunk a little more than usual proceeds to a brothel. The bawd asks him if he wants a fair one, a dark one or a red-haired one. Go on.

Vladimir: STOP IT! [*Exit Vladimir hurriedly. Estragon gets up and follows him as far as the limit of the stage. Gestures of Estragon like those of a spectator encouraging a pugilist*[6]*. Enter Vladimir. He brushes past Estragon, crosses the stage with bowed head. Estragon takes a step towards him, halts.*]

Estragon: [*gently.*] You wanted to speak to me? [*Silence. Estragon takes a step forward.*] You had something to say to me? [*Silence. Another step forward.*] Didi...

Vladimir: [*without turning*]. I've nothing to say to you.

Estragon: [*step forward*]. You're angry? [*Silence. Step forward*]. Forgive me. [*Silence. Step forward. Estragon lays his hand on Vladimir's shoulder.*] Come, Didi. [*Silence.*] Give me your hand. [*Vladimir half turns.*] Embrace me! [*Vladimir stiffens.*] Don't be stubborn! [*Vladimir softens. They embrace. Estragon recoils.*] You stink of garlic!

Vladimir: It's for the kidneys. [*Silence. Estragon looks attentively at the tree.*] What do we do now?

Estragon: Wait.

Vladimir: Yes, but while waiting.

Estragon: What about hanging ourselves?

Vladimir: Hmm. It'd give us an erection.

Estragon: [*highly excited*]. An erection!

Vladimir: With all that follows. Where it falls mandrakes grow. That's why they shriek when you pull them up. Did you not know that?

Estragon: Let's hang ourselves immediately!

Vladimir: From a bough? [*They go towards the tree.*] I wouldn't trust it.

Estragon: We can always try.

Vladimir: Go ahead.

Estragon: After you.

Vladimir: No no, you first.

Estragon: Why me?

Vladimir: You're lighter than I am.

Estragon: Just so!

Vladimir: I don't understand.

Estragon: Use your intelligence, can't you?

[*Vladimir uses his intelligence.*]

Vladimir: [*finally*]. I remain in the dark.

Estragon: This is how it is. [*He reflects.*] The bough...the bough...[*Angrily.*] Use your head, can't you?

Vladimir: You're my only hope.

Estragon: [*with effort*]. Gogo light—bough not break—Gogo dead. Didi heavy—bough break—Didi alone. Whereas—

Vladimir: I hadn't thought of that.

Estragon: If it hangs you it'll hang anything.
Vladimir: But am I heavier than you?
Estragon: So you tell me. I don't know. There's an even chance. Or nearly.
Vladimir: Well? What do we do?
Estragon: Don't let's do anything. It's safer.
Vladimir: Let's wait and see what he says.
Estragon: Who?
Vladimir: Godot.
Estragon: Good idea.

## Notes

1. We should have thought of it a million years ago, in the nineties: We should have committed suicide a long time ago.
2. blathering: talking nonsense for a long time
3. Hope deferred: hope delayed
4. Imbecile: a stupid person
5. wayfarers: travellers on foot
6. pugilist: a boxer

## For Study and Discussion

1. Who is Godot? What does Godot symbolise?
2. What is the relationship between Vladimir and Estragon? Why do you think they stay together, despite their frequent suggestions of parting?
3. Repetition is most striking in this play. Discuss how repetition is used to present the characters and develop its theme.

# Chapter 32

# Wystan Hugh Auden

## Life and Works

Wystan Hugh Auden (1907–1973) was born and raised in York, England. He went to Oxford University, where he studied and began to write poetry. At Oxford, Auden became familiar with modernist poetry, particularly that of T. S. Eliot. Then he went to Germany for a short period where he met his friend and later collaborator Christopher Isherwood. In the 1930s, he was deeply influenced by the social problems in England during the economic depression, and was interested in the theories of Karl Marx and Sigmund Freud. He offered to help the leftist republicans in the Spanish Civil War. He travelled a lot during this period of political turmoil. He left England in 1939 and became a citizen of the United States.

In 1956, he returned to England as a Professor of Poetry at Oxford. He held this post until 1961. Four years later, he returned to New York. He spent the rest of his life in New York City and his summer home in Austria.

Auden's early poems were concerned with revealing the ills of his native country and were intended to shock their readers. It was his impatience with the limits imposed by English society that prompted Auden to move to the United States. He later returned to the formal practice of Christianity, and his later poetry, though often as satirical as the early poems had been, became increasingly concerned with religious themes. Auden wrote three ambitious long poems: *For the Time Being*, a Christmas oratorio in which he explored the modern significance of the Nativity; *The Sea and the Mirror*, a discourse in poetic form on the relationship between life and art, which takes the form of a commentary on Shakespeare's *The Tempest*; *The Age of Anxiety*, which features four individuals attempting to find a way out of their spiritual dilemmas, won the Pulitzer Prize. Towards the end of his life, Auden's poetry tended to become mellower, reflecting a spirit that was less urgent in its denunciation of evil. His poetry never lost its moral quality, however, nor did it abandon its concern with the troubles of the modern world. His famous poems also include "Spain 1937", "Musée des Beaux Arts", "In

Memory of W. B. Yeats", "In Praise of Limestone" and many others.

## Brief Comment

In the early 1930s W. H. Auden was acclaimed prematurely by some as the foremost poet then writing in English, on the disputable ground that his poetry was more relevant to contemporary social and political realities than that of T. S. Eliot and William Butler Yeats, who previously had shared the summit. By the time of Eliot's death in 1965, however, a convincing case could be made for the assertion that Auden was indeed Eliot's successor, as Eliot had inherited the sole claim to supremacy when Yeats died in 1939.

Auden was, as a poet, far more copious and varied than Eliot and far more uneven. He tried to interpret the times, to diagnose the ills of society and deal with intellectual and moral problems of public concern. But the need to express the inner world of fantasy and dream was equally apparent, and, hence, the poetry is sometimes bewildering. If the poems, taken individually, are often obscure—especially the earlier ones—they create, when taken together, a meaningful poetic cosmos with symbolic landscapes and mythical characters and situations. In his later years Auden ordered the world of his poetry and made it easier of access; he collected his poems, revised them, and presented them chronologically in two volumes: *Collected Shorter Poems 1927–1957* (1967) and *Collected Longer Poems* (1969).

## Selections

### Petition

Sir, no man's enemy, forgiving all
But will its negative inversion, be prodigal:
Send to us power and light, a sovereign touch[1]
Curing the intolerable neural itch,
The exhaustion of weaning, the liar's quinsy[2],
And the distortions of ingrown virginity
Prohibit sharply the rehearsed response
And gradually correct the coward's stance;
Cover in time with beams those in retreat
That, spotted, they turn though the reveres were great;
Publish each healer that in city lives
Or country house at the end of drives;
Harrow the house of the dead; look shining at
New styles of architecture, a change of heart.

## Notes

1. sovereign touch: The "king's touch" was often regarded as a miraculous cure for disease (cf. "sovereign" as an adjective, meaning "supreme, all-dominating").
2. quinsy: tonsillitis

## For Study and Discussion

1. What is the concrete content of the petition?
2. Find the verbs used as predicates and discuss how they help illustrate the petition.

### Ballad

O what is that sound which so thrills the ear
  Down in the valley drumming, drumming?
Only the scarlet soldiers, dear,
  The soldiers coming.

O what is that light I see flashing so clear
  Over the distance brightly, brightly?
Only the sun on their weapons, dear,
  As they step lightly.

O what are they doing with all that gear;
  What are they doing this morning, this morning?
Only the usual maneuvers, dear,
  Or perhaps a warning.

O why have they left the road down there;
  Why are they suddenly wheeling, wheeling?
Perhaps a change in the orders, dear;
  Why are you kneeling?

O haven't they stopped for the doctor's care;
  Haven't they reined their horses, their horses?
Why, they are none of them wounded, dear.
  None of these forces.

O is it the parson they want, with white hair;
  Is it the parson, is it, is it?
No, they are passing his gateway, dear,
  Without a visit.

O it must be the farmer who lives so near,
  It must be the farmer, so cunning, cunning;
They have passed the farm already, dear,
  And now they are running.

O where are you going? stay with me here.
  Were the vows you swore me deceiving, deceiving?
No, I promised to love you, my dear,
  But I must be leaving.

O it's broken the lock and splintered the door,
  O it's the gate where they're turning, turning;
Their feet are heavy on the floor,
  And their eyes are burning.

## For Study and Discussion

1. The poet uses the traditional ballad form to describe the terror of the modern world. What narrative technique is used to increase gradually the poem's mood of terror?
2. The word "dear" is repeated in every stanza but the last. In what way is the use of this word ironic?
3. You must have noticed that the poet uses repetition in the second line of each stanza. Discuss the function of the repetitions.
4. Choose some lines that you like best and learn them by heart.

### Sonnet XVIII[1]

Far from the heart of culture he was used:
Abandoned by his general and his lice,
Under a padded quilt he closed his eyes
And vanished. He will not be introduced

When this campaign is tidied into books[2]:
No vital knowledge perished in his skull;

His jokes were stale; like wartime, he was dull;
His name is lost for ever like his looks.

He neither knew nor chose the Good[3], but taught us,
And added meaning like a comma, when
He turned to dust in China that our daughter

Be fit to love the earth, and not again
Disgraced before the dogs; that, where are waters,
Mountains and houses, may be also men.

## Notes

1. This sonnet was written in 1938 after the poet visited the front of the war against Japanese invaders in China, originally entitled "China Soldier".
2. tidied into books: written into books
3. the Good: kindness, everything that is good

## For Study and Discussion

1. What is the rhyme scheme of this sonnet? What is new in the stanzaic form of this sonnet?
2. What is the main idea of this sonnet?
3. Who is "he"?
4. Learn this sonnet by heart.

Chapter 33

# Dylan Thomas

## Life and Works

Dylan Thomas (1914–1953), poet, short-story writer and playwright, was born in Swansea, Wales, a mountainous and underdeveloped area to the west of England. His father was an English schoolmaster. Dylan attended a grammar school. After that he worked as a journalist in Wales and London. While still at school he began to write poems and in 1934, his first book of poetry, *Eighteen Poems*, was published in London. This volume won him immediate success. In theme, these poems and virtually all that followed seem obscure because they contain elements of surrealism and personal fantasy. But the freshness and vitality of his language draw the reader into the poems and reveal the universality of the experiences with which they are concerned.

The introspective tendency displayed in *Eighteen Poems* is less apparent in *Deaths and Entrances* and *In Country Sleep*, which are generally regarded as containing his finest writing. His other works include *Twenty-five Poems* and *The Map of Love*, containing both poetry and prose. *Portrait of the Artist as a Young Dog* is a group of autobiographical sketches, and *Adventures in the Skin Trade* published posthumously contains an unfinished novel and other prose pieces. During World War II Thomas wrote scripts for documentary motion pictures.

After the war he became a literary commentator for the BBC radio. *Under Milk Wood*, a play for voices, was originally written for radio broadcast. In 1950, he began to make successful tours in the United States, reading his poems. He became legendary in the United States, where he gave many lectures and gained a wide audience. Nevertheless, his last years were shadowed by an increasingly tragic view of his own tempestuous life. He died in the New York City of an overdose of alcohol.

## Brief Comment

An original poet of great power and beauty, Dylan Thomas is among the few modern poets recognised by the general public. At his early age, he displayed an unusual power in using poetic diction and imagery for his celebration of natural beauty. His refusal to ally with any literary group or movement has made it difficult to categorise him and his work. He was influenced by the modern symbolism and surrealism but he refused to follow their creed. However, he is viewed as part of the modernism and romanticism movements.

Thomas was always a highly individual stylist. Sound was as important as sense in his poems—some would even say more important. He made ample use of alliteration, assonance, internal rhyme and approximate rhyme. His major theme was the unity of life, the cycling process of life and death and new life that went on and on. In his eyes, life was a magical transformation producing unity out of diversity. So in his poetry he sought a poetic ritual to celebrate this unity.

## Selections

### A Process in the Weather of the Heart

A process in the weather of the heart
Turns damp to dry; the golden shot
Storms in the freezing tomb.
A weather in the quarter of the veins
Turns night to day; blood in their suns
Lights up the living worm.

A process in the eye forwarns
The bones of blindness; and the womb
Drives in a death as life leaks out.

A darkness in the weather of the eye
Is half its light; the fathomed sea
Breaks on unangled land.
The seed that makes a forest of the loin
Forks half its fruit; and half drops down,
Slow in a sleeping wind.

A weather in the flesh and bone
Is damp and dry; the quick and dead

Move like two ghosts before the eye.

A process in the weather of the world
Turns ghost to ghost; each mothered child
Sits in their double shade.
A process blows the moon into the sun,
Pulls down the shabby curtains of the skin;
And the heart gives up its dead.

## For Study and Discussion

1. The "process" and "weather" are the key words in this poem. Discuss how they are used to develop the theme.
2. What images strike you most? Why?
3. Learn the last stanza by heart.

### Do Not Go Gentle into That Good Night[1]

Do not go gentle into that good night,
Old age should burn and rave at close of day;
Rage, rage against the dying of the light.

Though wise men at their end know dark is right,
Because their words had forked no lightning they
Do not go gentle into that good night.

Good men, the last wave by, crying how bright
Their frail deeds might have danced in a green bay,
Rage, rage against the dying of the light.

Wild men who caught and sang the sun in flight,
And learn, too late, they grieved it on its way,
Do not go gentle into that good night.

Grave men, near death, who see with blinding sight
Blind eyes could blaze like meteors and be gay,
Rage, rage against the dying of the light.

And you, my father, there on the sad height,
Curse, bless, me now with your fierce tears, I pray.
Do not go gentle into that good night.
Rage, rage against the dying of the light.

## Notes

1. This poem was written in the form of *villanelle*, a French form of five three-line stanzas and a concluding four-line stanza. The first and the third lines of the first stanza are repeated in the second through the fifth stanzas, and the last stanza repeats both of them. So much repetition creates a mood of great intensity.

## For Study and Discussion

1. What is the rhyme scheme of this poem?
2. Why does the poet repeat the line "Rage, rage against the dying of the light"?
3. The sentence "Do not go gentle into that good night" is repeated four times. Why? What is a good night?
4. Recite the last stanza of this poem.

Part X

# The 20th Century Since 1945: Contemporary Literature

# Introduction

We refer to the period between 1945 to the present time as the contemporary period. This is the second half of the 20th century. World War II ended in 1945 and its conclusion marked an important shift in Great Britain's global role. For the first time, Britain was a secondary imperial power, something that was painful for many British citizens. The expectations after the war were that the economy would again rise, but inflation and unemployment led to an overall increase in national cynicism.

During this period, the writing was very diverse, and poets and novelists tended to develop new methods. They incorporated the idea that the world was in a state of incompleteness and gave up the style of such poets as Dylan Thomas and others in the 1940s. They saw the state of the world as dangerous, unstable and threatened. There appeared at Oxford a group of writers led by Philip Larkin, Kingsley Amis, known as "the Movement". They faced the global conflicts and uncertainties of the Cold War era and tried to regain a sense of rational control. Ordinary social relations did not bring satisfaction. They grated on and depressed the individuals. Nature was not kind but wild and predatory. Joy and pleasure were transitory and shallow. Hope and confidence were naive in the conflict-dominated world. Writers of "the Movement" preferred a civil grammar and rational syntax over prophecy, suburban realities over mythmaking.

On the other hand, the writers active in the late 20th century, as a matter of fact, did not form a group which marked out any definite trend. Doris Lessing wrote about the violence of the social conflict while Ted Hughes wrote mainly about the violence of nature. One of Larkin's better-known collections of poems was *The Whitsun Weddings* (1964). Within this collection, "The Whitsun Weddings" remained one of his more famous, one of his poems written about his train journeys. Seamus Heaney views contemporary violence through the lens of ancient myths, sacrifices and feuds, an oblique approach that gives his poetry about the troubles an unusual depth and resonance.

After World War II, things changed in the field of drama. The government helped to enlarge productions. Though commercial plays continued to be produced in London, there were more possibilities in provinces for the young protesting playwrights to produce their plays.

John Osborne, one of the "angry young men", wrote about the alienation of young men from petty responsibilities of middle-class society. His *Look Back* is typical of such plays. This play examines a marriage between a working-class man, Jimmy, and his middle-class wife, Alison. Their differences in class make it difficult for them to get along and when Alison becomes pregnant, their marriage falls apart. Another playwright considered part of "angry young men" is Arnold Wesker, whose kitchen sink drama, *Roots* (1959), addresses social concerns of the time. Kitchen sink dramas typically depict the living conditions of working-class Britons. They would often show cramped apartments, poor neighbourhoods, and the political and social issues of the working class, a turn-away from the "well-made" plays of the previous generation.

# Chapter 34

# Doris Lessing

## Life and Works

Doris Lessing (1919–2013), whose original name was Doris Taylor, was born in Iran to British parents. The family moved to Southern Rhodesia, now Zimbabwe, where she spent most of her childhood, and her father owned a 3000-acre maize farm. Following her education at the Dominican Convent in Salisbury, she held a variety of jobs—nursemaid, telephone operator, chauffeur and stenographer. At the same time, she was keen on politics. She married twice and had several children. She wrote novels using the surname of her second husband. After divorcing again, she was determined to begin a writing career. Armed with £20 and the manuscript of *The Grass Is Singing*, she arrived in England in the spring of 1949.

When the Swedish Academy announced on October 11, 2007 that Doris Lessing was the winner of the Nobel Prize for literature describing her as "that epicist of the female experience, who with skepticism, fire and visionary power has subjected a divided civilisation to scrutiny", the 88-year-old Doris Lessing was the oldest winner of the literature prize and the third oldest Nobel Laureate in all the categories. She became, at the same time, the 11th female writer who was awarded the Nobel Prize in its 106 years of history.

Doris Lessing started to practise writing at the age of seven when she was still a little girl, and at the age of fourteen, she had her own typewriter. Her writing career lasted for almost 80 years if her latest novel *Alfred and Emily* (2008) was included. Her first novel, *The Grass Is Singing*, was an immediate success upon publication. Her later works *Children of Violence* series (1952–1969) also gained great popularity upon publication, let alone her masterpiece, *The Golden Notebook*. Lessing's most brilliant ones also include *African Stories*, *The Summer Before the Dark*, *The Memoirs of a Survivor* and so on.

Lessing received a lot of prizes including the Somerset Maugham Award of the Society of Authors for her *Five: Short Novels*, the Booker Prize for *Briefing for a Descent into Hell*,

French Prix Médicis for Foreigners for her masterpiece *The Golden Notebook*, German Federal Republic Shakespeare Prize, Austrian State Prize for European Literature, and of course, the Nobel Prize in 2007. She was given the Honorary Degree of Harvard University in 1995. She was made a Companion of Honour by the British government in 1999, and was President of Booktrust, an educational charity promoting books and reading. In 2001 she received the David Cohen Prize for a lifetime's achievement in British literature.

## Brief Comment

During her long literary career, Lessing wrote extensively and the themes of her works covered various aspects of life. At the beginning of her writing, she attempted to solve the racial dilemma faced in Southern Rhodesia, a place where many of her writings set. With the increasingly widened horizons, her works covered various social, political and religious issues influencing and modelling the life of men on earth. She was engaged in such topics as racialism, generation gap, women's liberation, and sexual maladjustment in her early life. These problematic themes continued to nurture her talent and formed some parts of her later themes. "However, her mature vision basically centred around more sophisticated and unconventional themes like schizophrenia, inner fragmentation, nuclear holocaust, societal degeneration, cosmic consciousness, universal welfare and inter-stellar harmony." Doris Lessing's perception and strong mind, to a large extent, were closely associated with her frontier life in her childhood.

She is now widely regarded as one of the most important post-war writers in English literature. Her novels, short stories and essays focused on a wide range of 20th-century issues and concerns, from the politics of race—which she confronted in her early novels set in Africa—to the politics of gender, which led to her adoption by the feminist movement, and to the role of the family and the individual in society, which were explored in her space fiction of the late 1970s and early 1980s.

## Selections

### *The Grass Is Singing*

## The Story

The story in *The Grass Is Singing* takes place in Southern Rhodesia (now Zimbabwe) in Africa during the 1940s. It deals with the racial politics between whites and blacks in the then British colony. The novel created a sensation when it was first published and became an instant success in Europe and the United States. It is often described as a high-tension story of a woman whose life was changed by a few careless words which triggered the hate of the houseboy.

Mary Turner, Dick Turner's wife, has been murdered, and a houseboy has confessed to the crime. Dick and Mary are poor and do not socialise with the other white settlers in their farming district. When Mary's body is discovered, the Turners' neighbour, Charlie Slatter, sends a note to the local police sergeant, Sergeant Denham. Denham then sends six native policemen to the Turners' farm, and shortly after they arrive the houseboy, Moses, turns himself in. Charlie drives to the Turners' farm to find Moses in handcuffs, and puts Dick in the back of his car.

Inside the house, Charlie's assistant Tony Marston explains that he has found Mary's body on the veranda. Sergeant Denham arrives, and he and Charlie question Tony. However, Tony begins to feel that they are not actually interested in his testimony, and the interview ends abruptly. The policemen take Mary's body to the car, and Tony is left wondering whether he should insist on telling Charlie and Sergeant Denham his understanding about why Mary was killed. Moses will be hanged no matter what happens, but Tony wonders if by staying silent he is complicit in a "monstrous injustice". The next day, Tony packs his things and leaves the farming district. The trial takes place and it is decided that Moses murdered Mary while drunk and hoped to steal valuables from her house. Tony, meanwhile, briefly takes a job in copper mining, before reluctantly ending up in an office job.

## Brief Comment on the Novel

Doris Lessing's first novel *The Grass Is Singing* is a remarkable piece of work. It is mercilessly penetrating and casts a spell all its own. It touches upon the question of black against white which broods over the land like thunder. But above all, it is the story of Mary Turner who was rather a victim of her character and psychology.

The novel has its own special way of narrating the story. It is firstly presented as a murder: a white woman is killed, and the murderer is her native servant Moses. In the first chapter, Lessing makes Tony Marston tell the story. From the second chapter on, the murder is put aside and the author gives a chronological account of Mary's whole life.

The journal *New Statesman* says that *The Grass Is Singing* is "An extremely mature psychological study, full of touches of truth seldom mentioned but instantly recognised. By any standard, this book shows remarkable powers and imagination". *The New York Review of Books* says it is "Emotional unity and force...one of her best works". *St. Louis Post-Dispatch* says that "Her impressive first novel is told with all the intensity and passion Miss Lessing compacts into all her work". *The New York Times* says that in this novel "There is passion here, a piercing accuracy, a rare sensitivity and power". It blends Lessing's imaginative vision with her own vividly remembered early childhood to recreate the quiet horror of a woman's struggle against a ruthless fate.

## Chapter I
## MURDER MYSTERY
*By Special Correspondent*

Mary Turner, wife of Richard Turner, a farmer at Ngesi, was found murdered on the front veranda of their homestead yesterday morning. The houseboy, who has been arrested, has confessed to the crime. No motive has been discovered. It is thought he was in search of valuables.

*The newspaper did not say much. People all over the country must* have glanced at the paragraph with its sensational heading and felt a little spurt of anger mingled with what was almost satisfaction, as if some belief had been confirmed, as if something had happened which could only have been expected. When natives steal, murder or rape, that is the feeling white people have.

And then they turned the page to something else.

But the people in 'the district' who knew the Turners, either by sight, or from gossiping about them for so many years, did not turn the page so quickly. Many must have snipped out the paragraph, put it among old letters, or between the pages of a book, keeping it perhaps as an omen or a warning, glancing at the yellowing piece of paper with closed, secretive faces. For they did not discuss the murder; that was the most extraordinary thing about it. It was as if they had a sixth sense which told them everything there was to be known, although the three people in a position to explain the facts said nothing. The murder was simply not discussed. "A bad business", someone would remark; and the faces of the people round about would put on that reserved and guarded look. "A very bad business", came the reply—and that was the end of it. There was, it seemed, a tacit agreement that the Turner case should not be given undue publicity by gossip. Yet it was a farming district, where those isolated white families met only very occasionally, hungry for contact with their own kind, to talk and discuss and pull to pieces, all speaking at once, making the most of an hour or so's companionship before returning to their farms where they saw only their own faces and faces of their black servants for weeks on end. Normally that murder would have been discussed for months; people would have been positively grateful for something to talk about.

To an outsider it would seem perhaps as if the energetic Charlie Slatter had travelled from farm over the district telling people to keep quiet; but that was something that would have never occurred to him. The steps he took (and he made not one mistake) were taken apparently instinctively and without conscious planning. The most interesting thing about the whole affair was this silent, unconscious agreement. Everyone behaved like a flock of birds who communicate —or so it seems—by means of a kind of telepathy.

Long before the murder marked them out, people spoke of the Turners in the hard, careless voices reserved for misfits, outlaws and the self-exiled. The Turners were disliked, though few of their neighbours had ever met them, or even seen them in the distance. Yet what was there to dislike? They simply "kept themselves to themselves"; that was all. They were never seen at district dances, or fêtes, or gymkhanas. They must have had something to be ashamed of; that was the feeling. It was not right to seclude themselves like that; it was a slap in the face of everyone else; what had they got to be so stuck-up about? What, indeed! Living the way they did! That little box of a house—it was forgivable as a temporary dwelling, but not to live in permanently. Why, some natives (though not many thank heavens) had houses as good; and it would give them a bad impression to see white people living in such a way.

And then it was that someone used the phrase "poor whites". It caused disquiet. There was no great money-cleavage in those days (that was before the era of the tobacco barons), but there was certainly a race division. The small community of Afrikaners[1] had their own lives, and the Britishers[2] ignored them. "Poor whites" were Afrikaners, never British. But the person who said the Turners were poor whites stuck to it defiantly. What was the difference? What was a poor white? It was the way one lived, a question of standards. All the Turners needed were a drove of children to make them poor whites.

Though the arguments were unanswerable, people would still not think of them as poor whites. To do that would be letting the side down. The Turners were British, after all.

Thus the district handled the Turners, in accordance with that esprit de corps which is the first rule of South African society, but which the Turners themselves ignored. They apparently did not recognize the need for esprit de corps; that, really, was why they were hated.

The more one thinks about it, the more extraordinary the case becomes. Not the murder itself; but the way people felt about it, the way they pitied Dick Turner with a fine fierce indignation against Mary as if she were something unpleasant and unclean, and it served her right to get murdered. But they did not ask questions.

For instance, they must have wondered who that "Special Correspondent" was. Someone in the district sent in the news, for the paragraph was not in newspaper language. But who? Marston, the assistant, left the district immediately after the murder. Denham, the policeman, might have written to the paper in a personal capacity, but it was not likely. There remained Charlie Slatter, who knew more about the Turners than anyone else, and was there on the day of the murder. One could say that he practically controlled the handling of the case, even taking precedence over the Sergeant himself. And people felt that to be quite right and proper. Whom should it concern, if not the white farmers, that a silly woman got herself murdered by a native for reasons people might think about, but never, never mentioned? It was their livelihood, their wives and families, their way of living, at stake.

But to the outsider it is strange that Slatter should have been allowed to take the charge of the affair, to arrange that everything should pass over without more than a ripple of comment.

For there could have been no planning: there simply wasn't time. Why, for instance, when Dick Turner's farm boys came to him with the news, did he sit down to write a note to the Sergeant at the police camp? He did not use the telephone.

Everyone who has lived in the country knows what a branch telephone is like. You lift the receiver after you have turned the handle the required number of times, and then, click, click,

click, you can hear the receivers coming off all over the district, and soft noises like breathing, a whisper, a subdued cough.

Slatter lived five miles from the Turners. The farm boys came to him first, when they discovered the body. And though it was an urgent matter, he ignored the telephone, but sent a personal letter by a native bearer on a bicycle to Denham at the police camp, twelve miles away. The Sergeant sent out half a dozen policemen at once, to the Turners' farm, to see what they could find. He drove first to see Slatter, because the way that letter was worded roused his curiosity. That was why he arrived late on the scene of the murder. The native policemen did not have to search far for the murderer. After walking through the house, looking briefly at the body, and dispersing down the front of the little hill the house stood on, they saw Moses himself rise out of a tangled ant-heap in front of them. He walked up to them and said (or words to this effect): "Here I am." They snapped the handcuffs on him, and went back to the house to wait for the police cars to come. There they saw Dick Turner come out of the bush by the house with two Whining dogs at his heels. He was off his head, talking crazily to himself, wandering in and out of the bush with his hands full of leaves and earth. They let him be, while keeping an eye on him, for he was a white man, though mad, and black men, even when policemen, do not lay hands on white flesh.

People did ask, cursorily, why the murderer had given himself up. There was not much chance of escape. But he had a sporting chance. He could have run to the hills and hidden for a while. Or he could have slipped over the border to Portuguese territory. Then the District Native Commissioner, at a sundowner party, said that it was perfectly understandable. If one knew anything about the history of the country, or had read any of the memoirs or letters of the old missionaries and explorers, one would have come across accounts of the society Lobengula ruled. The laws were strict: everyone knew what they could or could not do. If someone did an unforgivable thing, like touching one of the King's women, he could submit fatalistically to punishment, which was likely to be impalement over an ant-heap on a stake, or something equally unpleasant. "I have done wrong, and I know it," he might say, "therefore let me be punished." Well it was the tradition to face punishment, and really there was something rather fine about it. Remarks like these are forgiven from native commissioners, who have to study languages, customs, and so on; although it is not done to say things natives do are "fine". (Yet the fashion is changing: it is permissible to glorify the old ways sometimes, providing one says how deprave the natives have become since.)

So that aspect of the affair was dropped, yet it was not the least interesting, for Moses might not have been a Matabele at all. He was in Mashonaland; though of course natives do wander all over Africa. He might come from anywhere: Portuguese territory, Nyasaland, the Union of South Africa. And it is a long time since the days of the great King Lobengula. But then native commissioners tend to think in terms of the past.

Well, having sent the letter to the police camp, Charlie Slatter went to the Turner's place, driving at a great speed over the bad farm roads in his fat American car.

Who *was* Charlie Slatter? It was he who, from the beginning of the tragedy to its end, personified Society for the Turners. He touches the story at half a dozen points; without him things would not happened quite as they did, though sooner or later, in one way or another, the Turners were bound to grief.

Slatter had been a grocer's assistant in London. He was fond of telling his children that if it had not been for his energy and enterprise they would be running round the slums in rags. He was still a proper cockney, even after twenty years in Africa. He came with one idea: to make money. He made it. He made plenty. He was a crude, brutal, ruthless, yet kindhearted man, in his own way, and according to his own impulses, who could not help making money. He farmed as if he were turning the handle of a machine which would produce pound notes at the other end. He was hard with his wife, making her bear unnecessary hardships at the beginning; he was hard with his children, until he made money, when they got everything they wanted; and above all he was hard with his farm laborers. They, the geese that laid the golden eggs, were still in that state where they did not know there were other ways of living besides producing gold for other people.

They know better now, or are beginning to. But Slatter believed in farming with the sjambok. It hung over his front door, like a motto on a wall: "You shall not mind killing if it is necessary." He had once killed a native in a fit of temper. He was fined thirty pounds. Since then he has kept his temper. But sjamboks are all very well for the Slatters; not so good for people less sure of themselves. It was he who had told Dick Turner, long ago, when Dick first started farming, that one should buy a sjambok before a plough or a harrow, and that sjambok did not do the Turners any good, as we shall see.

Slatter was a shortish, broad, powerful man, with heavy shoulders and thick arms. His face was broad and bristled; shrewd, watchful, and a little cunning. He had a crop of fair hair that made him look like a convict; but he did not care for appearances. His small blue eyes were hardly visible, because of the way he screwed them up, after years and years of South Africa sunshine.

Bent over the sneering wheel, almost hugging it in his determination to get to the Turners quickly, his eyes were little blue chinks in a set face. He was wondering why Marston, the assistance, who was after all his employee, had not come to him about the murder, or at least sent a note. Where was he? The hut he lived in was only a couple of hundred yards from the house itself. Perhaps he had got cold feet and run away? Anything was possible, thought Charlie, from this particular type of young Englishman. He had a rooted contempt for soft-faced, soft-voice Englishman, combined with a fascination for their manner and breeding. His own sons, now grown up, were gentlemen. He had spent plenty of money to make them so; but he despised them for it. At the same time he was proud of them. This conflict showed itself in his attitude towards Marston: half hard and indifferent, half subtly deferential. At the moment he felt nothing but irritation.

Half-way he felt the car rock, and swearing, pulled it up. It was a puncture: no, two punctures.

The red mud of the road held fragments of the broken glass. His irritation expressed itself in the half-conscious thought, "Just like Turner to have glass on his roads!" But Turner was now necessarily an object of passionate, protective pity, and the irritation was focused on Marston, the assistance who, Slatter felt, should somehow have prevented this murder. What was he being paid for? What had he been engaged for? But Slatter was a fair man in his own way, and where his own race was concerned. He restrained himself, and got down to mending one puncture and changing a tyre, working in the heavy red slush of the roads. This took him three-quarters of an hour, and by the time he was finished, and had picked the pieces of the green glass from the mud and thrown them into the bush, the sweat was soaking his face and hair.

When he reached the house at last, he saw, as he approached through the bush, six glittering bicycles leaning against the walls. And in front of the house, under the trees, stood six native policemen, and among them the native Moses, his hands linked in front of him. The sun glinted on the handcuffs, on the bicycles, on the masses of heavy wet leaves. It was a wet, sultry morning. The sky was a tumult of discoloured clouds: it looked like full of billowing dirty washing. Puddles on the pale soil held a sheen of sky.

## Notes

1. Afrikaners: South Africans of European descent whose native language is Afrikaans
2. Britishers: (American usage) people of Great Britain, especially Englanders

## For Study and Discussion

1. From the report "MURDER MYSTERY", what can you know about the relationship between the murdered and the murderer?
2. Why do the people in "the district" not discuss the murder? What are they interested in? Normally people would have talked about a murder for a long time. Why are they silent about this murder?
3. What are the Turners like? Why are they not popular with the neighbours? In what ways are they different from the other whites?
4. What are "poor whites"? Why does the author have to say so much about this?
5. Why do people hate Mary Turner and sympathise with Dick Turner? What is the author's attitude?
6. Who is the special correspondent? Why does he make the report that way?
7. Who is Charlie Slatter? From the description of the author, what can you see about the author's attitude towards him?
8. Who is Moses? Why does Moses not try to escape?

## Chapter 35

# Philip Arthur Larkin

### Life and Works

Philip Arthur Larkin (1922–1985) was born in Coventry in the English midlands. He attended school there and after that went to Oxford, where he was associated with the writers of "the Movement", a group of young poets and novelists who rejected the prevailing fashion for writing in the style of Yeats and Dylan Thomas. After graduating, Larkin undertook professional studies to become a librarian. He worked in libraries his entire life, in Shropshire and Leicester, and then at Queen's College in Belfast, and finally at the University of Hull.

Writers of "the Movement" were concerned with creating a less intense and colloquial experience and the changes in everyday English life. Larkin had proved to be one of the best poets of this group, while his best poems continued the tradition associated with Thomas Hardy. He had the rare gift of clarity and of casually suggesting the importance of the ordinary. He focused on intense personal emotion but strictly avoided sentimentality. His style is modern and precise, and he is widely regarded as one of the great English poets during the latter half of the 20th century.

His first book of poetry, *The North Ship*, was published in 1945, followed by two novels, *Jill* and *A Girl in Winter*, but he came to prominence in 1955 with the publication of his second collection of poems, *The Less Deceived*, followed by *The Whitsun Weddings* and *High Windows*. He contributed to *The Daily Telegraph* as its jazz critic from 1961 to 1971, articles gathered together in *All What Jazz: A Record Diary*, and he edited *The Oxford Book of Twentieth-Century English Verse*. He received many honours including the Queen's Gold Medal for Poetry. He was offered, but declined, the position of Poet Laureate in 1984, following the death of John Betjeman.

## Brief Comment

His poems are marked by a very English, glum accuracy about emotions, places and relationships, and are described as lowered sights and diminished expectations. Larkin himself said that deprivation for him was what daffodils were for Wordsworth. Influenced by W. H. Auden, W. B. Yeats and Thomas Hardy, his poems are highly structured but flexible verse forms. No other poet presents the welfare-state world of postimperial Britain so vividly, so unsparingly and so tenderly.

Larkin employed the traditional tools of poetry—rhyme, stanza and metre—to explore the often uncomfortable or terrifying experiences thrust upon common people in the modern age. Out of "the commonplace life" he fashioned uncommon poems. As Alan Brownjohn noted in *Philip Larkin*, the poet produced without fanfare "the most technically brilliant and resonantly beautiful, profoundly disturbing yet appealing and approachable, body of verse of any English poet in the last twenty-five years".

## Selections

### Going

There is an evening coming in
Across the fields, one never seen before,
That lights so lamps.

Silken it seems at a distance, yet
When it is drawn up over the knees and breast
It brings no comfort.

Where has the tree gone, that locked
Earth to the sky? What is under my hands,
That I cannot feel?

What loads my hands down?

## For Study and Discussion

1. Evening is presented as a metaphor for oncoming death. How is the metaphor developed?
2. Why is this poem entitled "Going"?
3. Why does evening seem "silken" at a distance?
4. Why does the poet stress the experience of hands?

## The Whitsun Weddings[1]

That Whitsun, I was late getting away:
Not till about
One-twenty on the sunlit Saturday
Did my three-quarters-empty train pull out[2],
All windows down, all cushions hot, all sense
Of being in a hurry gone. We ran
Behind the backs of houses, crossed a street
Of blinding windscreens, smelt the fish-dock; thence
The river's level drifting breadth began,
Where sky and Lincolnshire and water meet.

All afternoon, through the tall[3] heat that slept
For miles inland,
A slow and stopping curve southwards we kept.
Wide farms went by, short-shadowed[4] cattle, and
Canals with floatings of industrial froth;
A hothouse flashed uniquely[5]: hedges dipped[6]
And rose: and now and then a smell of grass
Displaced the reek of buttoned carriage-cloth
Until the next town, new and nondescript[7],
Approached with acres of dismantled cars.

At first, I didn't notice what a noise
The weddings made
Each station that we stopped at: sun destroys
The interest of what's happening in the shade,
And down the long cool platforms whoops and skirls
I took for porters larking[8] with the mails,
And went on reading. Once we started, though,
We passed them, grinning and pomaded, girls
In parodies of fashion, heels and veils,
All posed[9] irresolutely, watching us go,

As if out on the end of an event
Waving goodbye
To something that survived it. Struck, I leant
More promptly out next time, more curiously,

And saw it all again in different terms:
The fathers with broad belts under their suits
And seamy foreheads; mothers loud and fat;
An uncle shouting smut; and then the perms[10],
The nylon gloves and jewellery-substitutes,
The lemons, mauves, and olive-ochres that

Marked off[11] the girls unreally[12] from the rest.
  Yes, from cafés
And banquet-halls up yards, and bunting-dressed
Coach-party annexes, the wedding-days
Were coming to an end. All down the line
Fresh couples climbed aboard: the rest stood round;
The last confetti and advice were thrown,
And, as we moved, each face seemed to define
Just what it saw departing: children frowned
At something dull; fathers had never known

Success so huge and wholly farcical[13];
  The women shared
The secret like a happy funeral[14];
While girls, gripping their handbags tighter, stared
At a religious wounding. Free[15] at last,
And loaded with the sum of all they saw,
We hurried towards London, shuffling gouts of steam.
Now fields were building-plots, and poplars cast
Long shadows[16] over major roads, and for
Some fifty minutes, that in time would seem

Just long enough to settle hats[17] and say
  *I nearly died*,
A dozen marriages got under way.
They watched the landscape, sitting side by side
—An Odeon went past, a cooling tower,
And someone running up to bowl[18]—and none
Thought of the others they would never meet
Or how their lives would all contain this hour.
I thought of London spread out in the sun,
Its postal districts packed like squares of wheat:

There we were aimed. And as we raced across
  Bright knots of rail
Past standing Pullmans[19], walls of blackened moss
Came close, and it was nearly done, this frail
Travelling coincidence; and what it held
stood ready to be loosed with all the power
That being changed can give. We slowed again,
And as the tightened brakes took hold, there swelled
A sense of falling, like an arrow-shower
Sent out of sight, somewhere becoming rain.

## Notes

1. The poem is written in eight ten-line stanzas of iambic pentameter rhyming ababcdecde with the exception of the second line iambic dimeter. Whitsun (also Whitsunday, Whit Sunday or Whit) is the Christian festival of Pentecost in the UK, held on the seventh Sunday after Easter. In English tradition, Whitsun has long been a day of feasting and merrymaking.
2. pull out: depart
3. tall: hard to believe
4. short-shadowed: referring to the time in the early afternoon. cf. "Long shadows" in Line 59
5. uniquely: unusually
6. dipped: lowered
7. nondescript: lacking distinctive qualities
8. larking: having a merry time
9. posed: assumed a certain pose
10. perms: permanent waves
11. Marked off: distinguished
12. unreally: imaginarily
13. farcical: ridiculous
14. a happy funeral: an oxymoron. It's a happy beginning of a new life, but it's also an end of the past life.
15. Free: referring to leaving the station
16. Long shadows: implying the time in the late afternoon
17. to settle hats: part of the Western wedding ceremony, meaning "to settle down"
18. running up to bowl: moving swiftly and smoothly
19. Pullmans: the Pullman car or coach

## For Study and Discussion

1. Discuss the sound effect of this poem.
2. What's the poet's attitude towards these marriages?
3. How do you understand "all the power / That being changed can give"? What's the function of change in life as shown in this poem?
4. What does the image "rain" in the end of the poem imply?

# Chapter 36

# Ted Hughes

## Life and Works

Ted Hughes (1930–1998) was born in Mytholmroyd, in the West Riding district of Yorkshire, on August 17, 1930. His childhood was quiet and mainly rural. The harsh landscape of the moors in the north of England had a strong influence on his poetry. In his poetry, he often presented images of his experiences he had together with his brothers who liked fishing and hunting.

After graduating from high school, he entered the Royal Air Force and served for two years as a ground wireless mechanic. He then went to Cambridge to attend Pembroke College on an academic scholarship. While in college he majored in anthropology and archaeology, and studied mythology extensively. He published a few poems when he was at college.

He graduated from Cambridge in 1954. In 1956, he co-founded the literary magazine *St. Botolph's Review* with a handful of other editors. At the launch party for the magazine, he met Sylvia Plath. A few months later, they were married. Then they went to the United States. Hughes lived in Massachusetts with Plath and taught at University of Massachusetts Amherst. Plath encouraged Hughes to submit his first manuscript, *The Hawk in the Rain*, to the Poetry Centre's First Publication Book Contest. The judges awarded the manuscript first prize, and it was published in England and America in 1957, with much critical praise. Six more volumes of poetry appeared in the 1960s and 1970s.

They returned to England in 1959, and their first child, Freida, was born in 1960. In 1961 they moved to Devon. At the same time, Sylvia Plath's mental instability increased. Their second child, Nicholas, was born in 1962. In 1962, Hughes left Plath for Assia Gutmann Wevill. Less than a year later, in 1963, Plath committed suicide. Hughes did not write again for years, as he focused all of his energy on editing and promoting Plath's poems. He was also roundly lambasted by the public, who saw him as responsible for his wife's suicide. Controversy surrounded his editorial choices regarding Plath's poems and journals.

In 1965, Wevill gave birth to their only child, Shura. Four years later, in 1969, like Plath, she also committed suicide, killing Shura as well.

The following year, in 1970, Hughes married Carol Orchard, with whom he remained married until his death. He himself died of cancer on October 28, 1998. Hughes' books of poems include *Wolfwatching*, *Flowers and Insects*, *Selected Poems 1957–1981*, *Moortown Diary*, *Cave Birds*, *Crow* and *Lupercal*. His final collection, *The Birthday Letters* published the year of his death, documented his relationship with Plath.

## Brief Comment

Hughes has been named a "survivor-poet" by the critic Alvarez because he paralleled human beings with lower animals, creatures that would do anything to ensure survival. Hughes stated that poems, like animals, are each one "an assembly of living parts, moved by a single spirit".

Looking at the dark aspects of nature, he stressed the ferocious and demonic rather than the idyllic and beautiful. Within the cruelty and violence of nature, Hughes looked for an understanding of human life and its mysterious bonds with nature.

About his preference of poetic form, Hughes stated in *Poetry in the Making*, that there was no ideal form of poetry or writing. He wrote free verse as well as highly structured forms and rhyme schemes. He gradually abandoned traditional forms and stated that the "very sound of metre calls up the ghosts of the past and it is difficult to sing one's own tune against the choir".

His work is marked by a mythical framework, using the lyric and dramatic monologue to illustrate intense subject matter. Animals appear frequently throughout his work as deity, metaphor, persona and icon. Perhaps the most famous of his subjects is "Crow", a mixture of god, bird and man, whose existence seems crucial to the knowledge of good and evil. Hughes received all the major literary awards in Europe, but not the Nobel Prize. He also received the Order of Merit and was appointed Poet Laureate in 1984, a post he held until his death.

## Selections

### Snowdrop[1]

Now is the globe shrunk tight
Round the mouse's dulled wintering heart.
Weasel and crow, as if moulded in brass,
Move through an outer darkness
Not in their right minds,
With the other deaths. She, too, pursues her ends,

Brutal as the stars of this month,
Her pale head heavy as metal.

## Notes

1. Hughes was seriously interested in shamanism, hermeticism, astrology and the Ouija board. He examined in his animal poems the themes of survival and the mystery and destructiveness of the cosmos.

## For Study and Discussion

1. In what way is the theme of death presented?
2. Why is the earth shrunk tight?
3. What does "dulled wintering heart" refer to?
4. Who is "She" in Line 6?

### Hawk Roosting

I sit in the top of the wood, my eyes closed.
Inaction, no falsifying dream
Between my hooked head and hooked feet:
Or in sleep rehearse perfect kills and eat.

The convenience of the high trees!
The air's buoyancy and the sun's ray
Are of advantage to me;
And the earth's face upward for my inspection.

My feet are locked upon the rough bark.
It took the whole of Creation
To produce my foot, my each feather:
Now I hold Creation in my foot

Or fly up, and revolve it all slowly—
I kill where I please because it is all mine.
There is no sophistry[1] in my body:
My manners are tearing off heads—

The allotment of death.
For the one path of my flight is direct
Through the bones of the living.
No arguments assert my right:

The sun is behind me.
Nothing has changed since I began.
My eye has permitted no change.
I am going to keep things like this.

## Notes

1. sophistry: the use of clever but misleading arguments

## For Study and Discussion

1. Who is the speaker of this poem? What main idea does the speaker present in his soliloquy?
2. In the eyes of the hawk, what is the human world like?
3. Why does the hawk say "There is no sophistry in my body"? Where is sophistry?
4. Paraphrase the last stanza and recite it.

# Chapter 37

# Seamus Heaney

## Life and Works

Seamus Heaney (1939–2013) was born on April 13, 1939 in County Derry, Northern Ireland. He received his early schooling at a local primary school. He went on to Queen's University, Belfast and graduated with a BA in English Language and Literature. In 1962 he started work as a schoolteacher. He started writing while still studying at Queen's University in Belfast and some of his earliest poems were published in the college literary magazine, *Gorgon*, under the pen name Incertus (meaning Uncertain). He was a member of the Belfast Group, a gathering of young Northern Irish poets who met weekly to share and develop their work, under the guidance of poet and Queen's lecturer Philip Hobsbaum.

In 1964, three of Heaney's poems—including possibly his best-known, "Digging"—were published in *New Statesman*. Then in May 1966 his first poetry collection *Death of a Naturalist* was published. Over the next four decades, Seamus Heaney would publish eleven more volumes of original poetry. He was one of a generation of gifted poets to emerge from Ulster in the 1960s, among them his friends Michael Longley and Derek Mahon. He was also greatly influenced by the English poet Ted Hughes, who later became a close friend and with whom he edited two anthologies, *The Rattle Bag* and *The School Bag*.

Heaney's early volumes included *Door into the Dark*, *Wintering Out* and the landmark *North*, published in 1975 after the poet and his family moved from Belfast to Wicklow in the Republic of Ireland, as sectarian violence erupted in Northern Ireland. These early collections are firmly rooted in the landscapes and traditions of Heaney's native Derry, but in poems such as "Whatever You Say, Say Nothing", they also reflected the turmoil of the time. With his poetry writing in a following long period, he continued to mine his personal past while exploring themes of loss, memory and the changing world of the 21st century.

He also wrote several volumes of criticism, including *The Redress of Poetry*. As a translator, his translation works include the medieval Irish epic *Sweeney Astray*, Sophocles' *Philoctetes* (tr. as *The Cure at Troy*, 1990) and *Antigone* (tr. as *The Burial at Thebes*, 2004), the highly acclaimed *Beowulf* (2000), which won the Whitbread Book of the Year Award, and the libretto of Janáček's song cycle *Diary of One Who Vanished*.

In June 2012, Heaney was awarded the Lifetime Recognition Award from the Griffin Trust for Excellence in Poetry. He was also a foreign member of the American Academy of Arts and Letters and held the chair of Professor of Poetry at Oxford from 1989 to 1994. In 1995 he received the Nobel Prize. Heaney was a resident of Dublin from 1976 to 2013. Beginning in 1981, he also spent part of each year teaching at Harvard University, where in 1984 he was elected the Boylston Professor of Rhetoric and Oratory.

## Brief Comment

Heaney is widely recognised as one of the major poets of the 20th century. He has attracted a readership on several continents and has won prestigious literary awards and honours, including the Nobel Prize. His work is notable for its evocation of Irish rural life and events in Irish history as well as for its allusions to Irish myth. Part of Heaney's popularity stems from his subject matter—modern Northern Ireland, its farms and cities beset with civil strife, its natural culture and language overrun by English rule. He sought to weave the ongoing Irish troubles into a broader historical frame embracing the general human situation. Many of his works concern his own family history and focus on characters in his own family, which can be read as elegies for those family members.

During a career spanning fifty years, he became one of the most celebrated poets of his generation. While often rooted in the landscape of his native County Derry in the north of Ireland, Heaney's poetry has a universal appeal that is to find a worldwide readership. His work has been translated into 27 languages. Heaney's belief in the power of art and poetry, regardless of technological change or economic collapse, offers hope in the face of an increasingly uncertain future.

### Exposure

It is December in Wicklow:
Alders dripping, birches
Inheriting the last light,
The ash tree cold to look at.

A comet that was lost
Should be visible at sunset,

Those million tons of light
Like a glimmer of haws and rose-hips,

And I sometimes see a falling star.
If I could come on meteorite[1]!
Instead I walk through damp leaves,
Husks, the spent flukes of autumn,

Imagining a hero
On some muddy compound[2],
His gift like a slingstone
Whirled for the desperate.

How did I end up like this?
I often think of my friends'
Beautiful prismatic counselling
And the anvil brains of some who hate me

As I sit weighing and weighing
My responsible tristia[3].
For what? For the ear? For the people?
For what is said behind-backs?

Rain comes down through the alders,
Its low conductive voices
Mutter about let-downs and erosions
And yet each drop recalls

The diamond absolutes.
I am neither internee nor informer;
An inner émigré[4], grown long-haired
And thoughtful; a wood-kerne

Escaped from the massacre,
Taking protective colouring
From bole and bark, feeling
Every wind that blows;

Who, blowing up these sparks

For their meagre heat, have missed
The once-in-a-lifetime portent,
The comet's pulsing rose.

## Notes

1. meteorite: an individual chunk of rock falling from the outer space
2. compound: enclosed dwelling
3. tristia: personal griefs
4. émigré: originally someone who fled abroad to escape the French Revolution, extended to refer to political exiles in general

## For Study and Discussion

1. What is the setting of this poem?
2. What does the title "Exposure" mean? What is exposed?
3. What rhetorical devices are used in this poem? Pick some out and comment on how they are used in presenting the theme.
4. Which image do you like best? Why?

## Digging[1]

Between my finger and my thumb
The squat pen rests; as snug as a gun.

Under my window a clean rasping sound
When the spade sinks into gravelly ground:
My father, digging. I look down

Till his straining rump[2] among the flowerbeds
Bends low, comes up twenty years away
Stooping in rhythm through potato drills[3]
Where he was digging.

The coarse boot nestled on the lug[4], the shaft
Against the inside knee was levered firmly.
He rooted out tall tops, buried the bright edge deep
To scatter new potatoes that we picked

Loving their cool hardness in our hands.

By God, the old man could handle a spade,
Just like his old man[5].

My grandfather could cut more turf in a day
Than any other man on toner's bog.
Once I carried him milk in a bottle
Corked sloppily with paper. He straightened up
To drink it, then fell to[6] right away
Nicking and slicing neatly, heaving sods
Over his shoulder, digging down and down
For the good turf. Digging.

The cold smell of potato mold, the squelch and slap
Of soggy peat, the curt cuts of an edge
Through living roots awaken in my head.
But I've no spade to follow men like them.

Between my finger and thumb
The squat pen rests.
I'll dig with it.

## Notes

1. This is the first poem in the collection *Death of a Naturalist.*
2. rump: buttocks
3. drills: small furrows in which seeds are sown
4. lug: the upper edge of the spade on which one can put his foot and push down with force
5. his old man: his own father. The poet is telling the reader that his father worked as hard as his grandfather.
6. fell to: began to

## For Study and Discussion

1. To what is the poet's pen compared? Why is it so compared? What will he do with his pen?
2. What sound image can you find from the digging of the poet's father? Which words contribute to the construction of the musical effect of the father's digging?

3. Why does the poet mention his grandfather's digging? How do you understand the use of "Digging" in Line 24?
4. What is the difference between the three generations in their way of work? Between the two controlling images, the spade and the pen, which does the poet pour more feeling into? What does he want to do by describing digging? What is implied here?
5. Make your comment on the last stanza of the poem.